SUPERGRASSES

SUPERGRASSES

A Study in Anti-Terrorist
Law Enforcement
in Northern Ireland

STEVEN GREER

CLARENDON PRESS · OXFORD
1995

Oxford University Press, Walton Street, Oxford OX2 6DP
Oxford New York
Athens Auckland Bangkok Bombay
Calcutta Cape Town Dar es Salaam Delhi
Florence Hong Kong Istanbul Karachi
Kuala Lumpur Madras Madrid Melbourne
Mexico City Nairobi Paris Singapore
Taipei Tokyo Toronto
and associated companies in
Berlin Ibadan

Oxford is a trade mark of Oxford University Press

Published in the United States
by Oxford University Press Inc., New York

British Library Cataloguing in Publication Data
Data available

Library of Congress Cataloging in Publication Data
Greer, S. C. (Steven C.)
Supergrasses : a study in anti-terrorist law enforcement in
Northern Ireland / Steven Greer.
p. cm.
Includes bibliographical references and index.
1. Evidence, Criminal—Northern Ireland. 2. Informers—Legal
status, laws, etc.—Northern Ireland. 3. Criminal investigation—
Northern Ireland. 4. Terrorism—Northern Ireland. I. Title.
KDE550.G744 1994
345.416'02—dc20
[344.16052] 94-30996

ISBN 0-19-825766-X

1 3 5 7 9 10 8 6 4 2

Typeset by Datix International, Broad Street, Bungay
Printed in Great Britain
on acid-free paper by
Bookcraft Ltd., Midsomer Norton, Avon

To Susan, Cara, and Lucy

Preface

IN the first half of the 1980s a succession of high-profile and deeply controversial trials took place in Northern Ireland on the evidence of 'supergrasses' from loyalist and republican paramilitary organizations prepared to betray large numbers of their alleged former comrades-in-arms in return for immunity from prosecution, or lenient sentences, and new lives under new identities outside Northern Ireland. Some observers claimed that these proceedings, some of which involved more defendants than any other single trial in the history of British or Irish criminal justice, offered the first genuine opportunity to convict the 'godfathers of terrorism', the leadership of the various paramilitary factions, who had long evaded successful prosecution. Others warned that reliance upon such inherently untrustworthy evidence could seriously damage public confidence in the legal system, particularly since the special anti-terrorist 'Diplock' process had already suffered the removal of certain key due-process safeguards.

The Northern Ireland supergrass system, the effects of which spread far beyond those accused in the ten central trials, began hesitantly, experienced a brief ascendancy in 1983, and then suffered a lingering decline and fall, the bulk of the convictions eventually being quashed on appeal. However, although dead and buried, its ghost still haunts the Diplock process, in the form either of periodic rumours that a new supergrass has been recruited or of speculation, as in the autumn of 1993, that a return to such trials is under active official consideration. The central purpose of this study, pursued in Chapters 2–9, is to seek to trace the origins of the Ulster supergrass system in the context of security policy and intelligence-gathering since 1969, to chart its chequered career, and to consider its legacy. Chapter 1 compares and contrasts the role of the supergrass with that of various other kinds of police informant, Chapter 10 considers processes similar to the supergrass system in England, the United States, and several western European countries, while the concluding chapter summarizes the contribution of criminal justice agencies in the management of the supergrass system in Northern

Ireland and reflects upon the wider questions of successful institutionalization, accountability, and the importance of adherence to
due-process values.

The bulk of the data for the core of this study came from the
judgments delivered in the central supergrass trials and from an
extensive library of press cuttings collected while I was a research
student in Belfast in the first half of the 1980s, mostly from the
Belfast Telegraph, the *Irish News*, the *Guardian*, the *Observer*, the
Irish Times, *Fortnight*, the *New Statesman*, and *New Society*, as
well as various flysheets and pamphlets produced by organizations
involved in the anti-supergrass campaign. Additional information
was gathered in the course of formal and informal interviews with
many of those involved in the supergrass controversy, including
defence lawyers, the (now retired) Chief Constable of the Royal
Ulster Constabulary, Sir John Hermon, and the then Lord Chief
Justice of Northern Ireland, Lord Lowry. The Director of Public
Prosecutions for Northern Ireland declined to be interviewed and
instead cited two parliamentary statements made by the Attorney
General which, amongst other things, refer to the DPP's role in the
supergrass process. Regrettably, I was unable to obtain access to
any of the supergrasses themselves.

Since there were no written judgments in two of the central
trials, namely those involving, Allen (*R. v. Austin*) and Grimley (*R.
v. Connolly*), the accounts of these proceedings were constructed
largely from the press reports listed below. The other judgments
varied enormously in length, from a mere five pages in Gilmour (*R.
v. Robson*) to 501 pages in Kirkpatrick (*R. v. Steenson*). All the
appeal verdicts have been reported in the *Northern Ireland Judgment
Bulletin*, as have the first-instance decisions in Bennett (*R. v.
Graham*), McGrady (*R. v. Gibney*), and Quigley (*R. v. Crumley*).
Since virtually every sentence in the trial summaries derives either
from the relevant judgment or a press report, I have chosen to
confine footnotes to verbatim quotations, and to those points
which may be deemed particularly controversial. Some relatively
minor numerical inaccuracies which appeared in some of my previous supergrass publications have also been corrected.

Although responsibility for the views expressed here is entirely
my own, I owe an enormous debt of gratitude to many people
whose help and support ensured that this book saw the light of
day. The Cobden Trust (now the Civil Liberties Trust) and the

Faculty and School of Law at the Queen's University of Belfast each facilitated the Cobden Trust Research Studentship in Emergency Laws and Human Rights which I held from 1983 to 1985, the staff of the Northern Ireland Courts Service provided copies of judgments delivered in some of the supergrass cases; the Northern Ireland Office and the Belfast Central Library traced some useful information; Professor Ennio Amodio of the University of Milan made valuable documents about foreign processes available; Elizabeth Roberts translated some of the Italian literature; Julian Rivers helped with some German materials; Pat Hammond attended to corrections in the final drafts of the text; and the Faculty of Law at the University of Bristol provided a small grant to assist with some data collection. I should like to express a very special word of thanks to Professor Tom Hadden of the School of Law at the Queen's University of Belfast, who spurred me on to better things when I might have been content with less, and from whom I have learned a lot more than the remit of this study might suggest. Finally, my deepest thanks must go to Susan, my wife, and to Cara and Lucy, my little daughters who sacrificed much to enable this work to be completed.

S.G.

Contents

Abbreviations

AC	*Law Reports, Appeal Cases*
All ER	*All England Law Reports*
ASU	active service units
Ch D	*Law Reports, Chancery Division*
CLJ	*Cambridge Law Journal*
Cr App R	*Criminal Appeal Reports*
Crim LR	*Criminal Law Review*
DPP	Director of Public Prosecutions
DUP	Democratic Unionist Party
INLA	Irish National Liberation Army
IRA	Irish Republican Army
IRSP	Irish Republican Socialist Party
KB	*Law Reports, King's Bench Division*
LQR	*Law Quarterly Review*
MLR	*Modern Law Review*
NI	*Northern Ireland Law Reports*
NIJB	*Northern Ireland Judgment Bulletin*
NLJ	*New Law Journal*
PLA	People's Liberation Army
QB	*Law Reports, Queen's Bench Division*
RUC	Royal Ulster Constabulary
SAS	Special Air Service
UDA	Ulster Defence Association
UDR	Ulster Defence Regiment
UFF	Ulster Freedom Fighters
UVF	Ulster Volunteer Force
WLR	*Weekly Law Reports*
WPP	Witness Protection Programme, also known as Witness Security Programme (WSP)

Newspaper Sources for the Grimley, Gilmour, and Allen Trial Summaries

THE GRIMLEY CASE (*R. v. CONNOLLY*)

Belfast Telegraph 1983: 4 Mar.; 16 Sept.; 25 Nov. *Irish News* 1983: 14, 15, 20, 21, 22, 23, 24, 27, 28 Sept.; 4, 5, 6, 12, 26 Oct.; 9, 10, 11, 12, 15, 16, 25 Nov. *Newsletter* 1983: 24 Nov. *Guardian* 1983: 26 Oct.; 28 Nov. *Irish Times* 1982: 31 Dec. 1983: 24 Nov.

THE GILMOUR CASE (*R. v. ROBSON*)

Belfast Telegraph 1982: 18 Sept.; 8 Nov. 1983: 18, 20, 21 Apr.; 19, 26 July; 3, 5 Aug.; 2 Sept. 1984: 4, 17 Apr.; 8, 21, 22, 29, 30 May; 6, 12 June; 9, 10, 11, 16, 17, 23 Oct.; 5, 7, 8, 9, 14, 22, 27, 29 Nov.; 10, 11, 12, 19, 20 Dec. *Irish News* 1983: 20, 21, 23, 26, 27, 28, 29, 30 July; 4, 5 Aug. 1984: 5, 18 Apr; 9, 22, 23, 30 May; 7, 12, 23 June; 10, 16, 17, 18, 23 Oct.; 6, 7, 8, 9, 13, 22, 23, 29 Nov.; 11, 12, 19, 20 Dec. *Guardian* 1983: 20, 21 July. 1984: 22, 23 May; 17 Oct.; 19, 20 Dec. *Irish Times* 1983: 19, 21 Apr.; 23 July.

THE ALLEN CASE (*R. v. AUSTIN*)

Belfast Telegraph 1983: 9 July; 21 Oct. 1984: 16 Feb.; 26 March.; 6, 9, 13, 14 Apr.; 13 June; 7 July; 7, 8, 9, 17, 18, 21, Aug.; 23, 24 Nov. 1985: 10 Jan.; 15, 26, 27 Feb.; 14, 20, 27, 28, 30 Mar.; 17 Apr.; 1, 2, 3, 17, 21, 31 May; 7, 12 June; 5, 6, 31 July. *Irish News* 1983: 4, 22 Oct.; 16 Nov. 1984: 6, 10 Apr.; 3, 7, 8, 9, 10, 14, 15, 16, 17, 18 Aug.; 29 Oct. 1985: 10 Jan.; 16 Feb.; 2, 15, 21, 22, 28 Mar.; 18 Apr.; 1, 2, 4, 17, 18, 22, 31 May; 4, 7, 11, 12 June. *Newsletter* 1984: 14 Aug. *Guardian* 1984: 8 Aug. *Irish Times* 1984: 14 Aug.

1

Informers, Agents Provocateurs, *and* *Supergrasses*

THE term 'supergrass' was first coined by journalists in the early 1970s to describe those 'grasses' (informers) from the London underworld who testified against their alleged former associates in a series of high-profile mass trials[1]:—a modern instance of the age-old use of informants for the purpose of social control. It should be noted at the outset of this study, however, that 'police inform-ants' come in many forms, that the information they supply can be used by crime-control systems in a variety of ways, and that together these variables open up a range of opportunities and dilemmas, particularly for law enforcement professing committment to due process and the rule of law. There are two main difficulties. The first concerns the extent to which informants genuinely assist in the prevention, detection, and punishment of crime, and how this contribution can be measured. It should be stressed that this is not the same question as the extent to which the police consider certain types helpful in their investigations. The second problem concerns the establishment of effective mechanisms of democratic and legal accountability, especially since reliance upon certain kinds of informant appears to require a high level of secrecy and faith in police discretion. Political or administrative accountability involves the establishment of effective, thorough, systematic, and regular reviews by the legislature into internal police supervision of the use of certain types of informant by officers on the ground, while legal accountability involves finding answers to three ques-tions in particular: (1) when, if ever, is it appropriate to permit the police to refuse to disclose to a court that an informant has been used in a criminal prosecution or that his or her identity should be kept secret? (2) how can the reliability of the information which

---

[1] It is said that the nickname 'grass' for informer derives from the Cockney rhyming slang 'grasshopper' for 'copper' (policeman), but it may also owe something to the popular song 'Whispering Grass' and to the phrase 'snake in the grass'.

informants supply be assessed, particularly when it takes the form of testimony in criminal trials? (3) when, if ever, can police use of *agents provocateurs* be justified?

To date, remarkably few attempts have been made to discuss the problems presented by different kinds of informant, and virtually all the literature focuses on only one subcategory, police *informers*.[2] While the latter term carries with it certain cloak-and-dagger connotations considered more fully below, the term 'police informant' can be used to embrace everyone who provides the police with information about any matter whatsoever—from the irate householder who phones to complain about the noise made by a neighbour's dog, to the police agent who testifies in a criminal trial

---

[2] The police studies and sociology literatures include police manuals on informers, such as M. L. Harney and J. C. Cross, *The Informer in Law Enforcement* (Springfield, Ill.: Charles Thomas, 1960); J. H. Skolnick, *Justice without Trial: Law Enforcement in Democratic Society*, 2nd edn. (New York: John Wiley & Sons, 1975), ch 6; G. T. Marx, *Undercover: Police Surveillance in America* (Berkeley, Calif.: University of California Press, 1988); D. Campbell, 'Whisper Who Dares' (1991) *Police Review* 532; M. Findlay, '"Acting on Information Received": Mythmaking and Police Corruption' (1987) 1 *Journal of Studies in Justice* 19; G. T. Marx, 'Thoughts on a Neglected Category of Social Movement Participant: The Agent Provocateur and the Informant' (1974) 80 *American Journal of Sociology* 402; T. A. Reazer, 'Needed Weapons in the Army's War on Drugs' (1987) 116 *Military Law Review* 1–65; J. R. Williams and L. L. Guess, 'The Informant: A Narcotics Enforcement Dilemma' (1981) 13 *Journal of Psychoactive Drugs* 235–45; J. Q. Wilson, *The Investigators: Managing FBI and Narcotics Agents* (New York: Basic Books, 1978); N. Dorn, K. Murji, and N. South, *Traffickers: Drug Markets and Law Enforcement* (London: Routledge, 1992), ch 8; M. Maguire and C. Norris, *The Conduct and Supervision of Criminal Investigations*, Royal Commission on Criminal Justice Research Study No. 5 (London: HMSO, 1993), 75–83 and 89–95. The legal literature includes G. J. Wool, 'Police Informants in Canada: The Law and the Reality' (1985–6) 50 *Saskatchewan Law Review* 249; E. Haglund, 'Impeaching the Underworld Informant' (1990) 63 *Southern California Law Review* 1407; D. Katz, 'The Paradoxical Role of Informers within the Criminal Justice System: A Unique Perspective' (1981) 7 *University of Dayton Law Review* 51; L. E. Lawler, 'Police Informer Privilege: A Study for the Law Reform Commission of Canada' (1986) 28 *Criminal Law Quarterly* 91; E. Oscapella, 'A Study of Informers in England' (1980) Crim LR 136; R. Parker, 'Confidential Informants and the Truth Finding Function' (1986) 4 *Cooley Law Review* 562. The historical literature includes W. O. Weyrauch, 'Gestapo Informants: Facts and Theory of Undercover Operations' (1986) 24 *Journal of Transnational Law* 553; T. Bunyan, *The History and Practice of the Political Police in Britain* (London: Quartet Books, 1983); L. Radzinowicz, *A History of English Criminal Law and its Administration from 1750*, ii (London: Stevens, 1956); C. Hibbert, *The Roots of Evil* (London: Weidenfeld & Nicolson, 1963), 92–3; E. P. Thompson, *The Making of the English Working Class* (London: Victor Gollancz, 1980), 529–40; V. Navasky, *Naming Names* (London: Calder, 1982); N. Schleifman, *Undercover Agents in the Russian Revolutionary Movement: The SR Party, 1902–14* (London: Macmillan, 1988).

against several dozen of those upon whom he has been spying. It follows that many participants in the criminal justice process who are more familiar in other guises—for example the eyewitness, the accused who confesses, the suspect who turns Queen's evidence, and even victims of crime—can be regarded as 'police informants'. It may be thought that to recast these familiar figures in this manner obscures rather than clarifies universally acknowledged roles, and it would certainly be a mistake to suggest, for example, that the victim's role as informant is more important than his or her role as victim. But that is not what is intended. The point of making this observation, and the purpose of this chapter, is to seek to discover the contribution various kinds of police informant make to law enforcement, the sources of systematic distortion in the information they supply, and the ways in which reliance upon that information may be properly regulated. This will enable a general frame of reference to be constructed against which the supergrass system in Northern Ireland can then be compared. A method for identifying types of police informant is, however, first required.

INSIDERS AND OUTSIDERS

The few attempts which have been made to understand the police informer (as opposed to the informant) have tended to distinguish types by reference to motivation, criminal background, level of secrecy, and frequency of contact with handlers.[3] While it cannot be denied that these are important considerations with respect to both the informer and the informant, they can best be considered within a broader structural framework where the key to identifying types of police informant is to be found in two key variables: their relationships with the activities and people about which and upon whom they inform, and their relationships with the policing agencies to whom they supply their information.[4] Two further distinctions emerge when the first variable is considered: that between *outsiders* and *insiders*, and that between *single-event informants* and *multiple-event informants*. Together these yield a fourfold typology:

---

[3] See police studies and sociological literatures cited in n. 2.
[4] The latter can include, in certain circumstances, the military and other institutions charged with a social control function, e.g. the British security services MI5 and MI6.

the inside single-event informant (the 'confessor' and the accomplice witness), inside multiple-event informants (the informer, *agent provocateur,* and supergrass), the outside single-event informant (the 'casual observer'), and the outside multiple-event informant (the 'snoop'). Victims of crime can also be inside or outside informants, depending upon whether or not they were present when the offence in question was committed.[5] Whether an informant is on the 'inside' or the 'outside' of any activity, and whether they have knowledge of just one or a whole series of incidents, will critically affect the kind of information which they can supply, its accuracy and detail, and the correct identification of suspects. The events reported by insiders and outsiders may be either criminal or political or a hybrid of the two, but this distinction assumes greatest significance within the inside multiple-event informant category, where the relationship between informant and policing agencies critically determines whether the inside multiple-event informant remains a pure informer or becomes an *agent provocateur* or supergrass.

The Snoop and the Casual Witness

Recent research reveals the centrality of the outside informant to routine modern police work in Britain, 80–90 per cent of offences reputedly being brought to the attention of the police by victims, bystanders, or other members of the public.[6] However, outsiders have little direct relevance to the present study, since they merely observe activities which they then report to the police but do not participate in them directly.

The typical 'casual observer' is a member of the public who, on an isolated occasion and usually by chance, observes a crime or an activity which is brought to the attention of the police, either voluntarily or as a result of the observer's having been traced and interviewed in the course of a police investigation. Such information may prove crucial in the detection and prosecution of crime, or it may be of no significance whatsoever. It may also be systematically

---

[5] The information supplied by outsider victims may be unreliable, as a result of either deliberate or innocent distortions, but it is difficult to judge whether these follow any systematic pattern.

[6] *Report of Royal Commission on Criminal Justice* (The Runciman Report), Cm. 2263 (London: HMSO, 1993), 10. The Audit Commission has also recently suggested that the police should increase their reliance upon informants still further. See *Guardian,* 20 Sept. 1993.

unreliable, but usually for innocent reasons. The various psychological studies have, for example, sought to identify systematic sources of unreliability in the evidence of eyewitnesses: poor quality of light at the scene, the distance between the observer and the event, the duration of the observation, the contemporaneous awareness of the observer of what precisely was being observed, and the distorting effect of leading questions by investigators afterwards.[7] In the United Kingdom, juries are permitted to convict on the evidence of eyewitnesses alone, but judges must caution them about the possible defects in this kind of evidence.[8]

As the name suggests, the 'snoop' supplies the police with information about a number of incidents usually following a pattern—for example, drug dealing. Some snoops are merely nosy parkers who like to tell tales on their neighbours when the occasion arises. Others, whose occupations may put them in a position to observe other people without drawing undue attention to themselves—shopkeepers, bar and hotel staff, janitors, street sweepers, post office delivery workers, and taxi-drivers—provide a kind of informal police surveillance service. The motives of snoops are varied. A few may act out of a sense of civic responsibility, while others may seek revenge for having been victimized by their targets, for example in a protection racket which may or may not be connected with the activities they report to the police. 'Petty criminal snoops' may themselves be involved in criminal activity, usually divorced from the behaviour they report, and may hope to ingratiate themselves with the police in order that their own criminality will be overlooked.

The information supplied by any of these kinds of informant may be systematically unreliable. But with the petty criminal snoop, deliberate distortion, by the snoop and/or by the police, can occur more readily than with the casual observer, since the information may be supplied under pressure. There are also considerable opportunities for the police to share in the profits of the snoop's own criminality. The police will generally be strongly opposed to the disclosure of the identity of a 'serious snoop', especially as a trial

---

[7] See, e.g., E. Loftus and G. Wells (eds.), *Eyewitness Testimony: Psychological Perspectives* (Cambridge: Cambridge University Press, 1984); D. Farrington, K. Hawkins, and S. Lloyd-Bostock (eds.), *Psychology, Law and Legal Processes* (London: Macmillan Press, 1979) pt. 4; B. Clifford, *The Psychology of Person Identification* (London: Routledge & Kegan Paul, 1978).

[8] See *R.* v. *Turnbull* [1976] 3 All ER 549.

witness, unless the squandering of the source of information which this would cause is deemed cost-effective. The courts, for their part, have attempted to strike a balance between permitting non-disclosure, in order to protect vital police sources, and compelling disclosure when the defence of the accused demands it.[9] The common law treats snoops as eyewitnesses unless the court takes the view that their evidence is given from improper motives, in which case the judge may warn the jury of the dangers inherent in accepting their evidence.[10]

The Accomplice Witness

Inside informants are those who are directly involved either actively or passively in the activities they report to the police. Apart from certain victims of crime,[11] and the suspect who confesses and thereby 'informs' only on himself, there are two kinds of inside single-event informant: the 'confession informer' and the 'accomplice witness'. Typically, the confession informer will confess his own wrongdoing and implicate others, who are then prosecuted either upon their own confessions or other evidence. The accomplice witness, however, testifies against his alleged associates at trial. This kind of informant may emerge with respect to any offence which involves more than one offender, in any part of the jurisdiction, and under the influence of one or more motives, including: genuine contrition; the hope of striking a bargain with the prosecuting authorities in the selection of charges and/or with the courts in passing sentence; revenge against fellow accomplices; or a configuration of all three. However, the decision to co-operate with the police is generally taken only after arrest and may be influenced by police suggestions. Because the accomplice witness is an offender who is likely to become a defendant, there will generally be no problem from the police point of view concerning the disclosure of identity, and there will be no opportunity for the

---

[9] See, e.g. C. Tapper, *Cross on Evidence*, 2nd edn. (London: Butterworth, 1990), 473–4.

[10] See *R. v. Beck* [1982] 1 WLR 461.

[11] Some victims, e.g. those who are assaulted, may be directly involved in the activities which they report to the police. Questions surrounding the reliability of their information, however, resemble more closely those posed by the casual witness than those posed by the outsider victim, since similar systematically distorting processes concerning accurate observation and recall of events are likely to be present.

accomplice witness to be used by the police for surveillance purposes, much less as an *agent provocateur*, and little risk of police
corruption. The transformation from suspect to Crown witness is
amenable to quite a high degree of public disclosure and legal
accountability, although informal understandings regarding charge
and sentence may be reached 'off stage'.

From at least the seventeenth century, the common law has
admitted the evidence of those who have decided to betray their
erstwhile partners in crime.[12] Until 1954, subject to certain statutory exceptions,[13] the law for England, Wales, and Northern
Ireland gave juries in criminal trials absolute discretion to convict
upon the testimony of accomplices, whether their evidence was
corroborated or not, although from the nineteenth century onwards
it had become customary for judges to warn juries that, while they
could convict upon uncorroborated accomplice evidence, it was
dangerous to do so.[14] In 1954 Lord Simonds LC declared, in
Davies v. *DPP*, that the warning rule, until then one of judicial
practice, had become a rule of law.[15] Between then and the enactment of the Criminal Justice and Public Order Act 1994, including
the period in Northern Ireland to which this study refers, a failure
by judges to issue a warning in cases where an accomplice had
given evidence for the prosecution would generally have resulted in
the quashing of convictions on appeal.[16] Section 32 (1) (*a*) of the

---

[12] In *R.* v. *Turner* (1975) 61 Cr App R 67, 78–9, the Court of Appeal rejected the
argument that *R.* v. *Pipe* (1967) 51 Cr App R 17 had established a rule that trial
judges were obliged as a matter of law to exclude the evidence of accomplices who
could be influenced by continuing inducements, e.g. their own impending trial. See
also *Noor Mohamed* v. *The King* [1949] AC 182, 192; *Harris* v. *DPP* [1952] AC 694,
707. Today, such evidence can be excluded at the judge's discretion if, having taken
all the relevant factors into account, he or she considers that the inducement which
has encouraged compliance has made the testimony untrustworthy. This appears to
happen rarely, with the result that accomplice evidence called by the Crown is
unlikely to be ruled inadmissible. See *R.* v. *Rudd* (1775) 1 Camp 331; *R.* v. *Attwood*
(1787) 1 Leach 464; *R.* v. *Jones* (1809) 2 Camp 131; *R.* v. *Pipe* (1967) 51 Cr App R
67, 78–9; *R.* v. *Turner* (1975) 61 Cr App R 67, 77. See also L. Radzinowicz, *A
History of English Criminal Law and its Administration from 1750* (London: Stevens,
1956), ii, ch. 2; E. Oscapella, 'A Study of Informers in England' [1980] Crim LR
136.
[13] See Tapper, *Cross on Evidence*, 225–8.
[14] *R.* v. *Stubbs* (Deans 555); *Re Meunier* [1894] 2 QB 415; *R.* v. *Turner* (1975) 61
Cr App R 61.
[15] [1954] AC 378.
[16] Criminal Appeal Act 1968, s. 2 (1); *R.* v. *Turner* (1978) 66 Cr App R 6, 16.
The position in Scotland is more demanding still. Except in certain circumstances
prescribed by statute, Scottish criminal law prohibits convictions unless the evidence

1994 Act, which does not apply to Northern Ireland, removes the obligation for accomplice evidence warnings to be issued, although they may still be given as a matter of judicial discretion.

Accomplice evidence warnings, particularly the danger-warning, make heavy demands of both judge and jury. The judge's task of formulating the appropriate directions is not easy, and the jury's task of following them is more difficult still. If the witness in question does not admit to being an accomplice, the judge must explain the legal requirements.[17] Accomplices for this purpose include: parties to the crime charged either as principals or as accessories or as persons committing, procuring, or aiding and abetting; receivers of goods from a thief in the trial of the thief for theft; parties to offences allegedly committed by the accused on occasions other than that of the offence charged. The jury must decide whether the witness they have heard satisfies this test, and the judge must warn them that if they find the witness is an accomplice, it is dangerous to convict upon his or her evidence unless it is corroborated. There must be specific reference to danger, and a mere warning to be careful or cautious is not enough.[18] The judge is obliged to explain the nature of the danger,[19] to indicate which items of evidence are capable of amounting to corroboration, to draw the jury's attention to apparent weaknesses in the accomplice's evidence, and to ensure that jurors are left in no doubt that it is up to them to determine whether, in the circumstances, the evidence actually meets the required corroborative standard.[20] But beyond this the courts have not attempted to specify precisely the form the warning should take.[21]

The accomplice evidence rule is based upon the premise that accomplices as a class of witness are inherently untrustworthy and that their evidence, in consequence, must be presumed to be unreliable—hence the emphasis on corroboration. The following

---

of at least 2 witnesses implicates the accused in the offence with which he or she is charged. See *Morton* v. *HM Adv.*, 1938 JC 50, 55; *Lockwood* v. *Walker* (1909) 6 Adam 124; *Harrison* v. *MacKenzie*, 1923 JC 61; *Townshend* v. *Strathern*, 1923 JC 66.

[17] *R.* v. *Davies* [1954] AC 378, 400.

[18] *R.* v. *Beck* [1982] 1 WLR 461, 468 and 813.

[19] *R.* v. *Price* [1983] Crim LR 173; *R.* v. *Riley* (1979) 70 Cr App R 1.

[20] *R.* v. *Charles* (1979) 68 Cr App R 334; *R.* v. *Reeves* (1979) 68 Cr App R 331. See also E. Munday, 'Juries and Corroboration' (1980) 130 NLJ 352.

[21] *R.* v. *Thorne* (1978) 66 Cr App R 6, 16; *R.* v. *Price* (1967) 52 Cr App R 67, 79.

dangers have traditionally been cited.[22] First, accomplice witnesses are, by definition, criminals and therefore, in the eyes of the law, persons of bad character, whose evidence is 'not entitled to the same consideration as the evidence of a clean man, free from infamy'.[23] Secondly, they may have motives to fabricate chunks of their 'evidence'. Thirdly, the accomplice may tell the truth about the incidents in question but substitute the names of innocent people, or suspects whom the police are especially anxious to see convicted, for those who in fact took part.[24] Fourthly, the accomplice witness may change the roles of those involved, casting himself or herself in the most favourable light and the other suspects in the worst. Fifthly, spurious plausibility could be accorded false accomplice evidence by virtue of the accomplice's familiarity with the details of the crime or crimes. Sixthly, the real worry, according to Wigmore, is that the accomplice gives his or her evidence in the expectation of executive clemency.[25]

The accomplice evidence rule has been cogently criticized by a number of commentators from at least the 1840s,[26] primarily on the grounds that this brand of evidence is in principle no more dangerous than that supplied by other categories of witness. The unreliability of identification evidence by alleged eyewitnesses has, for example, long been recognized, but a caution rather than a danger-warning is required. It has also been argued that not all accomplice evidence suffers from the defects traditionally attributed to it. As Dennis asks: 'if the honesty of a particular witness is not expressly challenged by the defence nor called into question by the facts of the case, why should the presumption of suspicion automatically be applied?'[27] However, the fact that juries are permitted

---

[22] For an account of these dangers, see J. D. Heydon, 'The Corroboration of Accomplices' [1973] Crim LR 264.

[23] *People* v. *Coffey*, 39 LRANS 704, 706 (1911), *per* Henshaw J.

[24] As Maule J. stated in *Mullins*: 'it often happens that an accomplice is a friend of those who committed the crime with him and he would much rather get them out of the scrapes and fix an innocent man than his real associates', (1848) 3 Cox CC 526, 531, and as Lord Abinger CB said in *Farler*: 'the danger is, that when a man is fixed, and knows that his own guilt is detected he purchases impunity by falsely accusing others', (1837) 8 C & P 106, 108.

[25] J. Chadbourn (ed.), *Wigmore on Evidence in Trials at Common Law*, vii (Boston: Little, Brown & Co., 1978), § 2057.

[26] See, e.g., Chief Baron Joy, *Evidence of Accomplices* (London, 1844).

[27] I. Dennis, 'Corroboration Requirements Reconsidered' [1984] Crim LR 316. See also [1985] Crim LR, 143; J. D. Jackson, 'Credibility, Morality and the Corroboration Warning' (1988) 47 CLJ 428.

to convict upon uncorroborated accomplice evidence, even where the warning rule is mendatory, indicates that the presumption of unreliability is rebuttable in specific cases. Whether this occurs or not appears to depend upon the tribunal of fact's assessment of the credibility of the accomplice evidence and the degree to which it considers convincing independent evidence has been presented by the prosecution.

Informers, Supergrasses, and agents provocateurs

Inside multiple-event informants, the 'classic police informers', have been vilified in novels,[28] despised by diverse cultures, and are notorious under a host of nicknames in the English language alone: tout, rat, singer, finger, mule mouth, squealer, fink, snout, mut (apparently short for 'mutter'), snitch, stool-pigeon, stoolie, and nark (probably derived from the French *narquois*, mocking or derisive).[29] Judas Iscariot is, of course, the most notorious informer in the Christian tradition, while the Talmud prescribes harsh treatment—flogging, imprisonment, branding the forehead, cutting out the tongue, chopping off the hand, banishment, and death— for Jews who inform against other Jews to gentiles.[30] In modern Western societies the police informer or agent will typically be closely involved in criminal organizations or political/social associations which the police find suspicious and may be called upon to play one or more of three roles—pure informer, *agent provocateur*, or supergrass. It should be observed, however, that the informer is likely to be merely a cog, albeit a vital one, in a complex intelligence-gathering system in which a variety of other methods, such as technological surveillance, are also likely to be employed. But Dillon points out that, in Northern Ireland, and probably more generally: 'the most successful means of intelligence-gathering

---

[28] See, e.g., L. O'Flaherty, *The Informer* (London: Jonathan Cape, 1925), made into a film by John Ford in 1935, and Gerard Seymour, *Field of Blood* (London: Collins, 1985), a novel about a supergrass in Northern Ireland in the 1980s.

[29] *The Dictionary of American Underworld Lingo* has 68 words for informer. See D. Campbell, 'Splendour in Grassing', *Guardian*, 26–7 Oct. 1991.

[30] See Rabbi Abraham A. Rapoport, 'The Informer in Jewish Literature' (Ph.D. thesis, Yeshiva Univ., 1952), 3, 5, 96; D. Heller, 'Informing in Jewish Law' (paper prepared for Rabbi Rackman, New York Law School, Feb. 1977). The Aramaic word for informer, as found in the biblical Book of Daniel—*akhal kurtza*—literally means 'to eat someone else's flesh', and the so-called Minean curse, which was introduced as the 12th benediction to the daily Amidah prayer, says: 'and for the informer may there be no hope'. Navasky, *Naming Names*, p. xii.

still appears to be the traditional one—the use of informers, who are closer to terrorists than computers and thermal imagery and, unlike bugs can move independently.[31]

The pure informer merely supplies information to the police about the activities of any given political or criminal group and may do so with varying regularity. Some, generally described as police spies or agents, discharge what amounts to a professional informing role and may be either undercover police-officers or private citizens, although in certain contexts the distinction may be difficult to draw.[32] Infiltration by full-time professional police-officers is difficult to justify in a democracy, since it will involve the police in crime or the manipulation of legal political movements.[33] While also merely supplying information, the *agent provocateur* will, by definition, also seek to encourage the group's activities, whether or not authorized to do so by police handlers. The political *agent provocateur* may encourage both further legal and illegal activities, but his or her classic function is to push political groups which have been acting legally into committing crimes, in order to provide the police with a justification for making arrests and initiating prosecutions. The police may have other motives for using political *agents provocateurs*—for example, to encourage divisions within a given group between those who favour and those who are opposed to illegality, or to damage the group's public image. The classic function of the *agent provocateur* operating in purely criminal organizations is similar: to encourage offences to be committed at a time and place that will enable the police to make arrests. Strangely, and in spite of strong evidence that the information supplied by the *agent provocateur* is likely to be the most unreliable of that given by any type of police informant, an *agent provocateur* or spy is not regarded by the common law as an accomplice, with the result that the mandatory warning about accomplice evidence discussed above has not applied,

---

[31] M. Dillon, *The Dirty War* (London: Arrow Books, 1991) 417.

[32] The British army distinguishes between 'an *agent*: . . . one who is authorized or instructed to obtain or to assist in obtaining information for intelligence or counter-intelligence purposes' and 'an *informant*: . . . any individual who gives information. The term is generally used to describe a casual or undirected source as distinct from an *informer*, who is normally connected with criminal activities, can be directed, and receives payment for his services'. See Dillon, *The Dirty War*, 309.

[33] See Marx, *Undercover*.

although one may be issued at the trial judge's discretion.[34]

Supergrasses can fulfil the functions of both pure informer and *agent provocateur*. But their unique contribution is to allow the carefully cultivated results of sophisticated police intelligence-gathering systems to be presented in court for the purpose of convicting large numbers of suspected terrorists or organized criminals.[35] As the experience of Northern Ireland shows, however, this need not exclude the use of high-grade intelligence for other objectives, for example selective assassination. Since their central function is to obtain convictions in the courts, supergrasses can have no role in purely political organizations. The four key factors conducive to the construction of supergrass systems appear to be: mature informer and intelligence-gathering systems, the perceived failure of other methods to deal with a particular problem of crime or political violence, a crisis of allegiance on the part of at least some members of the target organizations,[36] and the attractiveness of the officially sanctioned rewards on offer—typically immunity from prosecution, reduced prison sentences, and new lives and new identities elsewhere.[37] The dangers associated with accomplice evidence, discussed above, are particularly acute with respect to supergrasses.[38] Each supergrass has been involved in serious, and mostly violent, crime and is therefore regarded by the law as of unusually

[34] Tapper, *Cross on Evidence*, 232; *R.* v. *Mullins* (1848) 3 Cox CC 526; *R.* v. *Bickley* (1909) 2 Cr App R 53; *Sneddon* v. *Stephenson* [1967] 2 All ER 1277; *Dental Board* v. *O'Callaghan* [1969] IR 181; *R.* v. *Phillips* [1963] NZLR 855, See also D. Miers, 'Informers and Agents Provocateurs' (1970) 120 NLJ 577 & 'Agents Provocateurs: The Judicial Response' (1970) 120 NLJ 597.

[35] While the term 'supergrass' need not necessarily be confined to those super-informers who go into the witness-box to testify for the prosecution, a convenient label is, none the less, needed to distinguish 'super-accomplice-witnesses' from mere 'super-informers', and the term 'supergrass' is as good as any. This is also the sense in which the term has come to be understood by the courts in Northern Ireland. See Ch. 8.

[36] The crisis of allegiance, which is particularly important in cultivating anti-terrorist supergrass systems, may also be present to a degree in supergrass systems targeted upon organized crime. For example, Tommaso Buscetta, the Italian and US Mafia supergrass, claimed that he turned state's evidence because the Mafia had breached its own rules of conduct. See Ch. 10.

[37] These may also be available to pure informers. Maurice O'Mahoney, one of the English supergrasses claims that another English supergrass, George du Buriatte, received plastic surgery in order to change his appearance. See M. O'Mahoney with D. Wooding, *King Squealer: The True Story of Maurice O'Mahoney* (London: W. H. Allen, 1978), 123.

[38] This was not fully recognized by the courts until *R.* v. *Crumley* (1986) 14 NIJB 30, the last but one appeal in the supergrass system in Northern Ireland in the 1980s.

bad character, even compared with other possible accomplice witnesses. The pressure to tell a story sufficiently appealing to attract the various rewards on offer is also likely to be more intense than with most other accomplices turning Queen's evidence. There is, in addition, ample time and opportunity during the many months spent in protective police custody for false evidence to be rehearsed in preparation for a convincing court-room performance. The risk of unreliability is greatly increased by the length of time it takes to prepare a supergrass for trial and the complexity of the issues which any case raises, even assuming incorrigible bona fides on the part of all concerned. As already noted, several studies illustrate how the accuracy of eyewitness testimony can be seriously, and unintentionally, distorted by the lapse of time between the event and the recording of statements[39] and by intervening suggestions as to what, and whom, the original event may have involved.[40]

THE CRIMINAL INFORMER

Criminal informers have played an important part in the development of modern policing, and the historical evidence reveals some of the dangers created by reliance upon their services. The criminal justice system in England in the seventeenth and eighteenth centuries relied heavily upon a variety of informal, and often privately organized, mechanisms of law enforcement,[41] and by the eighteenth century the paid agents of voluntary policing organizations[42] were using information supplied by 'common informers' to frame charges contained in warrants laid before the magistrates and then delivered to parish constables to be served upon the named miscreants. Widely despised by the populace, the common informer brought transgressions to the attention of the authorities not because he had been personally aggrieved or wished to see justice

[39] See, e.g., B. Clifford, 'Eye Witness Testimony: The Bridging of a Credibility Gap', in Farrington *et al.* (eds.), *Psychology, Law and Legal Processes*; E. Loftus, *Eye Witness Testimony*, (Boston: Harvard University Press, 1979), chs. 2–5.
[40] The problem of 'memory freezing' was raised by defence counsel in the Kirkpatrick supergrass trial and was noted but not discussed in depth by the Northern Ireland Court of Appeal.
[41] See generally, Hibbert, *Roots of Evil*, 92–3; Radzinowicz, *History of English Criminal Law*.
[42] W. E. H. Lecky, *History of England in the Eighteenth Century* (London, 1921), iii. 33.

done, but because the law offered him a share in any fine imposed.[43]

The ancient practice of 'approvement' also allowed an offender to confess both to a specific crime and to all other treasons and felonies in which he had been either principal or agent, and then offer to name his accomplices. If his offer was accepted, the accomplices were put on trial and if they were convicted, the approver received a royal pardon. But if the accomplices were acquitted, the approver was sentenced to death.[44] In the seventeenth century Hale denounced the bills of approvement on the grounds that: 'more mischief hath come to good men . . . by false accusations of desperate villains, than benefit to the public by the discovery and convicting of real offenders, gaolers for their own profits often constraining prisoners to appeal honest men'.[45] As the century progressed, the system became so restricted that it fell into disuse.

The appearance and growth of organized crime in England in the late seventeenth and early eighteenth centuries prompted the authorities to professionalize further the role of the common informer through an elaborate system of rewards, and through better incentives for accomplices to turn King's evidence. By the eighteenth century, approvement had been replaced by the 'equitable claim to the mercy of the Crown', a judicial recommendation for executive clemency in cases where an offender had confessed to all his treasons and felonies and had testified in the successful prosecution of his accomplices. Pardon could also be claimed as an absolute right under some fourteen major statutes enacted in the seventeenth and eighteenth centuries, provided the offender voluntarily gave himself up and his evidence secured one or more conviction. Throughout the eighteenth and nineteenth centuries the government also offered a free pardon to those who were instrumental in obtaining the conviction of their accomplices for certain specific offences, and Radzinowicz claims that 'there can be no doubt . . . that all these methods were employed upon such a scale that pardon ultimately became a major instrument for bringing criminals to justice'.[46]

Corruption was the clear by-product of most of these arrange-

---

[43] Radzinowicz, *History of English Criminal Law*, ii. 140. According to Hibbert the role of such informants is traceable to the 7th cent. Hibbert, *Roots of Evil*, 92.

[44] Radzinowicz, *History of English Criminal Law*, ii. 40–56.

[45] *Pleas of the Crown*, ii. 226.

[46] *History of English Criminal Law*, ii. 52.

ments. Some informers turned *agents provocateurs,* since the more serious the offence, the greater the rewards. Small and ruthless groups policed certain offences as their own private fiefdoms, with the result that the distinction between the professions of criminal, informer, and informal police-officer became blurred. For example, one of the most notorious criminals of the early eighteenth century, Jonathan Wild, plied his trade as informer in order to control his own criminal empire,[47] while the Bow Street Runners, the entrepreneurial progenitors of the British police, made deals with informers and thief-catchers in order to avoid competition for bounty.[48] However, the move towards the establishment of a professional police force in the early nineteenth century encroached upon the territory of the entrepreneurial informer. The Metropolitan Police, formed in 1829, was opposed to the use of informers as a means of laying charges,[49] and in 1839 magistrates in the metropolis were empowered to reduce the informer's share of the fine, or even to deny it altogether.[50] Nevertheless, statutes continued to be enacted which conferred powers upon, and granted privileges to, informers,[51] and it was not until 1951 that the Common Informers Act repealed, in whole or in parts, some forty-eight previous statutes, dating from 1382 to 1949, dealing with informers' rewards.

The classic empirical study of the modern criminal informer was conducted in the United States by Skolnick in the 1960s,[52] and several more recent studies suggest that little has changed in the processes described.[53] Skolnick found that informers are particularly useful to the police in identifying those responsible for victimless offences, for example those involving narcotics, with the police themselves typically playing the roles of complainant and witness. Narcotics policing tends to be highly pro-active, providing the police with a challenging, high-status, game-like job, and symbolizes efficient professionalism and thorough detective-work.[54] Attempts by the police to cultivate a relationship with the addict and

[47] See Hibbert, *Roots of Evil,* 47–50.
[48] Ibid. 103–4; Radzinowicz, *History of English Criminal Law,* ii. 151.
[49] Radzinowicz, *History of English Criminal Law,* ii. 153.
[50] The Metropolitan Police Courts Act, 2 & 3 Vict., c. 71, s. 34.
[51] Radzinowicz, *History of English Criminal Law,* ii. 155.
[52] Skolnick, *Justice without Trial.*
[53] See especially Marx, *Undercover*; Dorn, Murji, and South, *Traffickers,* ch. 8, and other sociological studies cited in note 2.
[54] See also R. Baldwin and R. Kinsey, *Police Powers and Politics* (London: Quartet Books, 1982), 64–74.

build dependence upon particular police-handlers hinge upon the bolstering of the informer's low sense of self-esteem and on the vital reinforcement of the undertaking that under no circumstances will his or her identity be disclosed to the underworld.

Skolnick also found that newspaper reports claiming that informers are paid large sums of money tend to be exaggerated. The police have an obvious interest in portraying themselves as generous paymasters, and this false picture may be sustained by the targets, who often find it hard to believe that they have been betrayed for so little. Although there are exceptions, the informer's primary interest tends to be lenient treatment by the criminal justice system rather than a financial reward.[55] Skolnick also claims that the allegation that the police grant informers a licence to commit crime tends to be untrue,[56] although myths to this effect are often cultivated by informers themselves in order to ingratiate themselves with their quarry. However, officers in one police department—narcotics, for example—tend to turn a blind eye to offences committed by their own informers which fall within the jurisdiction of another police department—burglary, for example.[57] Secrecy is a key ingredient in the management of the informer system, and even police records will often fail to record that an informer has been used in cases where, Skolnick claims, it is difficult to believe that this has not been the case.[58]

Skolnick argues that when the legal rules require the disclosure of the identity of informers in order to gain convictions, or where the case is too large or too important to be entrusted to addicts or to other civilians, the police themselves may play the role of *agent*

[55] In their police manual, Harney and Cross attribute 7 principal motives to the 'underworld informer': fear of associates or his fate in the criminal justice process; revenge; 'perverse' motives such as those possessed by the racketeer who informs on a rival to remove him from the scene; egotistical motives—the 'kick' of being regarded as a kind of celebrity; mercenary motives; dementia or eccentric motives; and, rarely encountered, repentance, *The Informer*, 37. See also J. Goodman and I. Will, *Underworld* (London: Harrap, 1985).

[56] See also Goodman and Will, *Underworld*, 49.

[57] This is supported by Baldwin and Kinsey's study, which found that professional rivalry and competition often make crime-patrol officers reluctant to pass on information and details about their sources and informants to other colleagues, *Police Powers*, 72.

[58] Skolnick maintains that, even though informers are almost invariably used in crimes of vice, only 9 per cent of 508 narcotics cases on the files of the Westville police from Dec. 1961 to Mar. 1963 mentioned that an informer had been involved in the investigation.

provocateur. The identity of an informer may have to be disclosed even in circumstances where the law does not always require it, where the informer participated in the crime charged, was an eyewitness to the offences in question, provided information which was the only justification for police suspicions, or would be a material witness on the issue of guilt in circumstances where non-disclosure would deprive the accused of a fair trial. In the second edition of *Justice without Trial,* published in 1975, Skolnick argues that court decisions such as that of *Theodor* v. *Superior Court*[59] have made it easier than hitherto for defendants to force the disclosure of an informer's identity and that this has resulted in the 'lateral snitch', where informers, knowing that their identities may be disclosed in some future proceedings, inform on small fry like themselves rather than take the risks which attach to the successful prosecution of the 'Mr Bigs'. This in its turn has caused friction between the police—who remain committed to the informer system because of its structural significance in the enforcement of victimless crimes, the functional need to keep the informer's identity secret despite the new legal developments, and the perceived organizational pressure on the vice squad to be productive through arrests—and the district attorneys, who regard the lateral snitch as having rendered informers largely useless.

Marx maintains that there have been two further important changes in the broader context since Skolnick's study. First, the technology available for covert policing in the United States has developed dramatically. Secondly, the scope of undercover police operations, including those in which informers are involved, has been greatly extended, and these methods are now increasingly being used by law enforcement agencies which never had recourse to them before—for example, the Immigration and Naturalization Service and the Internal Revenue Service—and in respect of offences never before a target of this kind of policing—for example, relatively unorganized street-crime and burglary, and white-collar crime. A tendency has also developed for covert operations to be

---

[59] (1972) 8 Cal. 3d 77. It was held that the identity of an informer can be kept secret if the purpose of disclosure is merely to show that the police did not have probable cause to make an arrest, but that if the defendant can make a plausible case that the informer may be a material witness on the issue of guilt or innocence, the name of the informer must be revealed. The informer can then be subpoenaed as a material witness and cross-examined, and if the prosecution refuses to comply, the judge must dismiss the case.

targeted upon individuals or groups to see what offences they may be committing, rather than upon offences to see who is committing them.[60]

The work of Skolnick and others shows, therefore, that although the criminal informer may make a genuinely positive contribution to the enforcement of the law against certain kinds of crime, since many of these are victimless offences, it is debatable whether they should be criminalized in the first place. The police maintain that secrecy is the cornerstone of any informer system and that even limited disclosure would destroy it. But secrecy is also the source of its most serious problems—police corruption, prosecutions on unreliable information, and the activities of *agents provocateurs*. The establishment of a standing commission on informers, which could periodically inspect internal police monitoring procedures but which would not look into any specific case might provide a partial solution to these problems.

THE POLITICAL INFORMER

In spite of the rich historical literature on informers in various political movements, little attempt has been made to study the phenomenon systematically. In some ways this is surprising, because, as the case-studies show, undercover agents can seriously affect the life of a movement by providing a means through which its activities are successfully repressed or contained. However, they can also, ironically, prolong a group's life-span and even channel it in directions which are more dangerous to the *status quo*. As with the study of other brands of police informant, social scientists can find access to data difficult because of the inherent secrecy of the political informer's world, because researchers sympathetic to the groups under analysis may be reluctant to admit that some of the movement's potency may have derived from planted agents rather than genuine devotees, and because some observers may attribute participants' accounts of infiltration to paranoia and an exaggerated sense of their own importance. The source of much social research, the printed word, may also not give much indication of the informer's occult role.

Given the absence of systematic research, it is difficult to draw

---

[60] Marx, *Undercover*, ch. 1.

many general conclusions other than that the role of the political informer is extremely complex and often highly paradoxical. However, a relationship appears to exist between political intolerance, heavy reliance upon political informers by policing agencies, and the absence of effective, genuinely independent supervisory institutions. A key factor leading to an increase in the use of political informers in any given state, including those in the liberal democratic tradition, is the regime's sense of security and its perception of the significance of challenges to its authority and interests.[61]

Non-Violent Political Movements

Navasky and Marx offer some of the most useful insights into the role of informers in modern non-violent political movements in the United States.[62] In his study of informers in the McCarthyite anti-communist witch-hunts of the 1950s, Navasky distinguishes four types according to motivation: the 'informer as patriot', who informs out of hostility to the group in question; the 'espionage informer', a police officer or other official who penetrates a given movement; the 'conspiracy informer', a member of the movement who regularly supplies official agencies with information; and the 'liberal informer', the non-political individual who likes to be helpful to the authorities when the opportunity arises.[63] Navasky argues that, in this period, the informer became a vital weapon, not only in the civil war between the self-styled guardians of internal security and the defenders of civil liberties in the United States, but also in the struggle within the liberal community between anti-communist 'liberals' and anti-anti-communist 'progressives'. The dubious information supplied by informers assisted in the conviction of many suspected subversives. The trial of eleven leaders of the Communist Party in New York in 1949, for example, 'wrote the script for a series of similar trials across the country' featuring a 'parade of FBI informants and ex-communists many of them professional informers'.[64] Informers were also instrumental in ruining numerous careers, particularly in the glamorous Hollywood

---

[61] Marx, 'Neglected Category'; Thompson, *English Working Class.*

[62] Navasky, *Naming Names*; Marx, 'Neglected Category'.

[63] *Naming Names*, ch. 1. Navasky (73–5) also identifies numerous other kinds according to a variety of other variables, e.g. the 'reluctant', 'enthusiastic', 'informed and philosophical', 'truth-telling', 'combative', 'denigrating', 'noisy', 'comic', 'husband-and-wife', 'volunteer', 'informer-by-dispensation', and 'resister-informer'.

[64] Ibid. 4.

film industry. Navasky concludes that apart from the shattered lives of those denounced as communists or fellow-travellers, 'the informer's particular contribution was to pollute the public well, to poison social life in general, to destroy the very possibility of a community; for the informer operates on the principle of betrayal and the community survives on the principle of trust'.[65]

In his study of informers in the radical US political and social movements of the 1960s Marx lists five principal motives— patriotism/ideological opposition to the group in question; coercion from the police (principally through the threat of arrest and prosecution followed by the prospect of offers of immunity from prosecution, leniency in the selection of charges, release from police custody, or help with various official problems, such as those concerning naturalization);[66] inducement; activist disaffection (caused, for example, by a transformation in beliefs, by personal vendettas, leadership contests, attempts to change the direction of the organization, or rivalry with other groups at the same end of the political spectrum); and the desire to become a double agent. While the line between the coercion and the inducement categories is blurred, the distinction is none the less important, the latter referring to those informers who were motivated purely by the prospect of financial gain. Federal agencies have traditionally had special funds with which to pay informers, while local police have had limited resources, if any. Apart from those in narcotics cases, informers at the local level were paid only nominal amounts, although in some political cases the rewards were considerable.[67] The desire to become a double agent can also be complex. Marx found that some double agents deliberately give the authorities false information and act as the movement's spy deep in officialdom, others are opportunistic and co-operate with, or mislead, either side as it suits their own interests, while others may be ambivalent about their true allegiances and shift their loyalties back and forth. The double

[65] Navasky, *Naming Names*, 347.

[66] Marx found that 6 of those involved in 15 documented civilian cases appear to have been coerced into this role as a result of arrest or threatened arrest. 'Neglected Category', 414.

[67] One student activist at a mid-western university, for example, went through her entire studies on what amounted to an FBI scholarship, receiving $300 a month in return for reports on student politics and the general mood on campus. In fact she was generally sympathetic to the student movement and claimed she wrote deliberately selective reports in order to protect it. Ibid. 415.

agent can, therefore, present problems for both the police and the movement to which he or she belongs.

In order to remain covert, the informer must appear credible to other activists, and in order to appear credible, he or she must appear to be willingly involved in the movement's activities. The informer's instructions may also be extremely vague, so it may be difficult in any given case to say what was, and what was not, authorized, with excesses taking the form either of exaggerated reports of the strengths of the subject group, intended to impress the police, or of unauthorized provocation. Marx discovered that, in two-thirds of the thirty-four cases he examined, informers went beyond passive information-gathering to active provocation. Certain kinds of agent may become *agents provocateurs* by another route, namely, by 'going native'—a particular risk with movements based upon distinct ethnic or socio-economic characteristics which the informer must share if he or she is to infiltrate effectively.

According to Marx, informers working on political cases were more likely to be subject to central supervision in the United States than informers operating in the field of organized crime. Controls included placing several informers, unknown to each other, on the same assignments to act as a mutual check, using electronic surveillance on the agent as well as on the activists, using police officers rather than civilians as infiltrators, and employing more developed organizational supervision rather than leaving decisions to individual officers. Marx argues, however, that even with strong institutional supervision, bureaucratic pressures, such as the need to increase productivity rates, can militate against the careful and thorough assessment of the reliability of the information which an informer supplies, and the efficiency of police checks on reliability is likely to diminish the more the information confirms police preconceptions of the nature of the group under surveillance.

The use of informers by the police in entirely lawful political movements is difficult to justify in a democracy. Marx argues that since most of the information gathered by political informers never features in court cases, and since successfully prosecuted political conspiracy cases are extremely rare, the 'latent reason' for the activities of the political informer in the United States in the 1960s may have been, 'to harass, control and combat those who, while technically not violating any laws [held] political views and

[had] lifestyles . . . at odds with the dominant society'.[68] In the United States, the jury system, the effectiveness of judicial review, and the defence of entrapment provide important safeguards against the abuse of police powers with respect to legal political movements. But considerable damage may none the less be caused to legal political organizations beyond the purview of the law by police informers and *agents provocateurs.* According to Marx this can be seen 'as one device whereby police may take action consistent with their own sense of justice and morality, independent of the substantive and procedural requirements of the law',[69] a danger compounded by the fact that the information supplied by political informers is often unreliable. Although police corruption, in the sense of bribery and profiteering, is not particularly likely in this context, there is a risk that distorted police perspectives will, in their turn, have a distorting impact upon the politics of the society in question, arguably a corruption of a potentially more serious kind.[70]

Violent Political Movements

In the nineteenth century, police penetration of subversive organizations was widespread, especially in the Austro-Hungarian empire during the Metternich period, in the France of Louis Philippe and Napoleon III, and in Prussia under Friedrich Wilhelm IV.[71] Schleifman's study shows that those who informed on the Russian Socialist Revolutionary Party in the early twentieth century fell into three broad categories: 'informers'—non-party members who passed on information to the police which they had picked up casually; 'secret agents' or *agents provocateurs*—party members who reported regularly to the police and were paid for their information; and 'external agents', 'filers', or 'shpiki'—low-ranking police-officers

---

[68] 'Neglected Category', 434.

[69] Ibid. 436.

[70] Civil libertarians have suggested various restrictions upon the use of undercover political agents, including: making their use in a preventive capacity a violation of the First and Fourth Amendments to the US constitution; subjecting the use of informers to the same restrictions the authorities now face with respect to wire-tapping and search-and-seize operations; and the establishment of a domestic intelligence advisory council to monitor intelligence activities. As far as social science is concerned, the researcher interested in social movements would be well advised to be alert to the possible distorting effects that a police interloper may be exerting. Ibid. 439.

[71] Schleifman, *Agents in the Russian Revolutionary Movement*, p. ix.

whose sole task was to tail suspects, known only by a code-name, and to monitor where they went and whom they met.[72] Although some were volunteers, many secret agents were recruited after arrest and confession and, in order to dispel suspicion, were released by way of a staged 'escape'.[73] Schliefman concludes that, although the number of secret agents operating in the Socialist Revolutionary Party was smaller than the party itself believed, they eventually became the linchpin of political police work, hastening the party's organizational and ethical breakdown, deepening rifts within the leadership, and bringing grass-roots discontent to the surface. However, in spite of this, police preconceptions exaggerated the party's importance, and the inefficiency of the police organizational structure resulted in poor co-ordination of intelligence, which prevented the full potential of this information from being realized.[74]

Informers and supergrasses have also played a prominent role in Irish history. The following are just a few examples and are not intended to provide a complete survey. During the Great Rebellion of 1641 Owen O'Connally, who was not in fact a party to the uprising itself, supplied information which led to the execution of Lord Maguire and Colonel McMahon, two of the rebel leaders. O'Connally received an annuity and a gift of money from the English parliament for his services, but did not live long to enjoy it, being killed in Ulster in 1643.[75] Informers also played a key role in defeating the United Irishmen by facilitating the arrest of many of the movement's leaders just a few weeks before the insurrection they had planned was due to take place in 1798. Despite heavy reliance upon informers, no trials on the evidence of supergrasses took place, largely because criminal trials were superfluous under the policy of military repression pursued in Ulster throughout 1797 and especially when martial law was declared throughout Ireland in March 1798.[76]

The parts played by several informers amongst the United Irishmen—Thomas Reynolds, Leonard McNally, Samuel Turner, Frederick Dutton, Captain Armstrong, Dr Conlan, James Hughes,

---

[72] Ibid. 29.

[73] Ibid. 37.

[74] Ibid. 194–8.

[75] A. Boyd, *The Informers: A Chilling Account of the Supergrasses in Northern Ireland* (Dublin: Mercier Press, 1984), 8.

[76] J. C. Beckett, *The Making of Modern Ireland 1603–1923*, 2nd edn. (London: Faber & Faber, 1981), 260–2.

and Edward John Newell—have been well documented.[77] Samuel
Turner, a lawyer from Newry, a man of property, and a member of
the United Irishmen, was one of the most effective of all. Turner
arrived on the doorstep of the London home of Lord Downshire
early in October 1797 indicating that he had some vital information
regarding the impending uprising in Ireland and enquiring if his
lordship would act as intermediary with the Prime Minister, William Pitt. Both Lord Downshire and Turner were descended from
Cromwellian settlers granted land confiscated from Irish Catholics,
and Turner's principal motive in informing seems to have been to
prevent his property being returned to a Catholic claimant. Pitt
greatly welcomed Turner's information and instructed Lord Downshire to give him every encouragement and to pay whatever he
asked. Turner, however, did not ask for much money and made
comparatively modest claims for expenses incurred on trips to
Ireland and the Continent, during which he met the top leadership
of the United Irishmen as well as General Hoche, who had led an
abortive French military expedition to Ireland in 1796, and the
French statesman, Talleyrand. The United Irishmen never suspected that Turner was an informer, and his treachery was not
revealed until the historian W. J. Fitzpatrick pieced together the
evidence from various sources. Following the defeat of the 1798
rebellion, Turner returned to a peaceful life outside Newry but died
a violent death in a duel on the Isle of Man in 1821. Another of the
movement's informers, Edward John Newell, a portrait painter
from Downpatrick, is alleged to have been responsible for the
arrest of some 227 people and for another 300 going to ground,
and, although it is assumed he was killed by the United Irishmen,
his body was never found. Leonard McNally, a successful lawyer,
author of plays and composer of operas and popular songs, betrayed the United Irishmen for financial gain and provided some
particularly suspect information, alleging, for example, that the
respectable and conservative Catholic Archbishop of Dublin, John
Thomas Troy, was a party to the republican conspiracy. McNally,
who, like Turner, was never suspected by those he betrayed, drew a
substantial pension from the state for the rest of his life, and it was

[77] See, e.g. W. H. Maxwell, *History of the Irish Rebellion of 1798* (London: 1845–
1903); W. J. Fitzpatrick, *Secret Service under Pitt* (London: Longman, 1892); R. R.
Madden, *Ireland in '98* (London, 1888); T. D., A. M., D. B. Sullivan, *Speeches from
the Dock* (Dublin, 1907).

not until the middle of the nineteenth century that the historians Madden and Lecky discovered his true colours.

Like the United Irishmen, the Fenian movement in the late nineteenth century was riddled with informers. For example, Peirce Nagle, a schoolmaster employed in a menial job in the Fenian press, supplied weekly reports to a police inspector in Dublin which led to the arrest and eventual conviction, in 1865, of O'Donovan Rossa, Thomas Clark Luby, John O'Leary, and other Fenian leaders. Herman Schofield, another informer, also became a supergrass and received £500 and a ticket to New Zealand in return for evidence given at trials in 1865.[78] The evidence of supergrasses also proved to be of vital importance in the trial of 'the Invincibles', the Fenian movement's inner circle of dedicated assassins, accused of the murders of Lord Frederick Cavendish, the newly appointed Chief Secretary for Ireland, and Thomas Burke, the Permanent Under-Secretary, in Phoenix Park, Dublin, in May 1882.[79] On 13 January 1883 the police arrested seventeen suspects in connection with the killings, and on 20 January it was disclosed that one of them, Robert Farrell, a veteran of the Fenian movement, had decided to give evidence against the others. Two other participants in the murder, the driver of the 'get-away cab', Kavanagh, and another key activist, Lamie, also turned Queen's evidence. But the biggest sensation of all, however, occurred on 17 February, when James Carey entered the court as a Crown witness. Carey, a businessman and member of Dublin Corporation, had been the ringleader of the whole conspiracy and had signalled with a white handkerchief that the attack should begin. On the basis of the evidence of these four supergrasses, five of the accused were sentenced to death, three to life imprisonment, and the remainder to long terms of penal servitude. Carey did not receive any money in return for his testimony but was held in protective custody in Kilmainham gaol until arrangements were made to resettle him with his family in South Africa. However, in July 1883, as the ship on which they were sailing neared Cape Town, he was shot dead by a man called O'Donnell from Donegal, who was later tried and executed in London. Another important Fenian informer, who remained undetected in the movement for some twenty-five years, was Dr. Thomas Beach, alias Major Henri le Caron, the physician

[78] Boyd, *The Informers*, 16.   [79] Ibid. 18–21.

to most of the Fenian leaders and often used as a messenger between London, Dublin, and Paris. For his services in warning the authorities of a Fenian plan to invade Canada in 1870, Beach received £500 from the British government and £50 from the Canadians. In 1889, when *The Times* held an inquiry in an attempt to prove Parnell's connection with political crimes, he proudly gave evidence and was reputed to have been paid £100,000 by the government and provided with police protection at a series of secret addresses afterwards. The inquiry, however, backfired, and Parnell's political reputation remained unscathed.[80]

The chaotic state of official intelligence-gathering in Ireland in the years following the First World War, and the success of the Irish Republican Army's counter-intelligence operations, were critical in hastening the south's independence. During all previous conflicts between the Crown and subversive movements, Dublin Castle had been able to rely upon informers deep in the rebel camp. But the general mood of hostility towards the British, expressed in the landslide vote for Sinn Fein in the elections of December 1918, together with the brutal activities of the IRA's anti-informer 'Squad', effectively reduced the flow of official intelligence to a trickle. Only in Protestant Ulster did it remain undiminished but here its 'prejudiced alarmism often made it useless'.[81] In 1919, under its director of intelligence Michael Collins, the IRA even managed to turn the tables and successfully infiltrated Dublin Castle. It was thus able to identify and then assassinate British agents and spies, and to stay one step ahead of the authorities itself.

CONCLUSION

While various types of informant can be distinguished the classic 'police informer', the inside multiple-event informant, has attracted most attention and is of most relevance to the present study. Two particularly pertinent conclusions can be extracted from the work of Marx, Skolnick, and others. First, it is clear that the role of such informers is complex and often highly paradoxical. While they can be invaluable assets in the prosecution of certain offences, their

[80] Boyd, *The Informers*, 17–18.
[81] C. Andrew, *Secret Service: The Making of the British Intelligence Community* (London: Heinemann, 1985) 251.

contribution to democratic law enforcement can be problematic and may ultimately even be counter-productive. The information which they supply may not be reliable, they may become *agents provocateurs*, and they can have a corrupting influence upon the police. Secondly, policing based on the use of officially sanctioned informer-systems tends to be insulated from effective democratic and legal accountability and provides the police with the opportunity to deal with certain political and/or criminal activities largely as they please. Supergrass systems are a refined version of informer systems yet they are, ironically, more legally accountable, because the identity and function of the supergrass will, by definition, be publicly exposed. However, as subsequent chapters will show, not all supergrass systems are equally accountable, and even those which are subject to thorough public accountability can nevertheless pose dilemmas about due process. The principal problem concerns balancing the powerful crime-control appeal of supergrass evidence with mechanisms to assess its trustworthiness and to redress the tendency for the police to be effectively in overall control of outcomes.

2

The Origins of the Supergrass System: 1969–1982

BROADLY speaking there are two ways in which modern states can respond to serious internal political violence: criminalization—modifying the criminal justice system in significant respects in order to secure convictions more effectively than under the regular process; and militarization—for example, in the form of martial law, detention without trial, selective assassinations, and shootings on sight—insulated as far as possible from effective supervision by judicial and representative institutions. However, although the focus may be more clearly on one approach than on the other, various mixtures between the two are likely to be adopted in practice. In liberal democracies criminalization will officially be the preferred strategy, since these societies must, by definition, find an effective response which does not destroy the fragile fabric of democracy itself. This does not, however, mean that distinctively military measures will not also be employed.

The key to the successful implementation of the criminalization alternative is the construction of an effective intelligence-gathering system—usually critically dependent upon informers—which will produce evidence capable of sustaining convictions in court. When accurate intelligence is acquired in advance of violent incidents, a choice of two courses of action may also present itself to those who receive it: arrest for prosecution, or interception by, for example, assassination or seizure of weapons. The selection will usually depend upon the nature of the anticipated incident, the need to protect a valued informer or agent, and the prevailing security climate. The emergence of the supergrass and 'shoot to kill' controversies in Northern Ireland in the 1980s amply demonstrates the centrality of intelligence-gathering to the management of the Ulster conflict, and, depending upon the circumstances, the attractions of prosecution and assassination to security chiefs. While the supergrass system marked a clear phase in the pursuit of a distinctive policy of criminalization, the 'shoot to kill' incidents indicate the ever-present temptation to use more direct military methods.

This chapter will explore the three processes which created the conditions out of which the supergrass system emerged: the maturing of the intelligence system throughout the 1970s; the difficulties which the police faced in obtaining confessions from key terrorist suspects following the Bennett Report in 1979; and a crisis of allegiance amongst certain paramilitary activists, especially the 'second-time-rounders', who, by the early 1980s, had already served one period of imprisonment and, having been arrested again, could not face another.

THE CONSTRUCTION OF THE MILITARY INTELLIGENCE SYSTEM: 1969–1975

Although the origins of the current conflict in Northern Ireland are well documented, its precise nature remains a matter of considerable dispute.[1] An attempt to provide a thorough summary of the extensive literature would be well beyond the scope of the present study, but some account of the background is none the less required. In the late 1960s activists from the Catholic/nationalist minority in Northern Ireland began agitating for the ending of institutionalized sectarianism, which had characterized politics and society in Northern Ireland since partition in the 1920s. The response, both from Protestant/loyalist mobs on the streets and from the Unionist state at Stormont, was hostile and at times violent. Spiralling sectarian disorder in the summer of 1969 prompted the British government to authorize the mobilization of units from the garrison force of the British army on 14 August. However, the violence did not abate and by the summer of 1971 it had escalated from street disturbances to endemic civil war as both loyalist and republican communities either revived dormant paramilitary organizations or created new ones.

On 9 August 1971, having obtained British government approval, the Stormont cabinet introduced internment without trial under

---

[1] For recent discussions of the various models, see, e.g., J. Whyte, *Interpreting Northern Ireland* (Oxford: Oxford University Press, 1990); B. O'Leary and J. McGarry, *The Politics of Antagonism: Understanding Northern Ireland* (London: Athlone, 1993).

the Civil Authorities (Special Powers) Act 1922. In the initial sweep the police and the army arrested 342 men, all but a handful from the nationalist community, and within six months 2,357 people had been arrested, 1,600 of whom were released after interrogation.[2] Poor police intelligence, particularly the failure to recognize that the Provisional IRA presented a much more serious threat than the Officials, from whom they had parted company in a bitter split in 1970, resulted in the internment of men who had little or no connection with organized political violence, or even civil rights agitation, and greatly increased nationalist resentment towards Stormont. Internment, and the fatal shooting by a unit of the Parachute Regiment of thirteen unarmed civilians attending a banned anti-internment rally in Derry on 14 January 1972, had a devastating effect upon the level of unrest, with more violence recorded that year than at any other point in the current conflict to date.[3]

In March 1972, by now convinced that the Stormont regime was incapable of either controlling the violence or providing the conditions for the emergence of a settlement, the British government suspended the Northern Ireland cabinet and parliament and instituted direct rule from London. Apart from a brief period of devolved power-sharing between unionists and nationalists from January to May 1974, this has been the form of administration in Northern Ireland ever since.[4] Throughout the 1970s successive British governments, both Labour and Conservative, sought to achieve three principal objectives. The first was to control the disorder through 'Ulsterization', that is to say transferring primary responsibility for law enforcement from the British army back to the local security forces, the Royal Ulster Constabulary (RUC) and the Ulster Defence Regiment (UDR), and through 'criminalization', a shift away from treating the violence as an expression of political discontent, which internment clearly suggested, in favour of securing convictions in the criminal courts. Secondly, repeated assurances were given that there would be no change in the constitu-

---

[2] P. Hillyard, 'Law and Order', in J. Darby (ed.), *Northern Ireland: The Background to the Conflict* (Belfast: Appletree Press, 1983), 37.

[3] There were e.g., 467 killings, nearly twice as many as in the next worst year, 1976, when the figure was 297.

[4] The Anglo-Irish Agreement of 1985 has modified this slightly by providing a channel for the government of the Irish Republic to express views about how Northern Ireland is governed.

tional position of Northern Ireland without the consent of the majority of the population there. Thirdly, attempts were made to create a viable devolved administration based on the principle of power-sharing between the more accommodating sections of the two communities.

In 1969 the army expected that swift and incisive intervention would help create a climate conducive to the reintroduction of routine civil policing. But frequent, often insensitive, and some-times brutal military arrest, search, and seize operations, concen-trated almost exclusively in nationalist areas, rapidly eroded the welcome which the British regiments had initially received. By 1971 it had become clear that the army would be involved in Northern Ireland, not only as a means of riot control but also in a counter-terrorist capacity, for much longer than had originally been envis-aged, and that a much more sophisticated intelligence-gathering system than that available would be required. From its recent experience in colonial wars, the army was acutely aware of the importance of a centralized intelligence network. As the military counter-insurgency bible, *Counter-Revolutionary Operations*, puts it:

Intelligence and security must be centrally controlled to ensure the efficient and economic exploitation of resources. Thus there should be a single integrated intelligence organisation under either a director of intelligence or the senior intelligence officer in the area of operations.[5]

But in the early 1970s intelligence-gathering in Northern Ireland was chaotic, with no co-ordination between the various agencies involved: MI5, MI6, the army, and RUC Special Branch.[6] More debilitating still was the lack of trust between some of these organizations, with Special Branch jealously concealing some of its information from MI6 and vice versa. Indeed it was not until the autumn of 1971 that Special Branch officers were allowed to talk to the army directly.[7] According to Lord Carver, Chief of the General Staff in the mid-1970s, liaison problems with Special

---

[5] See M. Urban, *Big Boys' Rules: The SAS and the Secret Struggle against the IRA* (London: Faber & Faber, 1992), 22.

[6] See M. Dillon, *The Dirty War* (London: Arrow Books, 1991), 198–9. Dillon claims that competition between MI5 and MI6 led to the deaths of 10 top-grade agents at the hands of the IRA in a single week. Ibid. 204.

[7] D. Hamill, *Pig in the Middle: The Army in Northern Ireland 1969–1985* (London: Methuen, 1986), 69.

Branch, distrust of the quality of Special Branch intelligence, and suspicion about connections between elements in the police and loyalist paramilitaries, led the army to seek self-reliance in intelligence in spite of its own received wisdom.[8]

In 1971 Brigadier Frank Kitson, a young military theorist then stationed in Belfast, published a book offering solutions to some of these problems.[9] Although Kitson's study was concerned with low-intensity operations in general, rather than with Northern Ireland in particular, many of his conclusions had clear implications for the role of the army in Ulster. Amongst other things, the author argued the case for using informers—particularly insurgents who had been 'persuaded' to work for the state—and for the gathering and analysis of routine 'operational intelligence', large quantities of apparently mundane information which, when collected and processed could be used to predict insurgent activities. Kitson also suggested that, as part of an overall military counter-insurgency strategy, the army should be prepared to engage in 'psychological operations', ('psy ops'), the formulation and dissemination of propaganda designed to win the 'hearts and minds' of the community, and to fulfil this objective the creation of 'psychological operations organizations' was recommended at every command level. The army was also advised to forge links with the civilian population by using whatever opportunities presented themselves—for example, by organizing discos and advising on construction or agricultural work. Whilst not suggesting that 'psy ops' units should be created throughout the United Kingdon before an insurgency had begun, Kitson recommended that the army should, none the less, have trained personnel available to establish them at short notice. Although Kitson's ideas initially met with some resistance from the army's senior command—not least because they ran counter to the expectation of early military withdrawal—as military entrenchment progressed, some of his proposals began to be implemented.

Internment provided the first opportunity for the army to experiment with intelligence-gathering methods in Northern Ireland. A group of internees was selected and 'interrogated in depth' with the assistance of sensory deprivation techniques developed in colonial conflicts in Kenya and Malaya. These included being deprived of

[8] Urban, *SAS and IRA*, 22.

[9] F. Kitson, *Low Intensity Operations: Subversion, Insurgency, Peace-Keeping* (London: Faber & Faber, 1971).

sleep and food and being made to stand spread-eagled against a wall for long periods, with radio hiss played through headphones. There was a public outcry when news of this broke, and the British government was forced to appoint a judge, Sir Edward Compton, to conduct an inquiry. In November 1971 Compton reported that the practice of sensory deprivation constituted physical ill-treatment but not brutality.[10] A further judicial inquiry chaired by Lord Parker[11] was commissioned to consider whether such techniques could be justified, and, although the majority decided they could be defended and that legislation should be passed to legalize the practice, in the event the government accepted the recommendations of Lord Gardiner's minority report that they were both immoral and counter-productive.[12]

From 1971 onwards the military intelligence system developed rapidly. The Special Air Service (SAS) began to train undercover Military (or Mobile) Reconnaissance Force[13] units for intelligence-gathering purposes, and, following their arrests, a group of former republican and loyalist activists and an army deserter known as the 'Freds' began to contribute to the army's intelligence-gathering effort.[14] However, some appear to have been double agents and were passing information about the army back to the IRA.[15] Accommodated in one half of a semi-detached house in the army barracks at Holywood, while their minders lived in the other half, the Freds would travel around Belfast in armoured personnel carriers, identifying people on the street for a photographer to photograph.[16] Early in 1972 a scientific officer at the Ministry of Defence developed an operational military intelligence-gathering system, as Kitson had recommended, the key to which lay in training the ordinary squaddie on patrol to notice and report minute changes in the pattern of daily life on the street which could

[10] *Report of the Enquiry into Allegations against the Security Forces of Physical Brutality in Northern Ireland Arising out of Events on the 9th of August 1971* (The Compton Report) 41, Cmnd. 4832 (London: HMSO, 1971).

[11] *Report of the Committee of Privy Councillors Appointed to Consider Authorised Procedures for the Interrogation of Persons Suspected of Terrorism* (The Parker Report), Cmnd. 4901 (London: HMSO, 1972).

[12] See generally J. McGuffin, *The Guineapigs* (London: Penguin, 1974).

[13] Also known as Military Reaction Force. See Dillon, *The Dirty War*, 46. According to Dillon these were amateurish and not tightly controlled. Ibid. 56.

[14] Ibid. 32 ff.

[15] Ibid. 63.

[16] Ibid. 37.

be indicative of terrorist activity. This information was then systematically processed in order to provide information for operational
military decisions.[17]

The Military (or Mobile) Reconnaissance Force was replaced in
1973 by the Special Military Intelligence Unit (Northern Ireland)—
SMIU (NI)—an organization of about fifty officers and non-com-
missioned officers involved in liaison with RUC Special Branch,
particularly over sensitive intelligence matters, and in early 1974
the elite 14 Intelligence Company, also known as 4 Field Survey
Troop, appeared.[18] In 1973 MI5 increased its activity in Northern
Ireland but initially had to rely upon police and army arrests to
recruit its informers.[19] Later, imaginative informer-recruitment
schemes were devised, including taking leading republicans on
foreign holidays, which they were told had been won in a competition, and making approaches to them as they relaxed in their
hotels.[20] From 1973 onwards the army increasingly targeted its
intelligence system upon the loyalist paramilitaries, but potentially
compromising relationships were also formed between certain army
intelligence officers and high-ranking loyalist terrorists which gave
rise to allegations of collusion in sectarian killings.[21]

Confusion about the army's legal powers was resolved in 1973
by the Northern Ireland (Emergency Provisions) Act, which overhauled the entire legal framework for the control of the emergency
and created the Diplock system. The Act put intelligence-gathering
on a much firmer statutory footing by, amongst other things,
giving soldiers the power to stop and question anyone to ascertain
their identity and their knowledge of terrorist incidents, and to
arrest and detain anyone suspected of any offence for up to four
hours. This allowed suspected terrorists and sympathizers to be
routinely 'arrested for screening', which involved keeping tabs on
suspects and updating files.[22] Although lawful arrest required
suspicion that an offence had been, was being, or was about to be

---

[17] Hamill, *Pig in the Middle*, 122–6.
[18] Urban, *SAS and IRA*, 21. See also Dillon, *The Dirty War*, 467–70.
[19] Urban, *SAS and IRA*, 97.
[20] Ibid. 105.
[21] Dillon, *The Dirty War*, 277 and 308. Dillon argues that loyalist paramilitaries
are easier to recruit as informers because their ostensible allegiance is already to the
Crown. Ibid. 379.
[22] K. Boyle, T. Hadden, and P. Hillyard, *Ten Years on in Northern Ireland: The
Legal Control of Political Violence* (London: The Cobden Trust, 1980), 43–5.

committed,[23] arrests for screening were effectively legally unchal-
lengeable, because it was virtually impossible to show that suspicion
had been absent. The legislation also provided extensive powers of
search and seizure.[24]

The early 1970s also saw the instalment of sophisticated surveillance equipment at key sites, and by 1974 the army computer was
said to have had data on half the population of Northern Ireland,[25]
although Dillon claims this did not occur until 1978–9.[26] By 1974
more than 100 army specialists were involved in intelligence work,
and by 1975 the figure had trebled.[27] The use of *agents provocateurs*, informers, and a variety of other undercover techniques was
also cultivated, although the details have remained obscure. The
result of all these developments was that throughout 1971–5 the
army became the eyes and ears of the law enforcement system in
Northern Ireland, especially in republican areas which were too
dangerous for the police to penetrate alone.

THE INSTITUTIONALIZATION OF THE DIPLOCK PROCESS: 1972–1975

Running parallel and somewhat counter to militarization in the
early 1970s was the increasing 'judicialization' of the official response to the unrest. The Detention of Terrorists Order 1972
altered the internment formalities so that the Secretary of State
could make 'interim custody orders' against suspects. These cases
were then considered by a judicially qualified Commissioner, whose
decisions could be appealed. A key element in the Commissioners'
hearings was the evidence supplied to the army and the RUC by
informers, and much of the cross-examination of army and police
witnesses concentrated upon the quality and reliability of their
evidence. Although informers could not be produced at the hearing,
and although their identity could not be revealed to the suspect's
legal representatives, some minor victories were won by defence
counsel. The Commissioners were persuaded not to accept 'double

---

[23] Northern Ireland (Emergency Provisions) Act 1973, s. 12 (1).
[24] See S. C. Greer, 'The Legal Powers of the Army', in B. Dickson (ed.), *Civil
Liberties in Northern Ireland: The CAJ Handbook*, 2nd edn. (Belfast: Committee on
the Administration of Justice, 1993); C. Walker, 'Army Special Powers on Parade'
(1989) 40 *Northern Ireland Legal Quarterly* 1.
[25] *The Times*, 5 Dec 1974.
[26] *The Dirty War*, 415.
[27] *Rose and Laurel: The Journal of the Intelligence Corps*, 1969–74.

hearsay' or 'hearsay upon hearsay', where the informer had merely passed on something he had heard, but the Appeal Tribunal narrowed this to cases in which the informer could not identify the source of his report. The evidence of specific informers was also impugned, on the grounds that on previous occasions it had turned out to be untrue, and attempts were made to show that the informer must have been an accomplice to the offence in question and that corroboration should therefore be required. However, the Commissioners nearly always accepted applications by the police and the army that, on security grounds, the hearings should be conducted in the absence of the suspect and his legal representatives, and the decision to intern remained largely an executive one with a judicial veneer, rather than one reached after a full-blooded judicial hearing.[28]

On 18 October 1972 the first Secretary of State for Northern Ireland, Mr William Whitelaw, announced that a commission chaired by Lord Diplock, a member of the Judicial Committee of the House of Lords, would consider what changes 'should be made in the administration of justice in order to deal more effectively with terrorism without using internment under the Special Powers Act'.[29] However, in November 1972, the government passed an Order in Council to ensure that internment would remain available whatever the outcome of the commission's deliberations. The Diplock Report, which was published in December 1972, proposed that the Civil Authorities (Special Powers) Act 1922 should be repealed, but recommended a fresh battery of special powers in its place. In addition to the army powers already mentioned, these included: extensive police powers to stop and question, search and seize, and arrest and detain; the relaxation of the legal test for the admissibility of confessions; and the suspension of jury trial for a list of serious offences associated with the activities of paramilitary organizations. In July 1973 the bulk of the commission's proposals were enacted by parliament in the Northern Ireland (Emergency Provisions) Act. In the period under discussion this legislation was revised twice: a new version was enacted in 1978 which remained the principal Act until 1991. In 1974 anti-terrorist provisions were enacted throughout the United Kingdom, including Northern Ire-

[28] Boyle *et al.*, *Law and State: The Case of Northern Ireland* (London: Martin Robertson, 1975) 67–9.
[29] HC Debs., vol. 855, col. 276.

land, in the wake of the Birmingham pub bombs.[30] In certain circumstances these anti-terrorist laws made informing in relation to terrorism compulsory both in Northern Ireland and throughout the United Kingdom. The Northern Ireland (Emergency Provisions) Act makes it an offence to fail to comply with the exercise of the police and army power to stop and question to ascertain identity and knowledge of terrorist incidents,[31] while the Prevention of Terrorism Act makes it an offence, without lawful excuse, to withhold information about terrorism even when no request has been made to divulge it.[32]

Two aspects of the judicial element in the Diplock process are of particular relevance to this study. First, the suspension of trial by jury transformed the judiciary into tribunal of fact and law.[33] Secondly, the power which the judiciary hitherto possessed under the common law to reject confessions which were not shown to have been made voluntarily, was restricted. In *R.* v. *Flynn and Leonard* in 1972, the Northern Ireland Court of Appeal declared that confessions obtained in the special anti-terrorist interrogation centres established by the police to question suspects were not voluntary for this purpose, under the common law, because the process was expressly designed to pressurize otherwise reluctant suspects into confessing.[34] Although the Northern Ireland (Emergency Provisions) Act changed the common-law admissibility requirements, placing the initial burden of proof upon the defendant to show that torture or inhuman or degrading treatment had been

---

[30] Amongst other things, this legislation, also re-enacted over the years, enables the police to arrest without warrant anyone reasonably suspected of being involved in the commission, preparation, or instigation of acts of terrorism, and provides for the detention of such persons for up to 48 hours, with further periods, of up to an overall total of 7 days, capable of being authorized by the Secretary of State. See C. Walker, *The Prevention of Terrorism in British Law*, 2nd edn. (Manchester: Manchester University Press, 1992).

[31] Northen Ireland (Emergency Provisions) Act 1973, s. 16 (2).

[32] Prevention of Terrorism (Temporary Provisions) Act 1976, s. 11.

[33] Lord Diplock recommended that the jury should be suspended from the trial of what became scheduled offences on the grounds of the vulnerability of jurors to intimidation and the tendency of juries to return perverse acquittals of loyalists because the property qualification for jury service ensured that the jury was a predominantly Protestant institution. However, subsequent research has shown that the evidence was at best equivocal and that other alternatives could have been considered, e.g. extending the jury franchise and protecting jurors' anonymity. See S. C. Greer and A. White, *Abolishing the Diplock Courts: The Case for Restoring Jury Trial to Scheduled Offences in Northern Ireland* (London: The Cobden Trust, 1986).

[34] (1972) NIJB (May).

used in order to induce a confession, the courts made it clear that a discretion to exclude confessions which had none the less passed the statutory test remained.[35] The net effect of the Act was to create a confession-based prosecution process centred on single-judge non-jury courts serviced by extensive police and army powers.

There were at least two supergrass cases in this early phase of the Ulster conflict, one of which occurred even before the Diplock process had been established. In October 1969 Sammy Stephenson, a fanatical loyalist and follower of the Revd Ian Paisley, was arrested in connection with bombings and a number of other offences, made a full confession, claiming to be Chief of Staff of the Ulster Volunteer Force (UVF), and named ten others. On 5 December he was convicted and sentenced to twelve years imprisonment, and in February and March 1970 three trials took place in which he appeared as the principal Crown witness. However, Stephenson, who had been in gaol twice for theft and seemed to have a score to settle with one of the accused, proved unconvincing, his uncorroborated evidence was rejected by the juries, and the accused were acquitted. Jurors' attitudes may, however, have been swayed by the fact that during the first court hearing a small bomb, allegedly planted by the Shankill branch of the Ulster Protestant Volunteers, exploded in the hall of the Crown Court building. Within a year Stephenson was transferred to Wakefield prison in England, where he served the rest of his sentence complaining that a deal in which he claimed to have been offered early release in return for his testimony had not been honoured.[36]

The second supergrass trial, which took place in October 1974, featured Albert 'Ginger' Baker, an army deserter active in the Ulster Defence Association (UDA) who had fled to England that spring when the organization became suspicious that he was an army or police agent.[37] Early on the morning of 31 May 1973 Baker turned himself in to Warminster county police station in England and told the duty sergeant that he wanted to confess to four murders and eleven armed robberies, committed in Northern Ireland, on the grounds of remorse stemming from a religious

---

[35] See, e.g. R. N. Corey [1979] NI 49.

[36] E. Moloney and A. Pollack, *Paisley* (Dublin: Poolbeg, 1986), 185–6.

[37] See Dillon, *The Dirty War*, 259–75.

conversion. But another motive became apparent in the course of interviews; he was prepared to turn Queen's evidence if assured he could serve his sentence in England. With no mention of where his sentence would be served, Baker was sentenced in October 1973 to life imprisonment by the Lord Chief Justice of Northern Ireland, Sir Robert Lowry, who recommended a minimum of twenty-five years. A year later Baker appeared as a Crown witness in the trial of some of his accomplices, but the trial collapsed without convictions. When the supergrass system developed in the 1980s, Baker attracted media interest by demanding a review of his case, claiming that promises of early release had not been honoured and implicating members of the RUC and UDR in the loyalist murder campaign of the early 1970s. He is later reputed to have written to Harry Kirkpatrick, the supergrass and member of the Irish National Liberation Army (INLA), warning that his expectations of early release were unlikely to be honoured either. An internal inquiry, ordered by the Chief Constable of the RUC, Sir Kenneth Newman, concluded that there was no truth in any of Baker's allegations.

POLICE PRIMACY AND THE REFINEMENT OF INTELLIGENCE-GATHERING: 1975–1979

According to Urban, the reorganization of the IRA into cells meant that 'the importance of the infomer to the security establishment, which had been growing since the outset of the Troubles, reached its zenith in the late 1970s and early 1980s'.[38] Although the army had by now been assigned a largely supportive role, its various specialist functions—the provision of bomb-disposal units, the manning of vehicle checkpoints, routine patrolling along the border and in republican strongholds, as well as mounting undercover surveillance and the collection of intelligence—remained of considerable importance. By this stage battalion intelligence units received intelligence from four main sources: their own informers,[39] patrols on the ground, RUC Special Branch, and the intelligence staff at brigade headquarters. The chief functions of battalion intelligence officers now also included building and maintaining an

---

[38] Urban, *SAS and IRA*, 101.
[39] Quartermasters in charge of arms, ammunition, and explosives dumps were particularly highly prized. Ibid. p. 107.

up-to-date 'rogues' gallery of all suspected paramilitary activists in an area, pin-pointing weapons and explosives dumps, providing the RUC with the necessary information to make arrests, and collating any useful information which could enhance the battalion's operational capability.[40] A new army computer was installed in 1978 which made possible 'the most extensive surveillance operation in any country'.[41] However, police primacy seems to have resulted in considerable military frustration and led to the development of 'alternative' strategies for the elimination of suspected terrorists. From 1976 to 1978 undercover soldiers shot dead ten people in ambushes; three of these were later admitted to have been killed in error. Two further shootings of this kind took place between December 1978 and December 1983.[42] Police primacy also increased the need for the RUC to gather its own intelligence and prompted the expansion of the confidential telephone service, the use of arrest and detention for intelligence-gathering purposes, and the recruitment of more informers. However, the army and police remained suspicious of one another's informer systems, a rivalry which became acute between 1977 and 1979, making the sharing of informer intelligence difficult.[43] The accidental arrest of one another's informers, the failure to notify other security organizations of movements of key IRA figures, and the compromising of one another's sources became routine.[44] In the mid-1970s the Director and Co-ordinator of Intelligence (DCI), appointed at Stormont in an attempt to overcome these difficulties, was rendered effectively impotent by the interminable feuding between the army and Special Branch on the ground. In 1977 Brigadier James Glover prepared a highly classified paper, *Future Organisation of Military Intelligence in Northern Ireland*, based upon recognition of the fact that the IRA had transformed itself into a more impenetrable cell-based structure. The report stressed the need for more centralized control over intelligence, with the DCI wielding greater authority, and for the creation of a system which would enable intelligence to be

[40] Lt.-Col. M. Dewar, *The British Army in Northern Ireland* (London: Arms and Armour Press, 1985), 186.
[41] D. Campbell, 'Society under Surveillance', in P. Hain (ed.), *Policing the Police*, ii (London: John Calder, 1980) 190.
[42] Urban, *SAS and IRA*, 81.
[43] Ibid. 19. See also Dillon, *The Dirty War*, 415.
[44] Urban, *SAS and IRA*, 23.

shared more easily at lower levels of the police and army command hierarchy.[45]

In the mid-1970s internal co-ordination of police activity was improved by the establishment of Regional Crime and Intelligence Units, and in the late 1970s these became a model for police–military intelligence co-ordination in Tasking and Co-ordination Groups (TCGs). According to Urban, this was 'probably the most important of all the steps taken during the late 1970s towards enhanced intelligence-gathering'.[46] Each TCG combined CID, Special Branch, and army specialists, plus MI5 agents on an *ad hoc* basis, and were commanded by a Special Branch officer. They soon attained a critical role in 'executive action' (integrating intelligence from informers with the information gleaned by undercover units in surveillance and ambush operations), thus eliminating duplication of effort, and in 'deconfliction' (tipping one another off about areas of covert activity in order to prevent accidental confrontations with uniformed patrols), thus reducing the risk of army or police units arresting one another's informers by mistake. However, because TCG commanders were permitted to hold back information, especially to protect the identity of an informer, they were sometimes faced with difficult choices between compromising the security of a source to facilitate a pre-emptive arrest, or concealing it and thereby jeopardizing the lives of security personnel or civilians. However, by the late 1970s joint TCG intelligence activities had led to some important successes, especially arms finds.

In 1976 the RUC's mobile anti-terrorist unit, the Special Patrol Group, set up a firearms and observation unit, Bronze Section, whose officers were trained in undercover activities, and in 1977 a special surveillance unit was formed in Special Branch's Operations Division E4. The appointment of Assistant Chief Constable Slevin as Head of Special Branch in 1976 did much to restore the Branch's reputation and, with the largest number of informers of any security agency in Northern Ireland, placed it in a pivotal position in the struggle against the IRA.[47] By the late 1970s paramilitary organizations in Northern Ireland were increasingly deeply penetrated by informers and by 1980 the IRA had taken the risk so seriously that it set up its own Security Department to hunt them down. Seven

---

[45] Ibid. 24.   [46] Ibid. 94.   [47] Ibid. 92.

IRA activists and a non-member were shot dead for suspected informing between 1979 and 1981, more than the number of Provisionals killed by the security forces (five) in the same period.[48]

The RUC has always been extremely reluctant to disclose details about its informer system, on the grounds that it would compromise a vital weapon in the war against terrorism. Home Office guidelines to mainland police forces on the use of informers[49] do not apply to Northern Ireland, where, according to Urban, 'all of these principles have been breached'.[50] However, the broad outlines of the RUC's informer system can be pieced together from press reports featuring the revelations of alleged ex-informers, some of the evidence given in the trial of Special Branch Sergeant Charles McCormick in 1982, the supergrass trials involving police agents Grimley and Gilmour, and in Walsh's research into the treatment of terrorist suspects in police custody.[51] The picture which emerges conforms broadly to that described by Skolnick and others, as set out in the previous chapter.

Considerable care goes into targeting the right individuals, who are then arrested and held for several days. Although informing can be inspired by different motives—disillusionment, the desire to pay off old scores, or the 'buzz' from leading a life of deception—most informers are recruited through police pressure, which typi-

---

[48] In the 10 years from 1978 to 1987, at least 24 alleged informers were killed—almost the same as the number of IRA activists shot dead by the SAS in the same period, Urban, *SAS and IRA*, 102. In 1982 the IRA announced an amnesty, giving informers a fortnight to turn themselves in. Dillon claims that between Sept. 1973 and 1990 the IRA killed 33 suspected informers. *The Dirty War*, 362.

[49] These deal with such things as: the need for supervision from senior officers, particularly in relation to payment, prohibiting activity as *agents provocateurs* and commitments from the police which could result in a court's being misled in any subsequent proceedings, allowing the informer to participate in crime only in a minor role and only when it is necessary to enable the police to arrest the principals, and informing the DPP and counsel of the fact that an informer had been used (although not necessarily of his identity) when it is proposed to prosecute his accomplices. See, e.g. P. Taylor, *Stalker: The Search for the Truth* (London: Faber & Faber, 1987), app. 3: 'Home Office Guidelines on the Use of Informers'. For more recent guidelines for police forces in Britain, see Association of Chief Police Officers, 'National Guidelines on the Use and Management of Informants' (ACPO Crime Committee Working Party on the management of informants: unpublished 1992).

[50] *SAS and IRA*, 107.

[51] D. P. J. Walsh, *The Use and Abuse of Emergency Legislation in Northern Ireland* (London: The Cobden Trust, 1983). See also Dillon, *The Dirty War*, ch. 13.

cally involves the offer of inducements such as the dropping of charges for usually minor and often non-political offences, offers of money, threats and blackmail based on intelligence gleaned from surveillance and information supplied by other informers. Once the informer has been persuaded to work for Special Branch, he or she will be given a code number and details of how to contact the handlers, usually at least two in number. Meetings generally take place away from republican or loyalist strongholds, and normally only small sums of money, £10 or £20 a week, are paid, with bonuses of £200–£300 for particularly useful tip-offs—for example, the recovery of an arms cache—although thousands of pounds have allegedly been paid into the bank accounts of high-grade informers.[52] Activity as an *agent provocateur* seems to be condoned if not encouraged.

While the claims of ex-informers must be treated with circumspection, a not untypical case is that of Michael Pius Devlin, from the Short Strand area of Belfast, whose story featured prominently in the *Irish News* in the early 1980s.[53] Devlin claimed that he was recruited as an informer when arrested, but not charged, in connection with the murder of a policeman in a proxy bomb-explosion. He claimed that, following his release, he was frequently stopped by the police on the street, his home was searched, and he was arrested six times and held on each occasion for a couple of days. With three convictions already on his record, including a six-year sentence for an IRA offence in the 1970s, he claimed the police frequently reminded him of his poor prospects if he were to be prosecuted again. Devlin said that although he was not physically assaulted by the police, the constant haranguing by CID officers, and the long periods he spent alone in his cell, pushed him to the brink of a nervous breakdown, and, in a weakened and frightened state, he agreed to become an informer, receiving £10 a week in return for information about the IRA and INLA in his area. As part of the deal, Devlin would call his Special Branch contact from a public phone-box, usually on a Wednesday, and arrange a meeting to pass on information and receive his payment. He claimed that the Special Branch became very excited when he reported that

[52] Urban, *SAS and IRA*, 106.
[53] Oct. 1983. Although Devlin claimed he was recruited as an informer in 1981, his account is typical of other, more fragmented accounts from other alleged informers in the late 1970s.

he had been asked to help with an INLA arms shipment; and he said he had been urged to become closely involved, but that in the event the delivery was called off. Devlin also alleged that the police persistently offered him £6,000 to kill someone whom, they said, was 'up to his neck' in IRA activities, and that he had been asked to report on Jimmy Brown, the chairman of the Irish Republican Socialist Party (IRSP), the political wing of the INLA. Having become heavily dependent upon drugs and alcohol, and beginning to suspect that he was being ripened for the role of supergrass, Devlin decided to go public in October 1983 and end his relationship with Special Branch.

Walsh's study of suspects arrested in Northern Ireland and released without charge provides some support for allegations like those made by Devlin and others. In the first ten months of 1980, 90 per cent of those arrested under both the Northern Ireland (Emergency Provisions) Act and the Prevention of Terrorism Act in Northern Ireland were released without charge, while the figure for routine criminal investigations in the rest of the United Kingdom was only 10–20 per cent. Walsh claims that the bulk of arrests in Northern Ireland were for intelligence-gathering purposes and that 48 per cent of his respondents had been subjected to verbal abuse under police interrogation while 35 per cent said they had been pressurized into becoming an informer.[54] Some claimed that the police promised to overlook a particular incident, while others said they were offered money or a job if they agreed to supply information.[55]

The change in the rules governing the admissibility of confessions occasioned by the Northern Ireland (Emergency Provisions) Act, the effective transfer of responsibility for intelligence-gathering to the RUC, and the ending of internment, all created enormous pressure on the police to produce evidence capable of securing convictions in the Diplock courts. The security situation presented serious problems regarding the collection of evidence from a wide range of sources: examination of the scene was often difficult because of the threat from paramilitaries, and witnesses were often reluctant to come forward. The outcome of all these factors was effectively to occasion a shift in the location of the decision regarding guilt or innocence from the court-room to the police station.

---

[54] *Emergency Legislation*, 33.   [55] Ibid. 68.

Put simply, the most critical point in the entire Diplock process was, and remains, whether the suspect confesses under interrogation or not. Only thirty-two confessions in a total of nearly 4,000 cases were declared inadmissible by the Diplock courts between 1976 and 1980[56] and between 75 and 80 per cent of the total number of convictions in scheduled offence trials in 1978, a not untypical year, rested on confessions alone.[57] If a suspect confesses to a scheduled offence under police interrogation, there is little chance that his confession will be ruled inadmissible at trial, and, once it is received in evidence by the court, little chance of an acquittal. Although an automatic right of appeal is available, few convictions are quashed.[58]

The number of complaints about the physical abuse of suspects during police interrogation rose from 180 in 1975 to 384 in 1976, and to 671 in 1977, as two new interrogation centres, one at Castlereagh RUC station in Belfast, and the other at Gough army barracks in Armagh, were opened.[59] A series of reports by several independent agencies, the Association of Forensic Medical Officers, the police surgeons at Gough, and Amnesty International, supported allegations that suspects were being physically ill-treated,[60] and in May 1978 the government instituted a judicial inquiry under a Scottish judge, Harry Bennett, which, despite limited terms of reference, concluded that while in police custody suspects had sustained injuries which had not been self-inflicted. A series of recommendations were made to restrict the opportunity for physical abuse: interviews should be monitored by closed-circuit television; the number of detectives involved in questioning suspects at any one time should be limited; questioning should not normally continue through mealtimes or after midnight; all suspects should have an absolute right of access to a solicitor after 48 hours; and a code of conduct for interviewing officers should become part of the

---

[56] D. S. Greer, 'The Admissibility of Confessions under the Northern Ireland (Emergency Provisions) Act 1978' (1980) 31 *Northern Ireland Legal Quarterly* 205, 233.

[57] Boyle *et al.*, *Ten Years on*, 1.

[58] See B. Dickson, 'Northern Ireland's Emergency Legislation: The Wrong Medicine?' (1992) *Public Law* 592, 608.

[59] *Report of the Committee of Inquiry into Police Interrogation Procedures in Northern Ireland* (The Bennett Report), Cmnd. 7497 (London: HMSO, 1979), app. 2.

[60] Boyle *et al.*, *Ten Years on*, 39.

RUC Code.[61] These recommendations were largely accepted by the government in June 1979 and the level of complaints dropped substantially.[62]

THE REORGANIZATION OF INTELLIGENCE GATHERING: 1979–1980

While the background conditions for the emergence of the supergrass system derived from the maturing of the intelligence-gathering system in the manner described above, the immediate conditions for its appearance lay in the government's response to a security crisis which occurred in 1979. In March of that year the British ambassador to the Netherlands was assassinated by the IRA, and Airey Neave, a Tory spokesman on Northern Ireland and a close confidant of the Prime Minister, Margaret Thatcher, was killed by an INLA car-bomb at the House of Commons. In the summer the IRA assassinated the most senior male member of the royal family, Lord Mountbatten, and three of his companions while they were boating in the Irish Republic, and, on the same day, eighteen British soldiers were killed by two IRA culvert mines outside the County Down village of Warrenpoint.

It was widely expected that the government would introduce selective internment in response to these disasters, but instead the appointment of Sir Maurice Oldfield as Security Co-ordinator for Northern Ireland was announced. Although the post had existed since 1970, its brief had been limited to the delineation of collection areas for different services ('tasking'), and arbitration in inter-agency disputes.[63] Oldfield, the head of MI6 between 1973 and 1978, then writing a book at All Souls College, Oxford, was put in charge of the entire intelligence operation in Northern Ireland and was said to have conceived a strategy deriving from his personal experiences in the Middle East and from cold-war spying. The former allegedly inspired the idea of 'taking out', by selective assassination, the 'middle management' of the republican paramilitaries, while the idea of 'turning', or converting key figures in the IRA reputedly came from experience with handling KGB double

[61]   The Bennett Report, para. 404.
[62]   Boyle *et al.*, *Ten Years on*, 40.
[63]   J. Block and P. Fitzgerald, *British Intelligence and Covert Action: Africa, Middle East and Europe Since 1945* (Dingle: Brandon, 1983), 231.

agents.[64] Although, as already indicated, some use had already been made of both strategies in the early 1970s, Oldfield's intention, shared by senior police and army officers, appears to have been to give each a higher profile. 'Turning' also appealed to many intelligence officers because of its capacity to create a climate of suspicion in the ranks of paramilitary organizations.[65]

The task of 'turning' people from their original allegiances to working for what they had hitherto regarded as the enemy involved two elements. First, suitable candidates had to be targeted and then subjected to a carefully administered mixture of ideological persuasion and the offer of various inducements. The ideal location for this to take place was the police station, following an arrest, since the police would be in complete control of the proceedings and the suspect would be at his or her most vulnerable. Furthermore, unlike a chat in a down-town pub or coffee-bar, such an interchange would not unduly arouse the suspicions of the movement outside. During the 1980s, methods of targeting and the choice of circumstance in which approaches could be made were refined.[66] The rewards available to high-grade informers were also said to have been substantially increased, and, as one senior army officer told Urban, 'a very special effort' was made 'to persuade some CTs [converted terrorists] to turn Queen's Evidence'.[67] Some suspects reported having been promised sums of up to £100,000 and a new identity, new home, and new job abroad, but as the supergrass system unfolded it became clear that few if any of these generous deals ever materialized, if indeed they had ever been on offer.

In order to create an effective system for gathering and collating intelligence an intelligence directorate known as 'the Department' was established, into which Oldfield reputedly moved a number of old MI6 operatives based in Ireland. The Department supervised the work of MI5 and MI6 throughout Ireland,[68] and its senior officer in Northern Ireland, also from MI6, worked under the direction of the Security Co-ordinator in London and chaired a committee known as the Ulster Security Liaison Committee. This comprised repre-

[64] F. Doherty, *The Stalker Affair* (Cork: Mercier Press, 1986), 31–2.
[65] Urban, *SAS and IRA*, 134.
[66] Ibid. 105.
[67] Ibid. 133.
[68] Block and Fitzgerald, *British Intelligence*, 232.

sentatives of MI6, MI5, the SAS, RUC Special Branch, and the plain-clothes Bronze Section of the RUC's Special Patrol Group.[69] The committee had a support staff of twenty drawn from the army, the RUC, and the Northern Ireland Office, and originally met at Stormont Castle but subsequently moved to conference rooms in RUC headquarters, near MI5 offices. Large sums of money from Whitehall were made available to support the intelligence-gathering effort, with more than £300 million reputedly spent on improving RUC intelligence-gathering equipment during Oldfield's brief time in Belfast.[70] Elaborate closed-circuit television systems using invisible infra-red floodlights to monitor even at night, were allegedly installed at vantage-points all over Northern Ireland, and the RUC's already sophisticated computer system was enhanced by the installation of a digital voice and data communications system called MSX, which linked every RUC outpost, as well as vehicles and individual officers, with the central computer.

The Ulster Security Liaison Committee organized tasking on a day-to-day basis for the army through a Defence Intelligence Staff colonel, and for the RUC Special Branch through a lieutenant-colonel on the staff of the Intelligence Corps.[71] In 1980 military intelligence was improved by the centralization of agent-running activities first from company to brigade level and then from brigade-level to headquarters (Northern Ireland) at Lisburn.[72] The new headquarters organization, known as the Field Research Unit, together with 14 Intelligence Company and the SAS, comprised the trinity of military intelligence units in Ulster at the time.[73] While the intelligence community wanted to increase the profile of 'turning', the RUC was in a position to provide ideas about how the information which this yielded could be used as evidence in court. However, continuing distrust of RUC Special Branch made both the army and MI5 reluctant to relinquish or downgrade their own informer networks.[74] The appointment of a new Chief Constable

[69] *Sunday Tribune*, 5 Apr. 1981.

[70] Block and Fitzgerald, *British Intelligence*, 232; Doherty, *Stalker*, 32.

[71] The Intelligence Corps officer, condenamed 'Echo Five', was responsible for yet another intelligence squad, named the Speical Military Intelligence Unit, to which, it has been alleged, Robert Nairac, an SAS Captain killed by the IRA in 1977, belonged. The unit's precise function remains obscure.

[72] Urban, *SAS and IRA*, 108.

[73] Ibid. 109.

[74] Ibid. 110.

of the RUC with effect from 1 January 1980 conveniently coincided with these developments and provided a clean break with the past, since Sir John Hermon was known to be opposed to the discredited policy of relying upon confessions to defeat the IRA.[75] But, although the Bennett inquiry had effectively closed the door on attempts to secure confession-based convictions of top-ranking paramilitaries, confessions continued to be used routinely to convict rank-and-file activists.

After only six months Oldfield retired from his new post on grounds of ill-health and under suspicion for alleged homosexual indiscretions, attributed by some to an MI5 or Special Branch smear campaign.[76] He died shortly afterwards. His successor, Sir Francis Brooks Richards, completed the studies ordered by Whitehall, and the planning staff was dispersed. Urban concludes that although Oldfield's mission was originally trumpeted as a major security shake-up, its effect was essentially to endorse police primacy and the centralization of intelligence while preserving the information-gathering autonomy of the army, RUC, and MI5.[77] However, while the Oldfield review may have largely endorsed the intelligence-gathering *status quo*, one of its principal effects appears to have been a marked increase in the supply of high-grade intelligence from 'deep' informers, especially to the police.[78] This concerned such things as the identification of other potential informers, which could be used to advantage in the psychological contest between suspects and investigating officers in interrogations, and in the selection of particularly prized defendants. Although supergrass trials may not have been actively contemplated, it was but a small step from deliberately recruiting highly placed informers to developing a system for their appearance as witnesses in court.

INAUSPICIOUS BEGINNINGS: 1980–1982

The 'demand side' factors considered in the previous sections probably would not have led to the construction of a supergrass system had it not been for the supply of informers and police spies

---

[75] Hillyard, 'Law and Order', 51.
[76] Urban, *SAS and IRA*, 111.
[77] Ibid. 110.
[78] See R. Deacon, *'C': A Biography of Sir Maurice Oldfield* (London: Macdonald, 1984) 233 and 247.

whose treachery had been discovered by the respective paramilitary organizations to which they belonged, and the 'second-time-round-ers', dedicated members of paramilitary organizations who had served sentences for serious offences in the early-to-mid-1970s, and who had returned to their various paramilitary organizations shortly after their release. Arrested again in the early 1980s, they faced the daunting prospect of returning to prison for even longer terms than before. For many, this factor, together with the attractive deals on offer, precipitated a crisis of allegiance: commitment to a cause which they had served at personal cost for many years with no victory in sight, against allegiance to family and/or the chance of a new life, either without having to go to prison at all, or after having served a relatively short and comfortable prison sentence.

Although, as already indicated, there were two isolated super-grass trials in the 1970s, it was not until the early 1980s that the supergrass system began in earnest.[79] However, the first successful trials were modest by comparison with what was to come, and in its early days the process was dogged by retractions and doubts about the prospects of many cases reaching the court-room. But, as the *Belfast Telegraph* noted, even if none of the supergrass cases had come to trial, the supergrasses would still have been of assistance to the RUC in providing fresh intelligence and enabling arms to be seized and confessions to be obtained.[80] In July 1979 the army rescued an informer, Stephen McWilliams, from IRA detention and interrogation. McWilliams later testified in the trial of seven men, including veteran republican Martin Meehan, on charges relating to the kidnapping. Three of the accused made confessions, and, although the judge described McWilliams's identification of Meehan as of 'poor quality', the fact that the accused's car had been seen in the street where the rescue took place was deemed to provide corroboration. In March 1980 six of the seven were convicted, but McWilliams later claimed that his evidence

[79] The *Belfast Bulletin* claims that in 1977 a third supergrass trial in Northern Ireland took place when, in return for immunity from prosecution and a new life elsewhere, UVF activist John Wright gave evidence which helped to convict 26 loyalists. Workers Research Unit, *Belfast Bulletin No. 11: Supergrasses* (Belfast: pub. authors, 1984), 4. However, in spite of research through local-history data-banks and newspaper archives by the staff at the Belfast Central Library, no other reference to this case could be found.
[80] 3 Sept. 1982.

about Meehan had been fabricated.[81] In June 1981 James Kennedy, also granted immunity from prosecution, gave evidence in the trial of ten alleged members of the IRA, eight of whom were convicted.[82] Kennedy, a taxi-driver on the fringes of the IRA but not himself a member, appears to have been a police informer who turned Queen's evidence when the IRA became suspicious. Both his and the McWilliams case differed from the subsequent high-profile supergrass trials in a number of key respects. In each there were comparatively few defendants and few charges, the latter revolving around McWilliams's abduction and, in the Kennedy trial, the possession and use of certain firearms. There was also more corroboration. Four of the eight convicted in the Kennedy case had been caught red-handed and Kennedy's uncorroborated evidence was instrumental in securing the conviction of only three accused—on arms-possession charges.

In 1982 not only did the supergrass issue gather momentum, but the 'shoot-to-kill' controversy reopened with the fatal shooting of seven people by the security forces in November and December.[83] In March Robert McAllister, who had implicated thirteen alleged members of the INLA in return for rewards the details of which were not disclosed, retracted his evidence, although the charges against twelve of those he had named were sustained. In April a trial on the evidence of an accomplice was completed in the Diplock system which, although independent of the supergrass process, was to provide both an important point of reference and a contrast as the supergrass system itself unfolded. In *R.* v. *McCormick* a detective sergeant in the Special Branch of the RUC was charged with a number of scheduled offences ranging from armed robbery to the murder of an RUC sergeant,[84] largely on the testimony of Anthony O'Doherty, a paid police informer who reputedly had connections with the CID, the Special Branch, the army, the IRA, and the INLA, and was then serving an eighteen-

---

[81] Dillon, *The Dirty War*, 388–9. *Belfast Telegraph*, 28 Mar. 1980. The 7th defendant found not guilty was Kevin Mulgrew, one of the central accused in the Black trial in 1983.

[82] *Irish News*, 13 June 1981.

[83] See A. Jennings, 'Shoot to Kill: The Final Courts of Justice', in id. (ed.), *Justice Under Fire: The Abuse of Civil Liberties in Northern Ireland*, 2nd edn. (London: Pluto Press, 1990).

[84] A detailed account of the background to this case can be found in Dillon, *The Dirty War*, 327–63.

year prison sentence for his own part in some of these offences. O'Doherty claimed that he and McCormick had stage-managed shootings at police officers which McCormick would then 'investigate' in order to enhance his professional status. He also alleged that Sergeant Joseph Campbell had been murdered in Cushendall on 25 February 1977 because he had begun to suspect that McCormick and O'Doherty were partners in crime. McCormick claimed that although O'Doherty had been 'hard to handle', he had produced some top-grade intelligence, which had led to the discovery of an arms dump in Cushendall, a mortar-bomb factory, and rocket launchers,[85] and he confirmed that the police would often 'turn a blind eye' to the activities of paid agents.[86]

The judge in McCormick's trial, Mr Justice Murray, held that: 'it would be highly dangerous and wrong to convict the accused on any of the crimes charged against him on the evidence of O'Doherty unless that evidence is supported by clear and compelling corroboration'.[87] He nevertheless found the defendant guilty on one count of armed robbery and three related counts. The judge inferred that discrepancies between the defendant's evidence and that of other witnesses indicated that the accused was lying and that, taken together, these things amounted to corroboration of the necessary standard. The defendant had found himself in a worsening financial situation at the time of the robbery in question and had made a statement admitting buying a van, claiming that O'Doherty gave him 'Nan's money'—some £600 or £700—to purchase it. Mrs McLaughlin ('Nan'), McCormick's girlfriend, denied in evidence that she had parted with such a sum. McCormick also denied possessing a hand-grenade, but his landlady found one in his room, a detective sergeant gave evidence that McCormick had taken one from a police security-cabinet, and O'Doherty alleged that one had been used in a robbery which he and McCormick had committed. An entry in the defendant's official diary referred to his having met

---

[85] Dillon, *The Dirty War*, 347.

[86] During cross-examination, Special Branch Inspector Jimmy Blair, who had been in contact with O'Doherty when he was in prison in 1981, was asked whether he had ever encouraged persons other than police officers to shoot in unwarranted circumstances. Blair declined to reply on the grounds that his answer might incriminate him. The proceedings were adjourned for 10 minutes and when they reconvened, the judge indicated that the witness did not have to answer this line of questioning. Dillon, *The Dirty War*, 352, 355.

[87] (1982) 3 NIJB 8.

O'Doherty on the day the robbery in question had been committed.

By June 1982 the appearance of the supergrasses was said to have brought many members of the IRA 'close to panic',[88] and in July, after disturbances at the preliminary inquiry, Clifford Mc-Keown retracted his accusations against twenty-nine alleged members of the UVF. Charges against six were dropped, but eighteen of the rest were eventually convicted and two others were later arrested and charged on the word of Joseph Bennett. McKeown, who had allegedly been involved in at least one sectarian murder, had himself been promised immunity from prosecution and was reported to have lived expensively in the south of England, and to have made a number of trips to France, during his time in protective custody. On 15 June 1983 he was sentenced to ten years' imprisonment for his part in an armed robbery, committed on 28 October 1981 and not included in the immunity deal, and claimed from his prison cell that he fabricated much of the evidence originally used to prosecute those he had implicated.[89] In August IRA supergrass Robert Brown retracted his evidence against eighteen suspects.

Some of the 'retraction cases' from 1982 are well documented and give a valuable insight into the life a fledgling supergrass could expect to lead. For example, on 14 March 1982 the RUC arrested Jackie Goodman, allegedly INLA operations officer in Belfast, responsible for co-ordinating the INLA's violence throughout Northern Ireland, and on the verge of becoming the organization's adjutant-general with a seat on its ruling army council. Less than two days after having been picked up by the police, and in return for immunity from prosecution, Goodman confessed to having been involved in the murder of an alleged informer, attempted murders, shootings, and robberies, turned supergrass and implicated twenty-three people in serious crimes. He later told the *Irish Times* that he had co-operated for only one reason—in order to avoid imprisonment—and that the other rewards on offer had had little or no effect upon his decision.[90]

Like all the supergrasses, Goodman was put through the 'confrontation' drill, which involved each of the principal suspects being identified in the police station by him in person. Afterwards the

[88] Urban, *SAS and IRA*, 135.
[89] *Guardian*, 29 July 1983.
[90] 21 Apr. 1983.

police collected Goodman's wife and children from their Ballymurphy home and for the next two weeks the Goodman family and
their minders stayed in ten hotels on the county Down and county
Antrim coast, with the RUC paying all the bills and Goodman
enjoying a £10 a day allowance. By mid-April Marion Goodman
was eight months pregnant and the family were moved to a house
in Thiepval army barracks in Lisburn. Here they had a weekly
living-allowance of £70 and went once a week with their minders
on shopping-trips to nearby towns and to the park, where, on one
such outing, they met and passed the time of day with one of
Goodman's old friends, who was not aware that he had turned
supergrass.

From Thiepval the Goodmans were moved with all their furniture to a house next to the police station in the small village of
Battle in East Sussex, their minders bring lodged in a house next
door. Relations between the RUC and the local police were strained
because the minders had been refused permission to carry firearms
and the RUC officers were reluctant to keep the local police fully
informed. When the Goodman baby, a boy, arrived, Marion's
sister and Goodman's brother were flown over from Northern
Ireland to attend the christening by a British army chaplain at
Aldershot barracks. But the visit fuelled Marion's growing home-
sickness. She asked if she could leave, was told she could but was
warned about the risk of being kidnapped by the INLA. Promises
of a house and a job in England, Canada, New Zealand, or South
Africa, plus £25,000 or £30,000 in the bank if her husband went
through with the trial, were also allegedly made at this stage.
Nevertheless, in mid-September 1982 Mrs Goodman left her husband and returned to Belfast.

The Goodman entourage then moved to Donnington in West
Sussex, where, unknown to his minders, Jackie phoned the INLA
and was assured that he would not be killed if he retracted. He
then phoned his solicitor, who informed him that all he needed to
do to end his association with the RUC was to sign an affidavit
withdrawing his evidence. As a result of these assurances, Goodman
decided that he would withdraw his co-operation and told the
RUC of his decision. An inspector flew out from Belfast with a
statement for him to sign saying that he no longer wanted police
protection. No attempt was made to talk him out of retracting and
he was assured that the DPP's immunity would still be honoured.

Only ten days after his wife had left England, he rejoined her in Belfast, and not long afterwards fourteen of those he had named were released without charge, although most were re-arrested on the evidence of other supergrasses.

A story similar to that of Goodman was told by Sean Mallon at a press conference in Belfast on 24 September 1982, convened a week after he had decided to withdraw his evidence against three suspects. Mallon said that he and his girlfriend, Patricia Hughes, were arrested by the police within a few days of each other in February 1982 and were taken from their flat in Armagh city via Gough army barracks to Bangor, County Down, where they were told they would be expected to give evidence against certain people. Two weeks later they were flown to a police training-centre in Guildford, Surrey, and accommodated in a house in the grounds, with two-man teams of plain-clothes RUC officers keeping watch on them from a house next door. Here they stayed for some seven months, on one occasion being taken on a day trip to France and on another to Cornwall for a couple of days, until being flown back to Belfast to testify at a remand hearing in September 1982. Mallon claimed that whilst in the Guildford police depot neither he nor his girlfriend had been allowed to make phone calls and that their mail had been read by detectives. Hughes said that they did not know that the police had no legal right to stop them from leaving and that they had been told they did not need a solicitor. It was during the remand hearing, which was marked by uproar from the public gallery, that Mallon decided he would not continue with his co-operation. However, despite his retraction, the three charged on his evidence, Oliver Grew, Roderick Carrol, and Kevin Crilly, were returned for trial on other evidence on a range of offences including attempted murder, possession of firearms, and membership of the INLA.

CONCLUSION

The supergrass system which unfolded in Northern Ireland in the early 1980s was no accident. The previous decade of conflict had seen the maturing of the intelligence and informer systems to the point where both supergrasses and defendants, particularly the second-time-rounders, could be confidently identified. The conviction-by-confession strategy had also clearly failed to put the 'godfathers of terrorism' behind bars. However, the supergrass process was not planned in the sense that its scale and subsequent trajectory were clearly foreseen by the security policy establishment. Even in its early stages it attracted considerable adverse publicity; particular concern being expressed about cases such as those of Goodman and McKeown, where immunities from prosecution for alleged murders had remained intact despite the retraction of the evidence for which they had been offered as a reward. This disquiet seems to have prompted a decision to offer reduced sentences instead as the key inducement. Beresford states that it was not until after the McKeown and Goodman cases that the RUC abandoned offers of immunity from prosecution for anyone who had 'pulled the trigger in a murder',[91] But it soon became clear that those who claimed to have played a secondary role—for example, as the driver of the getaway vehicle—could still have the slate wiped clean.

[91] *Guardian*, 29 July 1983. The adoption of this policy was confirmed by a police spokesman on the BBC's Panorama programme, 'Justice on Trial', broadcast on 24 Oct. 1983.

3

Ascendancy: January–October 1983

THE media dubbed 1982 'the year of the supergrass', since it was then that the majority came to public attention, but it was not until the following year that the first significant trials, on the evidence of Joseph Bennett, Christopher Black, and Kevin McGrady, concluded with the conviction of virtually all the accused. Between the beginning of 1981 and the end of 1983, at least eight loyalist and nineteen republican supergrasses had appeared and nearly 600 suspects had been arrested on the evidence which they had supplied.[1] Although supergrass defendants accounted for only 20 per cent of those tried by the Diplock courts in 1983,[2] they included those suspected of being amongst the top leadership of the IRA, the INLA, and the UVF. The RUC believed that the Black case had finished off the Provisional IRA in the Ardoyne area of Belfast, that the Bennett trial had destroyed the Ulster Volunteer Force in the city,[3] and that the ranks of the INLA had been decimated by the supergrasses, with morale dropping to a low ebb.[4] Only two new supergrasses, Eamon Collins and Angela Whorisky, emerged after 1983, neither recruitment resulting in a trial, and by that spring the rate of arrests on supergrass evidence had begun to slow down,[5] perhaps due to an exhaustion of the 'natural supply' plus the decision taken in the autumn of 1982 not to offer immunity from prosecution to anyone who had 'pulled the trigger' in a murder. By the end of 1983 another eleven people had also been killed in disputed shootings by the security forces.[6]

---

[1] The figure 593 for 1982–5 was given in a Commons written reply by Mr Nicholas Scott, Northern Ireland Junior Minister (HC Debs., vol. 73, col. 100).

[2] *Judicial Statistics for Northern Ireland* [*Jan.–Dec. 1983*] (Belfast: Northern Ireland Courts Service, 1984).

[3] *New Statesman*, 23 Sept. 1983.

[4] Statement of Dep. Ch. Cons. Charles Rodgers, *Belfast Telegraph*, 8 Aug. 1983.

[5] *Irish Times*, 6 Aug. 1983.

[6] A. Jennings, 'Shoot to Kill: The Final Courts of Justice' id. (ed.), *Justice Under Fire: The Abuse of Civil Liberties in Northern Ireland*, 2nd edn. (London: Pluto Press, 1990).

The decisions in the Bennett, Black, and McGrady trials seemed to bode well for the future of the supergrass system but in retrospect contained the seeds of its demise. Fifty-six of the sixty-four accused (88 per cent) were found guilty, thirty-one of these convictions (55 per cent of the total) resting on the supergrasses uncorroborated testimony. As in previous cases, the judges who presided over these three trials concluded that the common-law rule requiring them to warn juries about the dangers of convicting on the uncorroborated evidence of accomplices could be fulfilled in a non-jury court by the judge issuing the warning to himself and then proceeding to convict regardless of the absence of corroboration. The cultivation of supergrass evidence by the police appeared to be vindicated by these verdicts, since the courts seemed prepared to ensure the high conviction-rate that the supergrass system needed if the official justification for it was to be sustained.

However, 1983 was also marked by some further embarrassing retractions. By the end of the year the total number of known retractors had risen to sixteen, and in another case, involving UDA supergrass James Williamson, charges were withdrawn from all but two accused, who had made confessions. Two of the most important retractions in the autumn of 1983 were those of Robert Lean and Patrick McGurk. Lean, referred to in the press as second in command of the IRA's Belfast Brigade, had been arrested in March 1982 and held briefly with six others on the evidence of James 'Bimbo' O'Rawe but was released when O'Rawe retracted. He was arrested again on 6 September 1983 on the word of another supergrass, William Skelly, and later told Lord Gifford's unofficial inquiry into the supergrass system that the police had informed him that since his wife was also under suspicion, their five children risked being put in a home, but that if he turned supergrass, a high-powered team would negotiate his immunity with the DPP, he would be established with a new identity in any English-speaking country of his choice, and he would not have to work again.[7]

Having agreed to co-operate, Lean claimed that, over the following three days, the RUC prepared twenty-one statements based on intelligence information concerning various offences and said he would be familiarized with the details. Lean said he signed the

---

[7] T. Gifford, *Supergrasses: The Use of Accomplice Evidence in Northern Ireland* (London: The Cobden Trust, 1984), paras. 73–7.

statements and later that day was told he had been granted immunity. The next day he was 'formally released' and was housed, with his wife and children, in Lisburn army barracks, where the process of preparing him for his confrontations with each suspect began. Lean claimed he was shown photographs and told what the procedure for identification would be but that, of those he was supposed to identify, he only knew one vaguely and the others not at all. A few days later he was introduced to the chief inspector allocated to his case, who claimed also to have dealt with Christopher Black, and who said: 'We will build the statements up. It will be like a book, chapter by chapter. All fiction put across as facts. It's not me it's the man with the wig you have got to convince.'[8]

Some twenty-eight people were arrested and held on the evidence which Lean was said to have supplied to the police. These included: veteran republican Ivor Malachy Bell, said to have been the officer commanding the IRA's Belfast Brigade in the early 1970s and a participant, with Gerry Adams, then Sinn Fein MP for West Belfast, in talks with the British government in 1972; Gerry Brannigan, chairman of the Belfast executive of Sinn Fein and the party's director of elections in the Westminster poll of June 1983; and Eveleyn Glenholmes, who, some years later, was to become the subject of a famous débâcle over extradition from the Irish Republic. Describing the operation as a major strike against the IRA, the police claimed that Lean was one of the most important supergrasses to have given information.

On 30 September Lean's wife, Geraldine, left police custody expressing the hope that her husband would soon follow her. She was not to be disappointed. On 19 October Lean himself left his police minders in a stolen police car and visited his solicitor to sign an affidavit formally retracting the accusations against those he had implicated. He then appeared at a press conference, at which he claimed that he had made his decision some time before and had simply been waiting for the opportunity to make his escape, and that the police had intimidated him into fabricating evidence about suspects including Gerry Adams and other prominent Sinn Fein members. According to Urban, some intelligence officers were left with the impression that the Lean case had been a sophisticated

[8] Ibid. para. 74.

IRA plot to undermine the supergrass process.[9] After his press conference Lean was again arrested by the police and questioned about the theft of the police car he had used to make his escape. In October twelve of those he had implicated were released without charge, and three others were remanded in custody on the word of William Skelly. At another press conference following these developments it was alleged that all the Lean suspects had been offered sums of money if they would themselves turn supergrass, and one, Eddie Carmichael, claimed he had been offered £300,000 if he would testify against Gerry Adams. On 25 October Lean was himself released without charge with the immunity he had originally been offered apparently still intact. It is not clear what became of the thirteen others whom he implicated, but in August 1984 four were found guilty on their own confessions on comparatively minor charges and received suspended prison sentences. It is believed that others were tried on confession evidence and that the remainder were held on the evidence of other supergrasses.

On 24 October 1983 IRA supergrass Patrick McGurk retracted his evidence against nine defendants a few days before he was due to enter the witness-box to testify against them. In a police statement read out in court, McGurk said that the nervous strain caused by a last-minute postponement of the starting-date of the trial had prompted his decision. In September 1982 there had been disorderly scenes in court during the preliminary inquiry, which was eventually bypassed entirely when the Crown successfully applied for a voluntary bill of indictment—the first time one had been granted in a supergrass case.[10] Some observers claimed that this suggested that even a year before he finally retracted his evidence, McGurk may have been having second thoughts.[11] Seven of the nine defendants McGurk implicated, all of whom had been in custody for twenty months, were released with not-guilty verdicts entered on the record, a bench warrant was issued for the arrest of another who failed to answer his bail, and the ninth was subsequently tried and convicted on his own confession.

Also in 1983 a high-level RUC team including Assistant Chief

---

[9] M. Urban, *Big Boy's Rules: The SAS and the Secret Struggle against the IRA* (London: Faber & Faber, 1992), 137.

[10] For further details concerning the voluntary bill of indictment, see Ch. 11.

[11] See, e.g., Worker's Research Unit, *Belfast Bulletin No. 11: Supergrasses* (Belfast: pub. authors, 1984), 9.

Constable David Mellor and other senior officers paid a six-month visit to the US Marshals' Service to study the operation of the Witness Protection Programme, an initiative designed to protect vulnerable witnesses in trials concerning organized crime.[12] Their general conclusion was that the success of the US scheme hinged critically on the size of the United States, which enabled witnesses to be given new lives and new identities more easily than in a much smaller jurisdiction such as Northern Ireland or even the United Kingdom as a whole. However, for the RUC this did not necessarily imply that the supergrass system ought to be abandoned, but pointed rather to the need for less ambitious re-location arrangements.

THE BENNETT CASE: *R. v. Graham and others*

The Background

Joseph Charles Bennett was born on 19 July 1946 in east Belfast, trained as a welder after leaving school, and became involved in crime from an early age. When he was 11 he was convicted of larceny by a juvenile court, at the age of 15 he was found guilty of an offence involving dishonesty, and at the ages of 15 and 18 added convictions for firearms offences to his record. In his teens and twenties he also became a heavy gambler, and in 1972, while living with his wife and two children in Dundonald, on the outskirts of Belfast, he joined the UVF. In or around August of the same year, Bennett was charged with possession of firearms, ammunition, and explosives which he had agreed to keep on behalf of the organization, and in December he was released from remand on compassionate bail because his wife was terminally ill with cancer. When she died in April 1973, Bennett absconded, abandoning his two children in the process, and some months later, in the summer of 1973, he moved into a house in the Shankill Road area of Belfast with a married woman who was awaiting a divorce.

On 30 March 1974 Bennett was rearrested and the house in which he was living was found to contain a considerable quantity of firearms and explosives. He pleaded guilty to possession charges and received a twelve year prison sentence. But under the standard 50 per cent remission arrangements for terrorist offences then available in Northern Ireland, he served only six years, for the last

[12] See Ch. 10.

year and a half of which he was Commanding Officer of the UVF prisoners in Compound 21 at the Maze prison, then a 'special category' compound. Upon his release, on 30 March 1980, Bennett went to live in the Donegal Road area of Belfast with a single woman and her son and became a UVF company commander in the Sandy Row area of Belfast. He borrowed £600 from the Shankill UVF in order to tax and insure a car, and that summer and autumn he worked as a barman at the King's Inn, Dundonald. In December he became bar-manager of P. J. Lambe's at Ballyhackamore but was forced to leave in March 1981, having stolen some £1,350 from his employers. For this offence and for his failure to repay the borrowed £600, a UVF 'court martial' sentenced him to death in his absence.

On the evening of 5 May 1982 Bennett and two other men, Michael Campbell and William Clifford, took part in the armed robbery of Balloo Post Office at Killinchy in County Down. Bennett was armed with a loaded gun and Clifford carried a knife. The gang was confronted by the elderly postmaster and his two unmarried sisters; in the struggle which ensued, Bennett fired a shot, and one of the women, Miss Maureen McCann, was stabbed close to the heart and died soon afterwards. On 20 May Bennett was arrested by the police in connection with this incident and he later told the court at the trial of those subsequently accused on his evidence:

I did not want to go to prison again. I could not do another six. I volunteered to give evidence to the Detective Sergeant. I said I would like to make a statement of all the other crimes I was involved in and I asked if I did this would I be given immunity. I had read about immunity in the papers ... I knew I was in real danger of going down on a murder charge. I would be away for life and I was shocked. I was inside for life or sentence of death outside. The future was bleak. The police offered a third alternative ... My life depended on impressing the police. The police said they would take a statement first of my involvment and take it higher up ... The more you tell the better your chances of immunity. My safety depended on my ability to name as many as possible ... I was told I would be got out of here and looked after.[13]

Bennett made a series of police statements in May, June, October, and December 1982, and finally on 31 January 1983, which implicated eighteen suspects, including his two accomplices, in the

---

[13]   *R.* v. *Graham* (1983) 7 NIJB 25–6.

Killinchy post-office robbery, in a variety of offences ranging from murder to membership of the UVF. On 25 April 1983, at the conclusion of a trial in which Bennett was not called as a witness, Campbell and Clifford received prison sentences of fourteen and eighteen years respectively for the manslaughter of the elderly sister of the Balloo postmaster; and, in return for immunity from prosecution and a safe passage to an undisclosed destination, a new job, and a new life, Bennett agreed to testify against the remaining sixteen accused, who faced a total of sixty-six counts.

The Trial

The trial of *R. v. Graham and others*, which lasted from 16 February to 11 April 1983, attracted considerable public interest. Its high profile was graphically illustrated when, on 7 March, Mr Desmond Boal QC, defending fifteen of the sixteen accused, complained to the judge about remarks made by the Chief Constable, Sir John Hermon, in his annual report for 1982, which had been published just a few days earlier. The Chief Constable had stated that the outcome of the 'converted terrorist process' was crucial for the well-being of Northern Ireland.[14] Mr Boal claimed that, had there been a jury sitting, he would have asked for a ruling that the Chief Constable's report was in contempt of court, but the trial judge, Mr Justice Murray, assured the defence that the Chief Constable's remarks would have no effect upon his judgment.

Since *R. v. Graham* hinged almost entirely on the evidence which Bennett had given the police, the proceedings revolved around three central issues: Bennett's character, his credibility as a witness, and, in particular, the effect of the immunity deal upon the reliability of his evidence. The precise terms of the immunity were not disclosed, and Bennett's own testimony to the court remains the only evidence that he had, in fact, been granted immunity from prosecution. Mr Justice Murray outlined three strong criticisms of this state of affairs. First, he stated that the failure of the Crown to provide an 'official' version of the deal, despite specific queries about it from the bench, was 'most undesirable', although it had not affected his decision. Pointing out that in the English supergrass case *R. v. Turner*[15] the court had been able to see a letter from the

---

[14] *Chief Constable's Report 1983* (Belfast: HMSO, 1984).
[15] (1975) 61 Cr App R 67.

Director of Public Prosecutions to the accomplice's solicitor which indicated precisely what kind of immunity had been offered there, he added: 'the court should hear from a witness in authority what precisely has been promised to the accomplice witness in return for his testimony so that it may have a clear view of the extent of the inducement offered to the witness to give his evidence'.[16]

The judge's second ground for complaint was Bennett's claim that the promise of immunity had been made by a senior police-officer. Referring to remarks made by Lord Justice Lawton in *Turner*, Mr Justice Murray emphasized that such offers should never be made by the police:

the giving of a promise of immunity should be most carefully considered but it seems to me, as at present advised, that the precise mode in which it is to be done in any particular case is a matter of policy for the Crown rather than one of law for the courts. Of course the manner of its giving might become a vital matter for the courts in deciding the credibility or otherwise of the accomplice's evidence if ultimately given in court.[17]

Thirdly, there was considerable doubt about the offences which the immunity deal covered, and Bennett himself did not seem to know what was included. On one occasion he told the court that it encompassed 'murder and other crimes I was involved in', whilst at another point he claimed that it was limited to his 'participation in terrorist crimes'.[18] Mr Justice Murray concluded that 'whatever the precise terms of the immunity it must have been a highly potent incentive to Bennett to do what the police regarded as necessary to warrant a bargain being made with him'[19] and he doubted if the other benefits were of comparable importance. The inference was 'irresistible', he concluded, that Bennett's immunity was an integral part of the bargain involving his testimony in court.[20]

As far as Bennett's credibility was concerned, the trial judge indicated that he was aware that a person with Bennett's 'appalling' record 'would not . . . scruple at perjury if it suited him to commit it' and that he certainly had some motives for telling lies against at least some of the defendants, especially since he had admitted to fearing and hating the people he had implicated.[21] He was, Mr

---

[16] *R. v. Graham* (1983) 7 NIJB 23.   [17] Ibid. 24.   [18] Ibid. 28.
[19] Ibid.   [20] Ibid. 29.   [21] Ibid. 69.

Justice Murray said, 'a ruthless and resourceful criminal whose criminal acts extended to the use of his dead father's police uniform to carry out daring armed robberies from which considerable sums of money were stolen and divided amongst himself and his accomplices'.[22] Defence counsel argued that in order for an accomplice's testimony to be corroborated by a particular piece of independent evidence, *R. v. Baskerville*[23] required that it must both confirm that a crime had been committed and implicate the accused in it. Although he conceded that such evidence would be 'less cogent' than that which pointed to the participation of the accused in the crime, the judge dismissed this reasoning, on the grounds that it was sufficient for the evidence of an independent witness to place the accused at a time and place consistent with the accomplice's testimony, since this would amount to 'independent evidence which tends to show that the story of the accomplice that the accused committed the crime is true. It . . . confirms, or tends to confirm that part of the accomplice's story in a way that implicates the accused.'[24]

While the interpretation of *Baskerville* suggested by counsel for the defence may be unjustifiably narrow, what Mr Justice Murray seems to have overlooked is that unless at least one piece of independent evidence shows that a crime has been committed, charges fabricated by an 'accomplice' or supergrass may be 'corroborated'. An alleged accomplice could, for example, claim that he and a defendant charged with conspiracy to commit a murder which did not occur met at a particular time and place to plan it, while in fact the two met for some other, innocent purpose. Independent evidence confirming that the meeting took place at the time and location indicated by the accomplice's testimony can never implicate the accused in such an offence if no agreement to act unlawfully was even mooted, much less reached, and therefore cannot amount to corroboration.

Going through each of the incidents and the case against each defendant in turn, the judge concluded that Bennett's evidence had 'the ring of truth' and that it tallied with the supporting evidence offered by the Crown. Recognizing that the congruence between an

---

[22] Ibid. 25–6.
[23] [1916] 2 KB 658.
[24] *R. v. Graham* (1983) 7 NIJB 67.

accomplice's evidence and the bare facts of the events in question had limited probative value, he stated that it was significant that the independent evidence supported Bennett's general credibility. Mr Justice Murray was impressed by the 'terse and matter of fact way'[25] in which Bennett delivered his evidence and also with the way in which he withstood the 'forceful personality' and skilful advocacy of the leading counsel for the defence, Mr Desmond Boal QC.[26] He stated that the fact that none of the defendants had elected to give evidence should not be taken as evidence of their guilt, but that it could and had to be a factor in the assessment of the credibility of the testimony of an accomplice. He also concluded that Bennett risked being exposed as a liar if any of the defendants had a cast-iron alibi and that this could have resulted in the forfeiture of the protection the police might have provided, thus placing him at the mercy of the UVF 'execution' squad.

The Verdict

In Mr Justice Murray's opinion, there was technical corroboration of the charges against three of the defendants, Robert Wilson, Thomas Evans, and Brian Halliday, but none against any of the rest. When questioned by the police about a murder, Wilson was alleged to have said that the police could wait for six or seven days and 'I'll still not tell my part.'[27] The judge took this as 'a significant admission of involvement'.[28] Evans was also deemed to have made 'a most significant admission'[29] during a police interview about the Ballysillan UVF, when he was alleged to have said, 'I control the teams . . . I control the gear.'[30] At the time of his arrest, Halliday was found to be in possession of a key to a yard which contained explosives and wire-cutters which the prosecution claimed had been used to steal a car used as a car bomb.[31] A lie told by a fourth defendant, Norman Large, seems to have been treated by the judge as verging on corroboration.

Concluding his judgment, Mr Justice Murray listed a number of discrepancies in Bennett's evidence to which the defence had attached some significance. For example, Bennett claimed that he and the defendant John Irvine had flown to Amsterdam via London

---

[25] *R. v. Graham* (1983) 7 NIJB 77.   [26] Ibid. 78.   [27] Ibid. 74
[28] Ibid.   [29] Ibid. 76.   [30] Ibid.   [31] Ibid. 75.

in the summer of 1980 on an abortive trip to buy arms from a Dutch neo-Nazi organization,[32] while in fact the evidence showed that they had flown direct from Belfast. There was also some confusion over the identification of one defendant, Norris, and which defendants were known by which nicknames. Mr Justice Murray was also persuaded that Bennett had told a lie about a cheque for £200 from the North Belfast Mutual Aid Association, which he denied having received or having endorsed, claiming instead that, when he came out of prison, he had received £600 cash from the defendants Houston and Hewitt acting on behalf of the UVF. Although the cheque for £200 was produced in court and a handwriting expert confirmed that it bore Bennett's signature, the judge stated that Bennett's lie about it was 'an extraneous matter entirely as the evidence emerged' and that it would be 'wrong to allow that one offence to upset the whole view I have formed about the evidence'.[33] However, as Gifford points out in his report on the supergrass trials, the lie was highly relevant to the accusation that Houston and Hewitt were members of the UVF.[34] The judge attributed other inconsistencies in Bennett's evidence to his seven-day subjection to Mr Boal's skilful advocacy but, with the exception of the Norris case, concluded that none of these was of 'sufficient importance to raise a real doubt as to the credibility of [his] evidence'.[35]

Despite the marked absence of corroboration and having warned himself of the dangers of convicting on the uncorroborated evidence of an accomplice (a ritualistic exercise in all the supergrass trials), Mr Justice Murray convicted all but two of the sixteen defendants on 11 April 1983. William Davison was acquitted because, in the judge's opinion, the prosecution had not proved that he had the guilty knowledge necessary in a charge of failing to give information concerning a murder, and Robert Norris was acquitted on the

---

[32] Bennett claimed that, as part of the deal, the Dutch had insisted that the UVF carry out attacks on members of the Jewish community in mainland Britain, a commitment which they were not authorized to undertake. According to Bennett, 2 members of the Dutch group came to Belfast the following Christmas and received instruction in bomb-making. Curiously, Irvine was not arrested until 4 months after Bennett had begun giving his statements to the police.

[33] *R. v. Graham* (1983) 7 NIJB 87–8.

[34] *Supergrasses*, para. 39.

[35] *R. v. Graham* (1983) NIJB 83.

grounds that Bennett could have mistakenly confused him for someone else involved in the preparations for a bombing. Brian Halliday and Norman Large were found not guilty of the attempted sectarian murders of the clientele of two clubs in Clyde Street in the Short Strand area of Belfast between 24 and 27 April 1982, since the Crown had not proved an intention to kill, but they were convicted of causing the explosion in question. Robert Wilson and Robert Seymour were each found guilty of the sectarian murder of James Burns on 23 February 1981, and related offences. John Graham, allegedly the Commander of the UVF since 1976, John Douglas, and James Irvine were jailed for various offences including the no-warning bomb-attack on the Lakeglen hotel on 30 July 1980, which caused extensive damage and severe burns to a passing pedestrian, as well as possession of explosives and membership of the UVF.[36]

THE BLACK CASE: *R. v. Donnelly and others*

The Background

Christopher Black was born in 1955 and lived in the Ardoyne district of Belfast until his marriage in 1974, when he moved to the Oldpark area. He left school at 15, worked for periods as a builders' labourer and a semi-skilled machinist, and was also unemployed for long spells. He told the court in the trial of *R. v. Donnelly and others* that he joined the IRA in September 1975 in order to gain acceptance in his new neighbourhood and because he 'thought it would be a game really and there would be excitement'.[37] Black's first IRA operation had ended in disaster in December 1975, when he and two others were cornered by police during an attempted armed robbery of Dixon's, a builders' and timber merchant in Corporation Street, Belfast, where Black had previously been an employee. The gang took the managing director and bookkeeper hostage and, during a short-lived siege, demanded in turn a boat to Hong Kong and a car to Dublin, but eventually a priest persuaded them to give themselves up. At the trial arising

---

[36] At the trial, Bennett had said of Irvine: 'he sentenced me to death'. *R. v. Graham*, 26. But if the UVF 'court martial' had taken place in his absence, as Bennett himself alleged, he must either have fabricated Irvine's involvement or have been informed about it by a third party, in which case it would have been hearsay evidence.

[37] *Belfast Telegraph*, 3 Aug. 1983.

out of this incident Black refused to recognize the court. All three defendants were convicted and sentenced to ten years in prison, where Black acquired a reputation for aggression, apparently due largely to his behaviour on the football field. Having served the customary 50 per cent of his sentence, Black was released on licence in December 1980, immediately re-enlisted in the IRA, and was offered the choice of 'going company' or joining an active service unit (ASU). The 'company', nicknamed 'the Sweeney' after the Metropolitan Police flying-squad celebrated in the television series of the same name, was responsible for dealing with fights in pubs and clubs, stopping vandalism in republican areas, carrying out kneecappings, and acting as stewards at marches, while the ASUs carried out shootings, bombings, and other 'hard core' terrorist activities.

Black chose the company and for about five months was content being an IRA volunteer with a local reputation yet without having to participate in any risky terrorism. But all this changed during the hunger-strike of 1981, when the IRA stepped up its activities, in an attempt, as Black put it, to 'keep things on the boil'. Although the IRA's preferred policy was to keep the identities of ASU activists secret from those in the company, and vice versa, around April 1981 Black and Patrick Markey, another alleged member of the Sweeney, were called upon to assist an ASU in a sniping attack. Black claimed that the ASU members turned out to be either people he knew from his earlier period in the IRA, or neighbours, former school-friends, drinking-companions, or relatives of acquaintances. Black maintained that his 'active service' operations at this time were either dogged by ineptitude and his own half-heartedness, or thwarted by intervening events. He claimed, for example, that a sniping attack had to be called off when one of the gang realized that their getaway car could be seen from a nearby army observation post, and that the first time he had to use an Armalite rifle, for an attack upon a policeman emerging from Old Park RUC station, he fired to miss. He said that on another occasion he refused to shoot at an army bus because women were on board. Black maintained that, in 1981, riots were often started by ASUs to lure the police and army into ambushes and that he began to realize that it was only a matter of time before he himself became directly involved in a murder, a prospect he claimed not to relish. These qualms, he alleged, inspired him to supply false information about potential targets to those planning operations, and he claimed that the day before he was due to take part in an attempt to murder a reserve police constable, he deliberately picked a fight with an army patrol and injured his arm in order to be excused. He also maintained that in the one murder in which he confessed to having been involved, the shooting of UDR Sergeant Julian Connolly, his role was limited to taking the keys from the owner of the car the gang used and writing Connolly's name and address on a decoy registered envelope which was delivered by the gunman posing as a postman.

On 21 November 1981 Black was arrested by the police in the Ardoyne area of Belfast with two brothers, Kevin and James Donnelly, while the three were on their way to a drinking-club to read out a public statement about a road-block they had just staged to gain publicity for the IRA. They were all dressed in badly fitting combat-jackets taken from bemused customers in the High-field Club the day before, and their balaclava helmets and gloves were later recovered from where they had been discarded when the police approached. Two other men, Desmond Breslin, whom Black later claimed had photographed the road-block for the republican newspaper *An Phoblacht/Republican News*, and Kevin Mulgrew, said to have hijacked a car in furtherance of the offence, were also subsequently arrested. After two days of silence in police custody, Black started to make the first of a large number of statements implicating himself and others in a catalogue of IRA-related of-fences. On 24 November 1981 he was granted immunity from prosecution, and subsequently, in a trial occupying 120 court-sitting days, which lasted from 6 December 1982 to 5 August 1983, he gave evidence against thirty-eight accused, thirty-five of whom were ultimately convicted. Acting on Black's evidence, the police in the Republic of Ireland seized 4,000 rounds of ammunition and eleven Armalite rifles from an IRA training-camp in Donegal, and a senior RUC officer told the *Irish Times* that the arrests on Black's evidence had reduced the IRA in North Belfast to four members.[38] In their study of the IRA Bishop and Mallie claim that

Black's decision produced panic in the IRA. No one was sure how much he knew. The senior members of the Belfast IRA prepared to go on the run. After the initial hysteria had subsided, however, the leadership decided

---

[38] 6 Aug. 1983.

on the cooler but more risky tactic of staying put and gambling on being able to discredit Black and the immunity deal that was being struck.[39]

The committal proceedings in the trial of those Black implicated were bypassed by a successful *ex parte* application from the DPP for Northern Ireland to the Lord Chief Justice, Lord Lowry, on 5 October 1982, for a 'voluntary bill of indictment'.[40] The magistrate who presided over a remand hearing the day the voluntary bill was introduced said that the Crown was entitled to this procedure since there had been intimidation from the public gallery in other preliminary inquiries in similar trials. But some argued that this procedure had not been intended for use in such circumstances and the real reason it was granted was to spare Black the ordeal of having to give his evidence twice. A number of the accused dismissed their lawyers in protest.

While preparing for trial, Black spent a lot of his time with his wife, four children, and elderly mother-in-law in police protection in England, although their precise whereabouts have remained a mystery. He denied that he had learned his statements off by heart during this period, but admitted having been advised by a lawyer as to how he should give his evidence in court. He also denied that members of the RUC periodically arrived at his English retreat with fresh intelligence for him to confirm. The Chief Constable of the RUC, Sir John Hermon, was ordered to appear in court when other members of the family launched a habeas corpus action in an attempt to find out where Black's mother-in-law was, but the action was dismissed when a detective chief inspector stated in court that the 66-year-old woman was not being detained against her will and had chosen to be with her daughter and family.

The Trial

The Black trial was nothing short of a public spectacle. The thirty-eight defendants sat in rows around three sides of the court-room, guarded by a score of prison officers and more than seventy policemen, two of whom were armed with M1 carbines, and the judge, a former Stormont Attorney-General, Mr Justice Kelly, was reported to have worn a bullet-proof vest under his robes for the

[39] P. Bishop and E. Mallie, *The Provisional IRA* (London: Corgi Books, 1988), 407.

[40] See Ch. 11.

duration of the hearing. Although the indictment contained 184 charges, ranging from murder to failing to give information about terrorist activities, the offences had resulted in few victims. The bulk were based on forty-five separate incidents alleged to have occurred between December 1980 and February 1982, the majority of which related to the period of the republican prison hunger-strikes in the summer and autumn of 1981. There were: two murders, one of which did not involve Black's evidence; one knee-capping; eleven cases of false imprisonment, in which people had been held in houses taken over as vantage-points for shootings; twenty-three charges of conspiracy to murder, many involving alleged plans to attack the security forces, some of which had been attempted but had not caused death or injury; and thirty-nine charges involving possession of firearms. Over 150 members of the RUC were involved in the investigation, more than 550 witnesses gave evidence at the trial, and there were some 70,000 pages of trial papers. Black himself was on the witness-stand for fifteen days and it took the judge three days to read out his judgment. The *Irish Times* estimated that the trial, said to have been the biggest in Irish criminal legal history, had cost several thousand pounds a day and more than £1 million in total,[41] and the prison sentences which were imposed at the end of the proceedings totalled 4,022 years.

When Black first entered the witness-box to give his evidence, on 12 January 1983, the proceedings were immediately disrupted by his mother, who tried to speak to him from the public gallery. Black was led out of the court-room and the judge ordered both his parents to be removed. The camaraderie subsequently displayed in court between Black and his police bodyguards was regarded by some defence barristers as astounding. Knowing glances and whispered jokes were routinely exchanged and the minders even reassuringly touched Black on the shoulder when he seemed to be under particular pressure. In his report on the supergrass trials Gifford also commented upon the unusual rapport which Black seemed to have with the judge:

The witness box was close to the bench and slightly to one side of it. Black sat directly facing the judge, speaking directly to him, never turning away.

---

[41]   26 May and 8 July 1983.

In front of the witness, between Black and the rest of the court, stood two police officers. The effect was that even those barristers who were cross-examining Black could not see his face. To those who watched there appeared to be an intimate rapport between Black and the judge. (A wholly contrasting atmosphere was observed in the McGrady trial, continuing at the same time before the Lord Chief Justice, who treated the supergrass with coldness and at times hostility.)[42]

As in the Bennett case, the Black trial hinged upon Black's character, credibility, and in particular the arrangements concerning his immunity from prosecution. Refusing to believe Black's benign account of his involvement with the IRA, Mr Justice Kelly said that his commitment to terrorism was

active and wholehearted. He was in fact up to his neck in terrorist activity throughout 1981. In almost all the incidents he . . . recounted he played a major role . . . Clearly he was a dangerous and ruthless terrorist. If he had not been caught by the police . . . the probabilities are that by now his crimes would be multiplied and his terrorist activity unabated.[43]

As far as the offer of immunity from prosecution was concerned, Mr Justice Kelly stated that he believed the police evidence that it was not until the third interview that Black had said: 'Look, if I admit my part will you keep me right?' and that Black had offered to assist in the investigation of serious crimes provided there were 'guarantees as to his own safety and the safety of his family'.[44] Black was told that no promises could be made but that the matter would be brought to the attention of the relevant authorities, and a detective superintendent explained he could be dealt with in three possible ways, two of which would result in his avoiding punishment. He could be given immunity from prosecution, a prosecution could be brought but dropped, or he could be tried and sentenced.

The police record indicated, Mr Justice Kelly said, that before he gave any information to the police, Black was seeking immunity from prosecution and a safe passage out of Northern Ireland for himself and his family. But the RUC had given him no guarantees and had made no promises before he gave his information. The detective superintendent had, however, given him some hope when he outlined the three possibilities if he turned Queen's evidence

[42] Gifford, *Supergrasses*, Para. 49.
[43] *R.* v. *Donnelly* (1983) unreported judgment, day 1, pp. 71–2.
[44] Ibid. 72.

and, in the judge's view, by gaining Black's confidence and reducing his distrust the police had thereby advanced the interview process a stage further. Black hoped for immunity, Mr Justice Kelly said, but his participation in the Connolly murder caused him to think that he might not get it. At the trial the detective chief superintendent who was in charge of the Black investigation said that the RUC were not prepared to recommend immunity for anyone who had been directly involved in murder but that someone who had been less than directly involved might receive it.

It was apparently not until 24 November that a detective chief inspector came to Black's cell and told him that he had been granted a general immunity from prosecution but that he did not know 'the exact terms'.[45] However, Mr Justice Kelly believed that Black understood that the offer meant he would not be charged with any criminal offence, that he would not be returned to gaol and that he and his family would be resettled with a new identity somewhere outside Northern Ireland at public expense. The judge concluded that the immunity did not appear to be conditional upon Black's testifying, but clearly the police expected him to give evidence, and initially Black believed he was obliged to do so. However, Mr Justice Kelly said that some months before the trial, Black had formed the view that even if he recanted and stepped down from the witness-box, his immunity would remain intact and the judge, therefore concluded that 'Black's motives . . . in giving information to the police were entirely of self interest. The compelling reason was to escape imprisonment. He made no secret of this. Self interest also led him to turn Queen's evidence and a readiness to testify.'[46]

Mr Justice Kelly said that Black's expectation of being resettled and maintained for some time with his family probably created a sense of gratitude, and it was therefore important to be alert to the possibility that it might have affected his testimony against any of the accused. But he added that he was satisfied that Black had not given his evidence in return for future reward, although it was open to question whether his evidence had been given for past favours, and perhaps in return for the maintenance of his new identity.[47]

In assessing Black's credibility the judge considered several other issues. First, there was Black's admission that he had committed

---

[45] *R. v. Donnelly* (1983) 81.   [46] Ibid. 82.   [47] Ibid. 125.

perjury in a previous trial, *R. v. Crawford*,[48] over which Mr Justice Kelly had also presided. Although the precise nature of the perjury was not disclosed, it had clearly involved providing Crawford with a false alibi in connection with a charge of sectarian murder. Secondly, there were some questions about the reliability of Black's denials, which he later appeared to retract, that he had sought assurances or guarantees from the police prior to his decision to turn Queen's evidence. Mr Justice Kelly stated that some of his answers on this issue 'appear to be lies and are quite contrary to the police evidence ... At no time else during the trial did I find Black in this state of confusion and contradiction.'[49]

A possible reason for this, the judge suggested, was Black's confused, tired, frightened, and mixed-up state of mind, and his emotional state, particularly his fear of returning to prison, when he made his first statements to the police.[50] Thirdly, there was the question of Black's performance in the witness-box. Mr Justice Kelly concluded:

Throughout I was conscious of his bad character, his perjury, the motivations and benefits that preceded him to the witness box, the possible motivations while there, the inconsistencies and omissions revealed and indeed all of the infirmities that that cross examination exposed ... But at the end of the day ... my conclusion was that ... he was one of the best witnesses I have ever heard ... I am confident that any tribunal of fact sitting by who had heard him would have reached the same conclusion and the same degree of conclusion.[51]

The judge pointed out that, notwithstanding their strong attack upon his credibility, even defence counsel had remarked that Black had 'a phenomenal memory', 'a fantastic memory', that he was 'a careful and astute witness', and that 'there was a remarkable consistency between his depositions and his evidence'.[52]

Finally, Mr Justice Kelly stated that the credibility of Black's evidence had to be judged in the context of all the evidence of the case. He listed those items of evidence which the Crown claimed tended to confirm Black's general credibility because they showed, or tended to show, that the incidents Black related had taken place,

---

[48] Unreported.
[49] *R. v. Donnelly* (1983) unreported judgment, day 1, pp. 79 and 81.
[50] Ibid. 100.
[51] Ibid. 89–90.
[52] Ibid. 91.

and he remarked on the accuracy of some of the details. Defence
suggestions that this congruity was the result of Black's having
been coached by the police were rejected and the trial judge's final
conclusion on Black's credibility was 'that Black's evidence in this
trial is credible. I have not the slightest doubt in accepting it and
using it as a solid and reliable basis for my consideration of the
further issues in this case.'[53] Mr Justice Kelly said he found it
difficult to imagine what possible motive Black would have for
deliberately implicating innocent people and held that, although he
might have been honestly mistaken about one or two matters, it
was unlikely that he was mistaken about them all. Names might
have been suggested to him by the police, he added, but this was
unobjectionable provided it merely jogged the witness's memory
and stimulated his own evidence. Like Mr Justice Murray in the
Bennett case, he thought that Black's uncorroborated evidence
could be trusted because the possibility that any accused would
have had a cast-iron alibi would have discouraged Black from
giving false testimony. However, since many of the conspiracy
charges involved wide time-spans, alibis were out of the question
for most of the accused. In fact, only one defendant, Joseph Kelly,
claimed one, and this was disbelieved.

The Verdict

Eighteen of the thirty-five defendants found guilty in *R. v. Donnelly*
were convicted on Black's uncorroborated testimony. The 'big fish'
were of greatest significance in terms of their alleged position in the
IRA and their alleged offences, while the 'small fry' included those
convicted of less serious or less numerous IRA activities, as well as
those charged not with IRA membership itself but with various
offences of a supportive kind. In the first category, with their
alleged ranks in the IRA's Belfast Brigade were: Kevin Anthony
Mulgrew, known to the police as 'little Napoleon' (commander of
Black's ASU); Patrick Teer (second in command); Anthony Barnes
(officer commanding the Bone area); Patrick Markey (quartermaster for the Oldpark); Paul O'Neill (operations officer for the
Belfast Brigade); Thomas Prendergast (second in command of 'F'
Company in the Ardoyne); Samuel Graham (quartermaster for the
Ardoyne); Anthony McIlkenny (officer commanding the IRA's 3rd

---

[53] *R. v. Donnelly* (1983) 121.

Belfast Company); Patrick Fennell (IRA recruiting officer); Arthur Corbett (finance officer of the IRA's Belfast Brigade); and Paul Anthony Kane (a member of Black's ASU). Mulgrew, the central defendant, was found guilty of almost fifty offences, including having planned and directed the Connolly murder, conspiracies, and attempts to murder members of the security forces, as well as firearms and explosives offences, while Teer was convicted of forty offences, including attempts and conspiracies to murder members of the security forces, in addition to offences involving firearms and explosives. Apart from McIlkenny all these defendants were convicted on Black's uncorroborated testimony.

Serious doubts about the guilt of two of the principal defendants in particular were expressed after the trial. On Black's uncorroborated evidence Gerard Oliver Loughlin was convicted of the Connolly murder, firearms offences relating to this offence, conspiracy to kneecap, and of having been officer commanding the 3rd Belfast Battalion of the IRA, to which Black had belonged. Originally Black had implicated 'Gerry *Loughran*', whose address he gave as 118 New Lodge Road, and in his written statement Black added: 'His nickname is Lockey and he is about 27 years of age and he was in Castlereagh last week.'[54] On checking their records the police found that during the week to which Black referred, Gerry *Loughlin*, of 233 Spamount Street, had been detained at Castlereagh, but there was no record of Gerry Loughran of 118 New Lodge Road. Black changed his statement when he received this information from the police. Mr Justice Kelly described this as 'a significant error' and added that Black had not been 'at all frank about why he changed the address'.[55] Nevertheless, the judge concluded that the crucial factor in Black's identification of this defendant was the reference to his having been in Castlereagh the week prior to the one in which Black made his statements to the police, and he added: 'the use of the nickname "Lockey" might well have meant that the last syllable of the surname was rarely used and not clearly known' and pointed out that Black had made a clear identification of Loughlin in court.[56]

The other particularly controversial conviction of a major defendant was that of Tobias Charles McMahon, found guilty, on Black's uncorroborated evidence, of conspiring to murder members of the security forces with explosives, possessing explosives with intent,

[54] Ibid. 152.   [55] Ibid. 152–3.   [56] Ibid. 151–5.

and of having been the explosives officer of the IRA's Belfast Brigade, although there had, in fact, been no explosion on the occasion in question. Black claimed to have known McMahon well from the time they had been in prison together in 1976, and admitted to the court that they 'seemed to have an instant dislike for each other'.[57] No reference had been made to McMahon in the statements which Black had given the police in November 1981 and he was not included until 25 July 1982. In his evidence Black claimed that on one occasion McMahon had arrived to help Black's ASU plant a bomb but had become suspicious of a gap in a nearby bricked-up wall, had been concerned that it might have been the work of an army surveillance squad, and, on discovering that none of the ASU had checked this possibility, had left, taking his bomb with him. McMahon received a fifteen-year sentence.

The most controversial of the convictions of the 'small fry' was that of Joseph Henry Kelly, found guilty of having been a member of the IRA between 1 March and 31 August 1981, of hijacking, and of carrying an imitation firearm with intent. Black claimed to have been at an IRA training-camp in Donegal with Kelly in the pre-Easter period March/April 1981, while Kelly made a written confession admitting having joined the IRA in May 1981 and of having been at a camp from around 6 August that year. He also confessed to having hijacked a lorry with a plastic gun on the day in May 1981 on which hunger-striker Bobby Sands died. Black's deposition, served on Kelly in October 1982, stated that Kelly and Black had been at the same IRA training-camp in Donegal around March 1981, yet the indictment, as originally presented, alleged that Kelly had been at the camp between 1 June and 15 July of that year. In his testimony Black maintained that Kelly and he had been at the camp around March but added that he himself had been to another training-camp on two further occasions in July/August, which Kelly had not attended. The judge said that it remained a mystery why the police had originally given June/July as the relevant dates, and some days after Black had given his evidence but before he was cross-examined upon it, the Crown was granted leave to amend the dates on the indictment relating to the training-camp to 'between 1 March 1981 and 31 August 1981'.

In his defence Kelly claimed he had never been a member of the IRA, had never been to any of their camps, had never seen Black prior to an arranged police-station confrontation, and that his confessions to the police were false, having been induced by fear, a state of extreme nervousness, the shock of the confrontation with Black, and police aggression. But the judge said this account displayed a 'massive lack of credibility'.[58] Kelly showed an uncertainness about his whereabouts from 9–15 April 1981 in re-examination, and his work records showed that he had been absent between these dates, but over forty witnesses were called upon to support an alibi that he had been in Belfast in the Easter period 1981 and in August of that year. The judge, however, pointed out that it was not until Kelly's re-examination that the possibility of an alibi for the pre-Easter period in 1981 emerged, and, accusing the alibi witnesses of being 'hardly disinterested', he stated that 'their evidence was not always consistent or reliable' and 'it all seemed to be got together late in the day'.[59] In reaching his verdict Mr Justice Kelly held that he was satisfied beyond reasonable doubt on Black's evidence that Kelly and Black had attended an IRA training-camp together between 1 March and 31 August 1981, but he was not satisfied beyond reasonable doubt precisely when it was. There was a strong probability, he said, that it was the April period coming up to Easter and a possibility that Kelly may also have been at another camp in August 1981. He concluded that the defendant's verbal and written confessions had been voluntarily made and could be given full weight to corroborate Black's testimony.

THE McGRADY CASE: *R. v. Gibney and others*

The Background

Kevin McGrady was born in 1956 and lived with his parents, five brothers, and a sister in the Markets area of Belfast. He trained as a butcher after leaving school and, prior to joining the 4th (Markets area) Battalion of the Provisional IRA in 1975, had never been in trouble with the police. He claimed he enlisted in the IRA because he identified with the nationalist cause, distrusted the Protestant community, and because his brother Sean had been interned in the early 1970s. In his first few months as an IRA activist McGrady

[58] Ibid., day 2, p. 37.
[59] Ibid. 26.

participated in a series of serious incidents, including three murders, and in December 1975 he was arrested and charged with the last of these offences, the murder of Ernest Dowds. However, although the murder charge itself was dropped when the owner of the car said to have been used in the shooting withdrew his evidence, McGrady was nevertheless sentenced to three months' imprisonment for having assaulted a police officer during an interrogation. However, he was released immediately, having already been in custody on remand for seven months. McGrady left Belfast a month later and spent a year and a half in London before going to Amsterdam, where he got a job in a hotel, apparently underwent a religious conversion whilst staying at a Christian youth hostel, and, in March 1978, only five weeks after his arrival in the Netherlands, became involved with two religious organizations, one Dutch and the other American. He then worked with the latter, Youth with a Mission (YWAM), for about a year and a half.

In January 1982 McGrady returned to Belfast, gave himself up to the police, and, during the course of numerous lengthy interviews between 14 January and 24 May 1982, made ten written statements, with further statements in August and October 1982, about a series of terrorist offences committed in 1975. He told the court at the trial of those he implicated that he had given himself up because he wanted to clear his brother Sean and others of false charges and because, having failed in an application for the post of manager of a Christian youth hostel on account of his unpunished offences, he realized that he needed to set his criminal record straight in order to make progress in the religious movement he had joined. As in this case of other supergrasses, during his time at Castlereagh police station a number of 'confrontations' were staged between McGrady and various suspects. McGrady identified the suspect, provided an account of the crimes in which he claimed they had been involved, and a police officer made notes of what was said and how the suspect reacted. The session with the defendant James Gibney was to have particular significance. Whilst McGrady was in custody on remand awaiting trial, YWAM organized letters of support for him from all over the world and he was featured in the group's publications, becoming something of a celebrity to its readership. Later, representatives of the organization visited him in prison.[60]

[60] The *Belfast Bulletin* claims that McGrady received some 47 pre-trial visits from the police and members of YWAM. *Belfast Bulletin No 11*, 25.

On 26 June 1982, having pleaded guilty, McGrady was convicted and sentenced to life imprisonment on twenty-seven charges, including the murders of William Stephenson, Andrew Craig, and Ernest Dowds, and four attempted murders, in all of which he claimed to have played a secondary but willing role as a look-out or as a driver of the getaway vehicle. However, in the event, he was to serve only six years.[61] He also claimed that his brother Sean, who had already been sentenced to life imprisonment for the Dowds murder, had not in fact been involved. Later, at the trial of *Gibney and others*, McGrady maintained that Sean had been a look-out at the Craig murder in 1975, an offence for which Sean had not been prosecuted, and that he, Kevin, would be prepared to give evidence for the prosecution against Sean if required.

McGrady claimed that when he had given himself up he did not realize that he could give evidence in court against his accomplices and that it was only after having made his own confession, and having been told by the police that he could testify, that he decided to turn Queen's evidence. He denied that he believed giving evidence in court against others would help either his own case or that of Sean, but he acknowledged that giving evidence could help shorten his own prison sentence. During the course of the *Gibney* trial McGrady claimed that he had never suffered any remorse after the various murders in which he had been involved, and that God had spoken to him while he waited for the proceedings to begin.

The Trial

The trial of *R.* v. *Gibney and others*, presided over by the then Lord Chief Justice of Northern Ireland, Lord Lowry, began on 5 May 1983 with ten defendants and an indictment containing forty-five counts, including conspiracy to murder the former Chief Constable of the RUC, Sir Jamie Flanagan. The central defendant was James Gibney, a former national organizer of Sinn Fein, the party's director of elections in the Fermanagh-South Tyrone by-election in 1981, which returned IRA hunger-striker Bobby Sands, and a prominent member of the anti-H-Blocks campaign. Although Gibney was widely suspected of having been an officer in the IRA, Bishop and Mallie claim that by the time of the McGrady trial, his

---

[61] See Ch. 11.

activities in the republican movement were 'entirely political'.[62] The other accused were Brian Davison, John McConkey, Peter McKiernan, Philip McCullough, Thomas Pinkey, James Thompson, Malachy Murray, John Fitzpatrick, and Anthony McIntyre. During the trial McConkey claimed that the police had tried to recruit him as a supergrass, and that he had initially accepted the offer but had changed his mind when a new police-officer took over his case. A chief superintendent denied this and also indicated that he considered McGrady a 'truthful, frank and forthright person', whose claim that his brother Sean was innocent of the Dowds murder ought to be believed.[63]

The Lord Chief Justice's judgment in *R. v. Gibney* contained the first sustained judicial defence of the supergrass system and also attempted to show that the courts could reject the bulk of a supergass's testimony on most of the charges yet still find most of the defendants guilty at least of membership of a proscribed organization. It was in the public interest, Lord Lowry held, that criminals be brought to justice, and the more serious the offence the greater the need for justice to be done, even if this required, although not in the present case, the granting of immunity from prosecution to informers. He restated the accomplice evidence warning rule and noted that the law permitted defendants to be convicted on the uncorroborated evidence of an accomplice if the tribunal of fact was satisfied that it could be relied upon, but he did not consider how this rule was affected by the absence of a jury. Even accomplices who had been sentenced, or who had been granted immunity from prosecution, had to be treated with caution, the Lord Chief Justice said, because there would nearly always be something that executive authority could do, or which the accomplice believed it could do, which could affect the accomplice's future. He continued:

A person who has been granted immunity ... may fear ... that the immunity will be withdrawn or that the full terms of his bargain will not be implemented if he does not swear up to his proof. Someone who has been sentenced may believe—possibly quite mistakenly—that his actual stay in prison depends on the evidence he gives.[64]

But strong motives to misrepresent the facts were not a bar to

[62] *The Provisional IRA*, 408.
[63] *Belfast Telegraph*, 27 May 1983.
[64] *R. v. Gibney* (1983) 13 NIJB 5.

evidence being received in court, the Lord Chief Justice stated. He also affirmed that accused or suspect persons were entitled to remain silent at interviews without incurring any adverse inference, because, if it were otherwise, informing them of their right to silence would be illusory.

Referring to the use of 'supergrasses' in the trial of scheduled offences, Lord Lowry criticized suggestions that this amounted to a 'method of convicting suspected terrorists'. Although it could loosely be described as a 'method of prosecution', the term 'method of conviction' was a misnomer, because it gave the false impression that the executive and the judges were together implementing a trial process with the joint objective of convicting and imprisoning suspects, whereas in fact the two parts of the process were 'quite independent' of one another. The executive had the responsibility to bring prosecutions if that appeared to be the proper course, but the function of the judge, acting independently, was to decide whether or not in any individual case the allegations of the prosecutor had been proved. Quoting Cicero's famous remark that in time of war the law is silent, and Lord Atkin's famous dissent from this view in *Liversidge* v. *Anderson*,[65] the Lord Chief Justice asserted that, even though a war was being waged by paramilitary organizations outside, the rule of law would prevail in the courts in Northern Ireland, with two important consequences: the guilt of defendants had to be proved beyond reasonable doubt; and each case, sometimes involving difficult questions of credibility, had to be decided on its own facts.

At the close of the Crown case, referring to 'the manifest unreliability of Kevin McGrady',[66] the Lord Chief Justice acquitted Fitzpatrick and McIntyre of membership of the IRA on a defence application for a direction. McKiernan and Davison were also found not guilty of the Craig murder and, together with Gibney, were acquitted of the murder of William Stephenson. In statements to the police McGrady claimed that Stephenson had been bundled into the boot of a car, that he, McGrady, had driven him away to be shot, and that he had seen Davison kill Stephenson after they had arrived at their destination. But in his evidence to the court McGrady said that Stephenson had been in the back seat or on the floor of the car, that he, McGrady, had merely seen Davison point

---

[65] [1942] AC 206, 244.
[66] *R.* v. *Gibney* (1983) 13 NIJB 2.

a gun and had heard a shot, but could not confirm whether or not the victim had been killed. Although there was a prima-facie case against each of the defendants charged with these murders, and although it was 'very possible' that Fitzpatrick and McIntyre were members of the IRA, the Lord Chief Justice stated:

to have convicted on any of the counts in these groups of charges would have been a perversion of justice according to law, so contradictory, bizarre and in some respects incredible was McGrady's evidence and so devious and deliberately evasive was his manner of giving it.[67]

Lord Lowry stated that his assessment of McGrady's evidence on these counts would have a bearing upon the other charges where the only evidence against any of the accused was McGrady's uncorroborated testimony, since, as he pointed out, 'the absurdities were too great to allow the cases to stand and this must gravely affect this particular witness's credibility when he is unsupported by other evidence'.[68] Speculating on the reason for these absurdities, Lord Lowry outlined, four hypotheses: faulty memory (this was discounted on the grounds that McGrady 'dug pits for himself by trying to evade his pursuers'),[69] a foolish desire to improve a good case, a belief that those he implicated were genuinely guilty even though he had not been present at the incidents which he related, and deliberate fabrication. His lordship found it difficult to say which of these possibilities was correct, but indicated that the truth perhaps lay between the second and third alternatives. Lord Lowry also commented upon 'the extraordinary variations in the witness's power of recollection' with respect to the remaining charges on the indictment—variations which he had found 'revealing and unsettling'[70]—and he stated that he had also found the influence and authenticity of McGrady's religious experiences difficult to assess.

However, several positive aspects of the evidence which McGrady had given the court were also identified. In the first place he had been an active member of an IRA unit at a time when it was conducting a lot of local operations, and he must therefore have been very well acquainted with the other members; secondly, he had given himself up completely voluntarily. It was, therefore, natural to expect him broadly to associate those who committed

---

[67] *R.* v. *Gibney* (1983) 13 NIJB 11–12.   [68] Ibid. 12.   [69] Ibid.   [70] Ibid.

certain crimes with the particular offences, but caution had still to be observed, because 'there is an incentive to give good value if a bargain is contemplated'.[71]

The Verdict

Of the eight defendants who remained after the 'no case' submissions, seven were convicted on 26 October 1983. Thomas Pinkey was acquitted on the grounds that McGrady had originally implicated his brother Eugene as the driver in an attempted murder at a bookmakers but, having been told that Eugene was in prison at the material time, had substituted Thomas instead. Lord Lowry held that it would have been 'far too risky' to have convicted on the basis of such a substituted accusation. McConkey had made a written statement admitting to his part in the murder of Ernest Dowds, and its admissibility was unsuccessfully challenged at the trial. There were, in fact, acquittals on thirty of the forty-five counts, ten of which concerned McConkey and the other three defendants—Philip McCullough, Malachy Murray, and James Thompson—who had also made confessions. Murray and Thompson each confessed their parts in the non-fatal shooting of George Duff, while McCullough confessed to having participated in a bungled armed robbery at a bookmakers.

In arriving at a guilty verdict in Gibney's case, Lord Lowry attributed considerable significance to the police evidence about his reaction to McGrady in their police-cell confrontation. The police record indicated that Gibney had become uneasy and appeared flustered, that he had been asked to keep his voice down, and that he took his glasses on and off and rubbed his hands on his legs. He was also said to have accused McGrady of lying and to have issued the warning: 'Just before you give any more information, think about what you're saying. You know you are doing other people harm.' There was some confusion as to whether what Gibney said next was 'You know what you're saying is the truth' or 'You know what you're saying *isn't* the truth', and although the police recorded the former, Lord Lowry was prepared to accept that Gibney might have said the latter but was misheard. The Lord Chief Justice concluded that McGrady's testimony about Gibney's role in the shooting of George Duff had 'the ring of authenticity',[72] and

---

[71] Ibid. 13.   [72] Ibid. 21.

although Gibney's reaction in the confrontation could not corroborate McGrady's evidence in relation to any specific offence, it tended to confirm that McGrady was telling the truth when he alleged that Gibney was an intelligence or staff officer in the IRA. Gibney was acquitted of having briefed those who committed several other offences, including the murder of Ernest Dowds, on the grounds that the evidence against him, including that provided by McGrady, was too vague to prove guilt beyond reasonable doubt; but, on McGrady's uncorroborated evidence, he was convicted of having briefed the team responsible for the shooting and wounding of George Duff and, together with Peter McKiernan and Brian Davison, was convicted of membership of the IRA purely on McGrady's testimony.

CONCLUSION

The decisions in the Bennett, Black, and McGrady cases can be justly criticized on various grounds, as the Northern Ireland Court of Appeal later accepted. Over half the convictions rested on the supergrasses' uncorroborated evidence, despite clear evidence of bad character, specific evidential weaknesses, and expectation of rewards of various kinds in return for testifying. The contrast between the approach adopted by Mr Justice Murray in the Bennett case and his conclusion in *R.* v. *McCormick* did not go unnoticed either, many observers finding the difference between O'Doherty and Bennett, and the quality of the evidence which they each gave, difficult to detect. Although Mr Justice Kelly had shown considerable professionalism in presiding over the massive and complicated Black trial, he had also attempted to explain away defects in Black's evidence in terms of innocent human frailty—for example, his emotional and physical state when he gave his first statements—whereas the discrepancies in the evidence of defence witnesses were spotlighted and the witnesses themselves dismissed as either unconvincing or biased. The principal complaint about the verdict in the McGrady trial was that there was no rational basis for the distinction drawn by the Lord Chief Justice between those charges based on McGrady's uncorroborated evidence where convictions were justified and those, also based on McGrady's uncorroborated evidence, justifying acquittals. However, the three cases also appeared to indicate that the teething troubles of the previous two years were over, and the path looked clear for further supergrass trials to be concluded with a high conviction-rate. But, as the next chapter shows, this prospect became less certain even before the year was out.

4

Under a Cloud: November and December 1983

A SHADOW was cast across the supergrass system as 1983 drew to a close. In November William Skelly retracted his evidence against ten suspects, and the trial of *R. v. Connolly and others* ended in the acquittal of all seven of the fourteen defendants charged on the uncorroborated evidence of INLA supergrass Jackie Grimley, with the rest convicted on guilty pleas or confessions. On 19 December all five accused in the Morgan trial were also found not guilty.

THE GRIMLEY CASE: *R. v. Connolly and others*

The Background
John Patrick Grimley was born in 1943 in Craigavon, County Armagh, and had his first brush with the law at the age of 14, when he was convicted of burgling a bacon factory. Having served a probation order, he reoffended in each of the following two years and spent periods in a training-school, from which he escaped, and then in borstal. Soon afterwards he faked a suicide attempt and was committed to a mental hospital for six months. In 1961 or 1962, at the age of 18 or 19, Grimley joined the Irish Guards regiment of the British army and a year later allegedly again faked an attempted suicide, was discharged, and got married. In 1963 he joined another British army regiment, the Royal Irish Fusiliers, using his brother's name but, a year later, was again discharged after yet another faked suicide attempt. In 1970 or 1971, he served yet another year in the army, this time with the Pioneer Corps, but was discharged when his dishonesty concerning his previous enlistments was discovered. In 1972, having left the army, Grimley was soon in trouble with the police in London for theft. He then moved to County Longford in the Irish Republic and shortly afterwards embarked on petty crime again, stealing from his employer and

breaking into a shop and a café to obtain cigarettes and money. At the end of 1973 he was given a six month prison sentence by Dublin District Court for assaulting an elderly man in a homeless men's hostel and robbing him of £2 and two small bottles of whiskey, and a year later he was back in gaol for assaulting his girlfriend.

In 1975 Grimley moved back to Craigavon in Northern Ireland and started work in the Goodyear tyre factory. He stole a car in 1977 and, in the following two years, faced three charges of obstruction arising out of republican street marches and parades. He joined Sinn Fein but was soon thrown out for having sworn at the clientele at a republican supporters' dance through a microphone grabbed from the compère. He then joined the INLA and took part in a series of armed robberies and punishment shootings, in one of which he was said to have fired bullets into the arms and legs of two alleged thieves.

At the trial of those charged on his evidence Grimley admitted to having been beaten up by two of his cousins who suspected him of having sexually assaulted their seven year old sister, and it was another sexual assault to which he confessed, this time against a 23-year-old woman in 1979 or 1980, which brought him into contact with the police again and led him, in 1980, to become a police spy and *agent provocateur*. Grimley claimed that he was pressurized into informing by the Special Branch, who threatened him with a three-year prison sentence for having been a member of a Sinn Fein colour party at an illegal march. However, he changed his story twice under cross-examination, alleging, at first, that the threat was in connection with yet another sexual assault, and finally that his co-operation with the police was motivated purely by the £25 his police handler paid him each week or each time they were in contact.

In October 1980 Grimley met leading members of the Irish Republican Socialist Party from Belfast and was instrumental in setting up the first branch of the party in Craigavon. Some weeks later he swore two men into the first local unit of the INLA, of which he became the commanding officer. It has been suggested that the Special Branch were hoping to use Grimley to infiltrate the INLA's Army Council and to this end encouraged him to set up a branch of the IRSP and two units of the INLA in the Craigavon area while turning a blind eye to the offences which he then committed.[1] Grimley denied having received any encouragement from the Special Branch to embark upon these activities but said that his Special Branch handler was pleased when he told him the news. By his own admission, Grimley spent much of his time as commanding officer of the INLA unit in Craigavon swaggering around the Tullygally Tavern dressed in black to reinforce his terrorist image. Although it took him only eight weeks to drink his way through the £2,000 redundancy money he had received from Goodyear on being laid off in July 1981, he subsequently ran up yet more large drink-bills there. He admitted to having given one of the managers a forged bank-book to obtain money and accepted that his failure to mention this when quizzed about his previous convictions in the trial of Connolly and others made him a perjurer. In February 1982 the INLA discovered that Grimley knew about a bomb captured in transit by the RUC and concluded that he could only have found this out from the police and must therefore be a police spy. Grimley fled into police custody, arrests followed, and he was preened for appearance as a supergrass. As it turned out it was a role for which he was ill-suited.

The Trial

The evidence which Grimley supplied to the RUC led to twenty-two defendants from Derry, Strabane, Belfast, and Lurgan being prosecuted with twenty-eight offences ranging from attempting and conspiring to murder unionist politicians to membership of the INLA. One of the original defendants refused to answer bail and another three plead guilty leaving eighteen to stand trial on 13 September 1983. Although his name had been used freely earlier in the proceedings, when he took the witness stand to be cross-examined on 10 November, Grimley managed to obtain an assurance from the judge, Lord Justice Gibson, that from then on he would only be referred to, by lawyers and press alike as 'Witness A'.

The cross-examination began well for the defence, when Desmond Boal QC asked Grimley if he was a truthful person. He replied that, although generally he was, he sometimes lied to get himself out of trouble. Mr Boal highlighted eight features of Grimley's lifestyle which he suggested amounted to 'some form of

[1] Workers Research Unit, *Belfast Bulletin No. 11. Supergrasses* (Belfast: Pub. authors, 1984), 35.

emotional impairment or disability'.[2] He had admitted to being an exhibitionist, having committed a large number of crimes, consistently lying, being a habitual drinker who sometimes drank to excess, being given to acts of violence, having spent six months in a psychiatric hospital, being prone to irrational behaviour, and manipulating people to get himself out of unpleasant situations. Mr Boal also suggested that Grimley's refusal to be examined by a defence psychiatrist was motivated by a desire to conceal relevant aspects of his character.

The day after this cross-examination Grimley confessed to other crimes which until then had not been disclosed. He admitted having stolen £300 from a visiting American uncle, stealing timber, conspiring to rob a post office, having dishonestly cashed a social security cheque, and stealing from the Goodyear factory where he had worked. He told the judge that he had not owned up to these offences earlier because he thought the defence did not know about them. He then admitted to having lied to his Special Branch handler and to having the capacity to tell credible lies to various people in authority in order to get himself out of difficult situations. Boal suggested that the most 'unacceptable' situation he had yet encountered was the death threat by the INLA, following their discovery that he had been an informer. Later, when Grimley changed his story about the pressure allegedly exerted by the police to induce him to become a spy, he candidly conceded to the judge: 'I'm telling some lies, I'll admit.'[3] He also acknowleged that if the police had ever prosecuted him for INLA membership, he would have perjured himself in order to avoid conviction.

On Tuesday, 24 November the case against the seven men charged solely upon Grimley's evidence collapsed. Grimley began by claiming that the only motive he had in passing information to the police was financial, and then proceeded to describe an INLA conspiracy to assassinate unionist MP Harold McCusker and his UDR brother, as well as an attempt to assassinate Councillor David Calvert of the Democratic Unionist Party (DUP). Despite having earlier told the court that the McCusker conspiracy had been suggested by INLA activists in Belfast, under cross-examination Grimley admitted to having instigated it himself. He then

---

[2] A. Pollak, 'The Strange Tale of the Collapsing Supergrass and his RUC Accomplices', *Fortnight*, no. 200, Dec. 1983, 11.

[3] Ibid.

claimed that nobody had been arrested in connection with various crimes he had committed and that he found it 'damned funny' that he could have been given a licence by the police to carry out offences without the prospect of being caught.[4] He said he believed he could implicate anyone in these crimes, and no harm would come to them, and that the RUC would 'pull any police patrol or army patrol out of the area' so as not to interfere with his criminal activities.[5] He said he had told the police about his involvment in the Calvert attack, had implicated two other men, both of whom were in the dock, and had thought it 'very funny' that neither he nor the others had been arrested or charged.[6] He also alleged that he had given the Special Branch the date of an armed robbery at a local post office planned by three other named INLA members, but which, in the event, had been abandoned, and again no one had been arrested. He claimed that Special Branch detectives had never objected to his recruiting new members for the INLA, not even when he set up a second unit in late 1981, many of the recruits for which he subsequently named to the police; and he agreed with a defence suggestion that Special Branch officers had also committed offences by entering into these conspiracies with him. Only once, he claimed, after he had told them of his involvement in various kneecappings, had they become 'jittery' and told him that things were going 'a little bit too far'.[7]

Finally, late in the afternoon of 24 November, under relentless cross-examination, Grimley admitted that in return for this 'free hand' to commit crimes, he had supplied the Special Branch with the names of INLA suspects, and that the police had also suggested the names of those they suspected of being active in the INLA and wanted to prosecute. After considerable stonewalling, Grimley named one such man, the principal defendant in the trial, Gerard Steenson. He also alleged that Special Branch had suggested the names of Billy Browning, Sean Flynn, Jackie Goodman, and Harry Kirkpatrick, the last two of whom became supergrasses themselves, although Goodman retracted in September 1982.[8] Mr Boal put it to Grimley that his reluctance to reveal Steenson's name was

---

[4] Pollak, 'The Collapsing Supergrass'. Dillon makes similar claims about other informers. See M. Dillon, *The Dirty War* [London: Arrow Books, 1991), 80.

[5] Pollack, 'The Collapsing Supergrass'.

[6] Ibid.   [7] Ibid.   [8] See Ch. 2.

'because you realised that the conclusion that the court might draw from you, or from that, was that you in fact were setting Steenson up at the behest of the police?' Grimley answered, 'That would be right, yes.'[9]

The Verdict

The day after these disclosures, 25 November 1983, the seven defendants charged on Grimley's uncorroborated testimony, Gerard Steenson, James Tinney, John O'Reilly, Thomas Power, Bernard Dorrian, Patrick Moore, and Terence Robson, were acquitted of all charges against them, ranging from INLA membership to soliciting murder. However, five of those acquitted were held in custody on the evidence of other supergrasses, and only James Tinny and Patrick Moore walked free from the court. Eleven of those convicted had made confessions and the other three had pleaded guilty. Lord Justice Gibson said that he could place absolutely no reliance on Grimley's evidence, since he had admitted on numerous occasions that information he had given both to the court and to the police was a mixture of half-truth and lies. He was 'a person of anything but unimpeachable character', who had been 'a habitual criminal over a long period', with a record of forty convictions and who, from an early age, had lived 'a life of lies and deceit' in a 'half world between reality and charade'.[10] Describing the three contradictory accounts which Grimley had given of his recuitment by the Special Branch and his belief that the Special Branch had given him *carte blanche* to commit crimes for his own benefit, the judge said that 'under cross examination he trimmed his evidence to suit the moment, with little or no regard for the truth'. Lord Justice Gibson added that he found much of Grimley's behaviour difficult to understand and that it was impossible to accept his own explanations for it. His verdict was that Grimley's 'whole life and evidence was characterized by instability—if not of mind, then certainly of motive, purpose and behaviour'.[11]

The most intriguing element of the Grimley case concerns his claim that the police indulged his criminality. Some have argued that this was the real reason the trial collapsed, since the judge, caught between the devil and the deep blue sea, either had to

---

[9] Pollack, 'The Collapsing Supergrass'.
[10] Ibid.   [11] Ibid.

convict without corroboration, and by implication accept that the RUC condoned serious crime, or leave these accusations neither proven nor refuted, by acquitting suspects the police believed were deeply involved in terrorism. Alternatively, the 'free hand' Grimley alleged he had been given by the police to pursue his criminal activities may merely have been a further manifestation of the fantasy world which he inhabited, of which ample evidence had been given at the trial. However, whatever the truth, it is remarkable that Grimley's evidence was ever used as the basis of prosecution, and Lord Justice Gibson was clearly right to reject it.

THE MORGAN CASE: *R. v. Davison and others*

The Background

On Saturday, 24 April 1982 a young man, John Anthony Morgan, aged 24, in a confused state and bleeding from various superficial wounds, staggered into the Brook activity centre in the Twinbrook estate in south Belfast, anxious to contact the police. He subsequently claimed that he was a member of the Provisional IRA and that, the night before, he had been taken to a flat in Twinbrook on the pretext of being required to attend an IRA meeting but once there had been accused of being a Special Branch informer, had been set upon, bound hand and foot, and blindfolded. He claimed that during several hours of interrogation he had been severely beaten and kicked, and had been threatened by having the barrel of a gun passed along his jaw-line. Eventually his captors had allowed him to fall asleep on the floor and when he awoke it was daylight, his blindfold had slipped, and he was able to see two men who had apparently spent the night in a bed in the room with him. He said that when he peeped over his blindfold, he saw the face of one of the men, who was holding back a curtain to look through a window. Initially, Morgan said, he pretended not to have awakened, and his blindfold was replaced when he eventually informed his gaolers that it had slipped.

Morgan claimed that sometime later, possibly around lunchtime, he became conscious that he was alone in the room. Finding that his bonds had worked loose, he struggled to free himself, and when he removed his blindfold, he found that his captors had in fact gone. However, as he was attempting to escape through the window, the man whose face he had seen earlier that morning came in and tried to grab him. A chase ensued during the course of which Morgan claimed he was able to get a further look at this person's face as he glanced back over his shoulder. Outrunning his pursuer, he made it to the community centre, from where he gave himself up to the police.

John Morgan was born on 7 June 1959 in the Short Strand area of Belfast, and in the early 1970s he moved with his family to the Ormeau Road district, where he became a member of the Fianna, the junior branch of the IRA. In 1976, having incurred the hostility of some local members of the Official IRA, he went to live with a married sister in England. Not long after having arrived in his new home, he obtained a gun and killed his brother-in-law as he lay asleep in bed, because he had been ill-treating his sister. On 12 March 1976 Morgan was convicted of manslaughter on the grounds of diminished responsibility, and a psychiatrist who gave evidence on his behalf stated that his sense of responsibility was substantially impaired by his limited capacity for rational judgement in the exercise of will-power, and that the moral aspects of his mind were incompletely developed. He was sentenced to three years' imprisonment, was released after having served just two, and returned to Belfast a year later, in 1979. In November 1979 he joined the INLA and with John McConkey, another INLA activist, one-time supergrass, and defendant in several supergrass trials, moved into a flat off the Ormeau Road, where the pair kept two of the organization's pistols. On one occasion Morgan paid the rent with a dud cheque but eventually left the flat and moved back to live with his family. In April 1981 he left the INLA and joined the IRA and over the next year took part in a series of crimes including armed robbery, arson, throwing petrol bombs at police vehicles, and possessing firearms.

How Morgan came to be suspected of informing by the IRA remains a mystery. But on the evidence which he supplied following his dramatic flight into police custody seven people were arrested. Five of these, Brendan Davison, John Huddleston, James Clinton, Patrick Fitzpatrick, and Joseph McKee, were eventually prosecuted. The charges included those arising from Morgan's imprisonment and ill-treatment, while others involved armed robbery, arson, firearms offences, conspiracy to murder a police officer, attempted murder, and the murder of a soldier who had been lured to a flat in the Stranmillis Road in the university area of Belfast. From 24

April 1982, the day he gave himself up to the police, until 1 May, Morgan was intensively interviewed by detectives at Castlereagh police station. On or about 1 May the possibility of his being granted immunity from prosecution was discussed with Detective Chief Inspector Davidson, and around 5 May he was informed that it had been granted. In a clear change of policy in response to the criticisms delivered by Mr Justice Murray in the Bennett trial, two letters to this effect were sent to the solicitors representing the defendants charged on his evidence, but they gave few details and merely stated: that Morgan had been given immunity from prosecution for the offences to which he had confessed to the police; that he had been under police protection since 24 April 1982; that he had been provided with accommodation and that his rent, gas, electricity and all other bills in connection with his accommodation had been paid on his behalf; that since he had not been in receipt of state benefits, he had been paid a weekly allowance of £30, later increased to £80; that no bargains had been struck with him but that he had been told that in the interests of his safety, he and his family would be assisted in establishing a new life after the trial. The record of his manslaughter charge was attached to the first letter.

The Trial

Since he implicated comparatively few suspects, it is debatable whether Morgan should be regarded as a *super*grass at all. However, since the trial of *R.* v. *Davison and others*, which ran from 24 November to 19 December 1983, occurred in the midst of the high-profile supergrass cases, it would be difficult to justify excluding it on this ground alone. All the defendants except McKee testified in their own defence. In his judgment, the trial judge, Mr Justice Murray, pointed out that under cross-examination Morgan admitted 'apparently without the slightest indication of compunction that before his experiences in the flat of 23rd that he would have shot a soldier if ordered to do so and would have shed no tear over the death of a policeman'.[12] He also accepted that Morgan's imprisonment by the IRA happened just as he had described it and was satisfied that:

during the first few days of his interview in Castlereagh his main concern

---

[12] *R.* v. *Davison* (1983) (unreported), 12.

was to stay alive by having the police protect him from the Provisional IRA, and his next action was to disclose his involvement in that organisation and in crime generally in such a way as to minimise so far as he possibly could the actions in the matters that he was going to have to face.[13]

The prospect of immunity was particularly attractive to Morgan, the judge said, because of the double fear which prison presented, 'namely, the possibility of any terrorist being locked up for a long period of years but also, and worse for him, the possibility that Provisional IRA violence would pursue him into the very prison itself'.[14] It was therefore possibly 'not without significance', that it was on 1 May, when the prospect of immunity was first discussed, that Morgan first made his most serious allegation: that the defendant Davison had admitted murdering soldier Verdi in the Stranmillis Road flat.

The Verdict

Mr Justice Murray came to the conclusion that Morgan could not be trusted, since he was: 'at times a dishonest witness; at other times . . . a most unreliable one and of course there is the point . . . of the unexplained mental condition of the earlier years'.[15] McKee and Huddleston were found not guilty by a direction of no case to answer. There were marked inconsistencies between Morgan's description of McKee, the alleged captor whom he claimed to have seen at the window of the flat, and the defendant's actual appearance. Morgan said that McKee had a broad nose, and on one occasion he claimed that he had dark or black hair, while on another he said his hair was jet black with grey at the sides. In fact, as the judge pointed out, McKee had brown hair, no grey hair at all, and a perfectly normal nose. Huddleston, whom Morgan claimed had threatened him with a gun during the IRA interrogation, was identified purely by his 'rich', 'distinctive', and 'distinguished' voice, which Morgan claimed he recognized as that of 'Big Mick', a character he had met a number of times before. Mr Justice Murray was particulary critical of the way in which the police had dealt with this accused. Huddleston was not arrested until 24 July 1982, even though he had been going about his business as usual from the time Morgan had implicated him; and,

---

[13] Ibid. 13.   [14] Ibid.   [15] Ibid. 32

despite his willingness to take part in a police identification-parade, none had been organized. Of all the defendants, Huddleston was also the only one whom the police chose not to expose to a pre-trial confrontation, and no attempt was made to set up a straightforward voice-identification test. Although a bail application had been postponed in August 1982 to enable an identification parade to take place, in the event no parade was arranged and bail was refused. As the judge remarked: 'Huddleston spent some 17 months in custody when an identification parade in the summer of 1982 might well have produced a very different result.'[16]

One feature of the judgment in *R*. v. *Davison* is particularly worthy of note largely because of its absence in other supergrass trials. At the close of the Crown case the judge unhesitatingly acquitted Fitzpatrick of conspiracy to murder because there was no evidence that there had in fact been such a conspiracy, and although there was 'ample independent evidence of several of the crimes charged', there was 'no evidence to connect any of the defendants with any of [these] except one',[17] a reference to some remarks made by Clinton to the police which the judge said 'undoubtedly cast sinister overtones' and could 'possibly' be taken as corroborative,[18] although no final decision was taken on whether they were corroborative or not.

In assessing the case against Davison, Clinton, and Fitzpatrick, Mr Justice Murray stated that he had been influenced by a number of flaws in Morgan's evidence and by the fact that Morgan had lied to the court on a number of matters which were neither extraneous nor crucial, showing that he was prepared to tailor his testimony in order to make it conform with the statements he had made to the police. Morgan had also clearly indicated to the police the roles which the two Fitzpatrick brothers, Joseph and Patrick, had played in collecting information about the movements of a police officer on the Ormeau Road. However, he admitted to the court that he had difficulty telling which of the two brothers was which, and his testimony in this respect was described by the judge as 'confused and muddled'.[19] Although all five defendants were acquitted, Davison was held on other charges and Fitzpatrick was arrested on the evidence of supergrass Harry Kirkpatrick as he tried to leave the court-house.

---

[16] *R*. v. *Davison* (1983) 20.   [17] Ibid. 15.   [18] Ibid. 32.   [19] Ibid. 31.

CONCLUSION

The Grimley and Morgan trials raise two fundamental questions: why were prosecutions launched on the evidence of accomplices with histories of mental illness, and what did the verdicts mean for the future of the supergrass system? Assuming the IRA's suspicions about Morgan were correct, both he and Grimley were redundant as informers, but the police and the prosecuting authorities clearly thought it worth trying them out as prosecution witnesses and, in the pursuit of convictions, either underestimated or accepted the risk of the damage which the failure of these cases could cause the supergrass system. If the courts had convicted on their testimonies, the scope for future supergrass trials would have been enormous.

Those who defended the use of supergrasses in the Diplock courts pointed to these trials as a mark of the independence of the courts and an indication of a judicial readiness to reject supergrass evidence if it was not up to standard. However, others argued that the purpose of the Grimley and Morgan verdicts was to indicate to the police and to the prosecuting authorities that the judiciary would not tolerate convictions on the uncorroborated evidence of mental defectives or of informers who had been foolish enough to admit having been granted a licence to commit crime in return for spying on paramilitary organizations. Once these lessons had been learned, it was said, the supergrass system would be strengthened rather than weakened. One thing was clear, however. Convictions on supergrass evidence were no longer such a foregone conclusion as they had seemed at the end of the McGrady trial only a month or so before. But, at this point, the implications for the supergrass system remained uncertain.

5

The Public Controversy: 1983–1984

THE use of supergrasses in the Diplock system excited intense public controversy, both in Northern Ireland and to a lesser extent beyond, from the autumn of 1981, when the first mass arrests began. The debate gained momentum as the supergrass system itself unfolded, particularly after the convictions in the Bennett, Black, and McGrady cases in 1983. A central argument in this study is that the anti-supergrass campaign led to a judicial volte-face which terminated the supergrass system. It is appropriate, therefore, to deviate at this point from the chronological account of the key trials in order to consider the various viewpoints in the controversy which had already become clear by the end of 1983. The comparatively few important contributions made after 1984, for example the Attorney-General's second lengthy Commons statement in 1986, are considered in later chapters.

Unusually, the supergrass controversy cut across the traditional sectarian divide in Northern Ireland, where attitudes to anti-terrorist initiatives tend to reflect broader political and communal affiliations. Although the opposition of the Catholic/nationalist community was predictable, the criticisms which the supergrass system received from the Protestant/unionist community constituted a significant, though not unprecedented, exception to its customary support for anti-terrorist law enforcement.[1] A public opinion poll conducted by the Northern Ireland-based civil liberties organization the Committee on the Administration of Justice in Belfast in June and July 1984, found that 38 per cent of respondents approved of the supergrass process, while 40 per cent disapproved.[2] The major-

---

[1] Loyalists had protested against law enforcement initiatives introduced in Northern Ireland before. The Revd Ian Paisley, for example, had been an outspoken critic of internment in 1971 and of the suspension of jury trial in 1973.

[2] Eight wards were selected in order to give a class and sectarian balance. A quota sample, weighted in accordance with sex, age, and religion, yielded 233 respondents, of whom 131 declared themselves to be Protestants, 70 to be Catholics, and 32 refused to disclose if they had any religious persuasion. These ratios paralleled the 1981 census. *Fortnight*, no. 209, Nov. 1984.

ity of those who declared themselves Catholic (72 per cent) disapproved, while those who declared themselves Protestant were evenly split, with slightly more approving (56 per cent) than disapproving. About a fifth of those in each of the two communities said that they 'reluctantly approved' of the supergrass system but regarded independent corroboration as essential. Ninety per cent of declared Catholics stated that they did not think it was right that suspects should be convicted on the evidence of a supergrass alone, while 50 per cent of Protestants took a similar view. Most of the respondents were opposed to supergrasses receiving immunity from prosecution, and just over half (56 per cent) said they did not think it right for suspects to be charged and held for long periods on the evidence of supergrasses alone.

Views on the supergrass system were also expressed by political parties, community organizations, the churches, and by the various loyalist and republican anti-supergrass campaigning groups. Loyalists, as represented by the Democratic Unionist Party, the Ulster Defence Association, and Families for Legal Rights (the organization of relatives and friends of defendants in loyalist supergrass trials), found themselves arguing against it alongside civil libertarians, republican, nationalist, and left-wing political organizations, and the republican pressure-groups Stop the Show Trials, Relatives for Justice, and Concerned Community Organizations. Indeed, in October and November 1983 three joint protests were mounted by the largely women-led loyalist and republican relatives' organizations, but future co-operation became impossible because of pressure from their respective communities. Since the bulk of the Official Unionist Party supported the supergrass system[3]—subject to reservations about immunities from prosecution—a heated, and at times acrimonious, debate occurred within the Ulster Protestant community which was without parallel amongst nationalists and republicans. Inevitably, there were differences of opinion of various kinds within each of the 'for' and 'against' camps, and the boundaries between supporters and opponents were not entirely watertight, with some contributors to the debate capable of being regarded as either 'critical supporters' or 'mild critics'.

From the varied comments which the supergrass process gener-

---

[3] See, e.g. E. Graham, 'A Vital Weapon in the Anti-terrorist Arsenal', *Fortnight*, no. 198, Oct. 1983, 10.

ated, it is possible to distinguish three perspectives—one in favour
and two against. Each represents a distinctive synthesis of political,
legal, and moral ideas, and, given that this is the case, it would be a
mistake to suggest that every feature of any given perspective was
endorsed by everyone who could be said to have contributed to the
debate from that perspective. The supergrass process was defended,
by those who adhered to the 'official view', as an appropriate and
potentially effective means of responding to political violence in
Northern Ireland. It was criticized by conspiracy theorists as an
anti-republican strategy deliberately created and carefully planned
by the various components of the 'British war machine' in Northern
Ireland, and by civil libertarians for having fallen below certain key
democratic law enforcement standards.[4] The purpose of this chapter is merely to record the structure of the supergrass debate in
1983–4; an assessment of the strengths and weaknesses of these
views will be deferred until the final chapter of this study, when the
full story of the supergrass system has been told.

THE OFFICIAL VIEW

The 'official perspective' on the supergrass system emerged from
the various branches of the state in Northern Ireland, including the
courts. Its adherents maintained that the supergrass process was
not a 'system' as such, since it was largely spontaneous in origin
and had been managed by independent criminal justice institutions,
that although offers of rewards to the supergrasses themselves were
'distasteful', they could be justified in the public interest, and that
supergrass trials in the Diplock courts did not represent any significant departure from recognized standards of due process. In addition to judicial statements considered in previous and subsequent

---

[4] Although some loyalists criticized the supergrass system on civil libertarian
grounds, others—e.g. the UDA—attacked it as 'stupid' and indicative of 'the failure
of the criminalisation policy as a weapon to defeat terrorism'. The police and the
courts should not be used, the UDA said, in an attempt to deal with 'an organised
terrorist war' as if it were a huge crime-wave, and the IRA should instead be tackled
by special military units on a war footing. Although this view was not well
developed in the supergrass debate, it seems to imply that neither loyalist nor
republican terrorist suspects should be prosecuted at all, whether on the evidence of
supergrasses or otherwise, since the activities of the loyalists merely offer legitimate
defence which the state itself has failed to provide, while republican paramilitaries
should be dealt with as a military enemy, with all that this implies. *Irish News*, 22
Oct. 1983.

chapters, the clearest and fullest expressions of this viewpoint can be found in a statement of the Attorney-General, Sir Michael Havers, to the House of Commons on 24 October 1983, in Sir George Baker's review of the Northern Ireland (Emergency Provisions) Act 1978, published in March 1984, and in the 1982 and 1983 annual reports of the Chief Constable of the RUC, Sir John Hermon.

The Attorney-General's Statement of 24 October 1983[5]

The Attorney-General began his statement by saying that he wished to correct a number of misconceptions which had arisen on the use, in Northern Ireland, of the evidence of accomplices who had been granted immunity from prosecution. First, there was nothing new about the use of accomplice evidence in criminal trials, and the law in Northern Ireland was the same as that in England and Wales. The rule concerning the issuing of a danger warning by a judge to a jury required a judge sitting without a jury to warn himself that, although he might convict on the uncorroborated evidence of an accomplice, it was dangerous to do so. When someone involved in terrorist crime in Northern Ireland indicated his willingness to give evidence of the crimes about which he knew, it was the duty of the Chief Constable, the Attorney-General maintained, to put the facts before the Director of Public Prosecutions, and it was then the Director's duty to consider all the evidence and information before him, with a view to the initiation of criminal proceedings. Each case had to be considered by the Director on its own facts and in the light of the public interest that criminals should be brought to justice, and, where the evidence of an accomplice appeared to be credible and cogent and related to serious crime, it was the clear duty of the Director to put the case before the court, to determine if the evidence proved guilt beyond reasonable doubt.

Where the accomplice was himself to be prosecuted, the practice in Northern Ireland was that he should be tried and sentenced before testifying against others, so that there could be no suggestion that, in giving evidence, he was motivated by the hope of a sentence shorter than that which he might otherwise have received. But in other cases the accomplice would not give evidence unless he

[5] HC Debs., vol. 47, cols. 3–5.

himself was freed from the possibility of prosecution. In deciding whether or not to grant immunity from prosecution, the DPP for Northern Ireland had to evaluate the credibility and cogency of the accomplice's evidence, the number of alleged terrorists who could not otherwise be brought before the courts, the prospect of saving lives, and the prevention of further violent crime. The general criteria observed in Northern Ireland on the granting of immunity from prosecution were the same as those in England and Wales and included: (1) whether it was of more value in the interests of justice to have a suspected person as a witness rather than as a possible defendant; (2) whether, in the interests of public safety and security, obtaining information about the extent and nature of criminal activities was of greater importance than the conviction of a particular individual; (3) whether it was very unlikely that any information could be obtained without the offer of immunity, and whether it was also very unlikely that any prosecution could be launched against the person to whom the immunity was offered.

In every instance the scope of any immunity was limited and included only those offences which the accomplice had disclosed and of which he had given a truthful account. He remained liable to be prosecuted for offences which he had not revealed, and for those about which he had been less than truthful. If, during the police investigation, further offences were revealed, or further details of offences already disclosed emerged which tended to show that the original disclosure was misleading, the accomplice had to be cautioned before further questioning took place and the fresh information had to be referred to the Director for his consideration. The decision to grant or withhold immunity was for the Director personally and could not be taken by the police, although before any application to grant immunity could be made to the Director, the Chief Constable of the RUC had to recommend that the accomplice be called as a Crown witness. The Attorney General stated that in a number of instances, the Director had declined to grant immunity and that in others, although immunity had been granted, he had decided that the evidence was not sufficiently reliable to allow him to proceed. By granting immunity, the Director did all within his power to remove from the mind of the person upon whom it was conferred, any possible fear, hope, or expectation which might tempt him to give untrue evidence in court. When a prosecution witness was given immunity from prosecution, this fact was disclosed to the defence and to the court and there was no bargain or arrangement between the prosecution and the witness. The Director had given instructions that the Chief Constable would furnish him with a statement of all financial arrangements already made for, or to be made in the future for, the support of a witness and his family, and these particulars would be disclosed to the court and to the defence.

The Attorney-General said that, in respect of the decisions to initiate proceedings on the evidence of an accomplice and to grant immunity, the primary responsibility was vested in the DPP for Northern Ireland, acting under the superintendence and subject to the direction of the Attorney-General. However, the BBC's Panorama programme reported on 14 October 1983 that the Attorney General might informally consult the Secretary of State for Northern Ireland in any particular case where immunity was under consideration. Sir Michael Havers also told the House of Commons that the DPP for Northern Ireland 'keeps me fully informed of the general policies which he applies in this field' and added: 'we consult each other regularly on these matters, both as regards those general policies and as regards specific difficult cases'. The Attorney-General concluded his statement with the remark that he was 'entirely satisfied both as to the correctness of the principles in accordance with which the Director has taken his decisions' and with the information which he had received from the Director as to the decisions taken in individual cases.

While much of the statement is purely descriptive, parts of it are more contentious. It is correct to say that there is nothing new about accomplices turning Queen's evidence, but this is not the issue. As Chapter 1 showed, supergrasses can be distinguished from mere accomplices who decide to testify for the Crown not only by the scale of their accusations but by the inherent, rather than merely contingent, unreliability of their evidence. Secondly, the statement that the law on the judicial warning is the same in the Diplock courts as it then was in England and Wales begs many questions. The absence of the jury in the trial of scheduled offences transforms the warning on accomplice evidence, and the common law gives no clear indication of what the position should be in such trials. It is true that judges in the first supergrass cases in Northern Ireland decided that the rule on accomplice evidence required them to issue the warning to themselves. But it is not at all clear that this was the correct, or most legitimate, interpretation of the rationale which lies behind the rule. To state that the law regarding the warning is the same in jury and non-jury trials is to assume what needs to be proved. Thirdly, the terms of the deal between the supergrass and the prosecuting authorities were not disclosed to the court in the Bennett case, and in the Morgan and Quigley trials only minimal information about the arrangements between super-grasses and prosecuting authorities was revealed.[6] Finally, much of the statement refers to the DPP's taking decisions on the merits of each individual case, yet at the end there is a reference to the 'general policies' which the DPP follows 'in this field'. This may be intended to refer only to such elements of policy as are identified in the statement: the public interest requirement, the cogency and credibility test, and the practice of trying supergrasses who have not been granted immunity before they can testify against those whom they have implicated. But the use of the term 'policy' in this undefined manner is something of a hostage to fortune, since an important feature of the government's case was that there was no prosecution policy in this area at all, and no supergrass system as such.[7]

The Review of the Northern Ireland (Emergency Provisions) Act 1978 by Sir George Baker

In his report on the Northern Ireland (Emergency Provisions) Act 1978, published on 15 March 1984, Sir George Baker, a retired President of the Family Division of the High Court of England and Wales, considered some of the issues raised by the supergrass system. However, his conclusion, stated even before any of the counter-arguments were considered, was:

The overall benefit to the community from the conviction of many terror-ists who would otherwise be free to continue the murder and mayhem is such that, as a matter of policy, prosecutions with accomplices called as Crown witnesses will continue. The AG [Attorney General] has said so. I myself cannot see any objection to the Crown calling an accomplice . . .[8]

Items of 'disquiet' were then listed, with a perfunctory comment in

[6] See Chs. 3 and 6.
[7] See also Statement of 19 Mar. 1986, Ch. 8.
[8] *Review of the Operation of the Northern Ireland (Emergency Provisions) Act 1978* (The Baker Report), Cmnd. 9222 (London: HMSO, 1984), paras. 165–6.

parentheses attached to each. For example: '(2) there are possibilities of abuse; (there always have been); (3) there should be corroboration; (of course, if possible)'.[9] Some brief remarks about the origins of the judicial warning were also made, but on the question of its adequacy in trials without juries Sir George Baker stated that he was 'unable to accept that a different rule should apply in Northern Ireland'.[10] Judges, he said, normally get the feel of a case, and small points can be noticed which, although neither individually nor collectively amounting to corroboration, could afford 'a very good guide';[11] whilst jury decisions were inscrutable, a Diplock judge was required to give his reasons in writing and these could subsequently be attacked on appeal.

Sir George Baker advised any 'fair-minded person' seeking 'to be critical of the Northern Ireland judges' to read Lord Lowry's judgment in *R*. v. *Gibney* (the McGrady case).[12] It is difficult to determine why this decision was singled out for praise, however, since the distinction drawn by the Lord Chief Justice for Northern Ireland between those parts of McGrady's uncorroborated testimony which could be trusted and those which could not had been strongly criticized. It would seem that Sir George was more impressed by the rhetoric of the judgment than by its outcome. On the question of rewards to the supergrasses, Sir George Baker merely referred to the English supergrass cases *Turner* and *Lowe*, in which it was held that immunity deals could sometimes be granted in the public interest, and that substantial credit in sentencing should be awarded to supergrasses who plead guilty.[13] Concluding the brief section of his report on the supergrass issue, Baker sounded a solitary note of criticism. The 'one legitimate objection to the accomplice cases',[14] he said, concerned the wisdom of having 'so many defendants, so many charges, such delay in starting and such long trials'.[15]

The Reports of the Chief Constable of the RUC for 1982 and 1983

One of the earliest official defences of the supergrass system was contained in the annual report of the Chief Constable of the RUC for 1982, published in March 1983. Referring to supergrasses as

---

[9] Ibid., para. 167.   [10] Ibid., para. 169.   [11] Ibid.
[12] Ibid., para. 170.   [13] See Ch. 10.   [14] The Baker Report, para. 173.
[15] Ibid., para. 172.

'converted terrorists', Sir John Hermon said that the whole community had benefited 'immeasurably' from their appearance, and since they had been identified as a fundamental threat by both loyalist and republican paramilitary organizations, their supporters and fellow-travellers were using every means to frustrate this 'healthy trend'. The Chief Constable stated that 'the outcome is crucial to the well-being of Northern Ireland and it is essential that there should be general public understanding of this fact'.[16] Sir John Hermon also said that there was growing disillusionment in the ranks of terrorist organizations and that the informers had come to realize the true nature and futility of terrorism. Attacks on the use of supergrasses were indicative of 'the continuing ambivalence' of some sections of both communities to crimes committed by terrorists professing to represent their interests and had highlighted 'the unresolved problem of tribal prejudices and reactions, which sadly, on occasion, transcend support for the impartial process of law enforcement'.[17]

In his report for 1983, published in March 1984, Sir John Hermon repeated his defence of the supergrass process on the grounds that the supergrasses had 'dealt a severe blow to the morale of both republican and loyalist terrorist organisations and their ability to murder and destroy'.[18] It was not surprising, he suggested, that because of this, the terrorists and their supporters were trying to destroy what the police had been achieving. The report admitted that the granting of immunity from prosecution was 'distasteful' to many people, but stated that it must be borne in mind that 'the evidence and information so provided has contributed significantly to the removal from society of considerable numbers of persons convicted by the courts of the most appalling crimes'.[19] In one area of Belfast alone, which previously had suffered high levels of terrorist activity, Sir John claimed, there had been a 73 per cent reduction in the murder rate and a 61 per cent overall reduction in terrorist operations, and many people would not be alive had it not been for the 'converted terrorist process', which, he added, was an accepted world-wide practice.[20]

---

[16] *Chief Constable's Report 1982* (Belfast: Police Authority for Northern Ireland, 1983) p. xii.
[17] Ibid.
[18] *Chief Constable's Report 1983* (Belfast: HMSO, 1984) p. xiii.
[19] Ibid.   [20] Ibid.

Sir John Hermon's views on the supergrass system can be criticized for five main reasons. First, the term 'converted terrorist' seriously distorts the truth about the motives which the Ulster supergrasses had for giving evidence. Only one, Kevin McGrady, claimed to have undergone any recognizable kind of conversion before deciding to testify, while the others were clearly motivated by naked self-interest, many not even pretending to be sorry for the offences which they had committed. Secondly, the critical role of the police in cultivating supergrass evidence is not mentioned.[21] Thirdly, contrary to what the Chief Constable suggests, the use of supergrasses has been markedly different in other countries.[22] Fourthly, as the current chapter indicates, to equate criticism of the supergrass system with ambivalence towards terrorism and with 'tribalism' grossly distorts the breadth and depth of the anti-supergrass campaign. Finally, the Chief Constable's assessment of the efficacy of the supergrass system in countering political violence in Northern Ireland is open to dispute.[23]

THE CONSPIRACY THEORY

The conspiracy theory is eloquently put by Roisin McDonagh, a member of Relatives for Justice:

If the supergrass and shoot-to-kill systems have revealed anything to nationalist people it is that the Northern judiciary, like the Northern state, are irreformable and offer no justice to those opposed to Britain's rule. The administration of the law in the North has, in practice, shown the concept of judicial impartiality to be illusory ... High court judges are identified as the frontline in an organised political conspiracy involving the RUC, the Director of Public Prosecutions, the Northern Ireland Office and various security agencies intent on pursuing a British policy decision to scatter the Republican opposition in Northern Ireland.[24]

Conspiracy theorists regarded loyalist supergrasses as merely a ploy introduced by the authorities to give this essentially anti-republican initiative a veneer of even-handedness, and a key extract from Brigadier Kitson's *Low Intensity Operations* was repeatedly misquoted to support the view that the courts were merely another branch of the British war machine.[25] Kitson states that in an insurgency 'the Law should be used as just another weapon in the

---

[21] See Ch. 11.   [22] See Ch. 10.   [23] See Ch. 9.
[24] *Fortnight*, no. 216, Mar. 1985, 10.   [25] See Ch. 2.

government's arsenal, and in this case it becomes little more than a propaganda cover for the disposal of unwanted members of the public'.[26] But to see the supergrass system as a fulfilment of this theory is to misread the passage in question, because the author not only distinguishes, but clearly favours, a second alternative: 'that the Law should remain impartial and administer the laws [*sic*] of the country without any direction from the government', which he recommends as 'not only morally right but also expedient because it is more compatible with the government's aim of maintaining the allegiance of the population'.[27] While there is much in Kitson's theory which is worthy of criticism, and although he clearly maintained that the institutions of the state, including the courts, should work closely together to deal with an insurgency, he cannot legitimately be accused of recommending that the courts and the law become 'just another weapon in the government's arsenal'.

The motives of anti-supergrass activists subscribing to the conspiracy theory varied. Some appeared to be primarily interested in securing the release of a relative or friend as indeed did some loyalists, while others campaigned because they perceived the supergrass system to be a threat to the republican 'armed struggle' and sought to use the rhetoric about judicial independence to extract some minimal concessions in order to reduce the damage. But others believed that reformist demands alone were worse than useless, on the grounds that their implementation could result in a refined, and therefore more effective, rather than a critically weakened supergrass system. A key component of the republican opposition to the supergrass system lay on the international plane, with Relatives for Justice in particular proving themselves adept at attracting a series of prestigious critical foreign observers.[28]

---

[26] F. Kitson, *Low Intensity Operations: Subversion, Insurgency, Peace-Keeping*, (London: Faber & Faber, 1971), 69.

[27] Ibid.

[28] These included: Mr Peter King, publicly elected Comptroller of Nassau County in New York; Mr Gene Turner, senior aide to Congressman Mr Norman Kent from New York; Mr Noel Saint-Pierre of the Quebec Bar and Quebec Jurists' Association; Mr Charles Henri de Choiseul of the Paris-based International Federation for Human Rights; US Senator Alphonso D'Amateo and his assistant Mr Denis Dillon.

THE CIVIL LIBERTIES PERSPECTIVE

Civil libertarians saw the supergrass system as a further significant shift away from the standard of 'guilt beyond reasonable doubt' in the Diplock courts towards the notion that 'probable guilt' could be a sufficient basis for conviction. Two particularly important expressions of this view were the Gifford Report, published in January 1984, and the Tenth Annual Report of the government-appointed Standing Advisory Commission on Human Rights, which appeared in 1985.[29] As the final chapter of this study will argue, the civil liberties perspective not only provided the best normative critique of the supergrass system but, by stressing that its most indefensible feature—uncorroborated convictions—could be reformed by a properly organized campaign, also offered the most accurate analysis of the scope for change.

The Gifford Report

In the autumn of 1983 Lord Gifford QC, a Labour peer, was commissioned by the London-based civil liberties charity the Cobden Trust to conduct an inquiry into the supergrass system in Northern Ireland. On 12 January 1984 a highly critical report was launched at a press conference in the House of Lords which stated that the use of supergrass evidence had led 'to the telling of lies and the conviction of the innocent',[30] and warned that it could damage public confidence in the courts in Northern Ireland. In Gifford's opinion the supergrass trials had caused 'a dangerous anger and alienation among a broad section of both Protestant and Catholic populations',[31] and, although there was a need to combat terrorism, this could not be done effectively 'by twisting the course of justice'.[32] By an unusual coincidence, on the same day on which the press conference was held, the Northern Ireland Court of Appeal quashed the conviction of RUC officer Charles McCormick, originally found guilty on the evidence of IRA informer Anthony

[29] See also S. C. Greer, 'Supergrasses and the Legal System in Britain and Northern Ireland' (1986) 102 LQR 198, and D. Bonner, 'Combatting Terrorism: Supergrass Trials in Northern Ireland' (1988) 51 MLR 23. A report by Amnesty International outlined similar proposals in 1988, Amnesty International, *United Kingdom-Northern Ireland: Killings by Security Forces and 'Supergrass' Trials* (London: Amnesty International, 1988).

[30] T. Gifford, *Supergrasses: The Use of Accomplice Evidence in Northern Ireland* (London: The Cobden Trust, 1984), para. 95.

[31] Ibid.   [32] Ibid.

O'Doherty, adding impetus to the supergrass controversy and drawing extra attention to Gifford's conclusions.[33]

According to Gifford, the danger with supergrass evidence in Northern Ireland stemmed almost entirely from the absence of the jury in the Diplock system. The report states that, if the jury were to be restored to the trial of scheduled offences, 'possibly with some particular arrangements to ensure the security and anonymity of jury members'

I would not consider that any special measures need at present to be taken to deal with supergrass evidence. I would expect juries to appreciate the dangers of which the judge would be required to warn them. That would be the most effective means of doing justice.[34]

But some further recommendations were offered, on the assumption that jury trial would continue to be suspended for the foreseeable future. Gifford argued that there should 'be no further grant of immunity from prosecution to those who have repeatedly been involved in serious terrorist crime' and that 'the uncorroborated evidence of a supergrass should not be accepted as a valid basis for convicting a defendant'.[35] While recognizing that a corroboration requirement would not remove all the dangers of injustice, because, for example, alleged verbal admissions of guilt by defendants when in police custody could become common as a form of corroborative evidence, he concluded:

a requirement for corroboration would serve to put into general operation the standards of justice which were observed by Mr Justice Murray in the McCormick case and by Lord Justice Gibson in the Grimley case. Those judges were saying that there was some evidence that was so tainted, that even if parts of it had the so called 'ring of truth', it could not be relied upon on its own. I believe this to be true of the vast majority of supergrass evidence; and even if there was some such evidence which was worthy of belief, it is not right that a single fallible judge should be left to determine what it is.[36]

The report accepted that the existing law on accomplice evidence was clear but that much more could be done to ensure that in practice defendants were no longer convicted on uncorroborated supergrass evidence. First, the DPP for Northern Ireland should

---

[33] See Ch. 2.   [34] Gifford, *Supergrasses*, para. 96.
[35] Ibid., paras. 98 and 99.   [36] Ibid., para. 99.

not authorize prosecutions where the only evidence to implicate an accused was that of a supergrass, and if he would not take such action himself, the Attorney-General should intervene to prevent such prosecutions. Secondly, the judiciary should regard it as highly dangerous and wrong to convict on the uncorroborated evidence of any supergrass, a standard which should also apply to appeal-court decisions. If none of these things happened, the report concluded, parliament should enact legislation which would require. as a matter of law that in a Diplock court there must be corroboration of the evidence of an accomplice. At the press launch, Gifford said that he had 'no doubt that there are guilty men going free with immunity having been granted, with substantial funds to set themselves up in another country, while innocent people are being convicted.[37] He also said he had found that there was a practice, when people were arrested by the police in connection with paramilitary activities, for them to be asked if they wanted to become supergrasses. There was a strong impression that the police were relying heavily on supergrass evidence rather than on interrogation methods and that they had helped the supergrasses to 'concoct' statements and 'rehearse' evidence[38] although, he added, he 'did not altogether blame the police for seeking to obtain the convictions in this manner'.[39] The supergrasses, he added, were 'not repentant terrorists in any sense of the word' but 'hardened criminals caught in the act, facing another long term of imprisonment, who decide to strike a deal with the state'.[40]

The report made a number of other recommendations: magistrates and judges should exercise tight control over the remand period, by refusing adjournments and granting bail when necessary, in order to limit the time those awaiting trial had to spend in custody; the voluntary bill of indictment should no longer be used in supergrass cases; no more than ten defendants should be tried together in any supergrass trial without their consent; when giving evidence, supergrasses should not be shielded by bodyguards from the rest of the court; judges should guard against appearing to treat a supergrass giving evidence with particular deference or respect; and the names of supergrasses giving evidence should not be withheld from the public.

---

[37] *Belfast Telegraph*, 12 Jan. 1984.   [38] *Irish News*, 13 Jan. 1984.
[39] Ibid.   [40] *Belfast Telegraph*, 12 Jan. 1984.

It is difficult to gauge the effect the Gifford inquiry had upon public opinion in Northern Ireland and, more particularly, upon the fortunes of the supergrass system itself. The official response was muted. The Secretary of State for Northern Ireland, Mr James Prior, for example, maintained, when asked to comment, that the supergrass process had nothing to do with the government and was entirely a matter for the judiciary and the independent Director of Public Prosecutions. Immediate public reactions were fairly predictable: defenders of the supergrass system dismissed the Labour peer's conclusions as at best naïve and out of touch with the realities of the battle against terrorism, while the system's critics welcomed and endorsed many if not all, of the report's recommendations. But the Gifford report was, arguably, much more than just another of the many contributions to the supergrass debate which had by then been offered. It was the result of an inquiry which had lasted over two months, it outlined a series of trenchant and largely legalistic criticisms in a carefully measured and neutral tone, and, in particular, it invited lawyers and judges on 'the mainland' to conclude that in handling the supergrass issue, the Diplock courts had behaved in a way which could not be justified by reference to traditional common-law standards of fairness and due process. As subsequent chapters will seek to show the central argument was eventually subtly endorsed by the Northern Ireland Court of Appeal.

The Tenth Annual Report of the Standing Advisory Commission on Human Rights

In its Tenth Annual Report for 1983–4, the government-appointed Standing Advisory Commission on Human Rights recommended that 'if the method of dealing with scheduled offences remains trial by a single judge ... some further safeguards be introduced in favour of defendants in "supergrass" cases'.[41] It continued:

We have in mind some requirement of corroboration which falls short of the present technical legal concept—something which goes further than the present 'warning' requirement in that it involves the accomplice's evidence to be verified in some way, but does not in every case require 'corroboration' as presently defined in a very technical way by the courts.[42]

---

[41] *Tenth Report of the Standing Advisory Commission on Human Rights for 1983–84*, HC 175, para. 56.
[42] Ibid., para. 56.

The main body of the report states that in arriving at this view the commission had been assisted by a paper prepared by Mr John Jackson, Lecturer in Law at Queen's University, Belfast, which is reproduced in an appendix. Yet strangely, Jackson rejects the one modification to the supergrass trials which the commission recommended.

In his concisely argued paper Jackson sets out and considers six features of the Northern Ireland supergrass trials which 'give rise to particular concern and which arguably call for greater safeguards for defendants than exist at present'.[43] These were: the grants of immunity from prosecution and other inducements to the super-grasses; the lack of disclosure of the arrangements between the authorities and the supergrasses; the lack of corroborative evidence to support the supergrasses' testimonies; the absence of the jury in Diplock trials, with the result that judges have to warn themselves not to place too much reliance upon the supergrass's evidence; the delays in bringing the defendants in the supergrass cases to trial, and the length of time spent upon remand; and the size of many supergrass trials.

Having thoroughly reviewed each issue, Jackson came to the following conclusions. There were three approaches to the question of immunity from prosecution, which had given rise to concern that persons guilty of serious crimes were not being brought to justice and that there was a powerful motive to lie. The first was to continue to leave it to the DPP to decide on a case-by-case basis, in consultation with the Attorney-General and unfettered by any limitations except the public interest. Secondly, the grant of immunity could be prohibited for all crimes, 'the general practice though not the rule, now in England'.[44] The third option, the one Jackson himself favoured, was to exclude grave crimes, including murder, from the scope of immunity while leaving open the prospect of lenient sentences for such offenders. In addition to leniency it would be appropriate, Jackson maintained, that accomplices who turned Queen's evidence in terrorist cases, and their families, should be offered a safe haven after the trial, and police protection in the period before, during, and after the proceedings. But there should be no offers of large sums of money for resettlement, as this would be tantamount to allowing offenders to profit from crime.

---

[43] Ibid., para. 4, p. 84.   [44] Ibid., app. C, para. 9.

On the disclosure issue, Jackson argues that the public have a right to know what kind of deals are being made between the authorities and the supergrasses, and that judges also need to know what kind of incentive has been offered, in order to be able to assess their evidence. Although the broad terms of the immunity deals were revealed in the Black and McGrady cases, Jackson says the details should also be disclosed, and he recommends that the Crown be obliged to lead evidence concerning not only the substance of the deal but how it was negotiated, supported by tape-recordings of interviews. As far as corroboration is concerned, Jackson distinguishes three possible alterations to the position current at that time: the corroboration rules could be changed in order to require corroboration as a condition of conviction; the corroboration rules could stay the same but prosecutions on uncorroborated supergrass evidence could be prohibited; the meaning of corroboration could be altered in order to make it less technical and rigorous. Jackson rejects the last of these options on the grounds that it provides inadequate safeguards for the defendant because evidence which can support a supergrass's testimony—for example, that concerning such issues as the time and place of offences—may not be indicative of guilt. On the choice between the first and second alternatives he states:

Perhaps the best option is to encourage the prosecuting authorities to be very discriminating in instituting proceedings against defendants on the uncorroborated evidence of supergrasses and to try to aim towards adopting a practice of instituting proceedings in the main only when there is some corroboration. If there is little willingness on the part of the prosecutors to adopt a more discriminative attitude, then it may be that reconsideration should be given to making corroboration mandatory in accomplice cases.[45]

On the absence of the jury, Jackson takes the view that although the 'case hardening' thesis is difficult to prove, 'a defendant is more at risk when his fate depends on the judgment of one man rather than the collective wisdom of the jury',[46] and he points out that

---

[45] *Tenth Report of the Standing Advisory Commission on Human Rights for 1983–84*, app. C, para. 30.

[46] Ibid., para. 31.

non-jury trial is likely to remain for the foreseeable future. But in his view there is

a very strong argument, particularly in cases where the prosecution relies mainly or entirely on the evidence of an accomplice witness, for a judge to be able to discuss the evidence with another judge and for two judges to preside in court. No defendant could then be convicted unless both judges were satisfied of his guilt on the basis of the accomplice evidence.[47]

Jackson also recommends that the delay problem be tackled by an official inquiry and indicates his sympathy with the Baker proposal that any defendant who has spent a year remanded in custody should be granted bail without surety as of right. Another option, he suggests, would be to change the practice which allows a judge to grant bail to a remand prisoner on a second High Court bail application only when he can point to a material change in circumstances since the first application. Remand prisoners, he suggests, could be given a right after a certain period, say six months, to make a totally fresh bail application to the High Court, and could be given a right to make a fresh application after every further three months. There is a strong argument for legislation limiting the number of defendants in any one trial, the author maintains, because large trials involve a risk that the judge will confuse the evidence against one defendant with that against another, and because mass trials are open to the 'show trial' allegation.

[47] Ibid., para. 34.

6

Decline: 1984

On 12 January 1984 the conviction of RUC Special Branch sergeant Charles McCormick, secured largely on the evidence of IRA informer Anthony O'Doherty, was quashed on appeal.[1] The Northern Ireland Court of Appeal held that Mr Justice Murray, the trial judge, had been wrong to conclude that the evidence independent of O'Doherty's testimony reached the high corroborative standard he himself deemed necessary.[2] On 22 August it was announced that O'Doherty would be released by exercise of the royal prerogative, after having served only five years of an eighteen-year sentence on fifty-seven terrorist charges. Commenting upon his release, the Northern Ireland Office said that his sentence had been reduced as a reward for having supplied information which had led to the break-up of dozens of IRA units.[3] Although he was given a new identity, and a weekly wage, in another part of the United Kingdom, within a fortnight he had returned to his familiar haunts in the Ballymena area and was last seen in 1989, which suggests that, unusually, the IRA had no intention of punishing him.[4]

In February Stanley Smith became the seventeenth identifiable supergrass to retract, when he withdrew his evidence against nine alleged members of the UDA, including its two most prominent leaders, Andy Tyrie and John McMichael. All charges were dropped. However, in May 1984 all but one of the eleven defendants charged on Robert Quigley's evidence were convicted. But the year ended with the acquittal of thirty-five defendants in the trial of *R.* v. *Robson and others*—when IRA and INLA supergrass Raymond Gilmour was literally laughed out of court—and with the most serious set-back the supergrass system had by then received: the quashing of all the convictions, even those supported by

---

[1] See Ch. 2.
[2] (1984) 1 NIJB 12; [1984] NI 50.
[3] *Irish Times*, 22 Aug. 1984.
[4] M. Dillon, *The Dirty War* (London: Arrow Books, 1991), 357–8.

corroboration, secured on Joseph Bennett's testimony. Throughout the year the shoot-to-kill controversy raged, with ten more fatal shootings in disputed circumstances by the police and the army.[5]

THE QUIGLEY CASE: *R. v. Crumley and others*

The Background

Robert John Quigley was born in the city of Derry on 6 February 1958 and grew up in the staunchly nationalist Creggan estate. In the mid-1970s he joined the militant People's Liberation Army (PLA), a precursor of the Irish National Liberation Army, and on 15 March 1976 was convicted of possessing firearms and ammunition with intent and under suspicious circumstances. He was sentenced to concurrent periods of four and six years' imprisonment and was released from prison in December 1978. In June 1979 he married, and, at the time of the trial of Crumley and others, he and his wife had two children. By his own admission, he had been unfaithful to his wife with three or four different women.

With the exception of a job with Ulster Ceramics, Quigley had never been in steady employment for more than a short time. On occasions when he had been working he had fraudulently claimed and drawn unemployment benefit and had also received additional social security benefits by falsely signing a form that he and his wife were legally separated. In the early 1980s Quigley joined the IRA and soon became an active and dedicated member with, by his own admission

no feelings of compunction or remorse about the killing of policemen or soldiers by the IRA and . . . no feelings of sorrow for the widows and the families of soldiers and policemen killed by the IRA. He accepted that he would have killed a policeman without remorse. He said that he himself did not like no warning bombs, but if the bomb was directed against a military or police target he would have no regret if civilian casualties were caused.[6]

---

[5] See A. Jennings 'Shoot to Kill: The Final Courts of Justice', in id. (ed.), *Justice under Fire: The Abuse of Civil Liberties in Northern Ireland*, 2nd edn. (London: Pluto Press, 1990), 125–6.

[6] *R. v. Crumley* (1986) 7 NIJB. 77. In *R. v. Crumley and others* [1986] NI 66 Mr Justice Hutton held that notes taken at police interviews with Quigley could not formally be admitted as evidence nor did they constitute corroboration of Quigley's testimony in court. In *Re Quigley* [1983] NI 245, a habeas corpus application, it was confirmed that Quigley's wife and family were being held in protective police custody.

On 24 August 1982, along with some forty others, Quigley was arrested on the evidence of supergrass Raymond Gilmour and taken to Castlereagh police station in Belfast, where he was held for seven days and questioned about his involvement in a conspiracy to murder members of the security forces at Croby roundabout in Derry. Emphatically denying his involvement, he was said to have burst into tears in the course of one interrogation, and claimed that he had been ill at the relevant time and that his wife had had to call the doctor. The police checked his alibi and he was released. The conspiracy in question was one of the alleged incidents with which some of those he subsequently implicated were later tried.

Quigley claimed that after his release he was debriefed about his interrogation by an IRA man sitting behind a sheet which had been suspended across a room in a house in Derry, and that he was then ordered to go to Donegal, where he was hooded and taken to another debriefing session, the object of which was to determine if he had turned informer. Whether he had or not remains unclear. He claimed that this second interrogation lasted all night and at one point he thought he was going to be shot, but eventually he was released and given his bus-fare home. Quigley claimed that this experience disillusioned him about some of the IRA leadership in Derry and, although he remained committed to the cause, he became more wary. On one subsequent occasion he said he refused to take part in an IRA operation because he was concerned that if it went wrong he would be suspected of having informed.

On 1 November 1982 Quigley was arrested again. He claimed that on the way to Belfast he realized that, if he was held for a further seven days, it was unlikely that the IRA would believe that he had withstood pressure to inform a second time and he would probably be shot. Knowing that whatever happened he could not go back to Derry, he claimed that he arrived at Castlereagh in a state of considerable confusion and decided to ask the police for help. He stated that he indicated that he was concerned about his family and also wanted to get out of Derry. According to police notes, it was during the course of his third interview, from 4 p.m. to 6 p.m. on 1 November, that he admitted his involvement with the IRA and made several statements. He kept asking if 'anything was happening' and claimed that he believed the police would realize that he wanted immunity without its having to be specifically requested.

Quigley claimed that the first time he heard he had been granted immunity from prosecution was a week or two weeks after his arrest. The details, including the protection which the police were providing for him and his family, were given to the solicitors for the accused in three letters from the Director of Public Prosecutions, two of which were dated 14 November 1983 and the third 12 January 1984. These were in virtually identical terms to those submitted in evidence in the Morgan case, except that an additional item of correspondence indicated that a sum of £402.87 had been paid in discharge of a hire-purchase debt for some furniture.

The Trial

The trial, presided over by Mr Justice Hutton, began on 12 January 1984 and involved sixteen defendants indicted on eighty-four counts. Four of the accused were granted a separate trial when their defence counsel, Mr Richard Ferguson QC, withdrew for medical reasons and another defendant was acquitted on a minor charge. From 12 March 1984 the trial proceeded against the remaining eleven accused: Charles Gerard Crumley, Michael Joseph McLaughlin, James Doherty, James Leonard Cross, Eamon Anthony Doherty, James Martin Doherty, Gary Brendan Fleming, Brendan Mary Gerard Doherty, Gerard Majella O'Brien, Thomas Ashe Mellon, and Hugh Joseph Duffy. With the exception of Michael McLaughlin, all were charged with belonging to the IRA in Derry. The membership charge against Gerard O'Brien, who also faced other charges, was dismissed early in the proceedings on the grounds of no case to answer.

The Crown divided the offences into twenty-one principal events, but independent verification that the key offences had taken place existed in only six cases. Independent evidence was available that certain subsidiary offences had occurred which, it was claimed, were part of the preparations for more serious offences which themselves were abandoned or aborted—for example, planting a hoax bomb to lure the security forces into an ambush, and various hijackings. Apart from the membership charges, most of the other offences consisted of alleged conspiracies to murder members of the security forces, and offences concerning the possession of firearms and explosives. One of the counts, for example, charged

James Doherty with consipiring 'on a date unknown between 1st
and 29th March 1982, with persons unknown to murder a member
of the Royal Ulster Constabulary'.[7]

Duffy, Fleming, Mellon, O'Brien, and Eamon Doherty gave
evidence in their own defence. Duffy, a representative on the
Creggan Tenants' Association and Sinn Fein organizer in the
Creggan, denied being a member of the IRA and having given
Quigley IRA lectures. Mellon had worked in Sinn Fein advice
centres since 1976 and had been active in the hunger-strike campaign. Two alibi witnesses, called on behalf of Eamon Doherty,
supported his claim that he had attended a meeting of the Dungloe
Bar Fishing Club on the evening of 28 July 1982, when it was
alleged he had been one of the gunmen who shot at the RUC in
Linsford Drive. O'Brien claimed that on the night of 31 March
1982, when grenades exploded outside his home during an army
search, he could not have been responsible as charged, since he had
been inside the house at the time. His brother Adrian gave evidence
in support of this alibi, but a warrant officer from the Royal
Anglian Regiment testified that he knew both Gerard and Adrian
and that Gerard had not been in the house during the army search.
Mr Justice Hutton rejected O'Brien's alibi and described him as
'one of the most obvious and blatant liars, both by reason of his
demeanour and his answers that I have ever seen in the witness
box'.[8] If O'Brien's alibi was true, the judge said, it was a mystery
why he had waited until the middle of the trial to disclose it. Six
witnesses were called to support Charles Crumley's alibi that he
had been on the Dungloe Bar fishing-trip to Ballina, County
Mayo, between 15 and 19 July 1982 and therefore could not have
been guilty of offences allegedly committed between these dates.

Like all the supergrass trials, the case of *R. v. Crumley* revolved
around Quigley's character, his credibility as a witness, and in
particular the circumstances which led him to turn Queen's evidence. He was repeatedly pressed in cross-examination to admit
that giving evidence against alleged members of the IRA was part
of a deal made with the police in return for immunity from
prosecution. Quigley gave various inconsistent answers, claiming
first that he had merely offered to tell everything about the criminal
activities in which he had been involved and that this would

---

[7] *R. v. Crumley* (1986) 7 NIJB 152.
[8] Ibid. 158.

inevitably require naming the other participants; but later he said that, after he had started to make his statements, the police had asked him if he would give evidence against those he had implicated and he had come to an arrangement with them that he would do so. Later still he returned to his original story that he simply revealed the details of his own involvement and that this necessitated naming others also. The defence argued that Quigley felt that in order to secure immunity and police protection, he would have to outdo Gilmour and name high-ranking officers in the IRA. This, it was suggested, provided him with a motive for making false accusations, particularly against Mellon, Duffy, James Martin Doherty, and Brendan Doherty, who were members of Sinn Fein or prominent members of the local community. Mr Justice Hutton concluded that Quigley had decided to offer his services to the prosecution because he feared for his life if he were to return to Derry, but he rejected a defence suggestion that Quigley was motivated by the fear of being prosecuted and convicted on Gilmour's evidence, because, he said, Quigley had already withstood seven days' interrogation on Gilmour's statements. In the course of cross-examination, Mr Desmond Boal QC put it to Quigley that 'the most important purpose in this case is that you should save your own skin'. Quigley answered: 'That's why I decided to tell all, yes.'[9]

Mr Justice Hutton accepted that Quigley was probably 'frightened and in some confusion' during his first day at Castlereagh because he was afraid of what the IRA would do to him if he was released and returned to Derry. It was also probable that

his reluctance to accept under cross-examination that he offered to give information against other persons arose, in part, from an unwillingness on his part to admit to himself and to accept openly that he offered to become an informer or tout against his former friends and associates in the IRA.[10]

In his judgment Mr Justice Hutton accepted that in his evidence in the *Crumley* trial Quigley had perjured himself on several occasions and that he had also lied on other occasions. It was probable, he pointed out, that Quigley remembered much more of the interviews on 1 November and that he remembered making a more specific

---

[9] Ibid. 76.   [10] Ibid. 92.

offer to the police than he admitted. 'Therefore,' the judge said, 'to that extent I consider it probable that Quigley lied in the witness box when recounting his first day in Castlereagh in November 1982.'[11] Quigley had also given untruthful evidence at the preliminary inquiry, according to the judge, because he had accepted suggestions that he was a converted terrorist giving evidence out of conscience, whereas at the trial itself he had agreed under cross-examination that he was not a converted terrorist and that he was giving evidence out of self-interest and not remorse. Indeed, Mr Justice Hutton added, 'he appeared not to understand the concept of having a conscience'.[12] When cross-examined about his trial in March 1976 on charges of firearms possession, Quigley accepted that he had deliberately given false evidence under oath when he had stated that he had not known that rifles were in a car stopped by the army in which he had been a passenger. He also accepted that he had lied on other occasions when he considered it necessary to save his own skin. For example, in August 1982, when in police detention, he had interwoven fact with fiction in order to lie convincingly about his involvement in the IRA. He also agreed that he had feigned breaking down and crying in police interviews in order to persuade the police that he was not involved in terrorism. The judge also concluded that Quigley had lied in alleging that the occupier of a house had been unaware of an arms dump which he and Moore had spent two and a half days constructing, and in claiming that, during his seven days under police interrogation in August 1982, when Gilmour had been brought into the interrogation room, he had not realized who it was until Gilmour had left. He also lied when he told the court that he had not known who Gilmour was before 12 August 1982.

Nevertheless, Mr Justice Hutton concluded that, even when the dangers of accomplice evidence were taken into account, Quigley was 'a most impressive witness'.[13] He added that Quigley's evidence against Mellon was a little less impressive and that Quigley had had only a limited opportunity to observe the grenade-throwing incident with which O'Brien was charged, but that he described 'with remarkable consistency'[14] the other members of the IRA and the roles they had played in IRA meetings and operations. The judge stated that he was satisfied 'that in no case was he leaving

[11] *R.* v. *Crumley,* 92   [12] Ibid. 93.   [13] Ibid. 124.   [14] Ibid. 125.

out the names of the real IRA men who had taken part in the operation and substituting the name or names of the accused who had not, in reality, taken part in that operation'.[15] In responding to various defence suggestions concerning how the credibility of a witness such as Quigley could be tested, Mr Justice Hutton held that, in his opinion

the assessment of a witness depends to a very considerable extent upon the special circumstances of the particular case and there is no precise formula or set of conditions which must be met before a tribunal of fact can be satisfied that a witness's evidence against an accused person is true.[16]

Citing Eggleston's *Evidence, Proof and Probability*,[17] Mr Boal submitted that there were six factors which a judge ought to take into account when testing whether or not a witness was telling the truth: (1) the inherent consistency of the story; (2) its consistency with other witnesses; (3) its consistency with the undisputed facts; (4) extrinsic evidence concerning the general credibility of the witness—for example evidence of a relevant physical or mental defect or of bias against a party etc.; (5) observation of the witness's performance in the witness-box and such things as his ability to judge distance etc., should this be relevant; and (6) the inherent probability or improbability of his story. Mr Boal submitted that only factors 4 and 5 were available to test whether an accomplice's evidence was truthful and that these were inadequate tests. Mr Justice Hutton said that there was no set of tests or factors of universal application to decide whether or not an accomplice had been telling the truth but that the Eggleston check-list provided a useful guide. Applying each of the items in turn, he held that they pointed strongly to the conclusion that Quigley's evidence against each of the accused was true, except, in certain respects, for that against Mellon and O'Brien.

There was, he said, a 'remarkable inherent consistency' in Quigley's story (factor 1).[18] He had made certain errors in his evidence-in-chief: he had said, for example, that Eamon Doherty and James Doherty were to be the gunmen in the Croby roundabout attack and that Eamon Doherty was a party to two conspiracies when in

---

[15] Ibid.   [16] Ibid. 132.
[17] R. Eggleston, *Evidence, Proof and Probability*, 2nd edn. (London: Weidenfield & Nicolson, 1983).
[18] *R. v. Crumley* (1986) 7 NIJB 137.

fact this was not the case. But it would have been extremely difficult for any witness consistently to have maintained over a period of sixteen days in the witness-box, and subject to the relentless cross-examination of five eminent senior counsel, a false account which he had memorized. The defence submission that cross-examination could not expose a lying witness lacked weight in a case such as this, the judge said, where the witness was describing a very large number of criminal activities with many different participants. As far as factors 2 and 3 were concerned, Mr Justice Hutton conceded that, apart from the confessions, which were evidence only against the two accused who had made them, there was no other evidence to support Quigley's testimony that the particular accused had committed the offences alleged. But, he added, there was a large amount of evidence proving, or tending to prove, that an IRA unit had committed the offences which Quigley had described. As regards factor 4, it was true, the judge said, that Quigley was a man of 'deplorable character', who had lied both in the past and at the present trial.[19] But while this meant that his evidence had to be considered with the greatest care, caution, and vigilance, and with constant recollection of the warning on accomplice evidence, it did not mean that the court could not accept his evidence if it was wholly satisfied that it was true. In the witness-box (factor 5), Quigley was a 'tough and compact figure', who displayed 'an air of cool competence',[20] according to Mr Justice Hutton, and no one could have maintained under cross-examination such an immensely detailed account as that which he gave, if it were not true. As far as factor 6 was concerned, the judge said that he was convinced that Quigley's account was inherently probable and that it had 'the ring of truth about it'.[21] Apart from certain reservations which he had about Mellon and O'Brien, 'at the end of the case', Mr Justice Hutton concluded: 'I was not only intellectually wholly satisfied that Quigley's evidence against the accused was true, I believed and felt that his evidence against the accused was true.'[22]

The Verdict

Judgment in *R.* v. *Crumley* was given on 30 April and 1 and 2 May

---

[19] *R.* v. *Crumley* (1986) 7 NIJB 139.   [20] Ibid.
[21] Ibid. 140.   [22] Ibid. 141.

1984, when Mr Justice Hutton convicted all but one of the eleven defendants on virtually all counts. The only corroboration was to be found in the unchallenged verbal and written statements which James Doherty and James Cross had made to the police. Mellon was acquitted of the only charge he faced, membership of the INLA, on the grounds that, although he was probably guilty, there were certain parts of Quigley's evidence which 'raised an element of doubt' in the judge's mind; the dates of a meeting with Quigley and certain aspects of Quigley's description of that meeting, for example, were inconsistent with other aspects of Quigley's evidence and with items of independent evidence. Mr Justice Hutton denied that Mellon's acquittal cast any doubt on the guilt of the other defendants, because, he said, he was completely satisfied that Quigley's evidence against them was true beyond reasonable doubt. He added that he was almost convinced beyond reasonable doubt that it was true against Mellon too, but not quite.

Quigley, he held, was undoubtedly a member of the IRA and it was probable that he would have been instructed by an IRA education officer and would have been sworn in by the officer commanding and adjutant of the Derry Brigade. As there had been no suggestion that the police fed him names, there was no reason for him to have given false names to the police, nor were there any grounds for believing that he had made false accusations against the accused, either by substituting the name or names of one or more of the accused for the actual IRA member or members, or by falsely alleging that he had met high-ranking officers in the IRA. Regardless of whether Quigley's motive in giving evidence was a desire to avoid going back to Derry or to avoid a prison sentence on Gilmour's evidence, Mr Justice Hutton said that he was in a position to be able to give the police sufficient true and important information about the identities of members of the IRA in Derry and about their criminal activities. It would, in any case have been dangerous and contrary to his interests for Quigley to have given false names to the police, because he was astute enough to realize that if he had done so and the police had discovered that his information was unreliable, it might have cost him his immunity and protection. Mr Justice Hutton rejected as 'artificial and unrealistic' the argument that, by naming people from the Creggan, Quigley could have reckoned that there was no real risk of being refuted by an alibi,[23] and 'no reason of substance' had been given on behalf of any of the accused as to why he should have wanted to substitute them for the real IRA offenders.[24] Duffy had claimed that Quigley bore him malice because he had threatened to throw him out of a dance if he did not behave, and Eamon Doherty had warned Quigley to steer clear of his brother Michael, as he was giving the Doherty family a bad name. But neither of these were sufficient, in the judge's view, to provide a reasonable motive for Quigley to give false evidence against either of these accused.

Concluding his judgment, Mr Justice Hutton addressed the public debate about the supergrass process. There was nothing new, he stated, in accused persons being convicted on the evidence of an accomplice, since the law had permitted it for at least 200 years, although the modern slang term 'supergrass', used to describe an accomplice who gives extensive evidence against former associates in crime, might have given a mistaken impression that something novel was occurring. The concern expressed by some members of the public that a man like Quigley should be able to evade punishment for his own wrongdoing was understandable, he added, but it left out of account the fact that by reason of his evidence, Quigley had enabled ten terrorists, almost all of whom were highly dangerous, to be convicted.

THE GILMOUR CASE: *R. v. Robson and others*

The Background

Towards the end of August 1984 Lorraine Gilmour, a housewife from the Creggan estate in Derry, told friends that she, her husband Raymond, and their two children were going on holiday to Donegal. Not long after the family had departed, all their belongings and furniture were cleared out of their home and taken away under police and army escort. A few days later, on 26 August, about forty people were arrested in a pre-dawn swoop by 1,000 police and soldiers, in the biggest operation mounted by the security forces in the city since Operation Motorman in 1972. The Gilmour case had begun.

---

[23] *R. v. Crumley* (1986) 7 NIJB 131.   [24] Ibid.

Raymond Gilmour was born in Derry in 1961 and, according to the opening submissions by the prosecution in the trial of *R. v. Robson and others*, had been recruited as a paid informer by RUC Special Branch in September 1978 at the age of 17, following his arrest in connection with the armed robbery of a post office. During the course of police interviews about the robbery (which did not involve any paramilitary organization), Gilmour was introduced to two officers calling themselves Pete and Ian. Pete was said to have asked if he would be prepared to join the INLA and to supply information about terrorist activities in the Creggan. Gilmour said he would think about it and was given a telephone number to contact. Later, while on bail in connection with the robbery charge (for which he eventually received a two-year suspended sentence), he phoned the number, was put in touch with Pete, and began his career as a Special Branch spy. The Crown claimed that, as a police agent, Gilmour was expected to notify the police about the identity of IRA members and the location of arms dumps, and to provide intelligence which would enable operations to be intercepted. He was said to have provided the police with regular and reliable information about the INLA which had led to arrests and to the seizure of explosives. The prosecution claimed his evidence to the court would be of an equally reliable kind.

Precisely why Gilmour became a police spy remains a mystery, and he gave two contradictory reasons in the *Robson* trial. Mr Desmond Boal QC for the defence suggested that, at least seven months before the interviews about the post office raid, the police had pressurized him into informing, because of a homosexual liaison—at the time a criminal offence in Northern Ireland, even between consenting adults—and that information which Gilmour had supplied had led to the death of his friend Colm McNutt, shot attempting to hijack a car which turned out to be driven by a plain-clothes soldier. Gilmour denied both accusations and claimed that his main motive in becoming a police informer had been mercenary, although he added that he had not asked the police how much money he would receive. Later, under cross-examination from Mr Michael Nicholson QC, Gilmour said that he had agreed to join the INLA, and subsequently the IRA, as a favour to his police friend 'Pete' and not for the money. During the course of cross-examination, Gilmour also maintained that he would have worked for the Special Branch even if he had not been paid for it, and said that at some point in the future he would like to become a policeman because he felt that some of Pete's training had rubbed off on him during their association.

Gilmour's account of his involvement with the INLA at the first of three preliminary inquiries in the *Robson* case contained the familiar combination of botched operations and deadly violence which had characterized the evidence of all the supergrasses. Between November 1978 and April 1979 he participated in the INLA offences which were the subject of many of the charges against those tried on his evidence. Although the prosecution accepted that sometimes he had played leading roles, this had always been as a police agent. Gilmour told the court that his agreement with the police required him to supply information about any crime in which he was involved, or any impending operation. He was also supposed to try to prevent offences if he could, but there were times, he claimed, when he was unable to contact Pete because to do so would have blown his cover. He said that he and Pete had become very good friends and that he had kept him up to date on the whereabouts of his unit's arms dumps.

In 1979–80 Gilmour drifted out of his INLA cell, which by then had become less active, and in the late summer of 1980 he was again approached by the police and asked if he would join the IRA, whose activities in Derry had increased dramatically between 1980 and 1982 as the prison crisis unfolded. Gilmour agreed and approached the accused Hugh Duffy, who was in charge of Sinn Fein marches, claiming he was fed up with 'the army situation in Derry' and wanted to do something about it. He claimed that he met Duffy three times and that, on the third occasion, Duffy questioned him about his background and warned him that if he joined the IRA he would have to stay away from republican marches and bars and known IRA members. According to Gilmour, Duffy introduced him to James 'Ducksie' Doherty, alleged commander of the IRA in Derry. Gilmour told him about his involvement with the INLA and how his best friend Colm McNutt had been shot by the army and that he wanted to join the IRA to avenge his death.[25] Like Quigley before him, Gilmour said that

---

[25] For details of this incident, see M. Urban, *Big Boys' Rules: The SAS and the Secret Struggle against the IRA* (London: Faber & Faber, 1992), 43.

Doherty arranged for him to see Paul Elder, a teacher at St Peter's school, Creggan, where he learned anti-interrogation methods and was required to read extracts from the 'Green book', a history of Ireland from the Viking era until 1916, which, ironically, had blue covers.

Gilmour described various IRA operations, including five alleged conspiracies to kill members of the security forces between May and August 1982. On one occasion he said a plan to shoot soldiers at Butcher Gate had to be abandoned because the hit team arrived late and the gates had already been closed. He also related how he, and some members of another IRA unit, embarked on a mission to shoot policemen coming out of Strand Road police station but their car, which Gilmour was driving, encountered an army patrol and they panicked. Because they had all shouted at him to do different things, Gilmour said he had reversed the car into some railings and then crashed headlong into an oncoming vehicle. The unit abandoned the car and in their haste to escape threw two of their weapons away. Gilmour himself ran into a fish-and-chip shop, and the girl behind the counter told him that his colleague Martin Connolly was already hiding in the back, where Gilmour found him, dressed in a white coat. Doherty was said to have been so furious about this botched operation that he had threatened to hold a court martial. Gilmour also claimed that an attempt to shoot soldiers from the grounds of Magee College had to be abandoned because he managed to get the getaway vehicle stuck in mud, that the home of a Derry solicitor had been used as an arms dump, and that a weapon lost by a policeman had been used in a punishment shooting in which the victim bled to death.

Like Christopher Black, Gilmour maintained that, although he enjoyed the excitement of being in the IRA, he did not relish the possibility of people being killed. He claimed that during the attack upon soldiers at the Castle Gate security barrier on 20 January 1981 in which Private Shenton was killed and another soldier wounded, he had deliberately not released the safety catch on his Woodmaster rifle, and that later, he had told Doherty, the officer commanding, that his failure to press home the attack had been due to inexperience with the weapon, an explanation which, he said, Doherty appeared to have accepted. On another occasion, when acting as the driver of the car used by an active service unit, Gilmour claimed that he had jerked the clutch just as the gunman opened fire on a policeman whose car had been tailed from Strand Road police station. Like Grimley, Gilmour claimed that the police had declined to act upon the information which he had given about some impending terrorist incidents. These included the killing of Private Shenton, an attempted bombing of the army sangar on the roof of Rossville flats, a sniper attack on a police patrol in which an officer was wounded, a spate of bomb attacks on banks in Derry, an armed robbery, and the planting of a bomb in Magee College. He said that he could not explain why the police had taken no action since, he maintained, he had supplied the names of those involved. He also said that Pete had never told him that he was not to shoot, blow up, or kill anyone.

In November 1981, after a hijacking, Gilmour was arrested, along with Joseph Doherty and Catherine Moore. He maintained that, while in custody in Strand Road station, Pete had come to see him, had told him not to say anything to anyone, and had said that it would be necessary for him to go to prison for a couple of months in order to preserve his cover. With Pete's approval, Gilmour had given his wife Pete's name, and Lorraine had got in touch and had received cash through the post. After his release a few months later, when the hijacking charges were dropped, Gilmour joined another IRA cell and again provided the police with information concerning its activities. In August 1982, acting on information which Gilmour had supplied, a house which contained an M60 machine-gun was raided by the security forces. Gilmour said he contacted Pete soon after to let him know that 'things were getting hot' in the organization and that he had fallen under suspicion. Some days later Pete told him that he had two options. He could either leave Derry and get a new home and a new identity for himself and his family or give evidence against his accomplices. Gilmour claimed that he was not told he could be granted immunity from prosecution, and that he had chosen the latter option both as a special favour to his friend Pete and also to assist the fight against terrorism. He said that he expected to receive a house and a new job in England after the trial, but claimed that there had been no mention of a specific sum of money.

As a result of his decision to give evidence, on 24 August 1982 Gilmour was taken into police custody, along with his wife and two young children—a boy aged 3 and a girl aged 2. At the preliminary inquiry it was disclosed that he had received immunity from prosecution, but few details emerged. He had told his wife that he was taking the family on a holiday to Butlins and it was not until they were on their way to Lisburn army barracks that he confessed that he had been working for Special Branch and was going to give evidence in court. His wife, he said, had broken down in tears and had pleaded with him not to do it. In November 1982 Mr Patrick Gilmour, Raymond's 62 year old father, who was in poor health, was taken hostage by masked men, and a caller to the family threatened that he would be killed if Raymond did not withdraw his evidence. He was nevertheless released unharmed in September 1983.

Mrs Gilmour told the Gifford inquiry that, during the first four weeks in Lisburn army barracks, her husband spent a lot of time with the police, poring over papers in a portakabin. The family was taken to Ipswich, London, and Newcastle, and spent a four-week winter holiday with police minders in Cyprus, cut short when the RUC guards became suspicious of two other hotel guests. Lorraine Gilmour was not allowed to speak to strangers, not even to a priest at confession, and the children were prohibited from playing with other children lest she herself should come into contact with their mothers. Their son became quite unruly, and eventually quite ill, apparently as a result.[26] Mrs Gilmour told *An Phoblacht/Republican News*,[27] the weekly journal of the republican movement, that while in Cyprus Raymond had taken an overdose of drugs which had been prescribed for her because of nervous tension, and that their police minders had had to force open the couple's bedroom door in order to revive him. Feeling increasingly homesick after having seen her parents in March 1983, Lorraine Gilmour returned to her mother's home in the Creggan estate in Derry on 18 April 1983.

The Trial

The three preliminary inquiries in the Gilmour case were stormy affairs; the proceedings were disrupted several times and various members of Gilmour's family, as well as a number of defendants, were ordered out of the court-room. Press speculation suggested that Gilmour had implicated up to eighty suspects, and it was expected that there would be three separate trials, but, as it hap-

---

[26] T. Gifford, *Supergrasses: The Use of Accomplice Evidence in Northern Ireland* (London: The Cobden Trust, 1984), para. 82.

[27] 21 Apr. 1983.

pened, forty-one men and three women were indicated on 186
charges, allegedly committed between November 1978 and August
1982 and ranging from murder, attempted murder, and possession
of firearms, to assisting proscribed organizations. The trial of *R. v.
Robson and others*, which began on 8 May 1984, initially dwarfed
even the Black trial and was said to have been the largest trial in
British legal history. However, the number of defendants was
eventually reduced to thirty-five, facing 180 charges, when three
defendants did not answer bail and three others, Brady, Moran,
and Millar, were granted separate trials at various points in the
proceedings. Many of those implicated had already been in custody
for over twenty months by the time the trial started.

When Gilmour began giving evidence, on 16 October 1984, he
was visibly nervous and made a number of elementary mistakes,
including getting his own date of birth wrong, confusing the dates
when he first became involved in terrorist activity, and only being
able to remember the approximate ages of his two children. On 22
May 1984 the Lord Chief Justice, Lord Lowry, took over from the
trial judge, Mr Justice MacDermott, who dismissed himself from
the trial, having acceded to a defence submission that Crown
counsel's claim that Gilmour's evidence would be reliable was not
sustainable upon any admissible evidence and that had a jury been
sitting, he would have been obliged to discharge it and empanel a
fresh one. On 16 October 1984 three of the key defendants dismissed
their lawyers, claiming that the proceedings were a sham.

Gilmour's evidence was riddled with inconsistencies. For example, at the trial he initially denied that, before the preliminary
inquiry, he had refreshed his memory from a book of statements he
had given the police, and in fact had even denied that such a book
existed, claiming that his wife, the source of the defence's information, had been lying in order to protect herself from the IRA. Later
he accepted that there was a book of statements and that he had
had access to it in order to refresh his memory before the preliminary inquiry, but he continued to deny that he had rehearsed his
evidence with the police. He also admitted that some of the things
which he told the police could be regarded as second- or third-
hand hearsay.

In his evidence-in-chief Gilmour had said that James Doherty
had told him that he had organized the shooting of Inspector
Norman Duddy at Strand Road Presbyterian Church and that on

28 March 1982 he had sent two men on a motorcycle to carry it out. But during cross-examination Gilmour admitted that at the time of the Duddy murder he himself had been in custody and had not been released until May that year. He accepted that the IRA maintained strict secrecy about operational information and that he would not have been regarded as a full IRA member until he had been debriefed following release. Yet he claimed that at his debriefing Doherty mentioned these details about the Duddy shooting straight 'out of the blue'. He also claimed to have reported this information to his Special Branch handler, but Doherty had not been arrested at the time. Although he accepted that Doherty's alleged disclosure was extremely important, he was unable to account for the fact that he had omitted to mention it in the first two statements about this encounter which he had given the police in August and on 16 October 1982. In fact it was not until 21 October that Gilmour included it, and he told the court that 'things were coming back to me all the time. There were about 50 statements and my mind was clogged up.'[28]

Quizzed about the various conspiracies against the army and the police which he claimed he and his unit had hatched, Gilmour admitted that many of the details were impractical when examined closely. He was also unable to explain why the amount he claimed to have been paid by Special Branch differed substantially from the figures provided by the prosecution. He said that before he had been taken into protective custody, he had received at least £100 a week from his contact 'Pete', when in prison he had not been paid anything, but that when he had left, he had received a single payment of £250 or £300, and that since August 1982 he had been paid £120 a week. The defence produced figures provided by the Crown which showed that Gilmour had received £280 a month while in prison and that he had been receiving £40 to £70 a week whilst in protective custody. Gilmour agreed that by the time he left Derry in August 1982 he had accumulated debts for rent, hire purchase, clothes, and other items, amounting to over £2,000, and that he had made no effort to pay them, nor to discover if they had been paid on his behalf. He agreed with a defence suggestion that he had had to live a lie since becoming a police spy in 1978 and that he would have to tell lies about his past life in the new life

[28] *Irish News*, 9 Nov. 1984.

which lay ahead for him, but he denied he was an expert at lying and deception.

The Verdict

On 18 December 1984 all thirty-five defendants were acquitted on a submission for a direction. The decision was greeted with gasps from the court, then a stunned silence, which was broken by applause and cheering. Twenty-six of the defendants walked free, but the other nine had already been convicted on the evidence of other supergrasses. In a five-page unpublished judgment, Lord Lowry explained why he had decided to take 'this somewhat unusual course'. The Lord Chief Justice pointed out that the Crown case depended almost entirely upon Gilmour's evidence but that he had not reached his decision because Gilmour was an accomplice, an informer, a largely uncorroborated witness, or because 'of his scandalous character oblivious to every natural obligation of kinship, marital and fatherly affection and friendship'. It was rather, Lord Lowry said, that he considered Gilmour to be 'entirely unworthy of belief', since he was 'a completely selfish, self-regarding man, to whose lips in the witness box a lie invariably came more naturally than the truth'.

The Lord Chief Justice pointed out that 'an accomplice or informer, or someone who is both, can tell the truth and can command acceptance as a witness of the truth, but he requires to be impressive to overcome the handicaps inevitably associated with his position'. Refraining from going into detail about Gilmour's shortcomings as a witness, since, he said, this had already been very ably done by defence counsel, he stated that to have continued this trial would have been 'an abuse of the criminal process', since he knew what his decision was to be.

In a vein common to a number of his judgments in other supergrass cases, the Lord Chief Justice said that there was 'more than a trace of probability that many of those before [the court] are, or were, members of a proscribed organisation'. These were the people with whom Gilmour had been associating, he remarked, and no doubt the police believed them to be guilty of terrorist acts and terrorist plans. But, with the exception of those who had admitted their membership, the only way in which this could be proved was 'through the mouth of the witness whom I have condemned'. Lord Lowry stated that it could not be concluded that someone was a member of the INLA or the IRA simply because he had been implicated to the police by someone professing to be his accomplice, or because the police believed him to be guilty and wanted to bring him to book, since 'one must go by the evidence and by the weight of the evidence'. He had concluded, therefore, that on the overwhelming majority of charges it would not be safe to convict, and he was convinced a jury would also have acquitted on the remaining small number of charges where there was a prima-facie case, and on those other peripheral offences in respect of which statements of admission had been made.

THE BENNETT APPEAL: *R. v. Graham and others*

On 24 December 1984 all fourteen of the convictions obtained in *R. v. Graham* were quashed by the Northern Ireland Court of Appeal on the grounds that they were unsafe and unsatisfactory because the trial judge, Mr Justice Murray, had misdirected himself on the law governing Bennett's credibility. Delivering the judgment of the court, Lord Lowry considered a number of issues supporting this conclusion.

Matters Militating against Bennett's Credibility

The Lord Chief Justice noted how the trial judge had recognized that the central question was whether or not Bennett was 'credible', in the sense of 'capable of belief'.[29] The judge had then considered those matters which might have militated against Bennett's testimony and had cautioned himself as tribunal of fact concerning the dangers inherent in accepting the evidence of such a witness. 'On any basis', Lord Lowry said, 'the evidence of . . . Joseph Charles Bennett must rank among the most suspect'.[30] It was hard, he continued, to draw accurate distinctions concerning credibility between different criminals who are accomplices and paid informers based upon the variety of circumstances which can occur, but one must be prepared for the possibility that such a witness, whatever his motives, may tell the truth. But the circumstances in which Bennett turned informer 'did not constitute the most favourable augury for his reliability'. Since he was 'an unreconstructed villain' facing a murder charge and 'up against it from the start', there was

---

[29] *R. v. Graham* (1984) 18 NIJB 5.   [30] Ibid. 7.

'a special need for vigilance'.[31] He had been involved in criminal activities from an early age, as his criminal record showed, and had, moreover, committed perjury in the trial itself. Having purchased his own freedom by undertaking to give, and then giving, evidence against friends, acquaintances, and one-time comrades, he was 'hardly likely to scruple at committing perjury in order to secure the ends which he sought'; immunity from prosecution and a new identity and job outside Northern Ireland.[32] A man anxious to purchase immunity may attempt to curry favour with those in a position to secure such immunity for him, and in the light of Bennett's character and situation, Lord Lowry said, this was 'an obvious danger'.[33]

Possible Support for Bennett's Credibility

Having considered those matters which militated against Bennett's credibility, the trial judge had turned to those offences where clear, independent, and unchallenged evidence existed concerning some of the crimes alleged to have been committed. These were the Burns murder, the Lakeglen bombing, and the Clyde Street bombing. He had found, quite rightly, Lord Lowry said, that Bennett's evidence had tallied in all substantial respects with the independent evidence relating to these incidents and had concluded that this provided 'the best, though not the only, test of Bennett's credibility'.[34] But, the Lord Chief Justice remarked

consistency in this respect was hardly a reliable foundation for any confident finding in favour of credibility, much less could it be deemed 'the best . . . test of Bennett's credibility' [since]—an accurate description of the crime merely strengthens the inference that the witness who gives the description took part; this is important only where the witness's participation is in issue.[35]

Mr Justice Murray had then gone on to consider six other pieces of evidence which, in his view, tended to support Bennett's general credibility: (1) Wilson's alleged oral admission to the police: 'We could sit for six or seven days and I'll still not tell my part'; (2) the evidence which tended to corroborate Bennett's evidence that Halli-

---

[31] *R.* v. *Graham* (1984) 18 NIJB 7.   [32] Ibid. 8.   [33] Ibid. 9.
[34] Ibid.   [35] Ibid.

day had been involved in the Clyde Street bombing, and supportive evidence that Large had also been involved; (3) Evans's alleged oral admission to the police, with respect to the Clyde Street bombing: 'I control the teams; I control the gear'; (4) the supportive evidence that Bennett and John Irvine had gone to Amsterdam together; (5) Bingham's alleged admission to Bennett that he had bought a distinctive weapon in the United States and the fact that such a weapon had been found in Doherty's house; (6) Pritchard's arrest in possession of a large sum of US dollars, and Bingham's alleged admission to Bennett concerning an arms-buying trip to the United States.

Lord Lowry held that the out-of-court statements allegedly made by Wilson and Evans were admissible only against these defendants,[36] while the 'Doherty arms cache' and the arrest of Pritchard did not implicate Bingham or any of the other defendants, and could not be regarded as a crucial test of Bennett's general credibility. The evidence concerning Halliday and Large provided some corroboration of Bennett's evidence against each of them, but that concerning John Irvine's trip to Amsterdam was, at best, of doubtful support. Therefore, even if independent evidence against one defendant was capable of providing support for the general credibility of an accomplice in a multi-defendant trial, two of the trial judge's six examples were entirely inadmissible, and two more ineffective, to provide that general support.[37] The Lord Chief Justice concluded, therefore

that the learned trial judge might well not, indeed probably would not, have accorded to Bennett's credibility the necessary degree of acceptance, if he had considered that only two, and not six, of the specified items of evidence could be relied on ... It appears to us entirely unacceptable to characterise the evidence noted in items (2) and (4) as providing a 'crucial test'. Inconsistency is a most important factor, but consistency with independent evidence on one incident, whatever the admissibility of the material considered, is by no means a crucial test of the credibility of a witness's evidence on other incidents involving different accused persons.[38]

[36] *R.* v. *Daniel and Waton* [1973] Crim L. R. 627.

[37] Mr Justice Hutton held that, in principle, independent evidence which supported the accomplice evidence in relation to one or more defendant could bolster the accomplice's general credibility against all the accused, but Lord Justice O'Donnell was more doubtful.

[38] *R.* v. *Graham* (1984) 18 NIJB 5.

Eight Propositions

For the purposes of the present appeal, Lord Lowry continued, it was unnecessary to decide upon the relevance and admissibility for general purposes of the evidence in items (2) and (4) against Halliday, Large, and Irvine. Eight propositions relevant to the appeal in general were, however, reasonably clear: (1) the ultimate question for decision was how far, in a joint trial of more than one accused, the credibility of a witness's evidence against one, or several, defendants could be judged by reference to other evidence by the same witness, or by reference to the evidence of other witnesses (the same was true in trials of single defendants on more than one charge); (2) everything relevant which can logically enhance or detract from credibility is prima facie admissible; (3) where the accused were tried separately, much that would otherwise be admissible would be excluded from evidence because it was collateral (but this left open the question of how such evidence, which was admitted against one accused, should be treated in a joint trial); (4) oral and written statements by any given defendant are inadmissible for any purpose against other defendants; (5) corroboration against any given defendant is not corroboration against any other; (6) independent evidence which contradicts a Crown witness, even on an irrelevant point, has much more probative value against the Crown than evidence which supports the witness could have in its favour; (7) the way in which the witness gives his evidence against any one defendant is relevant to his general credibility in relation to all the defendants, although not decisive; and (8) in particular, points of evidence which militate against a Crown witnesses' credibility inure for the benefit of every defendant affected by that witnesses' evidence, and failure to discredit a witness, not least when cross-examination is directed to an irrelevant point, must to some extent help his credibility.

The Relevance of the Defendants' Refusal to Give Evidence

Mr Justice Murray had pointed out that the defendants had the right not to give evidence but that as far as Bennett's credibility was concerned, it was 'extremely important' that his evidence had gone uncontradicted.[39] According to *R. v. Sparrow*,[40] the Lord

---

[39] *R. v. Graham* (1984) 18 NIJB 18.
[40] (1973) 57 Cr App R 352.

Chief Justice said, in a case like this, where the finger is pointed directly at the defendants, a judge was entitled, 'indeed bound' to take account of the fact that the evidence against the defendants had not been challenged. The trial judge had indicated that he guarded himself against concluding that because the defendants had not gone into the witness-box, they must be presumed guilty. The Lord Chief Justice stated that the cases of *Mutch*[41] and *Sparrow*

show that, in order to justify an adverse inference by the tribunal of fact, on the failure of an accused to give evidence, there require to be uncontested or clearly established facts which point so strongly to guilt as to call for an explanation.[42]

But this was not the case here. Whatever *Sparrow* might have been able to justify with respect to Evans, Halliday, and Large, even they had been prejudiced, Lord Lowry said, since Bennett had been endowed with extra credibility against them also by the failure of the others to testify. *Sparrow* was not an authority for using a defendant's failure to give evidence as a test of whether a Crown witness *could* be believed, as opposed to the final question, *was* he to be believed. It was difficult to accept, Lord Lowry added, that when the credibility of a 'suspect witness' was completely put in evidence by the defence, the prosecution evidence could ever be so compelling as to require the defendants to testify under pain of certain prejudice.

Disclosure of Inducements

One of the appellants' grounds of appeal concerned the trial judge's ability to evaluate the inducements offered to Bennett in return for his testimony when the Crown had not made adequate disclosures about them. Lord Lowry said that it was not necessary to consider this issue in order to decide the appeal but that it was worthy of comment in its own right. In assessing Bennett's credibility, Mr Justice Murray had given full weight to the potential effect of the help which the Crown could grant or withhold, and if the appeal had depended upon this point, it would have failed. He recommended that the practice which had developed since then, by which the Crown informed the defence as precisely as possible of

---

[41] (1973) 57 Cr App R 196.
[42] *R.* v. *Graham* (1984) 18 NIJB 19.

the arrangements made with the informer witness, and the benefits
which he could expect, ought to continue and that both Crown and
courts should regard it as a duty.

The Verdict

Lord Lowry held that the convictions should be quashed on the
grounds that they were unsafe and unsatisfactory because in testing
Bennett's credibility the trial judge had applied three tests which
were unacceptable in law and logic. First, he had considered that
the independent evidence concerning the details of some of the
charges provided the best test of Bennett's credibility, when in fact
the consistency between Bennett's testimony and the independent
evidence did nothing to implicate any particular defendant. Secondly, two of the six pieces of evidence which he regarded as
supplying a crucial test of Bennett's evidence were inadmissible
except against the accused who made them, two others were logically unacceptable for any purpose, and the remaining two could
only provide a crucial or important test against the particular
accused involved in the incidents to which they related. Thirdly,
in the circumstances of the case, the trial judge had attached
unwarranted significance to the failure of the accused to give
evidence.

Lord Lowry said that the court had given serious consideration
to whether any of the membership charges should be allowed to
stand, since it was probable that many of the accused were members, indeed prominent members, of the UVF. But it had decided
that these convictions had to fall with the rest because, with the
exception of Evans, the sole evidence of membership was Bennett's evidence; but since Evans had already been in custody
long enough, the interests of justice did not require a new trial
in his case. Although the case against Halliday raised 'deep suspicion', a fresh trial, as in the case of any of the defendants,
would not have been appropriate, because it would have involved
Bennett testifying again and would have given the Crown a second
opportunity to negotiate the hazards of cross-examination on his
credibility.

Concluding his judgment, Lord Lowry affirmed that nothing
about the witness or his background necessarily precluded a 'favourable finding' as a matter of law but that the trial judge had applied
'faulty criteria' to evidence which experience showed to be, and

legal principle regarded as, dangerous.[43] However, his lordship emphasized that the evidence of 'a largely uncorroborated accomplice of bad character who has a great deal to gain by giving evidence can still be accepted'.[44]

CONCLUSION

Those who defended the supergrass system regarded the decisions considered in this chapter as further proof that supergrass evidence was being properly scrutinized by an impartial judiciary. However, some must have begun to wonder whether the supergrass system could continue to be justified if a few convictions eventually quashed on appeal was the best it could deliver. Conspiracy theorists regarded the Gilmour case as a further attempt by the judiciary to improve the quality of the prosecution case presented to the courts; Martin McGuiness of Sinn Fein, for example, described it as 'an elaborate attempt by the North's Orange judiciary to try to show the impartiality of British justice while, in effect, shoring up the whole paid perjurer strategy'.[45] Some predicted that ultimately all convictions obtained on the evidence of loyalist supergrasses would be quashed, while those obtained in republican cases would be confirmed on appeal. Civil libertarians tended to reserve judgement about the ultimate outcome of the supergrass system but saw these decisions as grounds for optimism that its days were numbered.

The Gilmour case had a number of unusual features. First, the fact that Gilmour, like Grimley, had been a police spy, did not bode well for the prosecution. Police agents, particularly in a terrorist organization, are obliged to play contradictory roles, and this can create difficulties in any testimony which they give in court. But, if Grimley and Gilmour are anything to go by, they also seem to suffer from severe character-flaws, which decrease further the chances of a good performance in the witness-box. As was the case with Grimley, one of Gilmour's fatal blunders was his allegation, whether true or not, that the police had declined to respond to his warnings about impending terrorist incidents. As Mr Desmond Boal QC defending said, there were only two possible

[43] *R. v. Graham* (1984) 18 NIJB 23.
[44] Ibid.
[45] *Belfast Telegraph*, 19 Dec. 1984.

explanations for this assertion: either Gilmour had been lying about giving the necessary information to the police, or the police were 'anti-social, ill-intentioned, destructive lunatics'. Clearly, most courts would be reluctant to accept the latter.

What the Quigley and Gilmour trials and the decision in the Bennett appeal showed above all else, however, was that judges in Northern Ireland could not agree on how to handle supergrass evidence, even when corroborated. It was also clear that the major inconsistencies between the cases heard up to this point would have to be resolved if the judicial system was to make a credible claim to a modicum of coherence. The Northern Ireland Court of Appeal's decision in *R.* v. *Graham* thus began the construction of a new judicial consensus around the proposition that to justify convictions in the Diplock courts, supergrass evidence had to be of such a high standard that it is doubtful if any flesh-and-blood supergrass can attain it. However, as the next chapter will show, there were some final ups and downs before this process was completed.

7

Final Ups And Downs: 1985

ALTHOUGH 1984 had ended with the supergrass system apparently in serious decline, 1985 closed with a partial resurgence. The year began disastrously for the authorities, with the almost complete failure of the loyalist Crockard and Allen trials, but in December all twenty-seven republican defendants charged on the evidence of Harry Kirkpatrick were convicted. However, as things turned out, this proved to be little more than the last flickers from a dying fire, since by the end of the following year all the uncorroborated convictions in every supergrass case, including that of Kirkpatrick, had been overturned on appeal.

Other developments in 1985 included the arrest, in Newry on 7 March, of seventeen men, implicated by former customs officer Eamon Collins. But within a fortnight Collins had retracted his statements and seven of the twelve who had by then been charged on his evidence were released. In the same month, UVF supergrass John Gibson decided to withdraw his evidence, a move which led to the dropping of charges against some thirty-five suspects; and ex-RAF pilot Owen Connolly turned Queen's evidence against two alleged accomplices in the IRA murder of deputy prison governor William McConnell in 1984. However, since he only implicated two defendants in a single incident, Connolly was more of a run-of-the-mill accomplice witness and not a true 'supergrass' at all. On 11 November 1986 his evidence was rejected by Lord Justice Gibson, and those he had implicated were acquitted. In October 1985 the information provided by Angela Whorisky, the last supergrass in the supergrass system, led to charges being brought against nineteen accused. But, on 15 October 1986, for reasons which have not been made clear, the DPP for Northern Ireland announced that they would not be prosecuted. In May 1985 an opinion poll carried out by Ulster Marketing Surveys for the BBC Northern Ireland current affairs programme Spotlight showed that, by this stage, only 26 per cent of Protestants and a mere 6 per cent of

Catholics supported the supergrass system.[1] In the course of the year, 'shoot to kill' incidents claimed five lives.[2]

THE CROCKARD CASE: *R. v. Sayers and others*

The Background

James Crockard was born in Belfast in 1953 and left school at the age of 13. Not long afterwards he was tried for a minor offence and was sent to Malone Training School, where he proved to be an unruly inmate and was soon transferred to another institution in Scotland. He reoffended following his release and was sent to borstal, where, at one time, he was classified as 'incorrigible'. According to Mr Justice MacDermott, who presided over the trial of those charged on his evidence, Crockard's 'appalling' criminal record revealed 'a virtual lifetime of crime'.[3] He was employed in a variety of jobs, but at the time of *R. v. Sayers and others*, he was described by the judge as a 'general dealer'. He admitted that from time to time he had helped himself to odds and ends around building sites or derelict premises.

In 1974 Crockard became involved with the UVF. Prior to joining, he scouted the bombing of the largely student pub, the Club Bar, on University Road, Belfast, in July 1974, and was sworn in as a member that August. Having been de-proscribed on 23 May 1974, the UVF enjoyed a brief period of legality, which ended on 4 October 1975 when it was re-proscribed. Although he lived in Fortuna Street off the Donegal Road, Crockard was attached to the UVF's A3 Platoon in the Shankill, and he claimed that in 1975 the defendant Sayers recruited him into the 'Provost Squad', a unit which performed a disciplinary function. But when counsel for the defence at the trial put it to him that Sayers had been in prison from 3 March 1972 to 26 April 1976, Crockard changed the date of his alleged induction to 'about 1976'. As a member of the Provost Squad, Crockard admitted to having taken part in four punishment kneecappings and a number of beatings.

---

[1] *Belfast Telegraph*, 13 May 1985.

[2] A. Jennings, 'Shoot to Kill: The Final Courts of Justice', in id. (ed.), *Justice under Fire: The Abuse of Civil Liberties in Northern Ireland*, 2nd edn. (London: Pluto Press, 1990).

[3] *R. v. Sayers* (1985) (unpub.), 9.

Like the testimonies of other supergrasses, Crockard's evidence indicated that loyalist paramilitary activities in Northern Ireland consisted of a combination of incompetence, cavalier casualness towards serious violence, and chillingly successful killings. The bomb at the Club Bar, for example, had been planted on 11 July 1974 but failed to go off and had to be re-primed, exploding two days later. On 1 January 1976 Crockard and three companions travelling in a hijacked car sprayed machine-gun and revolver bullets at six people standing at a bus-stop in the nationalist Ardoyne area of Belfast in order, according to Crockard, to test a home-made Sterling sub-machine-gun. Crockard told the court that the intended victims had not been singled out and that he and his colleagues would have considered, as a legitimate target, anyone in that neighbourhood 'who happened to be walking about'.[4] In the event the gun jammed shortly after the gunman opened fire, no one was injured, and an army patrol fired on the vehicle as it sped away. Crockard and others also attempted to booby-trap the car of Ardoyne republican Martin Meehan three times but without success, and the string of botched operations included two abortive armed raids on post offices. On one occasion the alarm went off before the robbers could seize the money, and on the other, the raid had to be hastily abandoned when the police arrived on the scene just as the gang pulled up in their car outside. Successful armed robberies were, however, carried out at the Maple Leaf Club and at Belfast Gas, and, on 21 January 1983, ten days before his arrest, Crockard was involved in a 'homer'—a robbery carried out by members of the UVF for private gain.

Crockard was arrested on 2 February 1983 in connection with another 'homer', the attempted robbery of Portland Jeweller's in Portland Avenue, Newtownabbey, in which Crockard's brother, Brian, and a man called Graham (not the defendant John Graham) were caught red-handed. For two days he remained silent under sustained interrogation when 'all the evidence pointed to his guilt',[5] later describing this reaction as 'instinctive'.[6] However, on the morning of his third day in custody Crockard made a statement admitting that he had organized the robbery and had driven the

[4] *Belfast Telegraph*, 21 Jan. 1985.
[5] *R.* v. *Sayers* (1985) (unpub.), 9.
[6] Ibid.

getaway car. Throughout his evidence at the trial of Sayers and others, Crockard claimed that he had made his initial confession as a result of an inducement from the police that his wife, who had also been arrested, would be released. Mr Justice MacDermott said that 'this part of Crockard's testimony always seemed unconvincing',[7] and, having heard testimony from the police, he concluded that it was in fact 'false lying testimony'.[8]

It had been put to Crockard by the defence that he had offered 'to do a Bennett', and, in Mr Justice MacDermott's view, Crockard was 'rather evasive about this'.[9] Crockard claimed that he did not recall having mentioned Bennett at all but admitted that it was possible that he might have. Mr Justice MacDermott was convinced by the evidence of a detective sergeant that, on the way back to his cell after having made his confession statement, he said: 'I could make Bennett seem like a wee boy.'[10] Crockard accepted that he was hoping to receive immunity from prosecution but stated that the police had told him they could make no promises; the question of immunity, he said, had then been discussed in a general way. 'It was explained to me that I would have to relate my past crimes', Crockard said, but 'there was no mention of numbers of people. I realised because I was naming the crimes I had committed, at the end of the day I was also giving the names of the people involved with me.'[11] It was put to Crockard by the defence that: 'before you made the first of your statements, your objective was to get freedom, a house and money'. Crockard replied that he was not interested in a house or money and only wanted to get 'back on to the street'.[12]

On 6 and 7 February Crockard made a large number of statements under caution, revealing, according to the judge, 'all his inherent dealing instincts—and especially a readiness to make the best of a very bad situation—a very long period in prison'.[13] On the evening of 8 February Crockard was informed that, as he had been involved in two murders, he would not be granted immunity, and he was then charged and lodged in the 'supergrass' annex of Crumlin Road prison. At one time Crockard weighed 22 stone and

---

[7]   *R.* v. *Sayers* (1985) (unpub.), 10.   [8] Ibid.   [9] Ibid.
[10] Ibid.   [11] *Belfast Telegraph*, 30 Jan. 1985.   [12] Ibid.
[13] *R.* v. *Sayers* (1985) (unpub.), 11.

was 'not loath to throw his weight about',[14] and while in prison awaiting the trial of Sayers and others he was disciplined twice by the prison governor. On one occasion he claimed he had struck another prisoner in self-defence, and on the other he said he was 'in the wrong place at the wrong time'.[15]

In September 1983 Crockard was tried and convicted on forty charges, including the sectarian murders of Carl McParland and Gabriel Wiggins (in which he claimed to have been the driver), three attempted murders, five conspiracies to murder, arms possession, armed robbery, causing explosions, and membership of the UVF. He received two life sentences, plus a number of other prison terms, and on 28 January 1984 he returned to court, where he was convicted of a number of further offences, including an attempt to murder six people at the bus-stop in Ardoyne, armed robbery of a butcher's shop, three conspiracies to rob, and possession of arms. For these further offences he received prison sentences of sixteen, twelve, and ten years. But in the went he was to serve only eight years in all.[16]

The Trial

It was rumoured that Crockard had implicated over 100 suspects, but, on the basis of statements which he made to the police, twenty-eight men and a woman were arrested and eventually charged with UVF activities. One of them was Crockard's brother, Isaac, allegedly his accomplice in the armed robbery of a post office in 1974. The indictment in the trial of Sayers and others, which began on 29 November 1984 and ended on 22 February 1985, contained a total of ninety-two counts arising out of twenty-four events relating to the activities of the UVF over almost a decade, from July 1974 to January 1983 and included murders, attempted murders, conspiracies to murder, causing explosions, possession of firearms and explosives, kidnapping, robbery, and membership of the UVF. Crockard claimed that Sayers, Nelson, and Graham, veterans of the Bennett proceedings, were his officers in the UVF, and that Graham had held the rank of Brigade Officer. Of the twenty-nine accused, seven (William Norman Mc-Clelland, William McFarland, Stephen McIlwrath, Robert Riddell

---

[14] Ibid. 9.
[15] *Irish News*, 2 Feb. 1985.
[16] See Ch. 11.

Harvey, Georgina Martta Nelson, John Kelly Hanna, and Walter McMurray Simms) made written statements the admissibility of which was not challenged, and two other defendants, William Kerr and Samuel Robert McCorkindale, made limited verbal admissions of membership of the UVF. Apart from this there was no corroboration of Crockard's evidence against the accused, and, as the judge said, these statements provided corroboration only against those who had made them. As in other supergrass trials, the preliminary inquiry in the Crockard case was marked by disturbances in the public gallery. The trial proper overlapped with the Gilmour case, which ran concurrently in another court-room and because a number of senior counsel were involved in both trials, twenty-six of the defendants briefly dismissed their lawyers on the grounds that their right to a fair trial had been compromised through their not being able to engage the lawyer of their choice. Legal representation was, however, soon restored.

Mr Justice MacDermott attempted to sum up Crockard's character in the following terms. He had 'street sense' and was 'shrewd, tough, able to look after himself, ready to aid an organisation proscribed because it was prepared to pursue its ends by vicious violence and preying on the population by endless robberies',[17] and, at the time of his arrest, he was a 'dishonest criminal who showed by his actions every inclination of so continuing'.[18] In cross-examination Crockard accepted that he had been a dishonest person in the past and that although he had a record of dishonesty, he was not an evil person. But the judge said he was 'a person of bad character, with a strong motive for giving evidence against his one-time friends and a man who will lie if and when occasion demands'.[19] He also stated that although the legal authorities seemed ambivalent on the question of whether a witness's character or his evidence was the important consideration, he took the view that it was a person's evidence which was important but that character had to be examined in order to see if the credibility of the evidence which had been given had been affected by it. It was 'an elementary fact of life', he maintained, that a person of bad character could give truthful and reliable evidence, and also that a person of exemplary character might give false or mistaken evi-

---

[17] *R*. v. *Sayers* (1985) (unpub.), 9.
[18] Ibid.
[19] Ibid. 15.

dence.[20] Crockard's bad character was, therefore, an important but not a determining factor in considering the credibility of his evidence.

During cross-examination Crockard had given two principal reasons for testifying at the trial of *R. v. Sayers*. First, claiming to be aware of his own poor past record, he said he wanted to clear his conscience, and maintained he had been seeking to mend his ways since about 1977. But when asked why he had participated in murders in 1979 and 1980, he replied that he had been acting under orders and had not had the courage to say no. 'Good intentions sometimes go astray,' he added.[21] Secondly, he said that he hoped his services would be recognized by the authorities in repayment of his debt to society and that he would be released at an earlier date than otherwise would have been the case; but he qualified this by saying that he believed his attitude to the authorities and his behaviour in prison were of equal importance. He told the court that he hoped to get out of prison at the earliest opportunity and that he had been given some privileges which had not been accorded other prisoners, such as having a television in his cell.

Crockard's first reason stretched credulity 'beyond any acceptable limit', Mr Justice MacDermott held, since the murders in which he had been involved, and his other criminal activities, were not 'the actions of a man seeking to climb out of the pit of crime and terrorism'. At times Crockard appeared anxious to water down 'this second, and in my view real reason' for his decision to turn Queen's evidence, by suggesting that everything really depended upon his behaviour in prison. But given that he had been disciplined by the prison governor twice since his first remand, this appeared to be 'a specious reason', which indicated 'that even in prison his ingrained characteristics of aggressive and anti-social behaviour lie shallow below his normal pattern of behaviour'.[22] Crockard's sole reason for giving evidence, the judge concluded, was his hope of securing early release,[23] and, the early release of O'Doherty, the informer who turned Queen's evidence in the case against RUC officer Charles McCormick, would justify such a hope, Mr Justice MacDermott added.[24]

[20] Ibid. 8.
[21] *Belfast Telegraph*, 29 Jan. 1985.
[22] *R. v. Sayers* (1985) (unpub.), 11.
[23] Ibid. 12.
[24] Ibid. 8.

Crockard admitted to having told one lie in the course of his evidence. At the preliminary inquiry he had said that, although he had had his caution statements, witness statements, and his own preliminary inquiry papers in his prison cell, he had not read them since the Saturday night prior to the beginning of the preliminary inquiry in June 1984. He later admitted that during the preliminary inquiry he had in fact reread one of his statements and that this had revealed an error about the weapons used in a murder. He told the Resident Magistrate the next day that he wanted to set the record straight, but 'the ingratiating way' in which he accepted that this was a lie 'was indicative', Mr Justice MacDermott said, 'of an anxiety to please, perhaps impress, the judge'.[25] While this particular issue was relatively trivial, Mr Justice McDermott said, it raised the important question: was Crockard's evidence a careful repetition of his thoroughly read statements, or was he trying to visualize and recall the events as they happened? Sometimes Crockard had given the impression that he was remembering a script—for example, in his account of the Wiggins murder—whereas on other occasions he did not convey this impression at all—for example, in his evidence about a bomb-planting episode in Alliance Avenue, which he had had to give twice because one of the accused had not been in court the first time. The judge's conclusion was that Crockard described events as he remembered them but that he probably had at least occasionally reread his documents since the previous June.

Crockard had also lied about the Club Bar bombing, the making of incendiaries for use in Ballycastle, and the shooting at the Ardoyne bus-stop, Mr Justice MacDermott said. As far as the Club Bar bombing was concerned, Crockard was unhappy about some aspect of his account of this incident, 'probably because it was untrue and he was constantly trying to foresee what Mr Boal's questions were leading to'.[26] The Ardoyne bus-stop shooting showed his performance as a witness at its lowest point. At first he had claimed to have been the driver, but later admitted that he had fired a .38 revolver, thus demonstrating the tendency, as counsel for the defence observed, when 'driven into a corner' for 'his "old vices" of deception and dishonesty' to take over.[27]

[25] *R. v. Sayers* (1985) (unpub.), 12–13.
[26] Ibid. 13.
[27] Ibid. 15.

Referring to a defence suggestion that one lie was enough to create 'a crack' in Crockard's credibility which would make it impossible to convict, Mr Justice MacDermott said that this 'overstated the position somewhat'. He observed that the expression 'a crack in his credibility' came from the judgment of Lord Justice Lawton in *R.* v. *Thorne*,[28] where it had been used to refer to evidence which had come to light since the jury had arrived at its verdict, and did not refer to defects in the accomplice's evidence which had been brought to the attention of the tribunal of fact at trial. The *Thorne* case also showed, Mr Justice MacDermott said, that a properly directed jury can convict upon the uncorroborated evidence of a villainous accomplice, although his evidence should first be examined with scrupulous care. Even a liar could be accepted as a credible witness, he added, since 'St Peter lied thrice but few would doubt that he could, if required, have given credible evidence.' But uncorroborated evidence in a case such as this had to be approached with 'extreme, but sensible, caution'.[29]

Although agreeing with the Crown's submission that 'in substance Crockard's factual account was accurate and reliable and that the inconsistencies were more consistent with truth than invention',[30] Mr Justice MacDermott stated that the issue at the end of the day was whether the Crown had proved beyond reasonable doubt that Crockard's partners in crime were the various accused he named. The great risk which a dishonest informer ran, the judge said, was that he could falsely associate certain people with crimes they had not committed, only to find that they had cast-iron alibis, and this would undermine his general credibility. But this prospect would be diminished, he added, where the charges were imprecise as to time and date, although only two of the twenty-four incidents in this case—the conspiracy to rob the Orangefield Post Office and the third attempt to murder Martin Meehan—fell into this category. It was clear, the judge said, that Crockard had 'perhaps understandably, difficulty in fixing past events accurately in time'.[31]

In his evidence to the court at the *Sayers* trial Crockard said that he had received no formal discharge from the UVF and that, as a result of having turned supergrass, the only other contact he was

[28] (1978) 66 Cr App R 6.
[29] *R.* v. *Sayers* (1985) (unpub.), 17.
[30] Ibid. 18.
[31] Ibid. 19.

likely to have with the organization would be if some of its members came to kill him. He told the court that it was strictly not possible to leave the UVF once one had joined, although some members drifted away by not attending meetings or leaving the area in which they used to live. During cross-examination Crockard also disclosed that his family was now living outside Northern Ireland and that their phone, electricity, and gas bills, and their travelling expenses when they came to visit him in prison, were being paid by the RUC. When asked if this was being done in order to keep him happy, so that he would continue to give evidence, he said that it might have been done to keep him happy but that he would have given evidence in any case. He told the court that he did not know if the police would continue to pay these bills when the trial ended.

The Verdict

Reaching his verdict, Mr Justice MacDermott said:

The burden of proof upon the Crown in any criminal case is a heavy one and my conclusion is that in this case Crockard's evidence has not measured up to that high standard. The corollary of that conclusion is <u>not</u> that I find that the substance of his evidence is false. Far from it—I think that it is at least probable that he has correctly identified the accused as being his partners in the serious crimes to which he, Crockard, pleaded guilty and which are the subjects of the charges before me. But these cases are not decided upon the balance of probabilities.[32]

Eight of the nine accused who had made statements were convicted. William Kerr, who was reported to have said that he had been in the UVF 'years ago' but had left when it became illegal, was acquitted, since there was insufficient evidence to convict him on the charge of being a member between the dates 31 October 1982 and 16 November 1983.[33] McIlwrath, Harvey, Hanna, Nelson, and McCorkindale walked free from the court, as their sentences were either recorded or suspended, and Walter Simms, convicted of robbery, had his sentence postponed. Of the remaining twenty-one defendants, seventeen others were set free, while the other four were detained on charges not connected with Crockard's allegations.

[32] *R.* v. *Sayers* (1985) (unpub.), 20 (emphasis in original).
[33] Ibid. 28.

THE ALLEN CASE: *R. v. Austin and others*

The Background

William 'Budgie' Allen, also known as William Reeves after his stepfather, was born on 25 August 1961 and grew up in the fiercely loyalist Shankill area of Belfast. He acquired the nickname 'Budgie' at primary school after the character played by Adam Faith in the television programme of the same name. But it assumed fresh significance in the trial of *R. v. Austin and others* because like a budgie, it was said, Allen was willing and able to repeat whatever he had been told.

In the late 1970s Allen became the commander of the Young Citizens' Volunteers, the youth wing of the UVF, where his responsibilities included taking other young members on firearms training-courses. He said that he had decided to join the UVF itself after having received a beating at the hands of the UDA in the Highfield area of Belfast, and maintained that in May 1978 the defendant Marchant had taken him to a short swearing-in ceremony in the Loyalist Club in Romford Street off the Shankill Road. He had been ushered into an upstairs lounge, where two hand-guns lay on a table covered in the Ulster and UVF flags and behind which stood two hooded men. The latter were called to attention when a man dressed in a black leather jacket, black face-mask, and beret with UVF badge came into the room. When asked by this man why he wanted to join the UVF, Allen replied that he wanted to fight republicanism, and confirmed that he would be prepared to carry out bombings, shootings, and robberies if required. Allen was then sworn into No. 2 Platoon of the UVF's 'A' Company, and a week later, he claimed, he was a member of the hooded colour party present when another new recruit was initiated. Allen soon found himself in trouble with his UVF superiors, and within his first twelve months he had been court-martialled three times. On the first occasion he was acquitted of having revealed the name of his commander whilst boasting to others about being a UVF member, but the second time he was found guilty of failing to report having been arrested while driving a vehicle which the UVF regarded as a 'staff car'. He received a beating as punishment and suffered a similar fate on the third occasion, when he admitted having talked outside UVF circles about his role in the attempted murder of Kevin Hannoway in December 1978. Allen admitted that, until his alleged conversion to Christianity in 1983, he had had little conscience, and had committed adultery without any qualms when his wife was pregnant and had signed on for social security benefit whilst working.[34]

Allen was arrested by the police in January 1983 in connection with a number of terrorist incidents. He admitted that he offered to turn Queen's evidence in the hope of being granted immunity from prosecution and was disappointed when he was told that he would have to stand trial himself. Although he was told by the police that 'no promises could be made' about his future, he said he had taken this to mean that his sentence would be reduced if things 'worked out alright'.[35] While the discussion about immunity was recorded in detail in the police notes, there was no mention of any possible reduction in sentence. Allen said that he found it difficult to understand why he had not been granted immunity, and he agreed with a defence suggestion that the absence of any record in the police notes that a reduced prison sentence had been discussed was also difficult to explain, and it was possible that the detectives had deliberately left it out. He acknowleged that his hope of securing an early release had been encouraged by learning, shortly before he had given his evidence in the preliminary inquiry, that Anthony O'Doherty, the IRA informer in the McCormick case, had been given an early date for release. Apart from O'Doherty and Kirkpatrick, Allen was the only inmate in the 'supergrass annex' of Crumlin Road prison then serving a fixed sentence, and for the eight months prior to the *Austin* trial he shared a cell with Kirkpatrick, with whom he developed a friendship. But he denied that they had ever discussed their respective trials, whether they would receive a reduced sentence, or how they would testify.

On 9 April 1984 Allen pleaded guilty to fifty-two offences arising out of twenty-six incidents, including attempted murder, conspiracy to murder, possession of firearms and explosives, giving and receiving training in the use of firearms and explosives, robbery, and membership of the UVF. Gaoling him for fourteen years, Mr Justice MacDermott said:

You have been used and abused by older people who were prepared to make use of people like you who ought to have known better. You

---

[34] *Belfast Telegraph*, 17 May 1985.
[35] Ibid.

admitted being involved in 26 incidents. Your part was often of a peripheral nature. All that you have done cannot be excused in any way, and lawless terrorist activity is bound to attract severe, but nevertheless, proper punishment.[36]

However, in the event, Allen was to serve only two years of his sentence.[37]

As in several other supergrass trials, there were repeated disruptions in the court throughout the preliminary inquiry, and on one occasion scuffles broke out and the court was cleared as Allen, apparently in tears, was ushered out by his police minders. Towards the end of the proceedings a woman in the public gallery hurled a packet of birdseed as Allen signed the lengthy deposition of evidence. Other missiles swiftly followed and a pitched battle erupted during the course of which four police officers were slightly injured and four members of the public were arrested. Magistrate Mr Basil McIvor then decided to exclude the public altogether from the remainder of the hearings. All forty-six of those accused on 227 charges on Allen's evidence were returned for trial, half being released on bail and half remanded in custody, and on 26 March 1984 some of these defendants, together with others in the Gibson and Crockard cases, dismissed their lawyers, claiming that they had no expectation of a fair hearing. On 15 February 1985 it was disclosed at a pre-trial hearing that, for administrative reasons, the proceedings against the forty-six accused on Allen's evidence would be divided into three separate trials.

The Trial

Twenty-five accused, some of whom had been in custody for over two years and who faced a total of 107 charges, went on trial on 20 March 1985 in *R.* v. *Austin and others*, the second of the three trials planned on Allen's evidence.[38] On 28 March 1985 all twenty-five

---

[36] *Irish News*, 10 Apr. 1984.

[37] See Ch. 11.

[38] The first trial, which began on 26 Feb. 1985, involved only 2 defendants— William Cowan and Robert Grainger—who faced a total of 62 charges, including the sectarian murder of a milkman, conspiracy to murder, UVF membership, possession of firearms, and receiving training in the use of firearms. Cowan was also accused of 2 other sectarian murders, and of conspiring to murder in revenge for the death of Lennie Murphy, the notorious Shankill Butcher responsible for the torture and sectarian murder of a number of Catholics. Grainger also faced charges of armed robbery. Both originally denied the charges, but on 14 Mar. 1985 Grainger

defendants dismissed their barristers because the trial judge, Mr Justice Higgins, was not prepared to grant an adjournment to enable Mr Desmond Boal QC, then appearing in the Kirkpatrick trial, which was running simultaneously, to be briefed for the defence. But by the end of April all the accused had reinstructed counsel, and, as things turned out, Mr Boal was able to join the defence team at the beginning of May. None of the defendants elected to give evidence.

When he began his evidence-in-chief, Allen appeared nervous and flustered, was unable to remember the age of his two-year old daughter, and at first claimed he joined the UVF in 1977 but then said it had in fact been in May 1978. The more serious of the accusations which Allen made included the following. He said that he had suggested that the UVF should murder a Catholic in November 1982 in revenge for the killing of Lennie Murphy, and that he had proposed that the gang should also mutilate the body, as Murphy had done with his victims, in order to show that although Murphy was dead, 'they had not killed the Shankill Butcher'. Allen told the court that, in pursuit of this plan, he had hijacked a taxi and had held the driver prisoner while three of the defendants had taken the vehicle to look for a victim. But the plot was abandoned when two intended victims who had been abducted managed to escape, and the murder gang refrained from giving chase in case they were seen. Had the murder attempt been successful, Allen said, it would have been claimed by the Protestant Action Force. Allen also admitted having opened fire from a hijacked car on a group of men on the Falls Road between July and September 1979 and, in his statement to the police about this incident, claimed that since the intended victim had not been present, he had deliberately aimed high in order to avoid hitting anyone.

changed his plea to guilty. Allen was not called to give evidence against either defendant, but each had made confessions to the police. Cowan was found guilty on 30 Apr. 1985, receiving a double life-sentence plus a concurrent term of 15 years. The judge, Lord Justice O'Donnell, said that he accepted Cowan's claim that he made his statements in the hope of becoming a supergrass and that the police had discussed this possibility with him. But it was clear, he concluded, that no promises had been made nor any deal struck. Even though Cowan's confession had been induced, the judge felt that this was not a case where the exercise of the judicial discretion to exclude a confession was warranted. Grainger received a twelve-year sentence for conspiring to murder, with concurrent terms ranging from 2 to 10 years. This included a seven-year sentence for UVF membership.

Allen also maintained that he had been involved in a plot to kill supporters of the republican hunger-strike camped around a bonfire in the Markets area of Belfast in October/November 1980 and that a machine-gun had been test-fired for the occasion but that when the gunman arrived, it was discovered that the bonfire had been abandoned. On another occasion Allen said he supplied the gun which was used to kill Mr John Hardy on 28 August 1979 and that, in November 1980, he had been assigned to murder a Catholic employee at Cliftonville Service Station in North Belfast whom the UVF believed to be an anti-H-blocks campaigner and member of the IRA. However, Allen maintained he had backed out of the operation, another man had been given the job, and the plan was abandoned when the hijacked car containing a sawn-off shotgun was found by the police. Allen also claimed to have supplied the sugar to make bombs and to have been present when it had been mixed with other ingredients and packed into five gas-cylinders intended for the Sinn Fein headquarters in Belfast and for other targets, including a chapel in Ardoyne.

Describing his involvement in the kneecapping of a friend and one of the accused, Robert Robinson, who was engaged to marry his sister, Allen claimed that initially the punishment had to be postponed because at the appointed time Lennie Murphy and another man had been too drunk to administer it. But the shooting had eventually been carried out by John Tweedie and Robert Spence, on the instructions of Lennie Murphy and of James Irvine, whom Allen described as provost marshal of the UVF. Allen at an Orange hall in Ballymena, followed by firearms practice at a farm, and that on another occasion he had attended a bomb-making lecture given by Norman Sayers, whom he described as commander of 'A' Company of the UVF, and Samuel Austin, whom he described as his platoon commander. Allen also maintained that after the shooting the gunman had told him that the original victim had not been at home when they called so they shot the man next door instead, on the grounds that he was a member of the IRA as well. The court was also told of UVF gun lectures which Allen alleged took place almost every week, and of an RUC man, known as 'Blinker' who was also said to have been involved in firearms training at New Mossley outside Belfast.

Asked by Mr Boal if he could give the court any proof that he was telling the truth in his testimony, Allen replied that he was prepared to give evidence against his former associates but beyond this the court had no way of knowing whether he was telling the truth or not. He also admitted that he had had no qualms about the Murphy revenge-murder plan when he suggested it but that, within a few weeks, when under arrest, he had told the police that he wanted to leave the UVF because he did not want to be involved in anything which could result in someone's death. Allen claimed that he made his original confessions for 'practical' rather than 'moral' reasons, namely to get out of the UVF.[39] He admitted, as already indicated, that he hoped to receive a reduction in his prison sentence in return for giving evidence, but he denied that he believed his helpfulness to the authorities would be measured by the number of people he put away. He said that when he thought about receiving immunity from prosecution he did not believe that it depended upon naming as many people as possible, even though, on the surface, this would appear to be a normal consideration. Allen also denied that there had been any discussion about his being paid for his services, although he said he thought he might be given some money for resettlement when he got out of prison but did not know for sure. He said he recognized that when he was released he would have to leave Northern Ireland and that, without some financial assistance in establishing a new identity, his life would be in danger. But he maintained he had not specifically asked about the prospective financial arrangements following his release, because he did not want people to think he was giving evidence just for the money.

Over the two-year period when Allen was in prison awaiting his appearance in the *Austin* trial, he claimed he was visited by the police about 100 times, most of these visits being social calls and some lasting an hour or more. He said he had become friends, and was on first-name terms with, a detective constable and a chief inspector. When asked if he would be prepared to conceal information the disclosure of which would be disadvantageous to a friend, he replied that it would depend upon the circumstances, but that he would not conceal anything from the court. He said that he did not believe his police friendship had been contrived to 'keep him

---

[39] *Irish News*, 18 May 1985.

sweet' in preparation for the series of trials in which he was to be the key witness. The defence suggested that Allen's relationship with the two police officers was improper and likely to have a distorting and corrupting influence upon the evidence which he gave in court, because a person who considered himself a friend of certain police officers was more likely to give the kind of evidence which he believed they wanted the court to hear.

Allen also admitted to being a liar. He accepted that, when arrested on a hijacking charge, he had lied to the police a number of times, and that he would have been prepared to perjure himself in court at his trial in 1980 if it had been necessary. But he denied that he was prepared to use the courts to suit his own ends, and when he was asked if he considered himself to be an experienced and accomplished liar, at first he replied 'no', and then 'probably'. He admitted that he had tried to present himself to the police as a pathetic character in order to produce a sympathetic reaction, and that he used tears and laughter on different occasions in an attempt to deceive the police about his involvement in crime. For example, when interviewed by the RUC in October 1982 about his involvement in the kneecapping of Robert Robinson, one of the *Austin* defendants, Allen laughed and told the officers that Robinson was one of his friends and that he could never have any intention of shooting him. Mr Boal put it to Allen that he had play-acted in order to convince the police that he was telling the truth, and Allen accepted that on occasions he had mixed fact with fiction in order to convince the police that what he was saying was true.

The Verdict

On 5 July 1985 Mr Justice Higgins rejected Allen's evidence as 'seriously flawed and unworthy of belief' and acquitted all but five defendants who had made statements to the police.[40] These were: John Dillon (charged with having acted as the driver of the motorcycle which took a gunman to murder John Hardy—the next-door neighbour of the intended murder victim—in August 1979, possession of the murder weapon, and membership of the UVF); James Greer (possession of a firearm on the day of the Hardy murder, possession of firearms on another occasion, and membership of the UVF); William Hunter (conspiring to murder hunger-strike protest-

---

[40] *Belfast Telegraph*, 5 July 1985.

ers in the Markets area of Belfast between September 1979 and August 1981, conspiring to wound, and membership of the UVF); Robert Spence, nephew of former UVF commander Gusty Spence (malicious wounding, UVF membership, and firearms offences); and John Tweedie (malicious wounding, possession of firearms with intent, and membership of the UVF). Following this débâcle, Allen did not appear in the third intended trial, and it is difficult to trace the nineteen defendants who were to have been prosecuted in these proceedings. Most were probably released, but some may have been tried independently on confessions.

THE KIRKPATRICK CASE: *R. v. Steenson and others*

The Background
Henry, alias 'Harry', Kirkpatrick, was born on 28 April 1957 in the Lower Falls, the son of a Catholic mother and of a Protestant father who converted to Catholicism, and the eldest of four children, the rest of whom were girls. The Kirkpatricks moved to the Ardoyne district, where, in 1969, their home was burned by loyalists an event which initiated an unsettled period in the family's fortunes. Kirkpatrick's mother ran off with her boss in 1969, and, after having lived at several different addresses, Kirkpatrick and his father ended up in Housing Trust accommodation in Belfast's staunchly republican Ballymurphy estate. Kirkpatrick's employment record was brief. He had a job for a period with Belfast Laundry but left because it was in an area considered unsafe for Catholics. He was also employed by Enterprise Ulster for a couple of months and worked for a time as a barman in the Whitefort Inn but gave this up because he found the hours uncongenial.

In 1970, at the age of 13, Kirkpatrick joined the Fianna, the junior branch of the Official IRA, acting as look-out during operations, collecting low-grade intelligence, attending meetings and lectures, selling republican papers, and collecting funds. He graduated to the Official IRA itself four years later but soon left to join the Irish Republican Socialist Party when the Official IRA declared a cease-fire in 1974. From the IRSP he found his way into the People's Liberation Army, the military wing of the Republican Socialist movement. In 1975 Kirkpatrick was arrested and charged with possession of a sawn-off shotgun, and while awaiting trial on bail he took part in a PLA armed robbery of the Northern Bank in

Andersonstown. He was convicted both on the original possession charge and for armed robbery and received concurrent prison sentences of two and nine years, of which he served six. In the trial of Steenson and others Kirkpatrick admitted that his defence in each of these cases was a tissue of lies and had involved an unfounded challenge to the admissibility of his confession statement based on untrue allegations about police misconduct, and a false alibi backed up by false testimony which he himself had arranged. While in prison Kirkpatrick was sworn into the Irish National Liberation Army, which had by this time replaced the People's Liberation Army as the military wing of the IRSP. He served part of his sentence in the Maze prison as an INLA compound quartermaster, becoming a close friend of Gerard Steenson, destined to become the INLA's second in command. On 17 October 1980 Kirkpatrick was released and went to live in the Twinbrook area of Belfast with his married sister, Michelle Dorian, whose husband, heartily disliked by Kirkpatrick, was in custody on remand. Keen to reinvolve himself in the INLA, Kirkpatrick approached Jackie Goodman at the IRSP offices in Belfast, but without result, and later he met Steenson again, who, he said, introduced himself as brigade operations officer of the INLA, and offered to take him on as an assistant brigade operations officer.

By his own admission, from this point until his arrest in February 1982, Kirkpatrick took part in half a dozen murders, attempted murders, bombings, hijackings, conspiracies, and robberies, and was unlawfully in possession of arms on numerous occasions. He also enjoyed apparently unlimited access to money, changing his car three times in one year, going on holiday to the United States with Steenson, and buying his mother an £850 bathroom suite. Clearly, much of the proceeds from the robberies had gone into his own pocket rather than into INLA coffers. In February 1981 Sean Flynn was ousted from his post as brigade officer commanding, and Kirkpatrick became brigade quartermaster and later, in August or September 1981, shortly before his marriage, brigade adjutant, second in command. In his evidence at the *Steenson* trial, Kirkpatrick claimed that this promotion tended to remove him somewhat from direct involvement with day-to-day INLA operations and that, although at the time he did not find this unwelcome, it marked the beginning of his growing disenchantment with the organization. Mr Justice Carswell, the presiding judge, said that he was 'somewhat sceptical . . . about this suggestion and inclined to doubt if there is as much substance in it' as Kirkpatrick made out.[41]

On 4 February 1982 Kirkpatrick was arrested and taken to Castlereagh police station for interview. Having been arrested and detained for questioning four times before, he was well aware of the procedure. At first, when interviewed about the murder of Reserve Constable McDougal in Great Victoria Street in Belfast on 9 January 1981, he employed the familiar anti-interrogation technique of saying nothing and staring at the wall. But things changed when John McConkey, his alleged accomplice, who had turned Queen's evidence, was brought into the room. Kirkpatrick admitted that the police had been talking to him about someone called McConkey before the confrontation but claimed that because they referred to him as 'John Francis' and not 'Seanie', as he knew him, he did not realize it was the same person until McConkey entered the room—although the interview notes for the period before the confrontation referred to McConkey as 'Sean'. Kirkpatrick also claimed that he did not know that Sean was Irish for John, Seamus for James, and Liam for William. Mr Justice Carswell said that his account of this episode was a 'good deal less than satisfactory',[42] that he found Kirkpatrick's evidence on the McConkey confrontation 'unreliable and his manner evasive', and that he did not accept that his evidence was truthful.[43] It was, he held, also impossible to accept, as Kirkpatrick alleged, that he, Kirkpatrick, was not sure whether or not McConkey had implicated him in the murder, or that he was unable to remember what McConkey had said.

Following a series of interviews, Kirkpatrick was charged with the McDougal murder and was remanded in custody. McConkey retracted his evidence, and, after a court hearing at the Maze Prison on 23 March 1982, Kirkpatrick was released. But as he tried to leave the court-room, he was rearrested, this time on the evidence of supergrass Jackie Grimley. Back in Castlereagh, Kirkpatrick reverted to non-co-operation tactics, but during his second interview he began to talk to detectives in a manner, as Mr Justice

---

[41] *R.* v. *Steenson* (1985) (unpub.), 16 Dec. 39–40.
[42] Ibid. 45.
[43] Ibid. 46.

Carswell later described it, 'of what can only be regarded as preliminaries to bargaining'.[44] He admitted to having said to his interviewers: 'Look, what's the score here?' and was told that he could possibly go to prison if convicted. It was at a later stage, he said, that he formed the view that he would go down on Grimley's evidence, and he also knew that Goodman had talked and was planning to turn Queen's evidence.[45] He told the police that Goodman was a nobody in the organization, that he, Kirkpatrick, was brigade operations officer for the North and added, 'but I'm saying nothing more', and asked to see someone higher.[46] Kirkpatrick then told the police that since he knew a lot more than either Goodman or Grimley, and could 'put a lot of ones away', he wanted complete immunity from prosecution, a move, Mr Justice Carswell said, that was indicative of an attempt to outdo other supergrasses. The police said that they could not give any guarantee, that it could well be decided that he would be charged and would appear before a court, that they were not in a position to give any assurances, and that Kirkpatrick should give them an account of all the incidents in which he had been involved. After some hesitation, Kirkpatrick made a number of admissions, which were recorded in interview notes, and from the evening of 24 March 1982 these were incorporated into written statements taken under caution. On 26 March, at the end of a sequence of interviews, Kirkpatrick was taken to Crumlin Road prison in Belfast and housed in the comparatively luxurious 'supergrass annex', where both republican and loyalist supergrasses freely associated, shared cooking-facilities and a colour television and video, and had black-and-white television sets in their cells. From information gleaned from loyalist supergrass William Allen, with whom he shared a cell, Kirkpatrick managed to smuggle notes to the INLA—on Rizla cigarette-paper—which were said to have been instrumental in the murder of the Shankill Butcher, Lennie Murphy.[47]

A short time after his decision to turn supergrass at the end of March 1982, Kirkpatrick changed his mind. He told the police, on or around 5 April 1982, that he was no longer prepared to give

---

[44] Ibid. 48.

[45] Ibid.

[46] Ibid. 49.

[47] Kirkpatrick was said to have evicted Allen from his cell when he suspected that Allen had tipped off the prison officers about his secret supply of marijuana. (M. O'Higgins, 'Harry's Game', *Hot Press*, 27 Mar. 1986, 30.)

evidence because of the threat to himself and his family. The INLA had kidnapped his wife, stepfather, and sister, the latter of whom was held for three and a half months. However, the defence at the *Steenson* trial suggested that this was not Kirkpatrick's real motive and that it was not until this date that he had found out for certain that he was not to be granted immunity from prosecution, having 'pulled the trigger' in at least five murders. Kirkpatrick nevertheless remained in the supergrass annex and eventually decided that he would give evidence after all. There was considerable confusion about when this second volte-face occurred, and two dates, 19 January 1983 and 19 April 1983, were discussed. It was also submitted that in January 1983, knowing the preliminary inquiry in his own case was approaching, Kirkpatrick sent for the police and told them that he would give evidence if the murder charge against him was dropped and he was given immunity from prosecution and a new life, but that this was turned down by the police on the grounds that a higher authority had already decided that he had to stand trial. The defence also maintained that in April 1983, as his own trial was approaching, Kirkpatrick made another attempt to obtain some assurances about his future and that this time he received enough encouragement to convince him that he should go ahead and give evidence and reveal further offences.

In June 1983 Kirkpatrick pleaded guilty to some seventy-seven counts, including five murders. The detective superintendent who had been present when he first decided to turn Queen's evidence testified on his behalf, and Kirkpatrick was sentenced to life imprisonment and substantial prison terms for a range of other offences but with no recommended minimum. However, he was eventually to be set free after completing only nine years of his sentence.[48] Kirkpatrick appeared in court again on 15 June 1983 for reasons which caused him 'some difficulty in his evidence', Mr Justice Carswell later remarked,[49] apparently confirming the suggestion that he tended to shift his ground and put forward unconvincing denials 'under pressure'.[50] Mr Justice Carswell added that it seemed probable that this further hearing was held at Kirkpatrick's own instigation and stemmed from concern that his involvement in another murder, that of William Henry McCullough, would be

---

[48] See Ch. 11.
[49] *R.* v. *Steenson* (1985) (unpub.) 16 Dec. 59.
[50] Ibid. 60.

revealed at some later stage, to his disadvantage. Throughout 1983 and 1984, while awaiting the *Steenson* trial, Kirkpatrick continued to make statements which covered not only the activities of the eight Belfast INLA units, but of those in Armagh and Derry as well, and two detectives paid him a total of 117 'social calls'. Kirkpatrick gave evidence at a preliminary inquiry which was disrupted by disturbances, and in June 1984 the Attorney-General, acting under s. 2 (2) (*f*) of the Grand Jury (Abolition) Act (Northern Ireland) 1969, directed that the defendants should be indicted for trial without committal proceedings.[51] None of the defendants elected to give evidence at trial, and the judge decided, quoting Lord Lowry in *R. v. Graham*,[52] that no adverse inferences would be drawn.

The Trial

Thirty-three defendants were originally charged on Kirkpatrick's evidence, on an indictment which contained 198 counts involving forty-two incidents, one of which was a conspiracy to plant a bomb at the wedding of Prince Charles and Lady Diana Spencer in June 1981. Incidents 31–42 involved only one defendant, Thomas Joseph Molloy, who had made statements of admission. A separate trial was ordered for Michelle Dorian and Bernard Denis Dorian, Kirkpatrick's sister and brother-in-law respectively. Three defendants, John Gerard O'Reilly, Kevin McQuillan, and Patrick Gerard McKeever, failed to answer their bail, while another accused, Eugene Thomas Cassin, changed his plea to guilty at the commencement of the trial. The remaining twenty-seven defendants, who stood trial in proceedings which lasted from 29 January to 18 December 1985, included the alleged top brass in the INLA's Belfast Brigade. They were Gerard Steenson (assistant brigade operations officer, becoming brigade operations officer, adjutant, and finally officer commanding the Belfast Brigade); Thomas Power (brigade intelligence officer); Thomas Molloy (officer commanding Andersonstown, later brigade quartermaster); Michael Kearney (officer commanding Ballymurphy); Dermot Drain (officer commanding Twinbrook); Hugh Torney (officer commanding Divis Flats, then brigade training officer); William Smith (assistant brigade quartermaster); Emmanuel Conway (officer com-

---

[51] For a further discussion of the voluntary bill of indictment, see Ch. 11.
[52] (1984) 18 NIJB 19.

manding Unity Flats); and Joseph Heaney (brigade finance officer).

Having reviewed the law on accomplice evidence, Mr Justice Carswell considered a legal issue which had been canvassed at some length in the trial—the degree to which it was legitimate to regard the supportive evidence, where it confirmed Kirkpatrick's accuracy on a specific incident, as enhancing his general credibility as a witness—and he concurred with the view expressed by Mr Justice Hutton in the Court of Appeal decision in *R.* v. *Graham* that supportive evidence given in respect of any incident could be relied upon to enhance the accomplice witness's general credibility provided that it was both relevant and probative, but only to a limited extent. However, he added that supportive evidence relating to some incidents could be used to enhance the credibility of an accomplice in respect of other incidents only where the issue with respect to these other incidents was one of accuracy and not truthfulness. Where the accuracy of Kirkpatrick's general description of any incident was not in dispute, but the participation of any given accused was, the issue was one of truthfulness, the judge held. But where there was some doubt about whether Kirkpatrick had described what had in fact taken place, or even that he had been there at all, the issue was, firstly, one of accuracy. Evidence that Kirkpatrick had accurately described certain incidents supported his general credibility only on the issue of accuracy but not on the issue of truth, the key issue, and therefore the consistency of his evidence with independent evidence was of little assistance to the court. Following remarks made by the Lord Chief Justice in the appeal decision in *R.* v. *Graham*, Mr Justice Carswell pointed out that inconsistencies between Kirkpatrick's evidence and the supportive evidence which the Crown had adduced would damage his general credibility.

In assessing Kirkpatrick's general credibility, Mr Justice Carswell said that he had given full weight to the witness's bad character in the many facets which were brought out in evidence, although he had reservations about the astuteness and speed of thought attributed to him by the defence. Kirkpatrick had been proved to have lied when it suited his book, whether in court or out of it, and to have shown little remorse over the consequences of his actions, or compunction about using other people to further his own ends.[53]

---

[53] *R.* v. *Steenson* (1985) (unpub.) 16 Dec. 105.

He had, however, been 'cool, composed and courteous' when giving his evidence and, even under vigorous cross-examination, never 'wilted or became flustered or lost his composure',[54] and the fact that he had delivered his testimony in a virtually unbroken narrative revealed 'quite remarkable powers of retention of facts'.[55] Mr Justice Carswell said that he received a good impression of actual recollection of events from Kirkpatrick's evidence rather than, as the defence had suggested, of the recounting of a script, but he did not say how he was able to tell the difference.

The judge did not accept that because Kirkpatrick tried to cover up mistakes by ready and resourceful invention, it followed that he 'set out to include in his account persons who had not taken part in the crimes for the purpose of making his own evidence more attractive.[56] Nor did he accept the suggestion that many of the incidents which Kirkpatrick related were based upon gossip and rumour in his neighbourhood rather than upon his own recollection. Kirkpatrick, he said, was 'a much bigger fish than any of his competitors' and his evidence was 'too circumstantial and accurate to have been invented.[57] However, his reluctance to admit having made mistakes even when this was demonstrably the case made it all the more necessary, Mr Justice Carswell said, that his evidence be approached 'critically and with caution'.[58]

Determining Kirkpatrick's motives for giving evidence occupied a substantial portion of the trial. During his cross-examination Kirkpatrick claimed repeatedly that he was motivated only by his desire to break his links with the INLA, because he no longer believed in what it represented, and to tell the truth in order to clear up his own crimes. He steadfastly denied that he had any element of self-interest to serve and, in particular, that his decision to turn Queen's evidence had been prompted by a desire to obtain immunity from prosecution or to ingratiate himself with the police in order to further his chances of executive clemency. However, Mr Justice Carswell concluded that Kirkpatrick realized in March 1982 that he would probably be convicted on the evidence of Goodman, Grimley, or some other supergrass, that he faced a stiff sentence for a long catalogue of offences, with a real risk that a

---

[54] Ibid. 40.   [55] Ibid.   [56] Ibid.
[57] Ibid. 70.   [58] Ibid. 43.

minimum term might be recommended, and that he had attempted
to pre-empt this by 'trying to get what he could out of turning
Queen's evidence.'[59] His second thoughts about giving evidence
could have been motivated by the risk to his wife or by the desire
to improve his bargaining position, but whichever was closest to
the truth

> Kirkpatrick's object in deciding finally to give evidence [was] likely to have
> contained an element, perhaps a substantial one, of self-interest, consisting
> of a hope for executive clemency in earlier release and assistance on his
> eventual discharge from prison. I am of opinion that this constituted and
> still constitutes a significant part of his motivation. It follows from that
> conclusion that Kirkpatrick has tried to conceal that part of his motivation
> from the court and has been prepared to lie to do so.[60]

Defence counsel had submitted that by its nature a case such as
this made false accusations extremely difficult to expose, but the
judge said they should have been able to adduce some evidence of
falsity if it had existed. Although in some places there was a
sufficient possibility of Kirkpatrick's having been mistaken to leave
the case 'inadequately proved',[61] he had not deliberately attempted
to mislead the court. Although he had made some errors in his
evidence, according to the judge these were 'remarkably few'[62] and
he had demonstrated 'a quite outstanding ability to remember
detail and to get it right when under pressure'.[63] The errors were
not sufficient to justify rejecting Kirkpatrick's evidence or to warrant regarding him as a less-than-credible witness. Referring to the
passage from Eggleston's *Evidence, Proof and Probability* which
Mr Justice Hutton had set out in his judgment in *R. v. Crumley*,[64]
Mr Justice Carswell indicated that he agreed with the conclusion
that there was no universal test by which the truthfulness of a
witness could be assessed and added:

> At the end of the process one must be intellectually satisfied and also
> subjectively believe and feel that the witness's evidence is true. Having
> carried out this process I am so intellectually satisfied and I do so believe
> and feel ... I also hold that his evidence is capable of satisfying the
> standard of proof beyond reasonable doubt. Whether it does so on any

---

[59] *R. v. Steenson* (1985) (unpub.), 67.   [60] Ibid. 68.   [61] Ibid. 106.
[62] Ibid. 107.   [63] Ibid.   [64] See Ch. 6.

count against any defendant will depend upon the totality of the evidence on that count against that defendant.[65]

The Verdict

The bulk of the judgment in *R.* v. *Steenson* consists of the careful documentation of a host of weaknesses in Kirkpatrick's evidence which the trial judge then ignored or sought to explain away before convicting all twenty-seven of the defendants on most of the charges. Not only was Kirkpatrick's evidence riddled with weaknesses and errors, but some of his accounts of the more serious incidents were based upon hearsay. Characteristically, Kirkpatrick would claim to have been a party to the conspiracy which preceded the offence in question, but would admit that his account of the incident itself had been based upon what one of the alleged participants had told him afterwards. On at least one occasion his knowledge of the event was based upon what someone else had said a participant had told him. Some of the most significant of these flaws are considered in the discussion of the Court of Appeal decision in the next chapter.

There was little corroboration, in the *Baskerville* sense, of Kirkpatrick's evidence, Mr Justice Carswell said. Molloy had made a number of verbal and written statements relating to many incidents which were capable of affording corroboration, but remarks by Smith, Connolly, Downey, and Power which the Crown submitted were capable of corroborating Kirkpatrick's evidence were not treated as corroborative, and there was some corroboration against two defendants on minor charges. John James Tumelty made a series of remarks during police interviews in which he admitted that he had once been in the INLA but had since left, and this constituted corroboration of Kirkpatrick's evidence on the membership charge. In an interview on 13 February 1982 part of a statement made by one-time supergrass Robert McAllister was read out to Martin Damien McKnight, who then signed a brief written statement confessing to having been in unlawful possession of a pistol and of having threatened to use it in a hijacking. However, the judge said that he would have convicted McKnight on this charge on Kirkpatrick's uncorroborated testimony anyway, and, in any case, each of these two defendants were convicted on more serious charges on Kirkpatrick's uncorroborated evidence, thus reducing the significance of their limited confessions.

CONCLUSION

The conspiracy theorists argued that developments from late 1984 to the end of 1985 showed that the supergrass system was being stripped of the last vestiges of non-sectarian even-handedness, since not a single conviction on the uncorroborated evidence of a loyalist supergrass remained, while the Kirkpatrick case indicated that the courts were still prepared to convict on the almost entirely uncorroborated evidence of republican turncoats. It is true that Mr Justice Carswell had been prepared to convict on Kirkpatrick's evidence, despite the kind of major inherent flaws which had resulted in acquittals in other cases, of which Crockard and Allen were particularly recent examples. But the fact that, at this point, the differences between loyalist and republican cases lay along sectarian lines was purely an accident of trial chronology rather than the outcome of an anti-republican judicial plot. However, the choice facing the Northern Ireland Court of Appeal in the remaining appeals was now stark. If it confirmed all the outstanding uncorroborated convictions, it would inevitably be condemned as sectarian, while if it confirmed only some, it would be criticized for unprincipled inconsistency. The only other alternative was to overturn all the remaining uncorroborated convictions, and, in the event, this is what it chose to do.

8

Collapse: 1986

ON 19 March 1986 the Attorney-General issued his second substantial Commons statement on the supergrass trials in Northern Ireland.[1] But by the end of the year the system itself had come to an end when the convictions secured in the McGrady, Black, Quigley, and Kirkpatrick cases, which were not supported by a confession or what was deemed to be an admission, were all quashed on appeal. The statement, which added little to the debate, was largely aimed at countering suggestions that there were differences between the law and practice on supergrass trials in Northern Ireland on the one hand, and in England and Wales on the other. The Attorney-General said that a judicial warning was issued by the judge either to a jury or to himself in both jurisdictions and neither DPP regarded himself bound by a rigid rule or practice regarding the need for corroborative evidence in the strict sense before authorizing prosecutions, although in the absence of either supportive or corroborative evidence it was unlikely that a prosecution would be brought. He also denied that supergrass trials were a 'routine and frequent occurrence' in Northern Ireland, and referred to the low conviction-rate which the supergrass system had by this stage achieved, together with Lord Lowry's judgment in the McGrady case, as evidence of the 'scrupulous care' which the judiciary had brought to bear upon supergrass evidence.

Although some of the judgments in the appeal decisions were concerned with the elaboration of formal legal doctrines, the general formula was remarkably straightforward. The Northern Ireland Court of Appeal simply accepted that the trial judge in each case had been too willing to believe the supergrass evidence and had paid insufficient attention to the specific weaknesses which had been exposed by the defence. No new evidence and no novel arguments were necessary to achieve this result, and indeed most of

---

[1] HC Debs., vol. 94, cols. 185–7.

the judges who sat in each of the appeal hearings had themselves convicted on the uncorroborated evidence of other supergrasses. Since there is also little evidence to suggest that this dramatic turn-about was due to the increasing skill of defence lawyers, these decisions appear to have been the result of a deliberate change in judicial policy, which had been gathering momentum from as early as the Grimley trial in October 1983, in direct response to the strong and cogent criticisms made of the supergrass system in the widely based campaign against it. This theme will be considered more fully in the final chapter, but at this point an attempt will be made to discover precisely how each appeal decision in 1986 was reached.

THE McGRADY APPEAL: *R. v. Gibney and others*

Four of the seven defendants convicted in the McGrady trial—Gibney, Davison, McKiernan, and McConkey—appealed against conviction. Murray had pleaded guilty and did not appeal, McCullough served notice of appeal but withdrew at the hearing, and Thompson did not actively pursue his appeal against sentence. Delivering the judgment of the majority of the court on 4 July 1986, Lord Justice Gibson allowed the appeals of Davison and McKiernan but dismissed those of Gibney, McConkey, and Thompson. McConkey and Thompson had made confessions, and Gibney's reaction to McGrady in a police-station confrontation was deemed by the majority (Lord Justice Gibson and Mr Justice MacDermott) to constitute an admission of guilt. Lord Justice O'Donnell delivered a short judgment dissenting from the majority view on Gibney's appeal.

One of the main topics for consideration, Lord Justice Gibson said, was the distinction drawn by the trial judge between those parts of McGrady's evidence which were held to be sufficient on their own to warrant verdicts of guilty, and those which were rejected as insufficient for this purpose. Lord Lowry had stated that McGrady's evidence on some of the charges would be 'gravely' affected by the absurdities of his evidence on some of the other charges,[2] and he also appeared to have accepted that there would be less danger of convicting on McGrady's uncorroborated evi-

[2] *R. v. Gibney* (1986) 4 NIJB 4.

dence if there was supportive evidence. Depending upon the nature of the supporting evidence, and the degree of reliance placed upon the accomplice testimony, Lord Justice Gibson said, a conviction on this accomplice's uncorroborated testimony could, on occasion, be safe, just as a conviction based on the uncorroborated evidence of any accomplice could sometimes be safe. The fact that the accuracy of the account of a crime given by an accomplice had been consistent and detailed would do little or nothing to rehabilitate his credibility if he had otherwise been exposed as inconsistent or had been shown to have lied, he continued. This was because, as an accomplice in any given crime, he would naturally know all the circumstances of its commission, although such evidence could not be regarded as supportive of his evidence regarding his associates in the offence. This rule was all the more pointed here, Lord Justice Gibson remarked, because on several occasions McGrady had been shown to have falsely identified a person as a participant—for example, by substituting Thomas Pinkey for his brother Eugene as the driver of the car used during a shooting, and similarly replacing Packie McMahon for his brother Gerard in another incident. He had also initially implicated Jackie Fitzpatrick as one of his companions on a week's IRA training-course in Dundalk, and also claimed that Fitzpatrick had been involved with him in an attack upon McKenna's public house but later retracted this and said that, on both occasions, it had been McMahon. These examples showed, Lord Justice Gibson said, that 'it clearly behoves one to look for positive independent identification of persons alleged by him as having been involved with him in less memorable circumstances'.[3]

The distinction drawn by the Lord Chief Justice between those parts of McGrady's uncorroborated evidence which could sustain a conviction and those which could not was, Lord Justice Gibson said, 'most unusual ... but ... quite credible'[4] and an appellate tribunal would need to have some reason arising from the evidence itself to reject such a judgment made by an experienced and perceptive judge who had watched and listened to the witness as he had given his evidence. This line of reasoning is, however, difficult to accept. Attempting to draw a distinction between those parts of McGrady's uncorroborated evidence which justified convictions and those which did not is both unusual and incredible because

---

[3] Ibid. 6.   [4] Ibid.

there is no reliable criterion by which such a distinction can be made, and an equally experienced judge seeking to do so might have come to very different conclusions. Lord Justice Gibson continued that, where the findings by the judge in the trial at first instance were of secondary facts which were not immediately dependent on what he himself had seen and heard, an appellate court was 'free to apply its own judgment, though considerable weight should be given to the conclusion of the trial judge when deciding whether to adopt a contrary view.'[5]

Lord Justice Gibson stated that the Court of Appeal also had a duty to reverse a conviction if it considered it unsafe and unsatisfactory due to a 'lurking doubt'—for example, where the trial judge had drawn an inference from primary facts while the Court of Appeal considered that reasonable alternative inferences consistent with innocence were also possible. But more was required than the fact that in certain cirumstances McGrady had proved to be unreliable. Four other reasons, indicated by *Thorne*[6] and *Turner*,[7] which could justify a reversal of the decision of the tribunal of fact on the evidence of an accomplice were outlined. In *Thorne* Lord Justice Lawton said that the villain's evidence should be examined to see if there were any weaknesses in it which the jury might have overlooked or not assessed properly in arriving at its verdict, while in *Turner* Lord Widgery, Chief Justice, held that, in matters of credibility, the Court of Appeal could only interfere in three circumstances: where the jury had been misdirected as to how to assess the evidence, where there had been no direction at all but should have been one, and where the jury had taken a perverse view of the evidence (likely to be rare). Having outlined these legal issues, Lord Justice Gibson then considered the cases of each appellant in turn.

Gibney

His lordship pointed out that there was no 'outside support'[8] for McGrady's accusation that Gibney had briefed the IRA unit which had attempted to murder Duff, nor for the claim that he had been in possession of the weapon used. But Lord Lowry had found support for McGrady's evidence in the words and demeanour of

---

[5] *R.* v. *Gibney* (1986) 4 NIJB 8. [6] (1978) 66 Cr App R 6.
[7] (1975) 61 Cr App R 67. [8] *R.* v. *Gibney* (1986) 4 NIJB 10.

Gibney in his sixteen-minute confrontation with McGrady on 23 January 1982 at Castlereagh police station, and the circumstances of this encounter, Lord Justice Gibson said, went 'a long way to substantiate the charges'.[9] Before the confrontation, Gibney had been informed of the general nature of McGrady's allegations, and, as soon as McGrady identified Gibney by name, he became uneasy and flustered and shouted at him: 'Just before you give any more information, think about what you are saying. You know you are doing other people harm.'

As the interview proceeded, Gibney continued to demonstrate his nervousness and attempted to stop McGrady's account from continuing. Lord Justice Gibson commented:

It is clear that each was well known to the other and Gibney's method of addressing McGrady was indicative of his having, or feeling that he had, some sense of authority over McGrady. These are considerations which would tend to corroborate McGrady's account that they were both in the Provisional IRA and that Gibney held a higher rank than he. The reference by Gibney to 'information' also tends to confirm the impression otherwise given that he knew from what the police had already told him that in at least some respects what McGrady was about to say was true, and his speaking of 'doing other people harm' would also point in the same direction. All this has, of course, to be read together with the later statement of Gibney that McGrady was lying, but that was undoubtedly a defensive retort to meet the accusations and does not seem to merit much weight.[10]

His lordship held that this, together with McGrady's evidence about the Duff shooting, supported McGrady's testimony as to Gibney's membership of the IRA, and that Gibney held a higher rank than he, since McGrady would not have been of sufficient rank to have organized the commission of terrorist offences himself, and, in his unit, there could only have been a few of the appropriate rank. The conclusion that Gibney was one of those of such rank was well justified, Lord Justice Gibson stated. There was, however, 'no such clear direct support'[11] for the evidence that Gibney had briefed the unit responsible for the Duff shooting, although Mc-Grady's account of the details was confirmed by independent evidence. Another pointer to Gibney's guilt in the Duff incident, according to Lord Justice Gibson, lay in the fact that Gibney had

[9] Ibid. 12.   [10] Ibid. 11.   [11] Ibid.

tried to stop McGrady from proceeding with his accusations. Two of the three occasions on which he tried to do so concerned the Duff shooting, the other was before McGrady had done more than identify him, and he had remained silent on all other matters. In appraising the evidence as to Gibney's part in the Duff shooting, Lord Justice Gibson said that Lord Lowry's remark that he was impressed by the ring of truth in this part of McGrady's evidence, an observation which he had not made with regard to any part of McGrady's evidence in relation to any other incident, should not be ignored. Lord Justice Gibson concluded:

A complete review of all the evidence on the matter raises no consideration which would make one doubt that the convictions of Gibney on all three counts were other than well founded having regard to the advantages which the learned trial judge had of discerning the truth which are denied to this court.[12]

Lord Justice O'Donnell's interpretation of the McGrady–Gibney encounter was, however, much more faithful to the criminal standard of proof and the *Baskerville* corroboration test. In his view, although the Lord Chief Justice had not misdirected himself on the law and had clearly found comfort and assurance in the inferences which he had drawn from the McGrady–Gibney encounter, he had not been present himself at the confrontation, and therefore the advantage which might normally exist from hearing witnesses did not arise. The Court of Appeal was, therefore, in as good a position to draw inferences from the primary facts as the trial judge. Lord Justice O'Donnell pointed out that, by Lord Lowry's own admission, there was at least a possibility that McGrady could have framed Gibney for the Craig and Stephenson murders and if he had done so: 'in my view no tribunal of fact could safely conclude that McGrady had rightly involved Gibney in the attempted murder of Duff, or as a member of the IRA, unless his evidence was corroborated.'[13] Lord Justice O'Donnell noted that Lord Lowry had appreciated that Gibney's reaction in the confrontation with McGrady did not technically corroborate but tended to support McGrady's allegations. But his lordship pointed out that supporting evidence was not a half-way house to corroboration, since it

---

[12] *R. v. Gibney* (1986) 4 NIJB 12.
[13] Ibid. 22.

did no more than merely support the general credibility of the witness, without connecting, or tending to connect, the accused with the crime charged.

The Lord Chief Justice regarded the confrontation as providing important support for McGrady's evidence in relation not only to the membership charge, but also in respect of the Duff shooting itself. But even if it established, as Lord Lowry thought, that Gibney was an intelligence or staff officer of the IRA, it did not prove, Lord Justice O'Donnell said, that Gibney had briefed the unit involved in this incident. This could just as easily have been done by Davison, who, McGrady claimed, had sworn him into the organization in the first place. McGrady was certainly capable of substituting someone else for the true offender, as his substitution of Thomas for Eugene Pinkey, and Packie for Gerard McMahon, showed.

The Lord Chief Justice had pointed out that a distinction should be drawn between the factual evidence—Gibney's shouting, the words he had used, his conduct in rubbing his hands on his trousers and removing his glasses—and on the impressions of those present as to what these various facts revealed or meant. Lord Justice O'Donnell stated:

> I consider it highly dangerous to rely (if it had been so alleged) on the impression that he was nervous or uneasy because of guilt, rather than nervous or uneasy because he was innocent and being wrongly accused. Even a trained psychologist would have difficulty making such a distinction. How much more dangerous then for someone not present to attempt to make deductions from conduct not witnessed but only described.[14]

Lord Lowry had drawn three inferences from the McGrady–Gibney confrontation: Gibney knew McGrady, Gibney was a member of the IRA, and Gibney was a person of authority and importance in the IRA. 'For my part', Lord Justice O'Donnell commented, 'I cannot see how these conclusions are either inevitable or even reasonable.'[15] There was no suggestion from any of those present that Gibney appeared to know McGrady, but what he did know was that McGrady was going to accuse him of involvement in the Craig and Stephenson murders, charges of which

---

[14] Ibid. 28.   [15] Ibid.

he was eventually acquitted by direction. If he was innocent, Lord Justice O'Donnell asked

was he not entitled to be uneasy and acutely nervous at being accused of a number of heinous crimes? Would it not be unusual for him to remind McGrady that false accusations were hurting a lot of people, not merely those accused, but their family and friends? Would it be remarkable if he lost his self control at being wrongly accused? Would it be unexpected if he shouted in an attempt to stop a series of lying accusations?[16]

Lord Justice O'Donnell said that he made these observations to show that the conclusions drawn by the trial judge were, at best, equivocal, and evidence which is equivocal cannot supply corroboration.[17] Even if it had been correct for the trial judge to infer from the confrontation that Gibney was an intelligence or staff officer in the IRA, that fact could not provide corroboration of Gibney's alleged involvement in the Duff shooting, and there was 'no evidence', his Lordship said

that Gibney addressed McGrady in a way which suggested a superior talking to a subordinate. Indeed, on the evidence of Chief Inspector Rawson, who was present, Gibney appeared to have lost control. This is hardly suggestive of a senior officer talking to a subordinate. Indeed it is hardly suggestive of a senior officer.[18]

Gibney's interruptions of McGrady's account of the Duff shooting were in no way probative of a desire to stop McGrady talking about that particular incident, and, since they all occurred at the beginning of the confrontation, it was much more likely that Gibney simply gained self-control as the encounter wore on.

Concluding his judgment, Lord Justice O'Donnell said that the most important feature of the evidence in respect of the McGrady–Gibney confrontation was that the trial judge and the Court of Appeal were totally dependent upon the words used and the impressions gleaned by the interviewing officers as to what had occurred. He pointed out that at no time during the course of their evidence at the trial at first instance did the interviewing officers confirm the impression of the Lord Chief Justice that Gibney's

   [16] *R.* v. *Gibney* (1986) 4 NIJB 29.
   [17] *Finch* v. *Finch* [1983] 23 Ch D 267, at 272; *Wiedmann* v. *Walpole* (1891) 2 QB 534 at 537; *R.* v. *Watson* (1913) 8 Cr App R 249.
   [18] *R.* v. *Gibney* (1986) 4 NIJB 29–30.

demeanour was suggestive of his being an officer or member of the IRA. Nor was it suggested that, at any subsequent interview, the officers present formed the opinion that Gibney had been giving orders to McGrady at the confrontation or that he had shown himself to be a member of the IRA on that occasion. The inferences drawn by the Lord Chief Justice from the confrontation were therefore nothing but 'mere speculation' and were 'certainly not legitimate'.[19] Lord Justice O'Donnell concluded that Lord Lowry's view that McGrady's evidence against Gibney had the ring of truth could do no more than merely confirm McGrady's evidence as to the general circumstances of the Duff shooting. It had a genuine ring because McGrady was there, but this was of no assistance in determining who else had been present, and in the absence of corroboration of McGrady's evidence Gibney was entitled to an acquittal.

Davison and McKiernan

Each of these two appellants had been found guilty on McGrady's uncorroborated testimony, which, in marked contrast to that in the case of Gibney, the court held, was unsupported and lacked detail. In convicting McKiernan Lord Lowry had said that he saw no reason to reject McGrady's evidence, but, Lord Justice Gibson held, the proven falsity of McGrady's evidence in other respects, and his undoubted policy of exculpating one, if not both, his brothers, made it difficult to eliminate the possibility that either or both appellants had been wrongly named, whether innocently or deliberately, and therefore each was entitled to have his conviction quashed.

McConkey

Two main arguments had been advanced in furtherance of McConkey's appeal against conviction for the Dowds murder. It was submitted, first, that his statement of admission should not have been admitted as evidence, because it had been made in expectation of becoming a supergrass, and secondly that there was a 'lurking doubt' as to his guilt, because there were three conflicting accounts of the incident: his own confession, the confession of Sean McGrady, and the testimony of Kevin McGrady. As to the first

---

[19] Ibid. 30.

matter, Lord Justice Gibson pointed out that Lord Lowry had accepted McConkey's confession as 'a perfectly normal statement taken in perfectly ordinary circumstances',[20] and although he might have been encourged to confess by the knowledge that McGrady had informed on him, this was not the same as saying he had confessed to a murder which he had not committed. Lord Justice Gibson said that in the light of the fact that the Lord Chief Justice had had the advantage of seeing and hearing McConkey, who had elected to give evidence, it would be difficult for the Court of Appeal to overturn the trial judge's findings.

The three versions of the Dowds murder were dealt with as follows. Sean McGrady had made a statement, given in evidence in his own trial, in which he confessed to having acted as look-out and in which he also claimed there were two other accomplices at the scene of the crime, apart from himself. During his own trial Kevin McGrady had exonerated his brother completely and had stated that he and McConkey alone had been involved, while in his confession McConkey had said that the participants had been himself and Kevin McGrady. Sean McGrady's case had been referred to the Northern Ireland Court of Appeal by the Secretary of State, but his conviction had been upheld on the grounds that Kevin's evidence was unreliable. In pursuit of his appeal McConkey's counsel argued that it was not open to the Crown to maintain that only two people had been involved in the Dowds murder, because it had already accepted, in the Secretary of State's reference, that there had been three. Lord Justice Gibson said that this submission was insupportable because McConkey had never maintained that only two persons had been involved in the murder, and in fact he had not been asked about Sean's participation at all, apparently because the police were concerned that if he had implicated Sean, Kevin's evidence against all the defendants tried with Gibney would have been undermined. His lordship quoted a passage from his own judgment in the Secretary of State's reference[21] to the effect that the different accounts could best be reconciled by assuming that Kevin McGrady had given untruthful evidence in an attempt to exonerate his brother, and that in fact Kevin, Sean, and McConkey had been involved in the Dowds murder. Independent evidence had been supplied by an eyewitness that three persons had

[20] *R.* v. *Gibney* (1986) 4 NIJB 15.
[21] (1984) 8 NIJB.

been at the scene, and some soldiers had claimed to have seen both Sean and Kevin in the locality where the van used had been returned. This contradicted Kevin McGrady's evidence at the Gibney trial that Sean was in bed until he had come back from the scene of the murder, a suggestion which was also incompatible with Sean's confession, aspects of Kevin's evidence, and some independent evidence—for example, that supplied by Bombardier Bogairt and others.

There was, therefore, Lord Justice Gibson concluded, no lurking doubt about McConkey's conviction. He added that Sean McGrady's conviction was conclusive evidence only of this fact, the date, and its legal consequences. Since the grounds upon which Sean McGrady had been convicted were technically inadmissible, there was no legal basis for considering any evidence given during the relevant proceedings, including the evidence of both Sean and Kevin McGrady. There was, in consequence, no valid ground for overturning McConkey's conviction.

THE BLACK APPEAL: *R. v. Donnelly and others*

Twenty-three of those convicted in the trial of *Donnelly and others* appealed against their convictions and sentence. The twelve who did not were all minor offenders, and only two of these, Elizabeth Ann McWilliams and Michael O'Neill, had received prison sentences. The number of appellants was reduced to twenty-one when Charles McKiernan withdrew his appeal and Kevin Barry John Artt escaped from prison. But Arthur Corbett, who had received a suspended prison sentence of two years for membership of the IRA, joined the appellants later and brought the numbers back to twenty-two.

On 17 July 1986 the Northern Ireland Court of Appeal upheld the appeals in all eighteen cases based on Black's evidence.[22] Delivering the judgment of the court, Lord Lowry, the Lord Chief

[22] The appeals of 4 appellants were not successful on some of the charges against them. Kevin and James Donnelly did not have their convictions quashed for offences arising out of the illegal road-block, since Black's evidence was corroborated by the gloves and the scientific match between the acrylic fibres in their hair-combings and the balaclava helmets which were found near the scene of their arrest. Anthony McIlkenny's confession sustained his conviction on the charges arising out of the Dixon robbery and the membership charge, and Terence McAllister's conviction for membership survived the appeal because of his oral admission to the police, but his other conviction was quashed.

Justice, said that the court had decided that the trial judge, Mr Justice Kelly, had greatly overestimated Black's honesty as a witness and that his assessment of Black as one of the best witnesses he had ever heard was 'a very ambitious and generous claim indeed in many respects'. Having reached this view at 'an unusually early stage' in the trial, Mr Justice Kelly had 'found it very difficult to attach any credence to evidence which conflicted with Black's or to any interpretation of the evidence which cast doubt upon Black's correctness'.[23] However, the Lord Chief Justice stressed that this decision did not rest on any

supposed principle or practice that corroboration will always be needed to support a conviction based on an accomplice's evidence. The point is that, having concluded that the learned trial judge assessed Black too favourably, not that Black's evidence generally was unworthy of belief, we cannot *in this case* safely affirm convictions based on that evidence alone.[24]

The appellants had referred to many inconsistencies in Black's evidence and had provided a profusion of examples which they submitted could not fairly be attributed to genuine mistake or lapse of memory on the part of someone who was rightly credited with excellent powers of recollection. Addressing a series of issues, Lord Lowry stated that the Crown had been unable to answer the best of the appellants' numerous and persuasive points.

Supportive and Corroborative Evidence

The appellants, Lord Lowry said, had complained that the trial judge had 'wrongly relied on evidence which supported Black on particular counts as supporting his general credibility and thereby supporting his evidence on every count',[25] a complaint which was wide enough to embrace a charge of reliance on evidence which was corroborative on one count in order to enhance a witness's general credibility and thereby support his evidence on other counts.

The admissibility of evidence against defendants tried together could not be determined according to what would have been admissible had they been tried separately, his lordship held, since in joint trials there was a broader spectrum of admissible evidence enhancing or detracting from the general credibility of all witnesses.

[23] *R.* v. *Donnelly* (1986) 4 NIJB 89.
[24] Ibid. 107 (emphasis in original).
[25] Ibid.

However, the credibility of a witness could be bolstered incidentally, but not expressly, by evidence which tended to support the witness's evidence, but not by mere evidence of competence (except for expert witnesses), or evidence of good character (except in the case of the defendants themselves). The Lord Chief Justice said that since anything which damaged the credibility of a witness's evidence on one issue would tend to damage it on all others, the opposite must also be true. A jury was bound to form impressions of a witness's reliability from all the relevant evidence in any given case, and the proper objection to wrongful reliance upon evidence in support of a witness's credibility was the weight which had been attributed to it, and not its admissibility as such.

On these matters Lord Lowry said judges sitting as tribunals of fact should bear three particular points in mind, and that the trial judge's approach to these issues was unobjectionable in principle. First, an accurate description of the crime tended merely to strengthen the inferences that the witness who gave the description took part, and this was important only where participation was an issue, although it could also tend to confirm accuracy of recall as opposed to veracity. Secondly, evidence corroborating a witness's evidence against one or more defendants would not provide support for finding a charge proved against others which arose out of the same or different facts. Thirdly, the essential thing to remember was that evidence which detracted from the credibility of a prosecution witness was much more important than evidence which enhanced it.

The Trial Judge's Assessment of Black's Credibility

The appellants had attacked Black's credibility at the trial and, in the appeal, had extended this attack to include the trial judge's assessment of his credibility. Mr Justice Kelly had stated the relevant legal principles precisely and accurately 'in a way that could not be improved upon',[26] Lord Lowry stated, but the appellants alleged that he had not acted upon these principles as he ought to have done, and that he had displayed a remarkable and unwarranted degree of trust in Black.

The appellants submitted that, in his interviews with the police from 22 to 24 November 1981, following his arrest, Black had

[26] Ibid. 70–1.

conducted a cool negotiation whereas the trial judge had accepted Black's evidence that he had been confused and mixed up at the time, and that this had then been used to explain everything which could not otherwise be accounted for. The judge's attitude to Black in connection with the interviews was, the appellants maintained, one of 'benevolent credulity',[27] at variance with the attitude of guarded suspicion which might have been expected in relation to such a witness. The appellants also cited the *Crawford* trial perjury and a 'very large number'[28] of defects in the descriptions which Black had given of various offences, in order to show that he was unworthy of belief and that the trial judge had been wrong to take such a favourable attitude. The 'Crawford perjury' indicated, they maintained, that the trial judge had given Black an almost completely clean bill of health, when it ought to have been plain to him that Black was an unscrupulous, cunning, and thoughtful liar, as well as a villain. Illustrations of the defects in Black's evidence which Lord Lowry singled out included: Black's account of the attempt to shoot soldiers entering and leaving Flax Street Mill from a house in Brompton Park, which would have involved removing a downstairs grill, resulting in the gunman looking down his sights onto a back-yard wall; the plan to attract police by exploding a bomb in a derelict barber's on the corner of Butler Street and Crumlin Road, which was absurd and impractical and also involved Black contradicting and correcting himself innumerable times; the Loughlin/Loughran confusion; Black's endorsement and embellishment of a mistake made by counsel for the defence, which showed his 'ability and readiness to invent colourful conversation to lend credence to his testimony'.[29]

The Lord Chief Justice pointed out that the Northern Ireland Court of Appeal was 'far from saying'[30] that on most of the main issues it had been demonstrated that Black was lying. In fact 'it still seems probable', he added, 'that he was in many cases not only telling what was done but also recounting accurately by whom it was done'.[31] The problem was that the trial judge had greatly overestimated Black's honesty as a witness, and it was impossible to say what conclusions would have been reached on the various charges by a judge who had assessed his evidence less favourably.

[27] *R. v. Donnelly* (1986) 4 NIJB 77.   [28] Ibid. 83.
[29] Ibid. 86.   [30] Ibid. 90.   [31] Ibid.

Such a judge would almost certainly have been bound to acquit on some of the charges upon which Mr Justice Kelly had convicted, and he might not even have convicted on what appeared to be the sounder charges, although, this was less certain. But since an appeal court could not form a fresh assessment, the convictions even on the membership charges had to be quashed.

Identification Parades and Dock Identifications

The Lord Chief Justice made some brief remarks about the importance of holding identification parades and the difficulties with dock identifications. The police were criticized for relying on Black's assertions that he knew the accused as a reason for not holding identification parades, and the court held that the police-cell confrontations were of no value for the purpose of confirming whether or not this was true, except for any reasonable inference which could be drawn from the reactions of those who were confronted. When an identification parade was not held, the ultimate question was not whether it should or should not have been, but whether 'the actual identification relied on by the prosecution is satisfactory and sufficient, so far as it is relevant to establish the guilt of an accused'.[32] The Lord Chief Justice said that although dock identifications were of greater value in multi-defendant trials than in single-defendant proceedings, the entire value of such identifications was called into question where each defendant occupied an allotted place in the dock throughout the trial, even if it was not assumed that the witness had been given improper assistance.

The Length and Complexity of the Trial

The Lord Chief Justice said that the judgment from the trial at first instance showed the 'enormous care and the remarkable and scrupulous mastery of detail'[33] which the judge had brought to his task, and demonstrated that no jury, no matter how carefully directed, could have coped, and probably would not have been asked to cope, with such a task. However, 'things were . . . overlooked from time to time, not merely or mainly by the learned trial judge, but by the teams of counsel and solicitors acting for the prosecution

---

[32] Ibid. 106.
[33] Ibid. 50.

and for the different groups of defendants'.[34] The Crown's omission to inform the defence that when Black was about to sign his 'deposition', he had made an oral confession of his part in the *Crawford* trial, and a small number of defects concerning dates in the indictment, were cited as illustrations. 'It is less likely that these mishaps would have occurred', Lord Lowry said, 'if there had been fewer defendants and fewer issues to consider.'[35] The lengthy *voir dire* on the admissibility of Artt's confession, the expansion of the case against Kelly, and the 'very tardy' organization of certain photographic evidence combined to increase the complexity and confusion. Quoting with approval dicta from Lord Justice Lawton's judgment in *Thorne*,[36] which deprecated mass trials with 'overloaded' indictments, Lord Lowry said that a judge, however, was more likely to be able to deal with the issues in such circumstances than a jury because he would have the benefit of a complete or partial transcript as well as his own notes, and he would also be alert from the beginning to the main issues of fact and law and would thus not require a summing-up. The view of the court in *Thorne* that the length of the trial and the complexity of the issues do not of themselves make the result unsatisfactory applied *a fortiori* to a trial by judge without a jury, but length and complexity had to be kept in mind when the appellants' other points were being considered.

A judge was bound to hesitate before suggesting, much less ordering, separation of the charges on an indictment unless he received an application for that purpose, the Lord Chief Justice held, otherwise he would run the risk of acting contrary to the will and interests of the defendants. In cases such as this, defence counsel might deliberately omit seeking separate trials rather than lose both the opportunity of subjecting the chief Crown witness to sustained cross-examination and also the chance that shortcomings in the witness's evidence with respect to one defendant could work to the advantage of the other accused. A further advantage of joinder was that the one tribunal assessed the witness by the same yardstick, although, on the other hand, it tended to increase the length and complexity of the trial and to introduce much inadmissible and prejudicial evidence, particularly dangerous to the defence

---

[34] *R.* v. *Donnelly* (1986) 4 NIJB 51.
[35] Ibid.
[36] (1978) 66 Cr App R 6.

if juries were involved. However, whatever the pros and cons of large trials, Lord Lowry stated, there was little to commend the inclusion on the indictment of the 'smaller fry', who often admitted their guilt and made confessions yet pleaded not guilty at the trial.

The Case of Joseph Kelly

Joseph Kelly's case stood somewhat apart from the others, the Lord Chief Justice said, because he was charged with membership of the IRA on the basis of an alleged stay at a training-camp with Black, and with hijacking a lorry, to which he confessed in properly admitted written statements. Lord Lowry said that the case against Kelly provided 'examples of the learned trial judge's reluctance to entertain evidence which tended to call in question Black's credibility'[37] and that the 'preparation, presentation, and proof' were 'greatly prejudiced' by the Crown's inability to decide upon the period during which the appellant had attended the training-camp.

Lord Lowry took the view that Kelly had been denied a fair trial, because the change of dates in the indictment indicated the Crown's uncertainty as to the precise charge which it required him to answer. Kelly's first statement, which dealt with how he had joined the IRA and attended the Donegal camp, differed in important respects from Black's evidence. The dates were different— Black said March/April, coming up to Easter, whereas Kelly said within a few days after 4 August—as was the place, which Black said was Gweedore while Kelly said Glenties. The Lord Chief Justice pointed out that forty alibi witnesses had been called to account for Kelly's movements in both the April and August periods and that the defence had explained why these had not been available until late in the proceedings.

The Crown accepted that the only time at which Kelly could have been at the training-camp with Black was during April and before Easter 1981. Yet the trial judge stated that he was not satisfied beyond reasonable doubt that they had been there together then, although he was convinced that there was a strong probability that it was true. Lord Lowry said that this inconsistency in the judge's approach meant that full weight could not be given to

---

[37] *R.* v. *Donnelly* (1986) 14 NIJB 93.

Kelly's first statement as a truthful account and that therefore the membership charge had to be overturned. Kelly's second statement, relating to the hijacking, was made a couple of days after his first and initially referred to a bus, although he later changed this to a 'vegetable lorry'. There was, however, no police record that a vegetable lorry had been hijacked on that particular day. The unreliability of Kelly's first statement made his second unreliable also, and required the hijacking conviction to be overturned as well.

THE QUIGLEY APPEAL: *R. v. Crumley and others*

The eight defendants found guilty on Quigley's uncorroborated testimony also successfully appealed against their convictions. James Doherty, who had been convicted upon Quigley's evidence and his own confession, lodged an appeal but withdrew before the hearing was completed. Delivering the judgment of the Northern Ireland Court of Appeal on 18 November 1986, Lord Lowry stated that while relying upon Quigley's impressive demeanour the trial judge, Mr Justice Hutton, had paid insufficient attention to his shortcomings, and although noticing many of these, had not been deterred by any. He had also set too much store by Quigley's consistency and was generally indifferent to his much more important inconsistencies, tending to confine consideration of these to the actual events instead of allowing them to affect his overall assessment. The trial judge's faith in the efficacy of cross-examination had also given undue weight to Quigley's survival as a witness in areas where it was well-nigh invulnerable to cross-examination. The judge had also been too ready to discount the unusual factor of Quigley's relationship with, and apparent determination to distance himself from, Gilmour. This remained an unresolved mystery and could only render unquestioning acceptance of his evidence more dangerous still.

Supergrass Trials

The appeal in *R. v. Crumley* provided the first clear judicial recognition of the term 'supergrass'. Lord Lowry stated that although it was a slang expression

we consider it permissible to use it in the present context to describe a terrorist informer who turns Queen's evidence against his alleged former associates, often, as in this case, having been granted immunity in respect of his own serious crimes and entertaining a clear expectation of a new life in different surroundings for himself and his family.[38]

It was essential in such trials, Lord Lowry said, that a judge should warn a jury, or, if he was the tribunal of fact, remember that it is dangerous to convict any accused on any count on the evidence of an accomplice if uncorroborated as to that accused on that count. A supergrass was, however, no ordinary criminal and no ordinary accomplice. If what was known of the supergrass's character and situation increased the probability that he would be an unreliable witness, the danger of relying upon his uncorroborated testimony was also increased. In this case the chief witness for the prosecution was, by his own admission

a man of lawless character, a member of an unlawful organisation dedicated to violence and to the principle that the end justifies any means including indiscriminate murder and a person who had wholeheartedly engaged in all the activities of that organisation.[39]

He was not just a 'cornered criminal reluctantly disgorging information' to avoid the penalty of one moderately serious crime; he had volunteered a large quantity of evidence against his alleged confederates. Whether his motive was fear, despair, hope of an enormously improved life in the future, or all three, it was an extremely powerful motive, and when his claim that he was a supergrass who would outshine Gilmour was added to this, the need for 'the greatest caution' in accepting his evidence became 'clear beyond doubt'.[40] 'It is manifest', Lord Lowry said, 'that the evidence of such a witness must stand up successfully to the sternest criteria before it can be acceptable and become the sole basis for being satisfied beyond reasonable doubt that any accused is guilty of any offence charged against him.'[41] If a suspect witness becomes even more suspect for any or all of these reasons, then 'the manner and extent of his rehabilitation to a state of credence must be clear' before his evidence can become the sole basis for conviction.[42]

---

[38] *R.* v. *Crumley* (1986) 14 NIJB 42.   [39] Ibid 43.
[40] Ibid.   [41] Ibid.   [42] Ibid. 44.

Quigley's Evidence

Lord Lowry pointed out that the trial judge had concluded that on a number of occasions Quigley had not told the truth in the witness-box, that in cross-examination he had admitted to having interlarded truth with fiction, and there were also self-confessed falsities, such as leaving Mickey Doherty and Eddie McIlhinney out of offences because of friendship and/or an unwillingness to get them into trouble. Quigley's overall credibility was also affected by the fact that the judge had not been convinced beyond reasonable doubt about Mellon's guilt on the membership charge, O'Brien's on the grenade-throwing charge, and Eamon Doherty's on the charges arising out of the Linsford Drive shooting.

The Lord Chief Justice said that there were 'important inconsistencies'[43] in Quigley's evidence concerning the participation of Eamon ('Ebby') Doherty in a number of incidents, and that the lack of any reference to him could either have been a revealing slip by an untruthful witness or merely a mistake. But its significance was enhanced by other important inconsistencies in Quigley's evidence about this defendant. For example, Doherty had been left out of Quigley's account of the conspiracy to shoot at the security forces at Croby roundabout, but he did say that although Ebby Doherty had not been a party to the plot, he was to be one of the gunmen, along with Terence Moore and Jim Doherty. Originally Quigley cast himself as the driver, but in cross-examination he claimed he had made a mistake and said that the gunmen were to have been himself, Moore, and Tommy Ward, with Jim Doherty as the driver. Lord Lowry took the view that

> If Quigley was a truthful witness, lapses of memory about what other people were to do would raise a question mark about the accuracy of his recollection; but the fact that in addition he was mistaken about his own role must create a real doubt about his evidence. At the same time these mistakes put in question the veracity of the evidence.[44]

In his assessment of Quigley's evidence Mr Justice Hutton had referred to Quigley's errors about Ebby Doherty but chose to stress instead the 'remarkable detail' and 'great consistency' of Quigley's testimony in general. Referring to the Croby roundabout incident,

---

[43] *R.* v. *Crumley* (1986) 14 NIJB 56.
[44] Ibid. 62.

he said that Quigley had made an error about the involvement of Ebby Doherty, but that he had corrected himself in the course of cross-examination, and, subject to the other inconsistencies, which he listed, Mr Justice Hutton had concluded that Quigley was 'remarkably consistent in his account of the events and of the persons who took part in them'.[45] Lord Lowry said that Mr Justice Hutton had overlooked the fact that Quigley had been given an opportunity during cross-examination by Mr Cahill, counsel for one of the accused, to mention any concern he might have had about the accuracy of the evidence which had so far been given and that he had not taken advantage of it. 'The possibility of Quigley having been prompted by someone cannot be ruled out,' Lord Lowry said.[46]

The Lord Chief Justice then spelled out the implications of these flaws in Quigley's evidence for the prosecution case in general and asked:

Could anyone be satisfied then that Quigley had not made other genuine mistakes in implicating any of the accused? Neither in this nor in any other part of the judgment did the judge consider the possibility that Quigley as a truthful witness might have made genuine mistakes, which Quigley did not remember. The judge's failure to do so has flawed his conclusion that without corroboration he could be satisfied beyond reasonable doubt of the truth and correctness of Quigley's evidence and could convict the defendants as he did.[47]

As far as Quigley's credibility was concerned, Lord Lowry stated:

'The general impression which we gather without doubt or difficulty from reading the entire transcript of Quigley's evidence is of an evasive, devious, inventive and lying witness, who often took refuge in allegations of forgetfulness and of having been confused, for example during his police interviews ... The transcript also shows his irresponsibility and lack of conscience as a witness and not only as a man, his avowed propensity for deception and play-acting, his self-confidence and aggression, in that he regarded himself as being in competition with his interrogators. None of these characteristics tend to promote truthful evidence and many of them typify a liar.'[48]

---

[45] Ibid. 7 NIJB 193.
[46] Ibid. 14 NIJB 67
[47] Ibid.
[48] Ibid. 80.

Quigley had started as a supergrass of very bad character and his evidence had sunk to 'the margin of credibility or indeed beyond it', yet he was believed by the trial judge, who marked with emphasis many of his shortcomings. It was important, therefore, the Lord Chief Justice maintained, to consider carefully the route by which Mr Justice Hutton had reached his decision.

The Trial Judge's Reasoning

Mr Justice Hutton had described Quigley as a compact figure who had given his evidence with an air of cool competence. Lord Lowry commented:

We observe that, not surprisingly, the judgment contains no tribute to the witness's frankness, openness, straightforwardness or willingness to admit error or uncertainty. Coolness, competence and determination, especially when they are those of a terrorist moved by self-interest, are not qualities necessarily or even probably associated with the truth.[49]

Mr Justice Hutton's conclusion, that it was 'probable' that Quigley had lied when recounting his first day in Castlereagh in November 1982, was 'surely an understatement by any standards',[50] the Lord Chief Justice remarked, and his evidence about the chance meeting when Gilmour and his wife gave him a lift in their car on 12 August was 'the most devious exhibition that could be imagined'.[51] As far as Quigley's demeanour was concerned, Lord Lowry said that although it was some help in determining a witness's veracity, 'judges have long recognised it as a doubtful indicator'.[52]

Mr Justice Hutton had been 'mightily impressed'[53] by the consistency and detail of Quigley's evidence, and counsel for the appellants had placed great weight on the argument that the trial judge had misled and misdirected himself on this point. The Lord Chief Justice said that consistency had assumed importance because there had been a more vigorous challenge than usual in this case to the contention that all the events had happened, and that, if they had, that Quigley had in fact taken part. Therefore, Quigley's ability to describe the events was important as a means of proving those events and his participation in them. But, Lord Lowry said,

---

[49] *R.* v. *Crumley* (1986) 14 NIJB 92.   [50] Ibid. 93.
[51] Ibid.   [52] Ibid.   [53] Ibid.

once the trial judge had been satisfied on this score, it simply meant that Quigley was a proven accomplice. This evidence against the various accused ought not to have been endowed with any special credibility, however, merely because he could describe the offences accurately, if that was indeed what he was doing. The result was that the Court of Appeal gained the impression that

Quigley, by winning on the issue (so far as it was contentious) of whether he was describing actual events in which he had taken part, acquired a degree of strength for his evidence *against the accused* which that evidence would not have had if the issue of participation had never arisen. The appellants pointed out (with justification, as we think) the irony of relying, as the learned trial judge did, on Quigley's consistency and detail to support the Crown case, when these features of an accomplice's evidence are the very things to beware of lest they deceive the jury on the real question, namely, whether the accused, or any of them, are guilty.[54]

Apart from information regarding a few events, the consistency in Quigley's evidence related only to his own claims, and, as Lord Lowry stated

this betokens a good memory, not veracity, and perhaps a good memory for a script or made-up version rather than a good memory for what actually happened. It cannot be denied that, from the time of reducing his accusations to paper, Quigley had a long time before giving his evidence and very little to occupy him.[55]

The court held that, in any case, the internal consistency of Quigley's evidence was not particularly impressive when the various mistakes and falsehoods were considered. Mr Justice Hutton had said that, with the exception of these defects, Quigley's evidence was remarkably consistent, but the Lord Chief Justice commented that this approach 'sets at naught'[56] the important principle enunciated in the appeal decision in *R.* v. *Donnelly* that evidence which detracts from the credibility of a prosecution witness is much more important than evidence which enhances it. Throughout the judgment, disproportionate reliance had been placed at first instance on consistency, and inadequate emphasis had been given to inconsistency, and this was all the more objectionable when the consistency

---

[54] Ibid. 94–5 (emphasis in original).
[55] Ibid. 95.   [56] Ibid. 96.

in question was only internal. Moreover, Mr Justice Hutton had not given any attention to the possibility that Quigley's recollection might have been faulty, as some of the evidence, particularly in relation to Ebby Doherty, suggested, and that if such mistakes had been made about other accused, 'consistency' would merely perpetuate and conceal the errors. This danger was all the greater in multiple-event and multiple-defendant trials, Lord Lowry stated, particularly when many of the events could be described as 'non-events'—for example, the 'non-productive conspiracies which constitute a substantial proportion of the charges and exhibit few features worthy of recall'.[57]

The Lord Chief Justice also pointed out that Mr Justice Hutton had taken the view that, as a member of the IRA, Quigley knew the real criminals and had no need to give the wrong names. Lord Lowry recognized that there was an 'attractive simplicity' to this approach but that if it were universally true, it would reverse the demand for the time-honoured warning that an accomplice may easily incriminate the wrong people; it also ignored the real possibility of mistakes due to faulty memory or some more sinister cause, and the possibility that Quigley might have been trying to 'out-Gilmour Gilmour' by naming prominent people. Lord Lowry outlined a number of objections to Mr Justice Hutton's conclusion that Quigley would not have named the wrong people, because if they had had alibis, this might have militated against his receiving immunity and police protection. The precise time of many of the events could not be checked, Lord Lowry held, and an intention to name only the right people would not remove the possibility that a genuine mistake had been made. The only effective alibi, given the largely uneventful lives of those concerned and the witnesses upon whom they would have had to rely, would have been something like being in prison or on a well-corroborated holiday. More importantly, Mr Justice Hutton's theory crediting Quigley 'with a degree of judgment which is belied by his way of giving evidence . . .' was not a 'sound proposition leading to a reliable inference, but could be regarded as an ex post facto justification unrelated to the witness himself'.[58]

The Northern Ireland Court of Appeal also deemed Mr Justice Hutton's emphasis upon the evidence which survived cross-examina-

[57] *R.* v. *Crumley* (1986) 14 NIJB.
[58] Ibid. p. 98.

tion and upon counsel's failure to cross-examine on certain issues unjustified, and concluded that it had led him to place 'excessive reliance' on those aspects of Quigley's evidence which were not demolished or impaired by cross-examination, since 'only very rarely can any counsel, however skilful, defeat a witness without the material . . . In cases like the present the adversary had no rival version of the facts to compete with that of the Crown witness.'[59]

By using some of the independent evidence in the case, Mr Cahill had succeeded in undermining Quigley's evidence with respect to the Linsford Road episode and, to a lesser extent, in relation to O'Brien's involvement in the grenade-throwing incident; but the trial judge's conclusion, as a result of these successes, was that Quigley's evidence ought to be accepted in those cases where the cross-examination had failed or had not been attempted. In relation to all or most of the incidents, Quigley had a story which was 'mainly based on reality and the time to perfect it',[60] and, while the stories were capable of being true, the acceptance by the trial judge of a fallible test as a reliable criterion of truth made the reasoning which derived support from such a test flawed.

Lord Lowry concluded that Quigley had started the trial as a highly flawed and suspect accomplice and in order for his evidence to have been worthy of acceptance it was vital that he performed with considerable credibility in the witness-box. Instead, Quigley 'told many lies . . . displayed signs of (at least) faulty recollection, took pride in his expertise as a deceiver and clearly remained an unrepentant terrorist'.[61] The danger against which a warning is obligatory remained, Lord Lowry pointed out, even when the witness performed adequately, and it had nowhere been described more forcefully than in the comments of Lord Alverstone CJ,[62] who said: 'Considering too the respect which is always paid by the jury to such advice from the Bench, it may be regarded as the settled course of practice not to convict a prisoner, excepting under very special circumstances, upon the uncorroborated testimony of an accomplice.'[63] The appellants, Lord Lowry stated, would con-

[59] Ibid. 99.
[60] Ibid. 100.
[61] Ibid. 101.
[62] *R. v. Tate* [1908] 2 KB 680, 682. The quotation was taken from *Taylor on Evidence*, 10th edn. 688.
[63] *R. v. Crumley* (1986) 14 NIJB 102.

tend that the 'very special circumstances' which were said to justify convictions in their case consisted mainly of the fact that because Quigley was an accomplice he was bound to be able to name the guilty men, and that this argument ran counter to the accepted precepts in any accomplice case. Lord Lowry said that the court recognized the probability that Quigley had been describing, to a great extent, crimes which were committed by many of those he had implicated. But he was 'a seriously flawed and frequently lying witness and therefore the better and safer view may be that, having regard to his deplorable character and his evidence viewed as a whole, he cannot truly be said to have achieved the degree of acceptability which is required to sustain convictions on his uncorroborated evidence'.[64] The convictions were therefore unsafe and unsatisfactory and had to be quashed.

THE KIRKPATRICK APPEAL: *R. v. Steenson and others*

All twenty-seven of those found guilty in *R. v. Steenson* appealed against their convictions, and, apart from Molloy, Tumelty, and McKnight, who had made written or verbal admissions, all were successful. Summing up the court's verdict, on 23 December 1986, Lord Lowry said that the appellants had been justified in arguing, as had those in *R. v. Crumley*, that the supergrass on whose evidence their convictions had been based was unworthy of belief and that the trial judge had assessed his evidence wrongly. Kirkpatrick had begun as, and never ceased to be, a suspect witness; the judge had formed the opinion that he had told several lies, that he had executed a deliberate plan to deceive the court, and that he had made so many mistakes on material points that accuracy as well as veracity were in issue. But despite his shortcomings, evasiveness, lies, and feigned loss of memory, it was the trial judge's opinon that he had decided to tell the truth about the material incidents. This, Lord Lowry held, was mistaken, and Mr Justice Carswell had failed to appreciate the importance of the many demonstrable errors in Kirkpatrick's testimony. Having regard both to Kirkpatrick's character as a man and as a witness, his evidence required corroboration in order for safe convictions to be based upon it. Examples of the unreliability of Kirkpatrick's evidence in

[64] *R. v. Crumley* (1986) 14 NIJB 102–3.

relation to specific appellants were cited in the judgment, and some of the most significant of these are recounted below.

McNamee

Two cases involving Henry Joseph McNamee were both enlightening and instructive, Lord Lowry said; enlightening as to the dangers involved in placing complete trust in Kirkpatrick's accuracy and reliability, and instructive in that they demonstrated his dogmatism and obstinacy even when confronted with evidence which clearly showed him to be wrong. Mr Justice Carswell had noted how easy it would have been for Kirkpatrick to have framed people if he had wanted to do so, but did not entertain the possibility that he had actually done so.

Lord Lowry pointed out that although McNamee had been in custody at the time of the conspiracy to shoot Desmond McBride at the Bass Charrington Brewery, Kirkpatrick had insisted that he had been involved. Mr Justice Carswell stated that Kirkpatrick's evidence against McNamee was 'clearly wrong'[65] but that his error had stemmed from mistake and not deliberate falsification. Lord Lowry commented:

whether the error did stem from mistake or from deliberate falsifying seems to be immaterial. It would seem also to be fair comment to say, that, but for the mischance that McNamee could not obtain bail on the day on which it was granted, he would no doubt have been convicted of participation in this incident.[66]

Kirkpatrick had also included McNamee in a robbery at Riverdale Post Office on another date when McNamee was in prison, but had corrected himself after the preliminary inquiry had started but before he testified. Lord Lowry said that the defence suggestion to Kirkpatrick that the correction stemmed not from a sudden recovery of memory but from the fact that he had been informed by the police that McNamee had been in prison at the time, was 'a very feasible explanation', which the judge appeared to have completely discounted.[67]

Mr Justice Carswell also did not appear to have considered it remarkable that when Kirkpatrick belatedly remembered that

---

[65] *R. v. Steenson* (1986) 17 NIJB 68.
[66] Ibid.
[67] Ibid. 69.

McNamee had not been part of the Riverdale Post Office conspiracy, his memory about the Bass Charrington murder had not
been jogged. The fact that Kirkpatrick had not only placed the
same man in two separate incidents in which he had clearly not
been involved, but given a detailed account of that person's participation, 'revealed at the very least an irresponsible witness with a
memory which was alarmingly deficient'.[68]

McKnight

The Riverdale Post Office robbery also raised a question about the
involvement of another of the appellants, Martin Damien Mc-
Knight. McKnight had an alibi for the time at which he was
alleged to have been involved in the conspiracy and the hijacking
in furtherance of the robbery; he had appeared at Belfast Magistrates' Court to be summarily tried for another offence. There was
some doubt about the precise times McKnight had been at the
magistrates' court, since some matrimonial cases had been dealt
with that morning and he himself had been unrepresented. But,
Lord Lowry stated, there was 'cause for concern, and a certain
irony, in the judge's reliance on Kirkpatrick's "clear evidence"
about McKnight, having regard to the clear evidence which at one
time he was prepared to give about McNamee in the same incident'
and which he did give about him in another.[69]

Although McKnight's alibi did not necessarily place him at the
magistrates' court at the material time, the Lord Chief Justice said
that to reject it involved accepting a number of unlikely propositions, namely: that McKnight was aware that matrimonial disputes
would precede the hearing of his case; that he was confident that
his case would not be called on, or called over, at 10.30 a.m. and
that the matrimonial cases would continue until he arrived; and
that he had taken part in a hijacking half an hour after the court
which was to try him for the other offence was due to sit. 'Had the
learned trial judge not been so convinced of Kirkpatrick's truthfulness and accuracy, despite the latter's mistake in the very same case
about McNamee,' Lord Lowry held, 'he would have been likely to
entertain a reasonable doubt as to McKnight's involvement in this
incident,'[70] and, more significantly, the trial judge's belief in Kirk-

---

[68] *R. v. Steenson* (1986) 17 NIJB 71.
[69] Ibid. 73.
[70] Ibid.

patrick's general reliability as an accurate and truthful witness would have been 'seriously eroded'.[71]

The Case of the Unexploded Bomb

Kirkpatrick had alleged that McAreavey, Kearney, and Bradley had been involved in detonating a bomb behind a wall in New Barnsley estate, Belfast. Mr Justice Carswell had assumed that Kearney had correctly related to Kirkpatrick that the bomb had not been detonated but that, for one reason or another, Kirkpatrick had claimed that it had in fact exploded. The Lord Chief Justice said that the difficulty in accepting this explanation lay in the fact that Kirkpatrick had claimed to have seen the command-wire cut, and rubble at the place which he took to have been the site of the explosion. This must have been a 'fabrication', and the incident served, Lord Lowry continued, 'to emphasise, by reliance on the learned trial judge's own findings, the fallibility of Kirkpatrick's recollection about conversations and conspiracies in which it is alleged that he and others took part'.[72]

The Murder of Reserve Constable McDougall

Kirkpatrick's firm evidence that the car used in the murder of Reserve Constable McDougall had only two doors was contradicted by the owner, proving, the Lord Chief Justice held, that it was 'an invention', bolstered by fictitious references to having pushed the front passenger-seat forward in order to let the gunmen into the back, which, together with his assertion that he had never used a two-door car in any other operation exposed his evidence as 'a deliberate falsehood'[73] not easily attributable to an honest loss of memory or the result of a confusion between the facts of two different incidents. It was also possible, Lord Lowry remarked, that Kirkpatrick had been wrong about precisely when the car had been returned to the address from which it had been taken, as his evidence on this matter diverged considerably from that given by the owner, and if this was the case, it confirmed the impression that he was 'seldom ready to admit a gap in his memory' and 'made good any deficiency by providing details drawn from some other source'.[74]

---

[71] Ibid. 74.   [72] Ibid. 77.   [73] Ibid. 80.   [74] Ibid.

Lord Lowry pointed out that Kirkpatrick's account of the Mc-Dougall shooting differed in five significant respects from that given in a statement by McConkey, and he selected for illustrative purposes the alleged involvement of the appellants Barkley, Brown, and Power. Barkley, a close friend of Kirkpatrick's, had been implicated by McConkey in the incident, but Kirkpatrick had denied that he had been involved. Yet Kirkpatrick maintained that, when he and Barkley were both under arrest on McConkey's evidence, he had not mentioned to Barkley that McConkey had implicated him. Brown had been acquitted on the grounds that Kirkpatrick's evidence was confused about whether Brown had introduced Kirkpatrick to McConkey or whether he had known McConkey already. This should also have raised a doubt about the participation of Power, and indeed of any of the alleged conspirators, Lord Lowry said.

The Attempted Murder of Reserve Constable Skillen

The occupants of the house which the gang had taken over for the attempted murder of Reserve Constable Skillen mentioned only two men, but Kirkpatrick had claimed that three had been involved. Kirkpatrick changed his account about how the unit gained entry several times, and it was not until the final version that he made reference to the conspicuous wire-netting over the back yard, which, he claimed, had prevented McAreavey from gaining access over the wall of the back yard. Kirkpatrick had referred to the back alley's having been blocked off at one end, but independent evidence showed that this was not true. At first Kirkpatrick claimed that Patrick Tohill was one of the participants but later implicated Robert, Patrick's brother, instead. Since both brothers were well known to him and he gave no explanation for having initially mixed them up, Lord Lowry commented:

Quite apart from the general character and reputation of Kirkpatrick as well as the numerous other indications that his evidence deserved to be treated with scepticism, there were clearly a number of features of his evidence in connection with this incident which, even taken in isolation, would have raised the gravest doubts as to its reliability and were, in our opinion, bound to give rise to the question whether Kirkpatrick himself took part.[75]

[75] *R.* v. *Steenson* (1986) 17 NIJB 87.

Verdict

After his review of some of these glaring discrepancies in Kirkpatrick's evidence, the Lord Chief Justice stated:

We accept the appellants' contention that the learned trial judge, while fully alert to most or all of the discrepancies, unjustifiably discounted their effect ... Kirkpatrick was already established as a witness who would lie when it suited, and yet the judge, despite all these mainstream mistakes and confusions, relied on him as a witness of truth on the incidents ... In our opinion the appellants' criticisms of Kirkpatrick's ability to be accepted beyond reasonable doubt and of the learned judge's rationalisation of his lying and unsatisfactory evidence on the side issues is justified. We are inevitably impressed by the number of mistakes made by Kirkpatrick when dealing with the main issues and by his disregard for the truth when confronted with his mistakes. Accordingly we consider that all the convictions which depend on Kirkpatrick's uncorroborated evidence are unsafe and must be quashed.[76]

On the question of the trial judge's advantage in having observed the witness's demeanour, Lord Lowry noted that Mr Justice Carswell had paid no tribute to Kirkpatrick's frankness, openness, staightforwardness, or willingness to admit error or uncertainty. His impressions of Kirkpatrick as a witness were that he was 'cool, composed and courteous and ... at no time wilted or became flustered or lost his composure', that he had never expressed any real uncertainty, that he avoided eye-contact with defence counsel, apparently as a deliberate policy, and that he was 'wary and defensive' in cross-examination.[77] But of paramount importance, Lord Lowry stated, was the fact that the judge could not have derived any significant help from Kirkpatrick's demeanour, even if he had purported to do so, since Kirkpatrick had given his evidence in the same 'cool, composed and courteous' manner, whether he was later clearly shown to have have been in error or not.[78]

Finally Lord Lowry addressed himself to potential critics of the verdict. It was probable, he said, that many, if not all, the appellants had been members of the INLA and that between them they had been responsible for most of the crimes which Kirkpatrick described. But being probably guilty was not enough, since the standard demanded by the law was guilt beyond reasonable doubt. This did not mean that no convictions could ever be sustained

---

[76] Ibid. 87–8.   [77] Ibid.   [78] Ibid.

again upon the uncorroborated evidence of a supergrass, and an accomplice witness could possibly be found who would be 'really impressive' (although the need for the warning would remain). But if such a witness were found

the acceptance of his testimony would not need to depend on an overgenerous assessment or (as in the present case) on a theory (for that is all that we can fairly call it) that the witness, having lied about almost everything else, has decided to be as accurate and truthful as possible about the incidents themselves.[79]

The ink had scarcely dried on the Court of Appeal's judgment when a violent feud between rival factions in the INLA erupted and a number of those whose convictions had been quashed in the Kirkpatrick case, including Steenson himself, were killed by their former comrades.

[79] *R.* v. *Steenson,* 103.

9

Legacy: 1986–1993

IN a sense everything which has happened on the anti-terrorist front in Northern Ireland since the mid-1980s could be said to have been influenced to some degree by the failure of the supergrass system. But since many subsequent developments—for example, amendments to anti-terrorist legislation[1] and refinements in the intelligence-gathering system[2]—might well have happened anyway, attention here will focus upon three particularly direct legacies: the effect of the supergrass system upon the level of political violence; the implications of the abolition of the right to silence for the prospect of further supergrass trials; and the enduring need for certain statutory reforms.

THE EFFECT UPON THE LEVEL OF POLITICAL VIOLENCE

While the supergrass system may be given some credit for contributing to a reduction in the level of political violence in the mid-1980s, this was fairly marginal and short-lived. The death rate, to take just one indicator, shows two high peaks, in 1972 (467) and 1976 (297), followed immediately by steep declines, with much smaller rises in 1979 (113) and 1981 (101), followed by a drop from 97 in 1982 to 54 in 1985 and then a rise from 61 in 1986 to 93 in both 1987 and 1988. The trough, therefore, roughly coincides with the ascendancy of the supergrass system and may be at least partly attributable to the arrest of large numbers of active members of

[1] See B. Dickson, 'Northern Ireland's Emergency Legislation: The Wrong Medicine?' (1992) *Public Law* 592; T. Hadden, K. Boyle, and C. Campbell, 'Emergency Law in Northern Ireland: The Context,' in A. Jennings (ed.), *Justice under Fire: The Abuse of Civil Liberties in Northern Ireland*, 2nd edn. (London: Pluto Press, 1990); J. Jackson, 'The Northern Ireland (Emergency Provisions) Act 1987' (1988) 39 *Northern Ireland Legal Quarterly* 235.

[2] See M. Urban, *Big Boys' Rules: The SAS and the Secret Struggle against the IRA* (London: Faber & Faber, 1992), pt. 4; M. Dillon, *The Dirty War* (London: Arrow Books, 1991), chs. 15–17.

paramilitary organizations on supergrass evidence. But it may also derive from other developments—for example, more careful targeting of victims by terrorist organizations, the political rise of Sinn Fein in the aftermath of the prison protests, and a brief flirtation with electoral politics on the part of loyalist paramilitaries. Ironically, the loyalist supergrass trials led indirectly to an increase in violence, since the IRA used them to identify influential members of loyalist paramilitary organizations for the purpose of assassination. By the beginning of 1990 five prominent defendants in loyalist supergrass cases, John Bingham, William Frenchy Marchant, John McMichael, Robert Seymour, and John Irvine, had been killed by the IRA.[3]

THE ABOLITION OF THE RIGHT TO SILENCE

The experience of the supergrass system seems to have discouraged the police and prosecuting authorities, not only from promoting any further supergrass trials, but also from placing such heavy reliance upon any one method of counter-insurgency law enforcement or type of prosecution evidence. Not a single genuine supergrass trial has taken place in Northern Ireland between the settling of the Kirkpatrick appeal, in December 1986, and December 1993, and the post-supergrass Diplock and security landscape lacks any obvious distinguishing feature comparable to that imposed upon it in the heyday of the supergrass system. However, a climate of uncertainty about the prospect of further supergrass trials lingers, sustained by the abolition of the right to silence in Northern Ireland in 1988 and by periodic speculation that a new supergrass is being preened for trial,[4] or that a refashioned system is actively under official consideration. For example, on 27 May 1993 at a press conference to launch his annual report for 1992, the Chief Constable of the RUC, Sir Hugh Annesley, outlined seven measures, including making accomplice evidence more readily admissible against the accused, which he said were being considered at a senior level within the Northern Ireland Office and which were necessary to tackle terrorism more effectively.[5] In the summer of

---

[3] *Independent*, 3 Jan. 1990.
[4] See e.g., 'Loyalist Accused Rejects Supergrass Offer', *Independent*, 19 Dec. 1989; 'Supergrass Fears May Have Prompted Poster Displays', ibid., 6 Feb. 1990.
[5] These were not mentioned in the report itself. See 'RUC Seeks Curbs on

1993 the RUC was also said to be reviewing its guide-lines on agents and informers, following the conviction of loyalist army agent Brian Nelson in February 1992 for his part in five conspiracies to murder, and allegations, published in the *Daily Mirror* in June 1993, that Declan 'Beano' Casey, a former Special Branch spy in the IRA, had participated in over a dozen killings.[6] Finally, the 1993–94 'peace process', especially the Downing Street Declaration of 15 December 1993 and the IRA ceasefire of 31 August 1994, has added further uncertainty. If it succeeds, the emergency in Northern Ireland will be over. But if it fails, the prospects of more draconian anti-terrorist measures, perhaps including supergrass trials, will increase. Therefore, although the old supergrass process may be dead and gone, its ghost can still be heard rattling its chains.

The most significant and most tangible legacy of the supergrass system has been the abolition of the right to silence by the Criminal Evidence (Northern Ireland) Order 1988. In the Bennett case, *R.* v. *Graham*, the Northern Ireland Court of Appeal criticized the trial judge, Mr Justice Murray, for concluding that the credibility of Bennett's evidence was strengthened by the failure of the defendants to testify in their own defence, and the Lord Chief Justice stated that it was difficult to accept that, where the prosecution rested on the evidence of a 'suspect witness', it could ever be so compelling that the accused would be required to testify under pain of certain prejudice.[7] Some four years later the Criminal Evidence (Northern Ireland) Order 1988 abolished the right to silence throughout the Diplock and regular criminal justice systems in Northern Ireland. Although capable of a variety of interpretations, the phrase the 'right to silence' is generally understood to refer to

Suspects Rights', *Guardian*, 28 May 1993. The other 6 measures were: further restrictions upon the right to silence; introducing an offence of refusing to answer questions from members of the security forces; previous terrorist convictions to be admissible at trial; the burden of proof to be shifted to the accused in certain circumstances; the admissibility of intelligence information; and the revision of the discovery process in criminal trials. See also, 'RUC May Call Supergrass Scheme Back', *Guardian*, 9 Sept. 1993.

[6] Ibid., 14 Nov. 1992 and 15, 16, and 24 June 1993. Other disclosures included those made in the trial at the Old Bailey in London of 2 INLA activists convicted on 16 Dec. on the evidence of MI5 agent Patrick Daly, who claimed, amongst other things, that his resettlement expenses after the trial amounted to £400,000 and that he had been promised a bonus of £40,000 'if good custodial sentences were handed out', ibid., 18 Dec. 1993.

[7] (1984) 18 NIJB 21–2.

the common-law principle that juries should not be encouraged to conclude that a defendant is guilty merely because he or she has refused to respond to allegations, particularly from the police, or has refused to give evidence in their own defence in court.[8] The 1988 Order allows courts in Northern Ireland to draw inferences from the silence of defendants where: (*a*) in the course of police questioning before being charged, they have refrained from offering an explanation which subsequently formed part of their defence at the trial, or, upon being charged, they have declined to mention any fact which they could 'reasonably have been expected to mention' to the police; (*b*) upon being called by the court to give evidence, they have either refused to be sworn or, having been sworn, declined 'without good cause' to answer any question; (*c*) under arrest they have failed or refused to account for an 'object, substance or mark' reasonably believed by the police to be connected with the offence; and (*d*) under arrest they have failed to account for their presence at the place where, and around the time

---

[8] In *R.* v. *Director of the Serious Fraud Office, ex parte Smith* [1992] 3 All ER 56, at 463–4, Lord Mustill distinguished 6 different meanings, some of which, as his lordship observed, have already been encroached upon by statute: 1. a general immunity, possessed by all persons and bodies, from being compelled upon pain of punishment to answer questions posed by other persons or bodies; 2. a general immunity, possessed by all persons and bodies, from being compelled upon pain of punishment to answer questions the answers to which may incriminate them; 3. a specific immunity, possessed by all persons under suspicion of criminal responsibility whilst being interviewed by police officers or others in similar positions of authority, from being compelled on pain of punishment to answer questions of any kind; 4. a specific immunity, possessed by accused persons undergoing trial, from being compelled to give evidence, and from being compelled to answer questions put to them in the dock; 5. a specific immunity, possessed by persons who have been charged with a criminal offence, from having questions material to the offence addressed to them by police officers or persons in a similar position of authority: 6. a specific immunity (at least in certain circumstances), possessed by accused persons undergoing trial, from having adverse comment made on any failure (*a*) to answer questions before trial, or (*b*) to give evidence at trial. For recent reviews of the debate about the right to silence, see F. McElree and K. Starmer, 'The Right to Silence', in C. Walker and K. Starmer (eds.), *Justice in Error* (London: Blackstone, 1993), 58; P. Thornton, A. Mallalieu, and A. Scrivener, *Justice on Trial: Report of an Independent Civil Liberty Panel on Criminal Justice* (London: Liberty, 1992); S. Easton, *The Right to Silence* (London: Avebury, 1991); S. Greer and R. Morgan (eds.), *The Right to Silence Debate* (Bristol: Bristol Centre for Criminal Justice, 1990); S. C. Greer, 'The Right to Silence: A Review of the Current Debate' (1990) 53 MLR 709; D. Dixon, 'Politics, Research and Symbolism in Criminal Justice: The Right of Silence and the Police and Criminal Evidence Act' [1991] 20 *Anglo-American Law Review* 27; J. Wood and A. Crawford, *The Right of Silence: The Case for Retention* (London: Civil Liberties Trust, 1989).

at which, the offence was alleged to have been committed, and the police reasonably believe that they were there in connection with it. The legislation also expressly allows such silences to be treated as corroboration of other evidence.

Introducing the Order to Parliament, the Secretary of State for Northern Ireland, Mr Tom King, said that these changes were necessary because of the increasing tendency of those involved in terrorism and other serious crimes, including racketeering, to shelter behind silence and thus evade conviction. Later, when the proposed legislation was debated in the House of Commons, Mr King told MPs that he had been informed by the Royal Ulster Constabulary that, of all those detained in Northern Ireland in connection with serious crime, including terrorism, just under half refused to answer substantive questions, while some refused to answer any questions at all, but no further details about the source of these figures was given. The Secretary of State said that 'many people would think we were mad' not to allow the courts to draw inferences from these facts.[9]

Two particular features of Diplock trials seem to have prompted the government to abolish the right to silence, although it remains unclear why it was also removed from the regular criminal justice process in Northern Ireland. The first is the fact that successive versions of the Northern Ireland (Emergency Provisions) Act have required Diplock judges to produce reasoned judgments.[10] It follows that while juries may draw inferences from a defendant's exercise of the right of silence even when not invited to do so, a judicial inference will be much more difficult to draw in the absence of legislative authorization. The second factor concerns the supergrass system itself. As already indicated in previous chapters, in many of the supergrass cases the Northern Ireland Court of Appeal went out of its way to point out that most of the defendants were probably guilty but that probable guilt was not sufficient to justify conviction. By allowing silence under police questioning and silence in court to constitute corroboration of other evidence, the Criminal Evidence (Northern Ireland) Order 1988 may have created the conditions for fresh supergrass trials in which supergrass evidence could be corroborated by the silence of the accused. There

---

[9] HC Debs., vol. 140, col. 187.
[10] Section 7 (5). This, together with the automatic right of appeal granted Diplock court defendants by s. 7 (6), it is held, provides safeguards to compensate for the absence of the jury.

are, however, two difficulties with this hypothesis. The first is that, strictly speaking, it would be difficult for the courts to regard the silence of the accused as constituting the kind of 'clear and compelling' corroboration which the evidence of supergrasses is now said to require, since there are many reasons other than an attempt to conceal guilt which explain why any suspect may have stayed silent[11]—for example, reluctance to become an informer. While there can be no doubt that members of paramilitary organizations in Northern Ireland are trained to maintain silence under police interrogation, it does not follow that everyone who does so is a member of such an organization.[12]

The second problem is that the trend created by the 1988 Order has been for the accused's silence to be used by the Diplock courts to fill gaps in prosecutions resting on a variety of types of evidence other than that of supergrasses, informers, or accomplices.[13] *R. v. Martin and others*,[14] which featured the testimony of IRA informer Sandy Lynch, rescued, in January 1990, from a weekend IRA interrogation session in a house in Belfast by the timely arrival of a combined army and police patrol, is a case in point. Eight defendants were charged in connection with the incident, and two others with related offences. These included the householder, his wife, and son, and the Sinn Fein Director of Publicity, Danny Morrison, who claimed he had gone to the address to arrange for Lynch to give a press conference in which his role as a Special Branch informer would be revealed and renounced. Significantly, and in spite of the fact that the evidence of an informer had been involved, the trial in May 1991 bore strikingly little resemblance to the supergrass proceedings. First, unlike in the high-profile supergrass cases, the offences concerned only one incident—Lynch's unlawful

[11] See J. D. Heydon, *Evidence: Cases and Materials*, 3rd edn. (London: Butterworth, 1984), 149.

[12] *An Phoblacht/Republican News*, the journal of the republican movement in Northern Ireland (i.e. Sinn Fein and the IRA) has published advice to its readers on more than one occasion not to talk to the police if they are taken in for questioning. See *Guardian*, 21 Oct. 1988.

[13] See J. Jackson, 'Curtailing the Right of Silence: Lessons from Northern Ireland' [1991] Crim LR 404; id., 'Inferences from Silence: From Common Law to Common Sense' (1993) 44 *Northern Ireland Legal Quarterly* 103; id., 'Developments in Northern Ireland', in S. Greer and R. Morgan (eds.), *The Right to Silence Debate*; Amnesty International, *United Kingdom—Fair Trial Concerns in Northern Ireland: The Right of Silence* (London: Amnesty International, Nov. 1992).

[14] (Unpub.), 8 May 1991.

detention and the possibility that there had been a conspiracy to have him shot as an informer. Secondly, the prosecution case was based upon confessions, and upon forensic, circumstantial, eyewitness, and other types of evidence. In fact Lynch's testimony was largely unchallenged by the defence.[15] Thirdly, there was no question about the identity of the principal defendants, since all had been arrested at the scene. Fourthly, the forensic evidence clearly showed that an interrogation had been in progress just before the security forces arrived. Finally, the trial judge relied upon the 1988 Order and used the silence of six of the accused in the face of police questioning and/or their refusal to testify in their own defence to bolster the case advanced by the Crown on the various types of non-informer evidence tendered.

THE NEED FOR STATUTORY REFORMS

However, despite its demise and the hopes inspired by the 'peace process', the supergrass system has left an enduring need for certain statutory reforms whether or not the mandatory accomplice evidence warning is abolished in Northern Ireland as it has been in England and Wales by S.32 (1) (*a*) of the Criminal Justice and Public Order Act 1994. Although a strong case can be made for the restoration of the jury to the trial of scheduled offences in Northern Ireland,[16] the following recommendations assume that this is unlikely to happen in the immediate future. First, there should be no further prosecutions upon the uncorroborated evidence of alleged accomplices in the trial of scheduled offences. As the previous chapter indicates, the Northern Ireland Court of Appeal has signalled that such prosecutions have little chance of success, and therefore the DPP for Northern Ireland would be ill-advised to seek to launch any on this basis. Secondly, the corroboration in question must be 'clear and compelling' in order to justify convictions.

[15] Ibid. 66. Although he identified the defendants Anto Murray and Gerard Hodgins as IRA members present in the house when the security forces arrived, the only accused against whom Lynch's evidence proved crucial were Erin Corbett, whose home he said he visited to attend an IRA intelligence meeting which provided the pretext for his subsequent detention, and Mike Maguire, whom he claimed had driven him to the address in Carrigart Avenue where the interrogation had taken place. Ibid. 54–5.

[16] S. C. Greer and A. White, *Abolishing the Diplock Courts: The Case for Restoring Jury Trial to Scheduled Offences in Northern Ireland* (London: The Cobden Trust, 1986).

Silences in police custody, alleged verbal admissions which are later challenged, and refusals to testify in court should not be deemed sufficient for this purpose, notwithstanding the Criminal Evidence (Northern Ireland) Order 1988. Thirdly, there should be no further grants of immunity from prosecution to any prospective witness in a Diplock trial who has been involved in serious offences. Fourthly, the sentencing discount due to supergrasses should be determined by statute in accordance with the seriousness of the supergrass's own criminal record, but with no reference to any other criteria, and should be seen as the principal reward for testifying. This would weaken the incentive for suspects to be implicated in alleged but unfulfilled conspiracies when they had not in fact taken part. Fifthly, large sums of money should not be available for super-grasses who have served their sentences, although minimal assist-ance with finding a job and accommodation in another part of the United Kingdom, or in another country, should be available. Sixthly, there should be no release of supergrasses by exercise of the royal prerogative. Finally, all accomplices should be tried and sentenced before giving evidence for the Crown, there should be no further use of the voluntary bill of indictment in supergrass cases, and no more than ten defendants should be tried together unless they so consent.

10

Distant Cousins

IN the 1970s and 1980s processes similar in various respects to the supergrass system in Northern Ireland appeared in England, the United States, Italy, France, Spain, and Germany, directed against terrorism, organized crime, and insider dealing. While the relevance of the English experience is self-evident, the American Witness Protection Programme is of particular interest because the RUC is said to have borrowed from it the idea of protecting vulnerable witnesses before trial and offering them new lives and new identities afterwards.[1] The Italian process is also worthy of particular attention because in the 1980s Italian supergrasses, the *pentiti*, were used to devastating effect against the terrorism of the Red Brigades[2] but with less success against the Mafia, and in Germany in the early 1990s, accomplice testimony has been effectively deployed against the once ruthless but now largely defunct Red Army Faction. Although no supergrass processes as such have been established in France or Spain, legislation has been enacted in each of these countries to encourage terrorists to co-operate in the prosecution of their erstwhile confederates.

ENGLAND

The use of supergrasses in England has differed from the experience in Northern Ireland in four main respects. First, the English supergrasses have been used against defendants charged with offences relating to organized crime rather than political violence. Secondly, supergrass cases have been heard by juries within the regular criminal justice process. Thirdly, convictions critically de-

---

[1] E. Malony, 'Supergrass Scheme Owes Much to US', *Irish Times*, 8 Oct. 1983.

[2] L. Weinberg and W. L. Eubank, *The Rise and Fall of Italian Terrorism* (Boulder, Col.: Westview Press, 1987), 130; C. Seton-Watson, 'Terrorism in Italy', in J. Lodge (ed.), *The Threat of Terrorism* (Brighton: Wheatsheaf Books, 1988), 114.

pended from the beginning upon the availability of corroboration. Finally, the English supergrass system was successfully institutionalized and, following the resolution of its initial teething problems, functioned largely beyond the spotlight of public controversy for over ten years before quietly declining into oblivion.[3]

The evidence suggests that the appearance of the English supergrass process was connected with a rise in the incidence of serious organized crime, principally in the London area, and an official perception that existing methods of dealing with it were ineffective. Reflecting this mood, the Criminal Law Revision Committee stated in its eleventh report in 1972: 'There is now a large and increasing class of sophisticated professional criminals who are not only skilful in organising their crimes and in the steps they take to avoid detection but are well aware of their legal rights and use every possible means to avoid conviction if caught.'[4] In a similar vein, and only a week before this report was published, Sir Robert Mark, Commissioner of Police for the Metropolis, claimed in a public lecture that 'only a small proportion of those acquitted by juries are likely to be innocent in the true sense of the word' and that the professional criminal was 'the very man most likely to escape society's protective net'.[5] However, as Zander, amongst others, argued at the time, these perceptions were at variance with

[3] The principal study is D. Seymour, 'What Good Have Supergrasses Done for Anyone but Themselves?' *Legal Action Group Bulletin*, Dec. 1982, 7. Other fragmentary accounts can be found in J. Goodman and I. Will, *Underworld* (London: Harrap, 1985), ch. 4; J. Slipper, *Slipper of the Yard* (London: Sidgwick & Jackson, 1981), chs. 11 and 12; D. Campbell, *The Underworld* (London: BBC Books, 1994, ch. 8. See also the largely self-serving autobiography of Maurice O'Mahoney, one of the original London supergrasses, M. O'Mahoney with D. Wooding, *King Squealer: The True Story of Maurice O'Mahoney* (London: Sphere Books, 1978). See also '£1m Scheme to Pay Drug Grasses', *Guardian*, 15 Feb. 1990; 'Yard Chief Makes Sure Supergrass Rules Are Obeyed', ibid., 4 Jan. 1991. However, allegations have surfaced from time to time that the evidence given by some supergrasses has been untrue, most notably in the scandal about miscarriages of justice which emerged in the late 1980s and early 1990s in relation to the West Midlands Serious Crime Squad. See, e.g. 'Supergrass Tells Police of Yard Link', ibid., 7 Aug. 1992; 'Supergrass Lied on Police Orders', ibid., 1 July 1993; 'Supergrass's Claims Leave Him Between the Dock and a Hard Place', ibid., 16 July 1993; 'Inquiry Plans to Examine the Use of Supergrasses', *Independent*, 13 Aug. 1990.
[4] Criminal Law Revision Committee, *Eleventh Report, Evidence General*, Cmnd. 4991 (London: HMSO, 1972), para. 21.
[5] R. Mark, 'The Disease of Crime: Punishment or Treatment?' (London: Royal Society of Medicine, 1972), 6 and 13. See also 'Minority Verdict', *The Listener*, 8 Nov. 1973.

the empirical evidence, which showed that few defendants in trials involving professional crime managed to evade conviction.[6]

Origins of the English Supergrass Process

The modern English supergrass system is generally dated from the arrest on 23 December 1972 of Derek Creighton (alias Bertie) Smalls, a key member of a network of gangs responsible for major bank-robberies in London and the south of England.[7] Within a few days, according to the police, Smalls offered to name all his accomplices in exchange for his freedom, the Director of Public Prosecutions was contacted, and a deal giving him a written guarantee of immunity from prosecution was struck. No prosecution evidence was offered when Smalls appeared in court on 13 July 1973 accused of a catalogue of serious offences. He was therefore released, and subsequently appeared as the key prosecution witness in three trials involving twenty-five defendants, sixteen of whom were ultimately convicted.

In *R.* v. *Turner*, by allowing three appeals and dismissing sixteen others, the Court of Appeal both endorsed the practice of prosecuting large numbers of defendants upon the testimony of a supergrass and indicated the appropriate parameters—a decision which was clearly of central importance in determining whether, and in what manner, other prosecutions would be launched upon similar evidence. The appellants maintained that since Smalls was a particularly villainous character, the trial judge should have given the jury a more adequate warning about the danger of convicting on his uncorroborated evidence. It was also argued that, since the immunity from prosecution which Smalls had been granted would have been jeopardized had he not repeated in the witness-box exactly what he had told the police, his evidence was elicited by a continuing inducement, and that trial judges were obliged by the rule established by *R.* v. *Pipe*[8] to exclude such evidence as a matter of law. Delivering the leading judgment, Lord Justice Lawton dismissed all these submissions. The jury was well aware, he said, that Smalls was 'one of the most dangerous and craven criminals who

---

[6] M. Zander, 'Are Too Many Professional Criminals Avoiding Conviction: A Study in Britain's Two Busiest Courts' (1974) 37 MLR 28.

[7] See Seymour, 'What Good Have Supergrasses Done?'. Campbell states that Leslie Payne, adviser to the Kray twins who testified against them in 1969, may have been the first genuine supergrass (*The Underworld*, 153). But the term *supergrass* seems unwarranted here, given the small number of defendants.

[8] (1967) Cr App R 17.

have ever given evidence for the Crown',[9] and their common sense would have alerted them to the dangers of convicting on his uncorroborated evidence without the judge's having to issue a warning differing substantially from that which is customarily given. He also held that *Pipe* simply affirmed existing practice that normally an accomplice charged with the same offences as the accused should not testify for the prosecution unless already tried for his own offences, and stated that the decision did not upgrade the practice to a rule of law. According to the Court of Appeal, the trial judge had a discretion in the interests of justice to exclude Smalls's evidence on the grounds that there was an obvious and powerful inducement for him to ingratiate himself with the prosecution and the court. But it was proper for all factors in the case, including the services rendered by witnesses such as Smalls, to be taken into account when deciding whether or not to exercise it. Lord Justice Lawton added that the guarantee Smalls had received excluded any real prospect of his being prosecuted, even if he had refused to give evidence, although the police could have withdrawn their protection. The Court of Appeal's endorsement of prosecutions on the evidence of supergrasses was based on the grounds that it was 'in the interests of the public that criminals be brought to justice' and that 'the more serious the crimes the greater is the need for justice to be done'. Employing Queen's evidence to accomplish this end was permissible, Lord Justice Lawton said, even though it was 'distasteful and has been distasteful for at least 300 years to judges, lawyers and members of the public'.[10]

There were three main lessons for the prosecuting authorities in *Turner*. First, the Court of Appeal indicated its preference for less complex trials.[11] Secondly, the Director of Public Prosecutions was rebuked for having granted Smalls, in writing, an extremely wide immunity from prosecution. Lord Justice Lawton stated:

the spectacle of the Director recording in writing, at the behest of a criminal like Smalls, his undertaking to give immunity from further prosecutions, is one which we find distasteful. Nothing of a similar kind must ever happen again. Undertakings of immunity from prosecution may have to be given in the public interest. They should never be given by the police. The Director should give them most sparingly; and in the cases involving

---

[9] (1975) Cr App R 67, 79.
[10] Ibid.
[11] Ibid. 76.

grave crimes it would be prudent of him to consult the Law Officers before making any promises. In saying what we have we should not be taken as doubting the well established practice of calling accomplices on behalf of the Crown who have been charged on the same indictment as the accused and who have pleaded guilty.[12]

Thirdly, it appeared that neither the Court of Appeal nor the jury was prepared to permit defendants to be convicted upon the uncorroborated and unsupported testimony of a supergrass. Lord Justice Lawton remarked that: 'if the jury found Smalls to be a credible witness, as they did, *and there was independent evidence supporting him* we can find no reasons for adjudging that verdicts based on his evidence were unsafe or unsatisfactory'.[13] However, the Court of Appeal took the view that the trial judge had been wrong to conclude that statements made to the police by one defendant, Kozak, were capable of amounting to corroboration of Smalls's evidence and that hearsay evidence had also been wrongly admitted with respect to another, Wilkinson. The conviction of Jones was, however, overturned on the grounds that

In the series of cases with which the Court has been dealing, this is the only instance in which the jury have convicted solely on Smalls' uncorroborated and unsupported evidence ... In short the conviction of Jones for the Ralli Brothers robbery was completely out of pattern, not only with the other verdicts of the same jury on this indictment, but with those of the two other juries who tried the indictments in the other two appeals.[14]

Refinements

The prosecuting authorities responded to the criticisms outlined by the Court of Appeal in *Turner* in two ways. First, the practice of granting immunity from prosecution was abandoned in England and Wales, in favour of a policy of prosecuting potential supergrasses prior to their appearance in trials as the key Crown witness.[15] Vital to the success of this modification was the readiness of trial judges to accept the police view of the utility of the

---

[12] Ibid., 79–80. His lordship also advised the DPP to remember Hales's caution that 'more mischief hath come to good men by these kinds of approvement by false accusations ... than benefit to the public', but added with respect to immunity deals; 'it is ... no part of our function to add to the weight of ethical condemnation or to dissipate it'.

[13] Ibid. 79 (Emphasis added).

[14] Ibid. 86.

[15] Seymour, 'What Good Have Supergrasses Done?', 9.

supergrass to law enforcement. The second alteration was not implemented until the day the appeals in the second supergrass case, *R.* v. *Thorne*, were heard, when, according to an exclusive report in the *Guardian*, the Director of Public Prosecutions issued instructions that there were to be no further prosecutions on the evidence of supergrasses unless their evidence was corroborated.[16]

Even before all the trials in which Smalls gave evidence had been completed, the next two supergrasses, Maurice O'Mahoney and Billy Williams, were already in custody at Chiswick police station, or as Williams preferred to call it 'Chiswick drinking club'.[17] O'Mahoney was allotted two cells, with a colour television-set and a record-player, and his mistress visited him frequently there. She later gave birth to a child conceived on one of these occasions.[18] Williams also had a colour television and a record-player, and the use of three cells. Three days a week he was taken out by Flying Squad officers, and, he claimed, the police plied him with drink at the police station.[19] His girlfriend also visited him for sex, and while in custody he was married, with Detective Superintendent Jack Slipper as best man.

O'Mahoney was arrested on 12 June 1974 and appeared in court three months later, admitting to 102 offences, including thirteen armed robberies and sixty-five burglaries. The only witnesses were two police officers who assured the court that he had provided even more information than Smalls. Accepting the value of O'Mahoney's co-operation, the judge sentenced him to five years' imprisonment, although on the basis of his record he could have expected at least fifteen. Between the summers of 1975 and 1976 O'Mahoney appeared as a prosecution witness in a series of trials, and in the spring of 1977 he was called by the Crown to support the evidence of Billy Williams. The appeals in the biggest of these cases, involving John Thorne and twelve others, were heard by the Court of

---

[16] 19 May 1977.

[17] *News of the World*, 16 May 1978.

[18] O'Mahoney with Wooding, *King Squealer*. Amongst other things, O'Mahoney claims that he turned supergrass while in custody on remand because of threats made to his girlfriend and children and because of ill-treatment received from his cronies, who already suspected him of having informed (128–30 and 134), and that he was given a new identity, but this was not supported by adequate documentation (214).

[19] See also Slipper, *Slipper of the Yard*.

Appeal in 1977 and provided a second opportunity for the court to exert some influence on the use of supergrass evidence.

As in *Turner*, the appellants in *Thorne* sought to impugn the credibility of the Crown's chief witness and also argued that, because the proceedings had taken 111 working days and had involved so many defendants, facing a multiplicity of charges, the appellants had been denied a fair trial. With the exception of those of Marks and Cook, all the convictions were upheld. The Court of Appeal's decision in *Thorne* followed *Turner* by endorsing the use of supergrass evidence as a method of prosecution, again criticizing the size of the trials, and once more underscoring the need for corroborative and supportive evidence. Delivering the judgment of the court, Lord Justice Lawton reaffirmed the utilitarian justification for reliance upon supergrass evidence as a means of gaining convictions and said that the cost of the trial—£313,977 in legal fees alone—had to be seen in perspective. What mattered most was the removal from society of a 'ruthless, dangerous and cunning gang of robbers'.[20] Although smaller trials might have reduced the cost, the court did not consider that the appellants' rights had been prejudiced by the scale of the proceedings. It was held that the function of the Court of Appeal in cases such as this was to examine the supergrass's evidence with care to see whether it disclosed any weaknesses which the jury might have overlooked or might not have assessed properly, and to take into account any new evidence brought to its attention by the Crown with the consent of any of the appellants. The Court of Appeal concluded that, with respect to all the appellants except Marks and Cook, the trial judge had correctly found that there was evidence capable of amounting to corroboration, at least on some of the counts. However, evidence from another case in which O'Mahoney had testified showed that he was prepared to cast the blame for his own crimes on to others, and this revealed a 'crack in his credibility', a 'lurking doubt' that his testimony about Cook was not true,[21] while Marks's conviction was quashed on the grounds that the prosecution had changed the date of the charge on the indictment late in the proceedings. Lord Justice Lawton also expanded upon the criticisms he made in *Turner* about the number of defendants being tried on one indictment:

[20] *R.* v. *Thorne* (1978) 66 Cr App R 6.
[21] Ibid. 17.

No more accused should be indicted together than is necessary for the proper presentation of the prosecution's case against the principal accused. Necessity not convenience should be the guiding factor . . . Our experience warns us . . . that in cases involving a number of accused, there is a danger that those on the fringes will be dragged down by those at the centre.[22]

On 15 March 1976, a mere twenty-one months after having been arrested, O'Mahoney was released on parole, having spent all his time in custody, with the exception of a few months, in a police cell. He subsequently failed to appear at the trial of the remaining accused charged on the evidence he supplied, and as a result all were set free, with verdicts of not guilty entered on their records.[23]

Institutionalization

The negotiations between courts and prosecuting authorities represented by the *Turner* and *Thorne* cases, and the subsequent alterations in prosecution policy, resulted in the establishment of a *modus vivendi* which allowed a succession of supergrass cases to be processed comparatively smoothly.[24] The terms of the agreement were, first, that the courts, including the Court of Appeal, would be prepared to permit convictions upon supergrass evidence provided it was corroborated by other evidence, although, as the Chard case shows, the weak support offered by the evidence of other supergrasses has, in some circumstances, been held to be sufficient.[25]

---

[22] *R.* v. *Thorne* (1978) 66 Cr App R 12–14.

[23] In his memoirs O'Mahoney records this fact but offers no explanation for it. See O'Mahoney with Wooding, *King Squealer*, 211. Some time later O'Mahoney re-emerged as a security man on Rick Wakeman and David Bowie tours, selling jewellery of dubious origin, and carrying out electrical work at the homes of his former police minders. In July 1993, and under a new alias—Peter Davies—he stood trial at the Old Bailey charged with possession of firearms and the robbery of a money-bag outside a post office in Shepherd's Bush. In his defence O'Mahoney claimed that the police had themselves asked him to commit the offence so that they could frame someone else with the stolen property. He named a former detective constable as one of his middlemen and said that, on previous occasions, he had lied in court on the instructions of his handlers in order to secure the conviction of others. He was acquitted and promptly attempted to sell his story to the *Sun*. Campbell, *The Underworld*, 157.

[24] Between 1 Jan. 1979 and June 1982 there were, e.g., 18 supergrasses ('resident informers') in the Metropolitan Police district. Letter of 21 June 1982 to Christopher Price MP from the Home Secretary, cited in Seymour, 'What Good Have Supergrasses Done?', 9.

[25] *R.* v. *Chard* [1984] AC 279. In another unpublished decision (*R.* v. *Turner*, 11 Feb. 1980) the Court of Appeal endorsed a direction by a trial judge to a jury that

A second clear message was that the courts were ready to facilitate the recruitment of future supergrasses by adopting a lenient sentencing policy towards the supergrasses themselves. In 1978 the Court of Appeal laid down some guide-lines when it reduced to five years an eleven-and-a-half-year sentence imposed upon Charlie Lowe, London's fourth supergrass.[26] Lord Justice Roskill held that a balance had to be struck between, on the one hand, the risk of deterring offenders from supplying vital prosecution evidence by the adoption of an overly severe sentencing policy and, on the other, properly punishing a 'massive number' of serious crimes such as those which Lowe had, by his own admission, committed. The court concluded that in order to encourage others, the public interest required 'substantial credit' to be given to accomplices such as Lowe who turned Queen's evidence, especially when they pleaded guilty and the only evidence against them was their own confession. Justification for reducing Lowe's sentence was also found in the fact that he testified in other cases after having been sentenced, and that the trial judge was not in a position to take this into account when he imposed the eleven-and-a-half-year term. Other subsequent cases have established that sentencing discounts from a half to two-thirds can be awarded, depending upon the circumstances and the assistance which the police claim the supergrass has provided.[27] The Home Office has also made its own contribution by reducing the level of punishment further. As a result of the exercise of the Crown prerogative of mercy, it seems that few, if any supergrasses have served more than two years of their sentences.[28]

Decline

The view taken by the police, the courts, and the government in the mid-1970s concerning the value of supergrass evidence was increas-

the evidence of 2 accomplices who had turned Queen's evidence could not supply mutual corroboration against the defendants but that the jury could take the congruence of their evidence into account in deciding whether or not to believe it, provided they were sure that the evidence of each of the witnesses was credible and that they had not put their heads together, nor each been told by the police what the other had said.

[26] *R.* v. *Lowe* (1978) 66 Cr App R 122.

[27] See, e.g., *King* [1985] Crim LR 748; *Davies and Gorman* (1978) 68 Cr App R 319; *Tremarco* (1979) 1 Cr App R (S) 286; *Rose and Sapiano* (1980) 2 Cr App R (S) 239; *Sinfield* (1981) 3 Cr App R (S) 258; *Preston* (1987) 9 Cr App R (S) 155.

[28] Seymour, 'What Good Have Supergrasses Done?', 9.

ingly in question as the 1980s progressed. Seymour maintains that comparatively few of the scores of people arrested on supergrass evidence were eventually convicted and that, although there was a definite drop in the number of serious robberies in the London area following the conviction of the Smalls gang, from the mid-1970s to the early 1980s the annual number of serious crimes almost trebled, while the number of supergrasses multiplied.[29] Campbell attributes the decline in the supergrass process to changes in the activities and structure of organized crime, and to the increasingly obvious unreliability of the supergrasses themselves.[30]

   From the late 1970s professional criminals became more interested in the illicit drugs market, which required close-knit organizations, and moved away from armed robbery which involved assembling hand-picked gangs for particular jobs. The more intimate nature of these new enterprises made it easier for informers to be detected and the underworld became much more willing and able to punish betrayal with murder or mutilation than hitherto. Although no supergrass had cut a particularly admirable figure, the characters of some in the later phases were particularly unsavoury; Billy Amies, for example, was a brutal offender with a history of mental illness who sexually assaulted his male victims. Several, in addition to O'Mahoney, re-offended and subsequently admitted having given perjured evidence at the trials in which they had been the principal Crown witnesses. Still others withdrew their co-operation once they reached the witness-box having wasted large sums of public money in the process. It was not surprising, therefore, that juries became increasingly sceptical of supergrass evidence. The result was that, by the early 1990s, supergrass trials—such as the major Triad trial at the Old Bailey in 1992, where the chief witness was the first Chinese supergrass in Britain—had become the exception where once they had been routine. Attempts to secure the safety of informers have, however, continued. Since 1978 new identities have been granted in 170 cases involving some 700 informers and their families. Some have been supplied with bogus documents for bank accounts, educational qualifications, and medical records to authenticate their new personae, as well as relocation

---

   [29] Seymour, 'What Good Have Supergrasses Done?', 9.
   [30] Campbell, *The Underworld*, 160–3 and 'Whisper Who Dares' (1991) *Police Review* 532.

to Australia or the United States. In some cases round-the-clock police protection has also been provided for several years.[31]

THE UNITED STATES

The US equivalent of the supergrass system, the Witness Protection Programme, differs from the supergrass system in Northern Ireland in three principal respects.[32] First, it has been successfully institutionalized and continues to function as a matter of routine because from its inception it was based upon statute and subject to effective Congressional scrutiny. Secondly, the jury remains central to the US trial system, and this appears to have made convictions more difficult, though not impossible, unless the protected witnesses' evidence is corroborated. Thirdly, although both the United States and Northern Ireland are common-law jurisdictions, there are sharp differences in the respective law enforcement contexts.

Origins and Structure of the Witness Protection Programme

The Witness Protection, or Witness Security, Programme (WPP or WSP), established by Title V of the Organised Crime Control Act 1970, authorized the Attorney-General to provide short-term or permanent protection and new identities, credit cards, indefinite subsistence payments, and fictitious work histories, military service records, and school reports, to vulnerable witnesses involved in trials concerning organized crime, and to their families. Prior to this legislation, federal officials had made only sporadic attempts to protect witnesses at risk from reprisal, with a variety of informal procedures, including relocation, developed by the Department of Justice. But it was not until the Task Force on Organised Crime reported in 1967 that inadequate protection for vulnerable witnesses was identified as a major shortcoming of law enforcement in this context. The attitude of the US courts to the disclosure of an informer's identity was a critical factor in this assessment. From the decision of the Supreme Court in *Roviaro* v. *United States* in

---

[31] Campbell, *The Underworld*, 163.

[32] For recent studies, see R. J. Harris, 'Note: Whither the Witness? The Federal Government's Special Duty of Protection in Criminal Proceedings after *Piechowicz* v. *US*' (1991) 76 *Cornell Law Review* 1285; J. M. Levin, 'Organised Crime and Insulated Violence: Federal Liability for Illegal Conduct in the Witness Protection Program' [1985] 76 *Journal of Criminal Law and Criminology* 208.

1957[33] both state and federal courts have upheld the principle that an informer's identity must be disclosed where it is relevant to the guilt or innocence of the accused, but not where it merely goes to the issue of probable cause in respect of an arrest or the issuing of a search warrant.[34] The prosecuting authorities were thus placed in a dilemma: either to proceed and risk disclosing an informer's identity or to protect his identity and forgo prosecution.

Following the enactment of the Organised Crime Control Act 1970, the Justice Department developed an administrative process for the WPP, including vetting prospective candidates, with the principal criterion for admission being whether the federal interest would be served by an offer of protection.[35] Other reforms followed, including: the replacement of temporary 'safe houses' by permanent relocation arrangements; the creation of a protection bureaucracy, which became the responsibility of the US Marshals' Service; and the implementation of written 'Memoranda of Understanding' between government and protected witnesses enumerating the rights and duties of each party. Between 1970 and 1983 over 4,000 witnesses and 8,000 family members were involved in the WPP, its annual costs were in excess of $30.9 million,[36] and the estimated average cost of relocation was between $45,000 and $50,000 per witness.[37] About half those participating joined after having been convicted of felonies, while the other half consisted, in the main, of Mafia hangers-on, 'juice loan' victims, and others who faced retaliation if they testified.[38] In 1980 between 95 and 97 per cent of the witnesses in the WPP had extensive criminal records.[39]

[33] 353 US 53 (1957).

[34] See, e.g., *McCray* v. *Illinois*, 386 US 300 (1967); *Theodor* v. *Superior Court*, (1972) 8 Cal. 3d 77; Anon., 'Testing the Factual Basis for a Search Warrant' (1967) *Columbia Law Review* 1529, 1532–4; J. Schlichter, 'The Outwardly Sufficient Search Warrant Affidavit: What If It's False?' (1971) 96 *University of California Los Angeles Law Review* 96.

[35] Justice Order OBD 2110.2 repr. in *Hearings on HR 7309 before the Subcommittee on Courts, Civil Liberties, and the Administration of Justice of the House Committee on the Judiciary, 97th Congress, 2nd Sess.* 309 (Washington, DC: US Government Printing, 1982).

[36] Comptroller General of the United States, *Changes Needed in Witness Security Program*, (1983) repr. in *Hearings on HR 7309*.

[37] See J. Coates, 'Another Bad Apple Spoils Witness Protection Image', *Chicago Tribune*, 2 Mar. 1986.

[38] Interview with G. Shur, Director of the WPP, reported ibid.

[39] Evidence of Howard Safir, Assistant Director of Operations, US Marshals Service, Acting Chief, Witness Security Section, in *Convenzione per una ricerca su*

Throughout the 1970s and early 1980s a number of problems with the WPP became apparent. Tensions arose between local officials within whose jurisdictions witnesses were relocated, who wanted more disclosure, and WPP officials who wanted maximum secrecy. Witnesses themselves expressed dissatisfaction about the adequacy of the programme and about their true identities being inadvertently revealed by careless administrators.[40] By insulating witnesses from their former lives, the WPP also made it easier for certain legal responsibilities—for example, liabilities to debtors—to be evaded and created difficulties in respect of the rights of non-custodial parents whose children were secretly relocated. It also became apparent that the government's 'discretionary function exemption' made it difficult to hold the US Marshals' Service liable for crimes and torts committed by protected witnesses. There were also problems with the selection of witnesses and their subsequent relationship with the programme.[41]

In 1984 the Witness Protection Programme was overhauled by Congress. According to Levin, the basic defect of the original legislation was that it 'focused almost exclusively on protecting witnesses from the wrath of organised criminals' while largely ignoring 'society's need to be protected from the wrath of the witnesses themselves'.[42] Up to this point more than 500 cases of crimes committed by protected witnesses had been recorded and the recidivism rate of protected witnesses was 22 per cent.[43] Title V of the 1970 Act was repealed and a new statutory foundation was provided by the Witness Security Reform Act 1984. The WPP was extended to include 'organised criminal activity or other serious offence',[44] and the admission criteria were also more fully specified. Before providing protection, the Attorney-General must now

---

normative ed esperienza di maxiprocessi e sulla utilizzabilita e gestibilita probatoria dei c.d. testimoni della corona e della relative tutela. Confronto con l'esperienza italiana. Rapporto finale, 2 Allegati, II (Milan: Centro Nazionale di Prevenzione e Difesa Sociale, 1987) (hereafter CNPDS).

[40] See evidence given by G. Baldwin, Assistant Counsel, and R. Warsham, Investigator, US Senate Permanent Subcommittee on Investigations, in *Hearings before the Permanent Subcommittee on Investigations on the Committee on Government Affairs, US Senate, 96th Congress, 2nd Session, 15, 16, & 17 Dec. 1980: Witness Protection Program* (Nunn Committee).

[41] Levin, 'Organised Crime'.

[42] Ibid. 249.

[43] Coates, 'Bad Apple'.

[44] Pub. L. No. 98–473 § 1208, 98 Stat. 2153.

obtain information about candidates' criminal history, psychological state, the seriousness of the case in which they are to be called
to give evidence, alternative sources of testimony, the risks which
their relocation would pose to the local community, and the effects
of relocation upon parent–child relationships. Protection is now
prohibited where the need for a person's testimony is outweighed
by the risk of danger which it would pose to the public. The
Memorandum of understanding has also been codified and its legal
force strengthened, and access by non-custodial parents to relocated
witnesses has been increased. A Victim's Compensation Fund has
been established for families or victims injured or killed by protected witnesses, while witnesses who fail to comply with judgments
against them in debt-recovery proceedings now risk having their
identities exposed.

Recruits found amongst the prison population are required to
pass a polygraph examination before gaining admission,[45] and
some WPP witnesses testify for the prosecution on more than one
occasion.[46] Most of those involved in the WPP co-operate in
return for one of three rewards: immunity from prosecution, a
lenient sentence, or early release from prison. By law, all inducements, including express or implicit promises of leniency, must be
disclosed to lawyers defending those implicated by a protected
witness's testimony.[47] Requests for immunity from prosecution are
reviewed by senior prosecutors but final approval needs to be
obtained from the Assistant Attorney-General. The general rule is
that immunity is to be given only as a last resort,[48] and, as Michael
DeFeo, Deputy Chief, Organised Crime and Racketeering Section,
Criminal Division, US Department of Justice, states, this is designed to ensure that 'only participants who are less culpable,
harder to convict, and potentially useful witnesses are given immunity'.[49] De Feo also maintains that

[45] Statement of G. Shur, Associate Director, Office of Enforcement Operations,
Criminal Division, US Dept. Justice, in *Senate Subcommittee on Appropriations for
the Departments of State, Justice, Commerce, the Judiciary and Related Agencies,
July 6, 1982*, reprod. *CNPDS*, 8.

[46] See statement of Art Beltram to the Nunn Committee.

[47] *Giglio* v. *United States*, 405 US 150 (1972); *People* v. *Westmoreland*, 58 CA 3d
32 (1976); *United States* v. *Oxman and others*, 3d Cir. No. 83–1531, Aug. 1, 1984;
S. S. Trott, 'The Successful Use of Informants and Criminals as Witnesses for the
Prosecution in a Criminal Trial', *CNPDS*, 232.

[48] Trott, 'Use of Informants', 159–61.

[49] Letter from Michael De Feo, Deputy Chief, Organised Crime and Racketeering

This review process is ultimately reinforced by the spectre of the trial jury's anticipated reaction to an immunity. If a defense lawyer can point out that his client faces trial while others more culpable received immunity, the jury may be tempted to informally 'immunize' the defendant by an acquittal because its collective conscience is shocked by, or simply disagrees with, the prosecutorial choice as to who should be prosecuted and who should be immunized.[50]

It is also possible for accomplice witnesses to be offered 'post-conviction use-immunity'—that is to say, immunity from prosecution *after* they have given their testimony[51]—while those convicted can also be placed on probation on condition that they co-operate with the prosecution.[52] Co-operative accomplices can also be convicted, their sentence being deferred until after they have testified for the prosecution in the trial of others. This is an option particularly recommended by Stephen Trott, Associate United States Attorney-General, who emphasizes, however, that it would be improper to offer favourable treatment to the accomplice contingent upon the successful outcome of other proceedings, since to do so would invite perjury.[53]

Yet, despite these reforms, some difficulties remain. Levin identifies four in particular: there is no mechanism for airing grievances over child custody once protection has begun; state and local officials lack the power to compel disclosure of witness information except in connection with specific investigations or pursuant to court order; it remains unclear whether the WPP will become a regular vehicle for obtaining testimony in cases not involving organized crime, and, if so, how this will affect the programme's contribution to the enforcement of the law against organized crime; and the exposure of WPP agents to federal tort claims could have an inhibiting effect upon the management of the scheme.[54]

Impact

An illustration of the importance of the WPP to the enforcement of the law against organized crime in the United States can be

Section, Criminal Division, US Dept. of Justice to Prof. Guido Modene, Turin, 8 Sept. 1987, in *CNPDS*.

[50] Ibid. 4.
[51] Trott, 'Use of Informants', 255–9; *People* v. *Stewart*, 1 CA 3d 339 (1965); *People* v. *Watson*, 89 CA 3d 376 (1979); *People* v. *Campbell*, 137 CA 3d 867 (1982).
[52] *United States* v. *Worcester*, 190 F. Supp. 548 (D. Mass. 1961).
[53] Trott, 'Use of Informants', 172; *United States* v. *Dailey*, 759 F. 2d 192 (1st Cir.) 1985.
[54] 'Organised Crime', 246–50.

Distant Cousins

found in the testimony of Richard Endler, Attorney in Charge of the Buffalo Strike Force, New York State, to the Nunn Congressional Committee. Endler claimed that in almost 60 per cent of cases concerning organized crime, at least one witness had been a member of the WPP, and these testimonies had all been crucial to the ultimate issues of fact. Some 80 per cent of the prosecutions in question could not have been brought, he maintained, had it not been for the evidence given in court by protected witnesses.[55]

The overhauled Witness Protection Programme has been a vital component in the success of the drive against organized crime which began in the early 1980s and culminated in the conviction on 2 April 1992 of John, the 'Dapper Don', Gotti, reputedly the last of the Mafia heads of family then still at large, in a trial which hinged around the testimony of protected witness Salvatore ('Sammy the Bull') Gravano, Gotti's underboss.[56] Between 1980 and 1985 2,254 mafiosi were indicted in 1,025 trials in New York, Chicago, Boston, and elsewhere[57] and between 1 October 1981 and 31 December 1986 the FBI reported that over 850 cosa Nostra members and their associates had been convicted.[58] Until 1986 some 10,000 'very serious criminals' had been found guilty in trials involving protected federal witnesses, and the sentences which they received have been, on average, twice as long as those in similar cases in which protected witnesses had not taken part.[59] By 1992 seasoned observers and the FBI were claiming that the Mafia was a spent force in the United States, twenty heads of family and a string of 'underbosses' having been sentenced to long prison terms over the previous decade. In 1985 'Fat Tony' Salerno and four other elderly members of the 'Commission', a consortium of organized crime bosses described as the US Mafia's 'Supreme Council', received sentences of 40–100 years for racketeering,[60]

[55] Nunn Committee Report.

[56] *Guardian*, 3 Apr. 1992.

[57] M. White, 'Cracks Appear in the Mafiosi Mob Code of Silence', ibid., 30 Dec., 1987.

[58] Information supplied by Organised Crime Section, US Dept. Justice to *CNPDS*.

[59] Ibid.

[60] Since the 1970s, scholars studying the Mafia have maintained that there is no national organization as such, but rather shifting alliances between Mafia families. See, e.g. D. C. Smith, *The Mafia Mystique* (London: Basic Books, 1975); F. A. J. Ianni and E. Reuss-Ianni, *A Family Business: Kinship and Social Control in Organised Crime* (London: Russell Sage Foundation, 1972); W. H. Moore, *The Kefauver*

while in 1987 a further eighteen mafiosi went to gaol in the $1.6 billion 'Pizza Connection' case, which involved the distribution of heroin through a chain of fast food stores.[61] In both trials the testimony of protected witnesses Tommaso Buscetta, arguably the most celebrated supergrass of modern times, and his colleague Savatore Contorno,[62] proved to be of critical value to the prosecution.[63]

Nicknamed the 'Godfather of Two Worlds', Buscetta had been close to the heart of a network of organized crime in Italy, Canada, the United States, Latin America, and Switzerland since the end of the Second World War. From 16 July, the day after his extradition from Brazil on charges of involvement with an international drugs-syndicate, until 12 September 1984, he gave a number of statements to Italy's leading investigative magistrate, Giovanni Falcone, which eventually led to the arrest of hundreds of alleged mafiosi in both the United States and Sicily.[64] Buscetta claimed that his decision to co-operate with law enforcement agencies in the 'two worlds' had been inspired by the vicious vendetta then being conducted by the Corleone family in Sicily, which had claimed the lives of two sons from his first marriage, his brother, nephew, and three other close relatives. He denied that he was motivated by revenge and maintained that he wanted to destroy the Mafia because it had abandoned its traditional code of honour in favour of unrestrained greed and cynicism.[65] In fact, as in the case of most of the supergrasses in Northern Ireland, it took an arrest and impending prosecution to galvanize Buscetta's commitment to the traditional Mafia code. Having testified in the Commission case and a huge

---

Committee and the Politics of Crime 1950–1952 (Columbia: University of Missouri Press, 1974); A. A. Blok, 'History and the Study of Organised Crime', (1978) 6 *Urban Life*, 455–74, Pennsylvania Crime Commission, *A Decade of Organised Crime* (St David's, Pa.: The Commission, 1980); *US Senate Governmental Affairs Committee (Permanent Subcommittee on Investigations), Organised Crime and Use of Violence, Hearings, Apr. 28–May 5, 1980* (Washington, DC: US Government Printing, 1980).

[61] White, 'Code of Silence'; R. Blumenthal, *Last Days of the Sicilians: At War with the Mafia—The FBI Assault on the Pizza Connection* (London: Bloomsbury, 1989); S. Alexander, *The Pizza Connection: Lawyers, Drugs and the Mafia* (London: W. H. Allen, 1989).

[62] T. Shawcross and M. Young, *Mafia Wars: The Confessions of Tommaso Buscetta* (London: Fontana, 1988), 26.

[63] M. Gwyther, 'Wall Street Crusader', *Observer Magazine*, 28 Feb. 1988, 26–32.

[64] Shawcross and Young, *Mafia Wars*, 307–8.

[65] Ibid.

Mafia 'maxi-trial' in Sicily (see below), Buscetta is now reported to be living somewhere in the United States under a new identity supplied by the Witness Protection Progamme, enjoying American television, Charles Bronson movies, and the occasional game of football.[66]

A major law enforcement drive against stock-market fraud was also launched in the United States in the mid-to-late 1980s, greatly facilitated by RICO, the Racketeering Influenced Corrupt Organisations Act 1970, which enables prosecutions to be brought for participation in a 'continuing criminal enterprise', and outlaws four activities: using income derived from a pattern of racketeering in order to acquire an interest in an enterprise; acquiring or maintaining an interest in an enterprise through a pattern of racketeering; and conducting the affairs of an enterprise through a pattern of racketeering; and conspiring to commit any of these offences.[67] Civil remedies, with the prospect of triple damages, run parallel to public prosecution, and assets may be seized prior to trial. However, the real power of the leglisation has proved to be its capacity to create super-informers and supergrasses from the world of white-collar crime. By encouraging defendants caught in an initial round-up to turn state's evidence through plea-bargaining, the net can be spread wider and wider to trawl what is likely to be a complicated criminal system. The threat of state-sanctioned 'asset stripping' is, ironically, a particularly powerful inducement for predatory Wall Street millionaires like inside dealers Dennis Levine and Ivan Boesky. Levine, an investment banker, pleaded guilty to fifty-four illegal transactions using privileged, non-public information which had made him $12.6 million, plea-bargained with the authorities, and then began informing on others. Later, in 1987, Boeskey gave himself up, was tried, was sentenced to only three years in prison despite a catalogue of stock-market offences, and reputedly provided the prosecuting authorities with so much information that it will take years to sort out.[68] The wheeler-dealers of New York and Chicago have no code of silence, no loyalty to their own kind, nor are they likely to pose any violent threat to any of

---

[66] Shawcross and Young, *Mafia Wars*, 307.

[67] USC § 1962 (a)–(d) (1976).

[68] Gwyther, 'Wall Street Crusader'; M. Brasier, 'How a Law to Curb the Mafia is Now Being Trained on Wall Street', *Guardian*, 4 Apr. 1989; (1988) 1388 NLJ 676. See also *Independent*, 2 Apr. 1990.

their number who turn state's evidence, so although accomplice testimony is an important part of the law enforcement effort in this domain, there is no need to protect co-operative defendants from the wrath of those they betray. The RICO statute, and the manner in which it has been used, have, however, given rise to some familiar civil libertarian criticisms, including concern about the reliability of the information supplied by such informants. For example, one city informer implicated three highly respected figures in the financial world, Robert Freeman of Goldman Sachs, and Timothy Tabor and Richard Wigton of Kidder Peabody, but the cases against all three were subsequently dropped.[69] Names of other stock-market suspects have been leaked to the media in advance of arrest, to the outrage of the firms concerned, and this has stimulated complaints that sound reputations have been ruined by rumour and inuendo and that innocent people have been tried and convicted by the media. It has also been argued that RICO was never intended to be used in the stock-market context at all, that it operates on a guilt-by-association principle, that both RICO and the Witness Protection Programme may increasingly be used against political 'conspiracies'[70] and that some prosecutors, using campaigns against organized crime and city fraud in pursuit of political ambitions, have trampled over standards of due process.[71]

Juries and Corroboration

Despite all these developments, mass trials of hundreds of defendants on the Italian model have not occurred in the United States. Although some cases concerning illegal business activities have involved forty to fifty defendants, prosecutors have generally declined to include large numbers of accused on a single indictment, in order to avoid the opprobrium of prosecutors and judges, who generally agree that trials involving more than fifteen or twenty defendants place an intolerable burden upon juries.[72]

The laws of the various states in the United States treat the evidence of accomplices differently. In about half, legislation pre-

---

[69] Gwyther, 'Wall Street Crusader', 31.
[70] See evidence to the Nunn Committee given by US Marshal John Partington.
[71] Brasier, 'Law to Curb the Mafia'.
[72] De Feo, *CNPDS*, 160–1. This is also reckoned to be the critical mass beyond which proceedings become procedurally inefficient, with long delays for roll-calls and other time-consuming formalities.

cludes convictions unless the accomplice evidence is corroborated,[73] in some of the remainder, judges are required to caution juries about the dangers of relying upon an accomplice's uncorroborated testimony, while in others the warning is discretionary.[74] The majority of federal courts have opted for a mandatory judicial warning in cases where the accomplice evidence is uncorroborated, even in those states which have a statutory corroboration requirement.[75] The corroboration test in the United States is similar to the *Baskerville* standard in the United Kingdom. The corroborative evidence must implicate, or tend to implicate, the accused in the offence charged and not merely confirm circumstantial details of the alleged offence.[76]

It is difficult to assess the degree to which the uncorroborated evidence of protected witnesses has led to convictions in the United States. Saverda argues that the stricter statutory corroboration requirement of some of the state jurisdictions should be the norm for all courts in the United States, together with a judicial warning requirement.[77] But there is some evidence to suggest that prosecutors, sensitive to the suspicion which juries attach to turn-coat evidence, are already reluctant to rely upon the evidence of protected witnesses alone. For example, in his guide to prosecutors, Associate Attorney-General Stephen Trott states:

Ordinary decent people are predisposed to dislike, distrust, and frequently despise criminals who 'sell out' and become prosecution witnesses. Jurors suspect their motives from the moment they hear about them in a case, and they frequently disregard their testimony altogether as highly untrustworthy and unreliable, openly expressing disgust with the prosecution for making deals with such 'scum'.[78]

---

[73] A typical example can be found in the Minnesota provision: 'a conviction cannot be had upon the testimony of an accomplice, unless it is corroborated by such evidence as tends to convict the defendant of the commission of the offence; and the corroboration is not sufficient if it merely shows the commission of the offence or the circumstances thereof.' (Minn. Stat. 634. 04 (1974)); J. Chadbourn (ed.), *Wigmore on Evidence in Trials at Common Law*, vii (Boston: Little, Brown & Co., 1978), § 414.

[74] *Wigmore on Evidence*, § 408; C. Saverda, 'Accomplices in Federal Court: A Case for Increased Evidentiary Standards' [1990] 100 *Yale Law Journal* 785.

[75] L. B. Orfield, 'Corroboration of Accomplice Testimony in Federal Criminal Cases' [1963] *Villanova Law Review* 15.

[76] *Wigmore on Evidence*, § 2059.

[77] Saverda, 'Evidentiary Standards'.

[78] Trott, 'Use of Informants'.

He also warns prosecutors about the dangers of using accomplice testimony even where other evidence would otherwise be fatal to the accused—for example, where there is strong eyewitness identification or a confession—since the informer's testimony will tend to contaminate the rest of the prosecution case.[79] As the monograph puts it:

The key to whether or not a jury will accept the testimony of a criminal is the extent to which the testimony is corroborated . . . the jury will not accept the word of a criminal unless it is corroborated by other reliable evidence. I cannot stress this point too strongly. If you are going to have to rely on the uncorroborated or even weakly corroborated word of an accomplice or an informant, get back out in the field and go back to work.[80]

Trott also advises prosecutors making their concluding statement in court to 'accentuate the corroboration' and to draw the jury's attention to the evidence 'which proves independently and conclusively' that X was guilty of the offence.[81] He also points out that juries tend to frown upon arrangements which benefit financially the accomplice who testifies.[82]

As already noted, the successful high-profile Mafia prosecutions have rarely in fact been based upon the testimony of protected witnesses alone. Extensive evidence gathered from surveillance— photographs, for example, and particularly recordings of phone-taps—have proved vital.[83] The importance of corroboration in the US context is also illustrated by those Mafia trials which failed. An earlier prosecution of Gotti, for example, based on the testimony of several protected witnesses, collapsed in 1987 when the jury refused to convict,[84] and several months later, in August 1988, twenty members of the Lucchese family were also acquitted. Some jurors told the press that they had been concerned that the prosecution had chosen to rely heavily upon the evidence of convicted criminals.[85] In the successful Gotti trial, which ended in April 1992, hours of recordings of wire-taps ensured that the accused would not fall through the net again.[86]

[79] Trott, 'Use of Informants', 156.
[80] Ibid. 168 and 178 (italicized section appears as block capitals in original).
[81] Ibid. 180.
[82] Ibid. 171.
[83] Shawcross and Young, *Mafia Wars*, chs. 16 and 17.
[84] White, 'Code of Silence'.
[85] *Guardian*, 28 Aug. 1988.
[86] Ibid., 3 Apr. 1992.

Four differences can be identified between the supergrass system in Northern Ireland and its counterpart, the *pentiti* process, in Italy. First, there are substantial differences between the criminal justice tradition in each jurisdiction, one inquisitorial and the other adversarial. Secondly, the *pentiti* process has been regulated by statute. Thirdly, *pentiti* have been used to devastating effect against violent political movements but with less success against organized crime. Finally, in Italy greater emphasis has been placed upon denunciation and dissociation by outlaws than has been the case in Northern Ireland. Denunciation secured with the offer of immunity, and often given in secret, was a vital element, together with confessions, in the medieval inquisitorial trial process in Spain and parts of Italy.[87] However, in spite of criticisms—for example, those made during the Enlightenment by the influential Italian penologist Cesare Beccaria[88]—informer evidence continued to be used. Article 62.6 of the Italian Rocco Criminal Code 1930 offered a reduced punishment for an offender who, as far as possible, voluntarily made good the damage caused by his crime and promised not to offend again, and the contemporary Italian Penal Code provides for reduced sentence and clemency provided such co-operation leads to positive results.[89] In the 1980s, new legislation was passed in Italy which greatly increased the rewards on offer for compliant terrorist offenders and in the 1990s attempts have been made to extend this more systematically to the campaign against the Mafia.

The Anti-terrorist Pentiti Process

Modern Italian terrorism has come in two phases: the first, from 1969 to the mid-1970s, was dominated by neo-fascists, who hoped to pre-empt a communist take-over by precipitating a military *coup*; in the second, from 1976/7 to 1982/3, various leftist organizations, particularly the Red Brigades, sought to ignite a workers' revolution by acts of 'armed propaganda'.[90] Although the most

---

[87] A. Vercher, *Terrorism in Europe: An International Comparative Legal Analysis* (Oxford: Clarendon Press, 1992), 261–3.

[88] C. Beccaria, *Of Crimes and Punishments*, trans. Juan Antonio de las Casas (Oxford: Oxford University Press, 1964), ch. 9.

[89] Vercher, *Terrorism in Europe*, 264.

[90] See Weinberg and Eubank, *Italian Terrorism*.

violent era was the late 1970s and early 1980s,[91] virulent right-wing terrorism has reappeared in the 1990s, linked with the mysterious P2 masonic lodge and elements in the state security services anxious to defeat judicial attempts to uncover the Mafia's connections with the political establishment.[92]

A key element in the construction of a *'pentiti* process' against the armed Left, as in the creation of the supergrass system in Northern Ireland, was the reorganization of the Italian intelligence-gathering system in the mid-1970s.[93] In 1974 Carabinieri General Carlo Alberta Dalla Chiesa took charge of a special anti-terrorist unit targeted upon the Red Brigade in Turin and was responsible for the arrest of its leadership, the 'historic nucleus', although the organization regrouped and was soon actively involved in violence again. In 1976, acting under public pressure created by revelations connecting elements in the security services with right-wing terrorism, Prime Minister Andreotti reformed the intelligence apparatus, taking overall responsibility for intelligence and security policy himself. The scandal-ridden Defence Information Service (SID) was split into two new bodies, the Service for Intelligence and Military Security (SISMI) and the Service for Intelligence and Domestic Security (SISDE), with an interministerial committee and an Executive Committee for the Security and Intelligence Services (CESIS) organized to provide the Prime Minister with intelligence information. In January 1978 the Interior Minister formed a Central Bureau for General Investigations and Special Operations (UCIGOS) the principal task of which was to co-ordinate the work of the Division for General Investigations and Special Operations (DIGOS), an anti-terrorist unit of the state police with branches attached to each regional police headquarters. In 1978 Dalla Chiesa took charge of the national offensive against the Red Brigades, both state police and Carabinieri developed special units known as 'leatherheads', trained in the assault of terrorist bases and hide-outs, and new maximum security prisons were built to prevent escapes of the kind which had occurred in the past.

With a more effective intelligence system in place, a series of laws, some of only temporary duration, was enacted to encourage terrorists to collaborate with the authorities. The first of these, law

[91] Ibid. 123.
[92] See, e.g. *Guardian*, 22 May, 29 July, 1 Oct. 1993.
[93] See Seton-Watson, 'Terrorism in Italy', 105.

N. 191, introduced on 21 March 1978, just a week after former Prime Minister Aldo Moro, Italy's elder statesman, was kidnapped by the Red Brigades, created various new offences, including the crime of 'terrorism or subversion of the democratic order', and contained further intelligence-gathering provisions. Special authority was granted for telephones to be tapped, and the police were given powers to detain any person who refused to identify themselves, and powers to conduct interrogations without a lawyer present. Landlords and property owners were required to notify the police within forty-eight hours of new tenants or purchasers, who could then be investigated to see if the property had been acquired in preparation for a terrorist incident. But of greatest importance for present purposes, dramatically reduced sentences of two to four years were offered to terrorist kidnappers who dissociated themselves from their organization and helped locate and free hostages. Significantly, the focus of this provision was upon *dissociation* and *collaboration* rather than *repentance* as such.[94]

In 1979 the so-called '7 April trial', involving some 200 defendants charged with subversion and membership of armed bands, began, and by 1984 4,000 suspects were being held in preventive detention awaiting trial in connection with these proceedings. However, one of the key witnesses, *pentiti* Carlo Fioroni, eventually absconded without testifying in the main trial.[95] The role of *pentiti* was increased by further legislation when, on 15 February 1980, the Cossiga Act (N. 15) was passed, making it an offence, punishable with prison sentences of up to fifteen years, to join, promote, constitute, organize, or direct an association which sought to subvert the democratic order by violent means. The police were also given extra powers to arrest terrorist suspects and, without warrant, to conduct searches of whole neighbourhoods in which they were thought to be hiding. Article 4 of the Cossiga Act stipulated that prison sentences could be considerably reduced for defendants who, having been found guilty of terrorist acts, dissociated themselves from their comrades and did all they could to prevent the continuation of criminal activity 'by giving concrete help to the police and magistrates in establishing decisive proof leading to the identification and arrest of conspirators'. Article 5

---

[94] See Vercher, *Terrorism in Europe*, 266.
[95] See *Guardian*, 9 Aug. 1984; Amnesty International, *7 April Trial—Italy* (London: Amnesty International, 1986).

provided that such persons who not only collaborated with the authorities in order to prevent crimes against the democratic state, but who also provided substantial evidence regarding conspiracies, including details of how exactly the crime was organized and the identification of the other conspirators, could be granted immunity from punishment. Radically reduced prison terms were also offered to those found guilty of belonging to terrorist organizations, provided they were willing to dissociate, renounce their terrorist activities, and help the authorities. The change in focus in the Cossiga provisions from dissociation and collaboration to *repudiation*, no matter what the eventual outcome of collaboration, has led some commentators to interpret the *pentiti* process as a symbolic attempt to reconstruct consensus in Italian society.[96]

By the early 1980s several *pentiti* had decimated the armed Right,[97] hundreds of left-wing suspects had been arrested, and whole armed leftist organizations such as Front Line had been dismantled.[98] The frequency of terrorist incidents declined, and terrorist targets shifted towards police officers and *pentiti* and their families, indicating that a struggle for survival had replaced the original purpose of leftist violence. In an attempt to regain the initiative, the Red Brigades kidnapped American General and NATO officer James Dozier from his home in Verona on 18 December 1982, but in January 1983, acting upon information obtained from informers, the police stormed the hide-out and secured the general's release. Further arrests followed when the leader of the Dozier kidnap, Antonio Savasta, himself 'repented' and many of those he implicated turned state's evidence in their turn.

The success of the 1980 legislation prompted the Italian legislature to pass a further temporary '*pentiti* statute'[99] which lasted until February 1983 and extended the possibility of immunity from punishment. Immunity from prosecution, on the other hand, was offered to those who had committed or attempted to commit minor crimes, and reduced penalties were made available to those guilty of more serious offences provided they dissociated themselves

---

[96] G. Mosconi and G. Pisapia, 'The Stereotype of the Repentant Terrorist: His Nature and Functions', in European Group for the Study of Deviance and Social Control, *Working Papers in Criminology*, 3 (1981), 190–9.

[97] See Seton-Watson, 'Terrorism in Italy', 105.

[98] Mosconi and Pisapia, 'The Repentant Terrorist', 201.

[99] N. 304 of 29 May 1982.

from their former activities, made full confession, and helped to reduce the impact of their offences. Penalties attaching to more serious offences were further reduced for those who confessed and took part in a reconstruction of the crime, or helped the police and judicial authorities to obtain crucial evidence leading to the capture of other offenders. Reduced sentences for terrorists who had 'collaborated in a very decisive way' were also made available, and the legislation also provided for a possible review of a court decision to reduce a penalty when the repentant statement upon which it had been based turned out to be false. A further shift towards symbolic repentance and away from instrumental collaboration occurred with Law 34 of 18 February 1987, which required dissociation, confession, repudiation, and reformation as the conditions of reduced penalties, but which made no mention of the utility of this to law enforcement.[100] However, the fact that no attempt was made in the 1980s to protect the political *pentiti* in the manner of the Witness Protection Programme of the United States, or even the less formal arrangements found in the supergrass system in Northern Ireland, was criticized by sympathetic commentators and by *pentiti* themselves. *Pentiti* who spoke to the *Sunday Times* in 1984, for example, said that in return for their co-operation they had been given immunity from punishment or reduced prison sentences, plus a hand-out of some £8,300, and then left to fend for themselves, forcing them to return to a life on the run the avoidance of which had been one of their original motives in betraying their comrades.[101]

The success of the Italian '*pentiti* strategy' against political violence has stemmed from a conjunction of 'supply' and 'demand' factors similar to those found in the supergrass system in Northern Ireland. On the demand side were effective intelligence-gathering, severe sentences for those captured who refused to co-operate, and the prospect of clemency for those who did, while a crisis of allegiance within the insurrectionary movement itself provided an abundant supply of willing collaborators. The experience of Patrizio Peci, a former member of the Red Brigades' Strategic Direction, the national leadership which replaced the 'historic nucleus' in

---

[100] Vercher, *Terrorism in Europe*, 267.
[101] D. Hallenstein, 'Walking Corpses', *Sunday Times*, colour supplement, 4 Sept. 1984.

1974, is typical.[102] As the 1970s drew to a close, Peci became increasingly disenchanted with the movement and with its prospects, and increasingly felt the stress of being a fugitive from the police. Weinberg and Eubank explain the conversion of so many former Red Brigade activists in the early 1980s as an inversion of the 'Stockholm syndrome' in which those taken captive by terrorists come to identify with their captors and their goals. In the case of Peci and others like him, arrest seems to have brought a welcome opportunity to confess, and to his surprise he found he could identify with the young and thoughtful police-officers who interrogated him and who were not at all like the ogres he had expected. The fact that Italian terrorism has a much weaker social base than its Irish equivalent has also been an important factor in the success of the *pentiti* strategy. By 29 January 1983, 389 terrorists had taken advantage of the *pentiti* laws and repented, and, according to Weinberg and Eubank, 'their assistance, along with the anti-terrorist apparatus put in place after the Moro assassination, brought an end to Italy's second episode of terrorist violence.'[103]

The Mafia Maxi-trials

Huge Mafia trials involving scores, and even over a hundred, defendants have occurred in Italy even without the involvement of *pentiti*. For example, 117 of the most prominent mafiosi in Sicily were tried in Catanzaro in 1968, and in 1974 114 Mafia defendants were tried in Palermó.[104] But it was not until Buscetta's appearance in the United States in 1984[105] that an anti-Mafia *pentiti* process could begin in Italy. However, as a result of political inertia stemming from collusion between the Mafia and elements within the Italian political establishment, a formal scheme of witness protection was not established until 1991.[106] Apart from Buscetta, the most important element in initiating and sustaining the Mafia supergrass trials was the work of Sicilian investigating magistrate

---

[102] Ibid.; Weinberg and Eubank, *Italian Terrorism*, 129. See Peci's biography, G. B. Guerri, *P. Peci, io, l'infame* (Milan: Mondadori, 1983).

[103] Weinberg and Eubank, *Italian Terrorism*, 130. However, the last Red Brigades trial did not take place until 1990 (See *Guardian*, 21 Apr. 1990).

[104] P. Arlacchi, *Mafia Business: The Mafia Ethic and the Spirit of Capitalism* (Oxford: Oxford University Press, 1988), 58. G. Falcone with M. Padovani, *Men of Honour: The Truth about the Mafia* (London: Warner Books, 1992), 22.

[105] See US section.

[106] Falcone with Padovani, *Men of Honour*, pp. xvi and 46.

Giovanni Falcone, himself a Mafia murder victim in May 1992. In a series of interviews with journalist Marcelle Padovani, Falcone offers some fascinating insights into the world of the Mafia and the Mafia supergrass,[107] and claims that Buscetta's decision to break the Mafia's code of silence, *omertà*, was a historic moment, which enabled the state to understand the Mafia from the inside for the first time.[108]

Buscetta's information, together with other evidence, including that of fellow *pentito* and US protected witness Salvatore Contorno, led to the first Italian Mafia supergrass trial held in 'the bunker' court-room specially constructed inside Palermo's ancient Ucciardone prison. The proceedings, which began on 10 February 1986, involved 475 defendants, nineteen of whom were alleged Mafia bosses. These included Michele 'the Pope' Greco, reputedly the head of the Mafia's multi-billion dollar heroin operation and head of the Sicilian Mafia's ruling 'commission' (*capo di tutt'i capi*), and Luciano Liggo, the head of the Corleone family, the victors in the bloody struggle for control of the heroin markets which had scarred the west of Sicily in the early 1980s. Since Buscetta had already been taken on to the US Witness Protection Programme, there was no need for any protection deals with the Italian state. On 16 December 1987, twenty-two months after it had begun, the trial's three hundred and fiftieth session ended with 338 convictions. Over 1,300 people had testified, photocopying machines had produced some 900,000 copies of documents, and a computer had been provided to help the jury and judges with their deliberations. However, it was reported that, while the evidence of the *pentiti* was not insignificant, the 'patient academic work' of the five investigating magistrates, spearheaded by Falcone, formed the backbone of the prosecution case.[109] The imprisonment of so many top mafiosi left a power vacuum which spawned a further cycle of bloodletting, and one of the trial judges was assassinated not long after

[107] Falcone with Padovani, *Men of Honour*.

[108] Ibid. 23–4. Falcone believed Buscetta's revelations and also claimed that he could tell the true from the false *pentiti*, for two reasons. First, he accepted that Buscetta was motivated by a grave wrong, the murder of his 2 sons, committed by other mafiosi against the Mafia code of honour, (44); as a fellow Sicilian, he also believed that true 'men of honour', while capable of callous killing and other serious wrongs, would be incapable of lying about certain matters. (42, 44, 53, 55). He nevertheless emphasizes the importance of verifying the accuracy of supergrass revelations with great care (25 and 41).

[109] *Independent*, 16 Dec. 1987.

the proceedings were completed. Whatever advantages over the Mafia may have been gained as a result of these proceedings seem, however, to have been fatally weakened as a result of the Mafia's influence in the corridors of power in Palermo and Rome.

Despite these difficulties, the maxi-proceedings have, nevertheless, continued, and a string of other major and minor supergrasses have followed in Buscetta's footsteps: Marino Mannoia, Sinagra, Trapani, De Riz, Marsala, Coniglio, Vitale, and Koh Bak Kin (a Chinese).[110] In October 1988 Salvatore 'Toto' Calderone gave evidence in a second trial in the Palermo bunker in which he implicated the alleged leaders of the Sicilian Mafia in the 1982–6 period, the years following those covered in the first trial; and in November 1988 a trial involving 198 Mafia defendants based upon the evidence of eight *pentiti*, who had received slightly reduced sentences, concluded in Turin with 130 convictions, including twenty-six life sentences for murder.[111]

The overall results of the Mafia maxi-trials have, however, been less positive than their anti-terrorist parallel. In February 1989, it was revealed that twenty of the top defendants in the first bunker-trial had been transferred from their prisons to luxurious hospital rooms, while others were convalescing from various mystery illnesses elsewhere. Three prison doctors were accused of issuing false reports to secure the men's release. The same month, eighty allegedly prominent mafiosi, including Michele Greco, charged with over eighty murders, including those of Dalla Chiesa and his wife, were acquitted in Palermo's third bunker-trial when the testimonies of the *pentiti* involved were rejected; and on 22 February 1992 forty defendants in the first bunker-trial, including Greco and other central figures, were set free under a new law which prohibited detention for longer than twelve months between conviction and appeal.[112]

In 1992 the Mafia war entered a further deadly phase with the murders, in May and July respectively, of Italy's two most experienced anti-Mafia investigating magistrates, Falcone and Paolo Borsilino, amidst suspicions of security service involvement. In June that year legislation was passed outlawing *omertà*, the Mafia code of silence, and refusal to dissociate from a Mafia clan, both of

---

[110] Falcone with Padovani, *Men of Honour*, 47–8.
[111] *Guardian*, 4 Oct. and 7 Nov. 1988.
[112] Ibid. 14 and 22 Feb. 1992.

which became punishable with a term of five years imprisonment. The contribution of *pentiti* was also formalized with guarantees of reduced sentences and protection, judges were given the power to impose a twelve-month freeze on any financial operation suspected of hiding Mafia assets, and the police were granted more time to conduct anti-Mafia investigations.[113] Following these developments, some 700 alleged mafiosi were swiftly arrested, and in the spring of 1993 Buscetta re-emerged from hiding, confirming suspicions that, when in power, former Italian premier and senior statesman Giulio Andreotti had protected the clans from successful prosecution.[114]

GERMANY

The use of accomplice evidence against terrorist organizations in Germany has differed from the supergrass system in Northern Ireland in three ways. First, the German trials have been much smaller; secondly, they have been targeted upon members of largely moribund organizations, which no longer present a real threat; and thirdly, legal authorization has been conferred by statute. Although *Kronzeugen* (Crown witnesses) or *Staatszeugen* (state witnesses) have a long history in the German legal system, modern measures to promote their contribution to anti-terrorist law enforcement date from 1976.

During the 1970s and 1980s West Germany was beset by serious violence from the extreme Left and, in the 1980s and 1990s, by the extreme Right. In May 1975 the four founding members of the Red Army Faction (RAF, or Baader-Meinhof gang), Andreas Baader, Ulrike Meinhof, Jan Karl Raspe, and Gudrun Ensslin, were tried on charges of murder, attempted murder, robbery, and forming a criminal association, in a case which at the time was described as the most important criminal proceedings in the history of the Federal Republic.[115] A key witness for the prosecution was Gerhard Müller, arrested with Meinhof in Hanover, whose evidence

---

[113] *Guardian*, 14 and 22 Feb. 1992, 10 and 13 July 1992.

[114] Ibid. 15 Apr. 1993.

[115] J. Becker, *Hitler's Children* (London: Michael Joseph, 1977), 12–14. A fifth member of the group, Holger Meins, died on hunger strike on 9 Nov. 1974. The controversy provoked by the trial was exacerbated when some defence lawyers were excluded shortly before the proceedings began, on the grounds of alleged collusion with the accused.

'ravaged the defence' since he 'told exactly who had laid the bombs, where and how'.[116] The fate of the accused was all but sealed, however, when, on 4 May 1976, Ensslin confessed to having been involved in three of the bombings on the indictment and, on 9 May, Ulrike Meinhof was found hanged in her cell. Rumours that she had been murdered by the state sparked riots in several German cities.[117] Raspe, Baader, and Ensslin were convicted and sentenced to long prison terms, but by the end of the 1970s they had also died in their prison cells, officially from suicide though state murder was again suspected by some.

Wardlaw claims that the response of the West German state to terrorism in the 1970s and 1980s diverged from that of any other liberal democracy because Germany's anti-terrorist measures have not been aimed exclusively at terrorist groups but at political dissent generally, and because there have been fewer legal and procedural impediments against the use of sweeping emergency provisions.[118] The *Berufsverbot*—exclusion from civil service employment on political grounds which originated in the Cold War climate of the 1950s—was applied with renewed vigour in the 1970s and 1980s, denying such employment even to mild critics of the regime. The Criminal Code was amended to include the offences of forming a criminal association and of incitement to commit offences prejudicial to the safety of the constitutional order, and the Code of Criminal Procedure was altered to permit surveillance of defence lawyers, their exclusion from trial, and the denial of contact with clients for initial periods of up to thirty days. Police powers of search and the power to carry out identity checks were also extended, and the Federal Criminal Office was expanded to incorporate a specialist anti-terrorist unit. Legislation was enacted which permitted the surveillance of suspects and the accelerated installation of surveillance devices and data banks. In 1976, at the height of the leftist terrorist campaign, the Law of Criminal Procedure was changed by the law of 18 August to enable the prosecuting authorities, with the authorization of the court, not to initiate any criminal proceedings against those suspected of certain offences, including the crime of 'organizing a terrorist association', when the

---

[116] Ibid. 13.

[117] Ibid. 280–2.

[118] G. Wardlaw, *Political Terrorism: Theory, Tactics and Counter-measures* (Cambridge: Cambridge University Press, 1982), 125.

suspect 'has acted in such a way as to prevent a threat to the
security of the Federal Republic or to the constitutional order'.[119]

Although more diffuse than its left-wing counterpart, the violence
of the extreme Right in Germany has been just as deadly, with
thirteen killed in the Munich Oktoberfest bombing on 26 September
1980 alone, and a rising tide of attacks against immigrants in the
1990s. In 1981 the Federal Parliament authorized a broad-ranging
census, not only to gain an accurate picture of the country for
demographic purposes but also to earmark possible terrorist suspects and to monitor their movements. However, following a
public outcry and an adverse decision by the Constitutional Court,
the census had to be modified and postponed until data-protection
legislation had been passed. In the mid-1980s a number of trials of
leading neo-Nazi activists took place in which accomplice evidence
was of some importance. According to Kolinsky: 'a mixture of
trying to save one's bacon and getting into the limelight and the
media may explain why, in contrast to their colleagues on the left,
right-wing terrorists have tended to name their accomplices, and
divulge information about their organisations and activities during
police interrogations'.[120]

Although the RAF had sunk into decline by the late 1970s, they
were revived in the mid-1980s by an alliance with their French and
Belgian counterparts, Action Directe and the Combative Communist Cells. But, after several high-profile murders in 1985 and 1986,
they again fell silent. With the demolition of the Berlin wall and the
reunification of Germany in 1989, a number of RAF suspects who
had enjoyed the protection of the Stasi—the East German secret
police—were arrested in the newly unified state. In June 1989 a
new temporary *Staatszeuge* scheme—which lapsed in 1992—was
introduced by the legislature,[121] enabling several to turn *Staatzeu-
gen* in return for greatly reduced prison sentences.[122] Under Section
1 the Federal Prosecutor-General was able, with the approval of a
criminal panel of the Federal Court of Justice, to refrain from
prosecution if a party guilty of a terrorist offence revealed facts to

[119] § 153e.
[120] E. Kolinsky, 'Terrorism in West Germany', in Lodge (ed.), *The Threat of
Terrorism*, 79.
[121] An Act to Amend the Criminal Code, the Code of Criminal Procedure, the
Assemblies Act and to Introduce the Regulation of Crown Witnesses in the Course
of Terrorist Offences, June 1989.
[122] See, e.g., *Guardian*, 4 June 1991, 11 Apr., 21 Apr., 4 May 1992.

the prosecuting authorities which were likely to prevent such an offence being committed, help solve it, or lead to the arrest of the offenders. In cases where a prosecution had been brought, section 2 empowered the court to refrain from imposing sentence or to mitigate it at its discretion. Section 3 prevented those charged with genocide from benefiting from these arrangements, and, in the case of those *Staatszeugen* charged with murder or manslaughter, limited their reward to a reduced sentence rather than immunity from prosecution. Section 4 provided that a third party mediating between perpetrator and prosecuting authorities was not under an obligation to report the offences disclosed, and section 5 stated that the benefits of the legislation would only be available to those *Staatszeugen* who had come forward by December 1992. The prosecuting authorities were permitted to stay proceedings, and the courts to refrain from sentencing or to impose lighter sentences, in respect of state witnesses who provided significant evidence likely to be of assistance in the prevention of offences more serious than those in which they themselves had been involved, and which also implicated those more culpable. Although this contravened the principle of equality in the German constitution by privileging the terrorist over the non-terrorist offender, it has been argued that it can be justified by the principles of necessity and proportionality. The limited duration of these arrangements makes it difficult to assess their effectiveness, but they have been criticized on various familiar grounds, namely the lack of credibility of the *Staatszeuge's* evidence, the need for corroboration, the possible damage which may be caused to the criminal justice system by the suspicion that a deal is being struck with criminals, and their doubtful efficacy.[123] In April 1992 the RAF announced an end to its twenty-year struggle, admitting to its own 'mistakes' and recognizing the 'fundamental changes in global politics over the past few years'.[124]

SPAIN

From the sixteenth to the nineteenth century, long after the notorious Holy Inquisition had ceased to function,[125] the Spanish crimi-

---

[123] Vercher, *Terrorism in Europe*, 284.
[124] *Guardian*, 21 Apr. 1992.
[125] See Vercher, *Terrorism in Europe*, 265.

nal justice system continued to rely greatly upon paid informers and upon accomplice evidence. Although, as elsewhere, the practice was subject to criticism, during Franco's dictatorship, from 1939 to 1975, exemption from punishment was offered to minor offenders who provided the authorities with useful information about offences connected with banditry and terrorism before they had been committed.[126] Article 9. 9 of the contemporary Spanish Criminal Code also recognizes 'spontaneous repentance' as a mitigating circumstance.

In 1981 a temporary law envisaging a variant on the Italian repentant-terrorist model was passed, but it was never implemented, and in 1984 Spain's principal anti-terrorist legislation outlined criteria for the reduction or avoidance of individual penalties for terrorist offences.[127] The offender must first give himself up to the authorities, confess his misdeeds, and voluntarily renounce his criminal activities, and the information which he or she provides must obviate or substantially ameliorate a dangerous situation, prevent a damaging outcome from occurring, or contribute significantly to the acquisition of decisive evidence leading to the identification or capture of other offenders. Those who can satisfy these conditions but who have already been sentenced become eligible for conditional release, but unlike its Italian counterpart the Spanish legislation does not provide for court decisions to be reviewed when the statement of an *arrepentido* is proved to have been false. The regime created by Article 6 lapsed on 4 January 1987, but it was re-enacted by Organic Law 3/1988 of 25 May.

In spite of this legislation and the considerable threat posed by the violent Basque separatist organization Euskadi ta Askatasuna (ETA), no repentant-terrorist process has developed in Spain, largely because a much more attractive alternative, 'reinsertion', has also been available. Since 1982 the Spanish government has attempted to reintegrate, by exercise of the executive pardon,[128] those members of ETA (or in principle any other terrorist group) who have not been involved in serious crimes of violence and who formally promise not to reoffend. Significantly, there is no obligation to 'repent' nor to renounce one's past. Every political party in the country, except ETA's political wing, Herri Batasuna, supports

---

[126] Vercher, *Terrorism in Europe*, 264.
[127] Art. 6.
[128] Under the Law of Pardon of 18 June 1870.

the programme, and on 14 June 1984 the Castellana Accords signed between the Spanish and French governments enabled the scheme to be extended to *émigrés* who had not been prosecuted for a terrorist offence in Spain, and to those who, although having been prosecuted, had not been responsible for any violent crime. The French government undertook that if ETA refused to negotiate with the Spanish government following the accord, those of its members wanted for violent offences would be expelled from French territory or extradited to Spain. In 1983 and 1984 119 former terrorists had been reinserted, only one of whom rejoined ETA, and by 1990 some 300 members of ETA had benefited from it.[129]

FRANCE

Like Spain, France has not developed a supergrass system as such, although legislation passed in the mid-1980s has sought to encourage members of terrorist organizations, particularly the left-wing Action Directe, to co-operate with the criminal justice process.[130] In 1981, following a period of relative calm, the Mitterand government adopted a softer approach to law and order. The death penalty and State Security Court were abolished, the granting of an amnesty for hundreds of prisoners 'effectively put many potential terrorists back into circulation',[131] and the open-door policy to political refugees was also reiterated. But in a four-month period in the summer of 1982 fifteen people were killed in terrorist incidents and the government felt obliged to show a sterner face. A Secretary of State for Public Security was appointed, laws on the sale of weapons were revised, Action Directe was banned, a stricter control on the influx of foreigners was announced, two Syrian diplomats were expelled—the first expulsions of Arab officials for ten years—and within the government a 'Council on terrorism' was formed.[132] In May 1986, at the height of a renewed murder campaign by Action Directe, in collusion with their German counterparts the RAF and the Belgian Combative Communist Cells, a further battery of emergency measures was approved by the law-and-

---

[129] Vercher, *Terrorism in Europe*, 268–9, 271–2, 275.

[130] E. Moxon-Browne, 'Terrorism in France', in W. Gutteridge (ed.), *The New Terrorism* (London: Mansell, 1986), 219–21.

[131] E. Moxon-Browne, 'Terrorism in France' in Lodge (ed.), *The Threat of Terrorism*, 226.

[132] Ibid.

order-conscious Chirac government, and this became effective on 9 September.[133] The key elements included new powers authorizing the police to demand proof of identity and enabling them to detain for questioning those whose papers were not satisfactory, extended prison sentences of up to thirty years, the institution of special non-jury courts for the trial of terrorist offences, the referral of all terrorist offences to Paris for a decision regarding the initiation of proceedings, an increase in the initial period of police detention for terrorist suspects from two to four days, and the offer of immunity from punishment and reduced sentences.[134]

The law of 9 September provides that punishment can be avoided entirely: (*a*) by anyone who has attempted to commit one of a list of crimes, provided, before they themselves are proceeded against, they notify the judicial or administrative authorities and identify other offenders, thus enabling the offence to be prevented and (*b*) by anyone who has been involved in one of a list of terrorist offences if, having notified the judicial or administrative authorities before they themselves are proceeded against, they identify the other culprits and enable a crime to be prevented which might have led to death or serious injury.[135] Life sentences can also be reduced to twenty years, and other sentences cut in half, where terrorists identify their accomplices before they themselves are proceeded against and when, if already in custody, they provide information leading to the arrest of their associates. As Vercher points out, although it has been claimed that this system is based on 'active repentance', its foundation is 'certainly not an act of repentance or even of dissociation, but rather an act of active collaboration with the authorities.[136] Unlike the supergrass processes in Northern Ireland and Italy, these measures have provoked little public controversy.[137] Although the legislation does not make any formal provision for the protection of *repentis*, police funds for the remuneration of informers have been increased[138] and the Ministries of the

---

[133] See J. Pradel, 'Les Infractions de terrorisme, un nouvel exemple de l'éclatement du droit pénal (Loi no. 86–1020 de septembre 1986)' (1987) *Recueil Dalloz Sirey, 7e Cahier-Chronique* 39.

[134] Laws no. 1019 and 1020.

[135] M. Cacciani and M. Bonetti, 'Normativa antiterrorismo e nuovi modelli di organizzazione processuale nell' esperienza francese', *CNPDS*.

[136] Vercher, *Terrorism in Europe*, 281.

[137] Ibid. 280.

[138] Cacciani and Bonetti, 'Normativa antiterrorismo', 79.

Interior and of Justice have provided the same kind of informal protection to informers and their families as that made available to the supergrasses in Northern Ireland—for example, changes of identity, occupation, and residence.[139]

The informer-oriented aspects of the law of 9 September ought not to be seen as innovations, since they merely apply to the domain of terrorist offences concepts of exoneration from punishment and reduction of sentence on the grounds of repentance and active collaboration which were already to be found in various parts of the French Penal Code in respect of counterfeiting,[140] conspiracies,[141] and destruction of, or damage to, property.[142] Under Article 2 of the Penal Code, for example, a would-be offender is not liable to punishment where he has voluntarily decided not to commit the offence between having contemplated it and having begun to carry it out; and, under the concept of *excuses absolutoires*, the code also enables sentences to be avoided altogether where, prior to any prosecution and before the completion of the offence, a guilty party informs the relevant authorities about it and identifies accomplices, or, where prosecution has already begun, information is provided which leads to the arrest of accomplices. The code also provides for the mandatory reduction of sentences on the grounds of 'extenuating excuses', detailed in the code itself, and 'extenuating circumstances', which are left to the discretion of trial judges. An example of the former can be found in Article 105, which enables an offender to secure a reduced sentence provided he is the first to warn the administrative or judicial authorities about a felony against the security of the state before it is completed or attempted, or in respect of crimes of abduction and kidnapping if the hostage is freed within five days.[143] A repentant attitude is generally expected to attract the benevolence of the judge, and judicial discretion on sentencing is wide enough to enable a life sentence to be reduced to a term of two years, and any other sentence to be varied to a term of one year.[144]

---

[139] Ibid. 95. [140] Art. 138. [141] Art. 266.
[142] Art. 435. [143] Arts. 341–3.
[144] Art. 463 as amended by the ordinance of 4 June 1960 and the law 81–82 of 2 Feb. 1981. See B. Bouloc, 'Le Problème des repentis: la tradition française relativement au statut des repentis' (1986) *Revue de science criminelle* 771.

On 4 December 1986, only three months after the law of 9 September had been passed, three of the alleged leaders of Action Directe stood trial in Paris under tight security in what was billed as France's first big terrorist trial in recent years. Joelle Aubron, her husband Régis Schleicher, and Claude Halfen, were accused of murdering two plain-clothes policemen and of attempting to murder another in central Paris in May 1983. A fourth defendant, Mohand Hammami, was tried in his absence, and Claude's brother, Nicholas, was accused of complicity. Much of the prosecution case rested upon the testimony of Claude Halfen's ex-mistress, Frédérique Germain, who had turned state's evidence, and all the accused were found guilty.[145] Although France witnessed another important anti-terrorist trial in January 1988, the case against the accused did not involve the evidence of informers.[146]

CONCLUSION

While there are undeniable similarities between the supergrass system in Northern Ireland and the parallels discussed in this chapter, it would be a mistake to underestimate the differences. Two principal categories can clearly be distinguished amongst these jurisdictions: those which have relied heavily upon the courtroom testimony of supergrasses to convict large numbers of defendants from terrorist and criminal organizations (England, Northern Ireland, the United States, and Italy), and those which have had the more modest aim of encouraging accomplices to provide information to the authorities (France and Spain), with Germany falling somewhere in between. These differences derive primarily from the kind of criminal or terrorist problem which each state has had to face, and the range of other measures invoked in an attempt to deal with it.

Various other differences cross-cut these two categories. There are, for example, different criteria for admission to the respective schemes. Entry to the US Witness Protection Programme is vetted by the Attorney-General and based upon a written memorandum of understanding between the authorities and the protected witness, and there is a further possibility of 'post-conviction immunity', deferred sentence, and probation until testimony is given. French

[145] *Guardian*, 4 Dec. 1986.
[146] Ibid. 11 Jan., 12 Jan., 19 Feb., 20 Feb., 23 Feb. 1988.

and Spanish accomplices must give themselves up or, if already in custody in France, provide information leading to arrests. The availability of immunity from prosecution also differs from jurisdiction to jurisdiction. In the Continental European systems surveyed here, for example, it is generally limited to less serious offences and is contingent upon formal dissociation, confession, and 'substantial collaboration' with the authorities—for example, identification of accomplices, the provision of evidence leading to their arrest, or the prevention of some serious offence.

There are also differences regarding the roles of courts and prosecuting authorities in deciding if immunity is justified and in determining the appropriate discount on sentence. The possibility of plea-bargaining in England, the United States, and Northern Ireland gives prosecutors considerable discretion in the preferment of charges. On the Continent, only the German system formally permits courts to refrain from sentencing accomplices entirely, and elsewhere it is a matter for the investigating magistrate. The arrangements for post-trial protection also vary widely, with little offered in Italy or Germany, an informal system in France, Northern Ireland, and England, and a highly developed programme in the United States. Some more general conclusions about the relationship between the supergrass and democratic legal systems are discussed in the next chapter.

11

Supergrasses and the Criminal Justice System

SOME reference has already been made in preceding chapters to the roles played by various agencies of the state, especially the courts, in the management of the supergrass process in Northern Ireland. The purpose of this chapter is to consider these contributions in a more systematic fashion and to reflect upon the broader issues of institutionalization, accountability, and due process which reliance upon supergrasses has raised in the various systems of criminal justice surveyed in this study.

THE COURTS

As already indicated, when the first supergrass cases came before the courts in Northern Ireland, the presiding judges reacted in a predictably conservative fashion by claiming that in legal terms nothing new was happening, and that the prescriptions of the common law could be fulfilled by issuing the danger warning to themselves. However, in the course of the ten major supergrass trials and the five appeals, a sea change in judicial attitude took place, reflected in the retreat from the high conviction-rate of the first phase, the reluctance to permit convictions on uncorroborated supergrass evidence which this betokened, and the overhaul of conventional legal wisdom which had subtly occurred.

The Conviction Rate

By the autumn of 1983 the three trials during the ascendancy phase had resulted in the conviction of fifty-six of the sixty-four defendants (88 per cent), with thirty-one of these convictions (55 per cent) resting on the supergrasses' uncorroborated evidence. However, in only two of the remaining seven trials at first instance, the Quigley and Kirkpatrick cases, were convictions secured purely on the supergrasses' testimony, while in the others the defendants were generally either convicted on their confessions or acquitted. The conviction rate in these cases plummeted to 42 per cent. By the end of 1986, sixty-six of the seventy-five appeals against conviction had been successful, virtually all the extant convictions being based upon a confession or alleged admission. Taking the appeal decisions into account, the overall conviction-rate from the Bennett to the Kirkpatrick trials stands at 24 per cent.

The supergrass system required a high conviction-rate in order to justify its heavy financial, policing, and political costs and was no longer viable as a method of prosecution when it became clear that the courts were increasingly reluctant to convict without corroboration, since it was precisely the prospect of uncorroborated convictions which had made it so attractive to the police and the makers of security policy in the first place. The fact that virtually all the outstanding convictions were ultimately sustained upon confessions means that in the final analysis the supergrass system remained faithful to the basic conviction-by-confession orientation of the Diplock trial process. Whether any of these confessions would have been forthcoming had it not been for the supergrasses will never be known, but it seems likely that at least some would not.

Credibility and Corroboration

Two questions arising from the fact that supergrass trials are in effect several separate trials rolled into one were explored in the appeal decisions in *Graham*[1] and *Donnelly*[2]: (*a*) to what extent could the testimony of a supergrass be generally supported, or damaged, by independent evidence which either tended to confirm or discredit his testimony against only certain of the accused; and (*b*) to what extent could the supergrass's general credibility be supported by independent evidence which merely showed that the offences in question had been committed? In *Graham* the Northern Ireland Court of Appeal decided that the trial judge had been wrong in law to use certain independent evidence as a 'best' or 'crucial' test of Bennett's credibility, because evidence which merely confirms that particular offences were committed can only bolster the credibility of a supergrass when his participation is in doubt. The Court also concluded that evidence which damages the super-

[1] (1984) 18 NIJB.
[2] (1986) 4 NIJB.

grass's credibility would be more to the advantage of all the accused than evidence supporting him would be to their disadvantage. The right of the defendants not to give evidence without this being taken as improving the supergrass's credibility was also affirmed, and the court stressed that admissions of guilt are only evidence against those who make them.[3]

But there was no clear decision in *Graham* regarding the degree to which evidence which supports the supergrass's testimony against specific accused can enhance the general credibility of his testimony against all the defendants. Mr Justice Hutton argued that, had the accused been tried separately, independent evidence which tended to confirm the supergrass's testimony against one would have been inadmissible against them all, not because it was logically irrelevant, but because it was collateral and its admission would tend unduly to lengthen and confuse the smaller separate proceedings. However, in a joint trial, he stated, it was, in principle, possible for such evidence to be properly admitted, since the objection from complexity and confusion no longer applied. But he refrained from attempting to resolve the issue further, since the basis of the appeal was not the admissibility of the evidence in question but the use to which it had been put by the trial judge.[4] Lord Justice O'Donnell doubted the validity of this reasoning but reserved his opinion until such time as the issue required a more considered answer. The fact that an accomplice was proven to have told the truth on one or two occasions, he said, was no reason for concluding that he would probably tell the truth on all occasions, and even if independent evidence relating specifically to a particular defendant, or defendants, were to be admitted, its evidential value in the cases against the rest would be slight.[5]

In *Donnelly* the question of the admissibility and relevance of supportive evidence to the general credibility of a witness in a joint trial was discussed more fully. Lord Lowry held that in joint trials there was a broader spectrum of admissible evidence than there would have been had all the defendants been tried separately. The general credibility of a witness could be bolstered incidentally, but not expressly, by evidence which tended to support his evidence, but not by mere evidence of competence (except for experts), nor

---

[3] (1984) 18 NIJB.
[4] Ibid. 37.
[5] Ibid. 41–2.

by evidence of good character (except in the case of the defendants themselves); and, since evidence which damaged a witness's testimony inured for the benefit of all the defendants, the converse must also be true. The proper objection to wrongful reliance upon evidence in support of a witness's general credibility in a joint trial was the weight which might be attributed to it and not its admissibility as such.[6] A similar view was taken by Mr Justice Carswell in *R.* v. *Steenson*,[7] where it was held that at best supportive evidence confirmed only the accuracy of a supergrass's evidence and not its truth against particular accused, and that it was therefore of little assistance to a court on the question of guilt or innocence. However, the identification of weight rather than admissibility as the key issue is of little consequence given the importance which corroboration has since assumed.

While the implications of the appeal decisions in *Crumley* and *McCormick* are not altogether clear, they suggest that not only must a supergrass's evidence now be corroborated, but the corroborative evidence itself must be of a particularly convincing kind. In *McCormick*[8] the Northern Ireland Court of Appeal suggested, when it endorsed the trial judge's assessment that a high standard of corroboration was required in this case,[9] that apparently, in some cases, the lower the credibility of the witness's evidence, the stricter the corroboration test. At a certain point on this continuum, to be determined by the view the tribunal of fact takes of the credibility of the accomplice evidence, circumstantial evidence will not be considered corroborative. Lord Lowry did not make clear whether the Court of Appeal's decision rested solely upon the trial judge's view that the evidence of the particular accomplice in question required especially compelling corroboration, or whether there is, or should be, a presumption that the evidence of *certain classes of accomplice* cannot be sufficient to sustain a conviction without independent evidence which is corroborative in the higher sense. However, this uncertainty has since been resolved by *Crumley*,[10] where it was judicially recognized for the first time that, by

[6] (1986) 4 NIJB 64–5.

[7] See Court of Appeal's decision (1986) 17 NIJB.

[8] (1984) 1 NIJB; [1984] NI 50.

[9] For a further discussion of this point, see S. C. Greer, 'Supergrasses and the Legal System in Britain and Northern Ireland' (1986) 102 LQR 198 and id., 'Corroboration and Suspect Evidence' (1988) 51 MLR 121.

[10] (1986) 14 NIJB.

its nature, the evidence of a supergrass is more dangerous than that of an ordinary accomplice, and that the character of particular supergrasses, and the circumstances in which they came to give their evidence, can make their testimony more dangerous still. If this were the case, Lord Lowry held, the 'sternest criteria' would have to be fulfilled before their evidence could provide the sole basis for conviction, and if any 'suspect witness' became even more suspect for reasons specific to his own case, but yet was rehabilitated by the tribunal of fact, 'the manner and extent of his rehabilitation to a state of credence' must be clear before his uncorroborated evidence could sustain convictions.[11] Although this appears to leave open the possibility of convictions on the uncorroborated evidence of supergrasses, and thus superficially avoids any radical departure from the regular common-law test, it is, in effect, tantamount to a prohibition upon convictions on uncorroborated supergrass evidence in the Diplock courts, since it is difficult to imagine any flesh-and-blood supergrass being able to meet this rigorous standard.

THE POLICE

The police played five principal roles in the supergrass system: recruiting the supergrasses, preparing them for trial, protecting their families, building the case against the accused, and defending the process in the public debate. The responsibilities of the RUC in the prosecution of any indictable offence in Northern Ireland are formally limited to the apprehension of suspects and the gathering of evidence, while the decision to proceed rests with the Director of Public Prosecutions for Northern Ireland.[12] The Attorney-General has stated that it is up to the Chief Constable to recommend that any given supergrass be called as a Crown witness, but that the final decision rests with the DPP.[13] However, there can be little doubt that the police are the linchpin in this process, and, as Gifford states: 'their recommendation will be virtually decisive, and the supergrass knows it.'[14]

[11] (1986) 14 NIJB 44.
[12] The Prosecution of Offences (NI) Order 1972, ss. 5 and 6.
[13] HC Debs., vol. 47, col. 4.
[14] T. Gifford, *Supergrasses: The Use of Accomplice Evidence in Northern Ireland* (London: The Cobden Trust, 1984), para. 78.

Whether the initiative to turn Queen's evidence comes from the police or the suspect has been hotly disputed. The police have consistently maintained that theirs was a reactive role, responding to initiatives which always came from the suspect. In contrast, supergrasses who retracted, and other one-time suspects, have claimed that they were pressurized to turn informer. Walsh found that 35 per cent of respondents in his survey of suspects interviewed by the RUC from September 1980 to June 1981 claimed that pressure had been exerted upon them by the police to pass on information, and some claimed that they were threatened with being framed, while others were offered money or a job.[15]

The particularly close relationship which tends to develop between the supergrass and the police in the long period between arrest and appearance at trial has given rise to four principal concerns. First, it is highly impenetrable to outsiders and has resulted, for example, in displays of support, and even affection from the police to supergrasses in court and to the kinds of pre-trial socialising documented in previous chapters. The police need the supergrass to sustain the charges, while the supergrass needs the police to gain his rewards. Having severed links between himself, his friends, and the movement to which he once dedicated his life, he is not in a strong position to resist police suggestions. The fear that police protection may be withdrawn is also likely to be considerable.

Secondly, it has been alleged that suspects have been named by the police for inclusion in supergrasses' statements, especially in cases where the accused have faced charges involving conspiracies vague on time, place, and intended victims. It has been suggested that an extra conspirator may have been inserted here or there in order to secure the conviction of those the police believed to be guilty of terrorist offences but against whom there was a frustrating lack of legally admissible evidence. Gifford states that he has no doubt

at least of this, that the police when interrogating suspects, and when putting to them the possibilities of immunity if they give information, mention specific names of people whom they wish to see convicted. It would be wholly natural for them to do so; indeed, it could be argued that

---

[15] D. P. J. Walsh, *The Use and Abuse of Emergency Legislation in Northern Ireland* (London: The Cobden Trust, 1983), 68. See Ch. 2.

they were not doing their duty if they did not press for information about those whom they believed to be terrorists.[16]

Some of Gifford's respondents also claimed that the police had asked them to sign statements which had been prepared in advance and which named certain individuals and detailed their alleged offences. Although recognizing the suspect nature of his sources, and the enormous range of possibilities between the accounts given by the police and by those who supplied evidence to his inquiry, Gifford concludes that there are grounds for concern that some, if not all, of these allegations are true.

The control which the police have over this critical aspect of a supergrass process raises, thirdly, a central complaint about the role in Northern Ireland of the supergrass system. It has been argued that the lengthy remands in custody of those implicated amounted to 'internment by remand', that is to say a form of administrative detention without the suspect's guilt having been proven beyond reasonable doubt in a judicial process. Periods of eighteen months or two years were not uncommon and a number of defendants were shunted from one supergrass to another, either as a result of having been acquitted or the evidence against them having been retracted.[17] Three Belfast men, Thomas Power, John O'Reilly, and Gerard Steenson, for example, spent just one month short of four years remanded in custody on the evidence of five successive supergrasses before being found guilty on the evidence of Harry Kirkpatrick only to be released a year later, when the Northern Ireland Court of Appeal quashed their convictions. The long remand periods were exacerbated by the general problem of delay in the Diplock process, an additional source of which in some supergrass cases was the determination of the accused to wait until the counsel of their choice, generally Mr Desmond Boal QC, became available.[18]

---

[16] Gifford, *Supergrasses*, para. 71.

[17] For a discussion of the distinction between 'internment' or 'preventive detention' and detentions obtained in the regular criminal justice system, see S. C. Greer, 'Preventive Detention and Public Security: Towards a General Model', in A. Harding and J. Hatchard (eds.), *Preventive Detention and Security Law: A Comparative Survey* (The Hague: Martinus Nijhoff, 1993).

[18] Various suggestions have been made as to how delay could be reduced. In his report on the Northern Ireland (Emergency Provisions) Act 1978—*Review of the Operation of the Northern Ireland (Emergency Provisions) Act 1978* (The Baker Report), Cmnd. 9222 (London: HMSO, 1984)—Sir George Baker stated that the

The fourth difficulty concerns the problem of 'post-perceptual' information replacing the original recollection of an event. Psychological research has shown that recollections of an incident can be affected, or even displaced, by subsequent suggestions—not necessarily intended to have this effect—as to what may have happened, and that after such interference the subject 'remembers' the distorted recollection rather than the original memory without being aware that anything has changed. This problem is particularly acute in police–supergrass interaction for two reasons. In the first place the supergrass will typically be attempting to recall a host of separate incidents, some of which happened rapidly and under conditions of extreme stress years before, and in which various parties were involved—factors widely recognized as conducive to memory warping. Secondly, as already noted, the police may have a motive to attempt deliberately to distort any given memory in order to include someone they particularly want to see prosecuted.

THE PROSECUTING AUTHORITIES

There is some ambiguity about precisely which agencies the term 'prosecuting authorities' includes in Northern Ireland. On a narrow view it refers solely to the Director of Public Prosecutions for Northern Ireland,[19] but the term can also be taken to include the Attorney-General for Northern Ireland, whose responsibilities have been discharged, since the imposition of Direct Rule in 1972, by

'one legitimate objection to the accomplice cases' (para. 173) concerned the wisdom of having 'so many defendants, so many charges, such delay in starting and such long trials' (para. 172). He regarded the internment-by-remand accusation 'difficult to refute' and, in his view, it was 'impossible to conclude that there is no injustice' in cases where defendants had been held for long periods on the evidence of supergrasses who later retracted (para. 174). The report makes a number of recommendations designed to alleviate the delay problem: the prospect of further judicial appointments should be kept under review; not all scheduled offence trials need be held in Belfast; sympathetic consideration should be given to any request that the DPP may make for more staff. But the most important proposal concerned the implementation of a version of the Scottish principle that prisoners held in custody beyond a specified time without having been committed for trial should be entitled to bail as of right. The time-limit suggested for scheduled offences is 12 months and the report recommends that no more than 20 defendants should be indicted in any given proceedings (paras. 179–87).

[19] The office of DPP for Northern Ireland was created by the Prosecution of Offences (NI) Order 1972 in order to establish an independent service for the prosecution of major criminal offences and certain types of less serious case. However, the police remain the 'prosecuting authority' for many minor offences.

the Attorney-General for England and Wales. The Northern Ireland Constitution Act 1973 gives the Attorney-General for Northern Ireland the power to appoint and remove the DPP for Northern Ireland,[20] and under the Prosecution of Offences (Northern Ireland) Order 1972, the Director is required to 'discharge his functions under the direction of the Attorney General' and to be 'subject to the directions of the Attorney General in all matters'.[21] The Attorney-General's office and responsibilities are varied and have grown organically, like the British constitution itself. As a Member of Parliament he or she has the usual political duties towards constituents and party, as well as being head of the Bar and the chief Law Officer, the government's in-house legal adviser. Although not a member of the cabinet, the Attorney-General may be invited to cabinet meetings to advise on the legal implications of government decisions. He or she is also constitutionally accountable to parliament and can make statements and answer questions in the House of Commons.[22] The responsibilities of the office also include deciding whether the 'public interest' warrants prosecution, or the discontinuation of prosecution, in any given case, and certain criminal proceedings, such as those under the Official Secrets Act, cannot be instigated without the Attorney-General's permission. This fusion of undeniably political responsibilities and ostensibly independent professional legal functions has made the precise role of political considerations in the management of the supergrass system difficult to determine.

The role of the DPP for Northern Ireland in the supergrass process was spelled out by the Attorney-General, Sir Michael Havers, in two statements to the House of Commons on 24 October 1983 and 19 March 1986, considered in Chapters 5 and 8 respectively. Put simply, without the DPP's imprimatur the supergrass system would never have got off the ground. Three specific aspects of this role can be distinguished: the decision to prosecute on the evidence of supergrasses, the decision to grant immunity from prosecution, and the use of the voluntary bill of indictment to bypass the committal proceedings in certain cases.

---

[20] Section 34 (2).
[21] Sections 3 (2) and 5 (2).
[22] See generally J. Ll. J. Edwards, *The Law Officers of the Crown* (London: Sweet & Maxwell, 1964) and id., *The Attorney General, Politics and the Public Interest* (London: Sweet & Maxwell, 1984).

The Decision to Prosecute

The specific criteria brought to bear by the DPP for Northern Ireland in determining if a prosecution should be brought on the evidence of a supergrass remain unclear, and the Attorney-General has stated that, in a number of cases, the DPP declined to prosecute. Yet the fact remains that prosecutions were initiated on the evidence of witnesses with histories of mental instability, Grimley and Morgan, and upon vague conspiracy charges which were difficult to defend with anything other than a blank denial. According to the Attorney-General's statement of 19 March 1986, the DPP's constitutional function is restricted to predicting how a court will treat the evidence presented to it and that prosecutions are justified if there is a 'reasonable' expectation of conviction. The DPP for England and Wales told the Royal Commission on Criminal Procedure in the late 1970s that a 'reasonable prospect of conviction' meant 'whether . . . it seems rather more likely that there will be a conviction than an acquittal'.[23] Consequently, it could be argued that although criticisms could be made of the DPP's deference to the police in deciding to prosecute on the evidence of certain supergrasses, the DPP acted properly when these cases did in fact result in convictions. However, it could also be argued that once the courts changed their minds and indicated their reluctance to convict on the uncorroborated evidence of supergrasses, the DPP again responded in an appropriate manner by withdrawing the Whorisky prosecutions and by refusing to sanction any further prosecutions on supergrass evidence. Since the courts in Northern Ireland have now signalled their refusal to convict on supergrass evidence unless it is corroborated by particularly compelling independent evidence, this appears to imply that the DPP for Northern Ireland should not mount any further supergrass prosecutions unless corroboration of this standard is available. To do so would violate the principle that only prosecutions which have at least a greater than even chance of resulting in convictions should be initiated. As already established, silence in response to police questions or a refusal to testify cannot be regarded as fulfilling the particularly stringent corroboration-test now required for supergrass evidence in the Diplock courts.

[23] *Royal Commission on Criminal Procedure* (The Phillips Report), Cmnd. 8091–2, (London: HMSO, 1981), app. 25.

Immunity from Prosecution

Dillon claims that, in the early 1970s, at least three informers were granted immunity from prosecution in return for their information.[24] Thirteen of the supergrasses in the 1980s received such immunity (Bennett, Black, Lean, Grimley, McGurk, Mallon, Goodman, O'Rawe, McKeown, Gilmour, Quigley, Williamson, and Morgan), while a further eleven (McGrady, Collins, McConkey, Skelly, Dillon, Kirkpatrick, Gibson, Allen, Smith, Crockard, and Whorisky) were denied it. The position of the others is not known.

The granting of immunity from prosecution was discussed in Chapter 5. A particularly vexed question, which the Attorney-General did not address in his first substantial Commons statement on 24 October 1983, concerns whether immunity from prosecution can be, or ever has been, offered to anyone who has 'pulled the trigger' in a murder in Northern Ireland. The police have maintained that a *de facto* policy operated to deprive those in this position of this particularly attractive reward, but Beresford claims that this was only instigated after the McKeown and Goodman cases in the autumn of 1982, and was apparently in response to growing concern, particularly from unionists, that this was morally unacceptable.[25] However, there is no doubt that immunity from prosecution has been granted to those who admitted having been involved in murder or attempted murder but allegedly only in a secondary capacity—for example, Black, Bennett, Grimley, and Gilmour.

A key problem here is the reliability of the supergrass's claim that his involvement in murder has been ancillary rather than primary. Unscrupulous accomplices can clearly alter roles in any given account of an incident in order to cast themselves in the best, and their associates in the worst, light, as the claims made by Black, Gilmour, and Allen that in certain shooting incidents they shot aiming to miss tend to confirm. This risk is increased by the fact that successfully being able to downgrade one's role in this manner may be crucial in determining whether immunity is granted or not, and it is therefore possible that immunity from prosecution has in fact been given to those who have pulled the trigger in

---

[24] See M. Dillon, *The Dirty War* (London: Arrow Books, 1991), 50, 62, 79.
[25] *Guardian*, 27 July 1983.

murders, but that this has been successfully concealed, either by the supergrass alone or by the supergrass and the police together.

The precise legal status of offers of immunity from prosecution is uncertain.[26] By coincidence the immunity issue re-emerged in public discussion in 1981, as the supergrass system began to unfold in Northern Ireland, when Sir Anthony Blunt was exposed as the 'fourth man' in the notorious pro-Soviet spy-ring which had operated within the British establishment in the years following the Second World War. When it was revealed that Blunt had been granted immunity from prosecution in 1964 by Attorney-General Sir John Hobson, Sir Michael Havers was obliged to make a statement to the Commons.[27] The key elements of this were quoted again in the statement on the supergrass system delivered on 24 October 1983. Sir Michael Havers stated that 'true immunities are uncommon, because it is now the practice not to go further than an undertaking that any confession obtained as a result will not be used against the maker. If other evidence to justify his prosecution becomes available then proceedings may be brought.'[28] A distinction can therefore be drawn between: (*a*) 'confessional immunities', undertakings given by the Attorney-General or the DPP to a suspect that, if he confesses, no proceedings will be brought on the basis of his confession; and (*b*) 'true immunities', more general guarantees that no prosecution will ever be brought in respect of certain offences. If the prosecuting authorities want to renege on a confessional immunity, the immunized suspect could only be successfully prosecuted on evidence other than his confession, since it is likely that the confession which secured the offer of immunity would be ruled inadmissible on the grounds of potential unreliability.[29] 'True immunities' are of two kinds: the advance pardon and the *nolle prosequi*. The former was traditionally given after the criminal act had been committed but before the indictment had been laid, and although, according to Smith, it is 'clearly moribund', it cannot be considered legally dead.[30] The *nolle prosequi*, on the other hand, is much more alive. The Attorney-General

---

[26] For a full discussion, see A. T. H. Smith, 'Immunity from Prosecution' (1983) 42 CLJ 299.

[27] HC Debs., vol. 19, col. 12.

[28] Ibid.

[29] See Police and Criminal Evidence Act 1984, s. 76 (2) (*a*); Police and Criminal Evidence (NI) Order 1988, s. 74 (2) (*b*).

[30] Smith, 'Immunity from Prosecution', 303.

possesses the power to enter a *nolle prosequi*, a formal means of informing the court that any given prosecution will not be pursued, and the DPP can also discontinue prosecutions. The 'true immunity' in the modern era therefore consists, in practical terms, of a promise by the Attorney-General to exercise the *nolle prosequi* should the need arise. As such it is deficient as a complete immunity in two important respects. First, it can only come into operation after a prosecution has been initiated either privately or by the DPP, and secondly, it is not binding upon successive Attornies-General.

The immunities granted to the supergrasses in Northern Ireland seem to be of the *nolle prosequi* kind, since it would appear that confessional immunities need to be offered *before* confessions are made, and officially offers of immunity were not made to the supergrasses in Northern Ireland until *after* they had made their statements. Although this sequence of events has been challenged, it is the official version which is likely to determine the status of the immunity. It follows that the supergrass immunities are not entirely legally watertight. The courts could be invited to exercise their inherent power to stay vexatious and oppressive proceedings if a prosecution were to be brought against a supergrass who had been granted immunity, a decision which would hinge on what was deemed to be in the public interest. But apart from this, no procedural or other formal impediment precludes the prosecution of any of the immunized supergrasses, including both those who retracted and those whose evidence has been instrumental in securing convictions. But such prosecutions are such a remote possibility that they can be discounted, since to prosecute a supergrass who has received immunity would effectively rule out the recruitment of any further supergrasses on this basis, and although there is no real prospect of this happening in Northern Ireland in the foreseeable future, the authorities are unlikely to want to foreclose this option unless doing so would achieve tangible gains.

The Voluntary Bill of Indictment

Another contentious aspect of the role of the prosecuting authorities in the supergrass system concerned the use of the voluntary bill of indictment in the Black, McGurk, and Kirkpatrick cases. Under Section 2 of the Grand Jury (Abolition) Act (NI) 1969, and Schedule 5 of the Judicature (NI) Act 1978, an accused can be sent for trial on indictment without having to go through the committal proceedings if (*a*) leave of a judge of the High Court, the Crown Court, or the Court of Appeal is granted, or (*b*) the Attorney-General or the Court of Appeal so directs, or (*c*) an order under Section 8 of the Perjury Act (NI) 1946 is made. Applications are made *ex parte* so an accused cannot be represented at the hearing, and the right of appeal is also limited because the Court of Appeal will not inquire into the exercise of the judge's discretion provided it is clear that in dealing with the application the judge has not exceeded his jurisdiction.[31]

The voluntary bill of indictment is not part of Northern Ireland's anti-terrorist laws and has, in fact, been available in England and Wales since 1933, although rarely used. In his study of the criminal prosecution process in England and Wales, Lord Devlin found that between 1951 and 1956 the voluntary bill tended to be employed as a stop-gap emergency measure where, for unusual reasons, the committal proceedings could not be completed, because, for example, an examining magistrate had died after a full hearing but before committal.[32] As Walsh argues, these are poor precedents for their use in supergrass trials in Northern Ireland, since the disruption of committal proceedings in previous supergrass cases provides little justification for the peremptory introduction of voluntary bills in others, as preliminary inquiries can be held in camera if it appears that justice cannot be served by a public hearing. As Walsh states:

Since it would appear that there are no other likely grounds on which the Crown could justify its decision to proceed by voluntary bill of indictment . . . [in the trial of scheduled offences] . . ., the suspicion inevitably arises that it . . . was . . . being used solely to shield the supergrass from cross-examination and to prevent the likely collapse of the prosecution case at the committal stage.[33]

This, as he points out, has two adverse effects upon the accused. First, it denies defendants their first opportunity to challenge the evidence upon which their remand in custody is typically based, and, secondly, it prevents the defence from securing the removal of

---

[31] See Walsh, *Emergency Legislation*, 88–90.
[32] P. Devlin, *The Criminal Prosecution in England* (Oxford: Oxford University Press, 1960).
[33] Walsh, *Emergency Legislation*, 90.

inadmissible evidence prejudicial to the accused from the written statements of prosecution witnesses. Although it is possible for defence counsel to apply to a judge other than the trial judge to have such material excised from the committal papers, this is not a facility to which defendants are entitled by right.

In his review of the Northern Ireland (Emergency Provisions) Act 1978 Sir George Baker considered the voluntary bill of indictment, although there is nothing in the relevant section of the report to indicate that 'the two scheduled cases' in which, until then, it had been used were, in fact, supergrass cases. He concluded that, while it was legitimate for the voluntary bill procedure to be adopted in cases where associates of the accused had disrupted proceedings, it was generally unwise to do so, because this afforded 'yet another opportunity for attacking the judiciary'.[34] Sir George added that it also deprived the defendant of a safeguard and that it was undesirable to stray too far from normal practice, and he recommended that the voluntary bill procedure should be employed in a scheduled case only by the Attorney-General.

THE GOVERNMENT

Apart from the Attorney-General's role in prosecutions, the government's contribution to the supergrass system came in two main forms. First, it provided the necessary financial resources and other facilities, such as documents with which to authenticate the new identities for those supergrasses who had received them, and early release from imprisonment. Secondly, it offered ideological support to the agencies who managed the supergrass system on the ground, the RUC, the DPP, and, in the 'conviction phase', the courts.

Early Release from Prison

Four supergrasses, McGrady, Kirkpatrick, Allen, and Crockard, were tried and sentenced before being called to testify against those they had implicated. Critics of the supergrass system alleged that tacit undertakings were reached in all of these cases and that only a short portion of the long sentence which was imposed would be served. Indeed, it has been claimed that, in the summer of 1983, the RUC trawled the prisons for supergrasses, offering the chance of

---

[34] Baker Report: *Review of the Operation of the Northern Ireland (Emergency Provisions) Act 1978*, Cmnd. 9222 (London: HMSO, 1984), para. 59.

early release as the incentive. On 27 August 1983 Fr. Denis Faul, a Catholic priest with a long track-record of humanitarian interest in the Diplock process, claimed that this deliberate policy singled out the most vulnerable candidates, and that he had been told of five prisoners who had been taken on the same day from the Maze prison and Crumlin Road gaol to the RUC's holding-centre at Castlereagh apparently for this purpose.[35]

Father Faul's accusations were supported by a claim from a republican prisoner, Thomas McCrystal, that he was offered early release by the police if he agreed to testify against a number of men. McCrystal, who was then serving a life sentence for the murder of a member of the UDR, made a detailed statement to this effect to his solicitor in the middle of August 1983, claiming that he had been taken to Castlereagh RUC station, where detectives had told him that if he gave evidence in court he would be released as soon as those he implicated were convicted. 'A proper standard of living' for the rest of his life, relocation in Britain, police protection, and education and financial security for his two children were also said to have been promised. The fact that McCrystal had severed links from, and had been ostracized by, other republican prisoners in the Maze, had refused to take part in the H-Blocks protest, and was housed in a mixed non-political block, gave his allegations extra credibility. The Northern Ireland Office denied his allegations and said that it was not in anyone's power to offer him such a deal. The RUC declined to comment specifically upon the McCrystal case, but a police spokesman denied the general allegations and stated that the RUC already had its hands full with supergrasses and had no need to enlist prison-inmates as recruits. It was pointed out that the police could only support an application to the Northern Ireland Office for early release if a prisoner offered to give evidence and that normally the police interviewed prisoners in only two circumstances: when they requested an interview or when police investigations required it.[36]

However, even if these accusations against the police are discounted, there are other reasons for believing that tacit understandings regarding early release from prison were reached between the authorities and those supergrasses who failed to secure immunity. First, while it is true that no single agency in the criminal justice

---

[35] *Irish Times*, 28 Apr. 1983.
[36] Ibid.

system is capable of giving such guarantees, a clear chain of responsibility was established in supergrass trials in England, making such outcomes relatively predictable. In English supergrass cases the police characteristically indicated to the supergrass that the assistance they gave the law enforcement process would be brought to the attention of the court at their own trial, and the courts, in their turn, typically imposed lenient sentences, usually with no minimum recommended term. Finally, the Home Office released the supergrasses by exercising the Crown prerogative of mercy even before these terms expired, and, as already indicated in the previous chapter, the evidence, incomplete though it is, suggests that no English supergrass has served more than two years in prison. Secondly, and more to the point, McGrady, Allen, Crockard, and Kirkpatrick all served comparatively short sentences. Allen was released only two years into a fourteen-year sentence, McGrady completed six years of a triple life sentence, Crockard served eight years of a double life sentence, and Kirkpatrick completed just under nine years of a life sentence for five murders.[37] Moreover, in comparison with the bulk of the prison population, all had enjoyed a remarkably leisurely custodial regime, accommodated in Maghaberry state-of-the-art prison in a cell-block equipped with videos, television, private bathrooms, a gym, easy chairs, and a library.[38]

Financial Rewards

The question of how much money the supergrasses received was a recurrent theme in the debate. The government and police consistently denied both that the total sum was particularly large and that significant sums were paid to given individuals. Against this, those claiming that their services as informer or supergrass were sought by the RUC have alleged that tens of thousands, and even hundreds of thousands, of pounds were offered.[39] As indicated in Chapter 2, it is clear that the RUC, in common with police forces the world over, regularly pay small sums to informers for information about certain suspects and certain localities. But this leaves open the possibility that different rules came into operation once the supergrass system began. As previous chapters indicate, most, if not all,

---

[37] Information supplied by the Northern Ireland Office.
[38] *Guardian*, 11 Aug. 1986.
[39] See Ch. 2.

the supergrasses received cash hand-outs for clothes and other essentials while preparing for trial, and that some went with their families and their police minders on expenses-paid trips abroad. However, following the judgment in the Bennett trial in April 1983, the RUC vigorously denied allegations that up to £100,000 had been offered to each of the defendants if they would turn supergrass in their turn. Commenting upon such allegations, a police spokesman said that 'money is not offered but we have a duty to protect [the supergrasses] not only at the time but afterwards and anything we would do for them would be in the light of this objective'.[40] The statement also denied claims made earlier by UVF supergrass Clifford McKeown that he had been offered £80,000 for his services.

On 16 November 1983 Mr Prior, then Secretary of State for Northern Ireland, told the House of Commons that the cost of protecting police informers in Northern Ireland had amounted to just over half a million pounds in the previous five years. However, a month later, after having been pressed to disclose how much money had been paid to each accomplice who had turned Queen's evidence, he refused to go into details on the grounds that to do so 'might prejudice the security of individuals'.[41] But in a written reply on 26 February 1985, a later Secretary of State for Northern Ireland, Mr Douglas Hurd, disclosed that providing protection for people who had given evidence against former accomplices in terrorist organizations had cost the tax-payer £1.3 million over the previous seven years,[42] although it would appear that the bulk of this sum was spent on the supergrasses in the last four years of this period.

New Lives Abroad

Both the supergrasses who received immunity from prosecution and those sentenced were provided with new identities and new lives together with their families somewhere outside Northern Ireland. Again, the nature of these arrangements has provoked controversy. A police spokesman admitted that the RUC was involved in getting supergrasses out of the country to 'somewhere they would be reasonably safe', and that 'part of the undertaking would be

---

[40] *Belfast Telegraph*, 18 Apr. 1983.
[41] *Irish News*, 15 Dec. 1983.
[42] HC Debs., vol. 74, col. 126.

helping them to get a home and a job'.[43] Others have alleged that luxurious new lives have been arranged in exotic places like Australia or South Africa, although the South African ambassador to the United Kingdom denied that supergrasses had found new homes in his country.[44] The truth is difficult to determine. The available evidence tends to suggest that the provisions have been reasonably generous, but that the eventual destinations have not been as far from Northern Ireland as speculation has suggested. A report in the *Belfast Telegraph* on 14 February 1985 claimed that Christopher Black had been refused admittance by Australia and New Zealand and had been forced to go into hiding in England; and the whereabouts of one former immune supergrass, Joseph Bennett, were revealed when, in 1986, he was convicted of armed robbery in the English Midlands. It appears that, following the Belfast trial in 1983, RUC Special Branch had supplied Bennett with new documents under a new name, including a passport and birth certificate, and had provided him with a furnished house and job. Firearms found in Bennett's home had been licensed in Northern Ireland and were apparently sanctioned by the RUC for use in his own protection.[45]

INDEPENDENCE, CONSPIRACY, OR NEGOTIATION?

In Chapter 5 it was noted that the official view of the supergrass system emphasized the independence of the Diplock system from government and, within it, the independence of the judiciary from the DPP for Northern Ireland and the police, while the conspiracy theory claimed that the supergrass process unmasked these institutions as compliant parts in a conspiracy masterminded to defeat republicanism in both its political and military manifestations.

The theory of institutional independence can be criticized on three principal grounds. First, it confuses the vital distinction between accomplices who turn Queen's evidence and supergrasses which was considered at length in Chapter 1. Secondly, it is implausible in the extreme to suggest that nearly thirty supergrasses inexplicably volunteered to turn Queen's evidence between 1980 and 1983 without some prior change in security policy, while in the

[43] *Belfast Telegraph*, 18 Apr. 1984.
[44] *Irish News*, 13 Apr. 1985.
[45] *Guardian*, 7 Apr. and 3 July 1986.

previous twelve years only a handful surfaced, and over the past ten years only two (Whorisky and Collins) have made an appearance, neither lasting the course. Thirdly, the theory fails to explain the sharp differences between the supergrass system's principal phases—construction and ascendancy on the one hand, and decline and fall on the other—and the fact that the same judges who quashed the uncorroborated convictions on appeal had previously been responsible for convicting without corroboration in other cases.

The conspiracy metaphor, on the other hand, is quite simply inappropriate and misleading. First, it implies the absurd conclusion that the low conviction-rate which the supergrass system achieved is all that the security and intelligence establishment expected in the early 1980s. Secondly, and more seriously, it underestimates the possibility of important differences of opinion between the institutions of the Diplock system, especially between the courts and the others, and therefore misinterprets them when they occur. It is undeniable that one of the central functions of the courts in any jurisdiction is to uphold the existing constitutional order, and it cannot seriously be suggested that judges in any system possess the 'independence' which would allow them to choose radically different constitutional arrangements. However, in liberal democracies a broad judicial commitment to the prevailing constitutional order does not exclude the possibility of a significant degree of judicial autonomy on given issues, and the supergrass system in Northern Ireland is a case in point. The abolition of the right to silence, even if deemed to have increased the risk of future supergrass trials, adds little credibility to the conspiracy theory for two reasons. First, a second supergrass system based upon supergrass testimony corroborated by the silence of the accused would be the result of a *negotiation* and not a *conspiracy* between the different agencies involved. Conspirators agree on a goal and set about achieving it but do not destroy the original objective as a means of renegotiating the terms. Secondly, as already suggested, it is not at all clear that a fresh supergrass system will be based upon the 1988 Order.

The 'negotiation theory' provides the best explanation for the rise and fall of the supergrass system in Northern Ireland and can be interpreted either as a version of liberal-democratic theory or as an application of the stream in Marxist jurisprudence which Collins and others have labelled 'law as ideology'.[46] Both approaches take the fact of judicial autonomy seriously and share a common recognition that judicial independence is more limited than the strong theory of institutional independence suggested by the official view, but more substantial than that described by the conspiracy theory. In liberal political theory judicial autonomy is understood in terms of the doctrines of the separation of powers and the rule of law, while under 'law as ideology' the focus shifts from the *fact* of autonomy to its *function* in stabilizing and defending the dominant set of values and ideas.

The negotiation theory maintains, as Chapter 2 of this study demonstrates, that the conditions for the construction of a supergrass system were created by policy decisions taken by the government and its security advisers, including the police, in 1979–80. But, for two reasons, this was not a 'conspiracy'. First, the courts and the DPP were not privy to these decisions, and secondly, the agreement in question appears to have been about increasing reliance upon informers rather than instituting supergass trials as such. The successful construction of a supergrass system depended upon unpredictable 'supply side' factors and the co-operation of the prosecuting authorities and the judiciary. The initial success of the supergrass system was underwritten both by the judiciary and the DPP. The DPP's role was largely a filtering one, and, as already suggested, the authorization of at least some of the early prosecutions was constitutionally justified in so far as the test was the likelihood of convictions. It would seem that the courts initially adopted a 'crime control' rather than a 'due process' approach, which placed a higher premium upon believing the supergrasses' accusations than upon the application of the full implications of principles of due process concerning the burden of proof and the particular risks posed by supergass evidence in non-jury trials. Later, when the damage this caused the reputation of the courts, not only in Northern Ireland but much further afield, began to be appreciated, the priorities were switched, first by individual judges and then more systematically by the Northern Ireland Court of Appeal. This required an awareness of public opinion, an appreciation of the threat posed to the legitimacy of the legal system by inconsistent judicial decisions, and the skilful manipulation of the

---

[46] H. Collins, *Marxism and Law* (Oxford: Oxford University Press, 1984), ch. 3.

'open-texturedness' of legal rules and principles to impose uniformity of decision-making while appearing not to depart from the 'seamless web' of 'institutional history'.[47] Legal criteria even more strict than those of the regular common law were eventually observed, even though this resulted in the acquittal of those deemed 'probably guilty' of serious terrorist offences in Northern Ireland. However, the substitution of due process for crime control was uneven and, ultimately, incomplete, as the Gibney conviction shows.

It is impossible to identify precisely the factors which produced the judicial U-turn. It could be argued that Northern Ireland's judges, drawn largely from Protestant backgrounds,[48] recognized the dangers inherent in the disenchantment of large sections of the loyalist community with the courts which the supergrass system inspired. Lord Gifford's unofficial inquiry in 1983 was probably of considerable influence, since it demonstrated that the decisions in the Bennett, Black, and McGrady cases were open to criticism on purely legal grounds. The broadly based anti-supergrass campaign, particularly in its international manifestations, also seems to have had some impact. However, contrary to what some have claimed, the Anglo-Irish Agreement of 1985 had little if anything to do with the decline and fall of the supergrass system, since the latter had been in terminal decline for reasons internal both to itself and to Northern Ireland for at least a year before the accord was signed.[49]

INSTITUTIONALIZATION, DUE PROCESS, AND ACCOUNTABILITY

Finally, certain tentative conclusions about the nature of supergrass systems and the relationship between their successful institutionalization on the one hand, and the provision of effective due-process constraints and mechanisms of public accountability on the other, can be derived from this study. In Chapter 1 it was suggested that, in the first instance, types of police informant should be distin-

---

[47] The 'open texture' of legal rules is one of the metaphors used by H. L. A. Hart in *Concept of Law* (Oxford: Clarendon Press, 1961), while the terms 'seamless web' and 'institutional history' are Dworkin's. See R. Dworkin, *Taking Rights Seriously* (London: Duckworth, 1978) and id., *Law's Empire* (London: Fontana, 1986).

[48] See, e.g., the thumb-nail sketches in Workers' Research Unit, *Belfast Bulletin No. 10—Rough Justice* (Belfast: publ. authors, 1982).

[49] See, e.g., the dispute between Garrett Fitzgerald and Sir Barry Shaw, former DPP for Northern Ireland, in *The Times*, 7 and 15 Oct. 1987.

guished not by reference to motivation, as other commentators have suggested, but by their relationships with their targets and the agencies of the state to whom their information is supplied. In the case of supergrasses, these unique relationships crystallize in their role as pivotal witnesses in mass trials of those allegedly involved in violent political or non-political crime. Three principal factors are strongly correlated with the creation of supergrass systems: the maturing of intelligence and informer systems to the point where sufficient information is available to identify potential supergrasses and defendants; the actual or perceived failure of other methods hitherto employed to tackle the given problem; and the exploitation of personal and/or systematic crises of allegiance on the part of members of target organizations. Employing the services of super-grasses is a high-risk strategy for the police and other agencies in the prosecution process, since, if it succeeds, the punishment of tens, if not hundreds, of suspects is assured. But if it fails, a valuable source of intelligence, as well as considerable resources, will have been squandered, exposing the police and criminal justice system to considerable public criticism. It follows that the decision to promote supergrass trials in any jurisdiction is likely to be taken at a high political level, resources being made available in advance for its successful administration.

The key agency in any supergrass process is the police, since they will be most instrumental in deciding whom to recruit and whom to prosecute. Supergrass systems are based upon pro-active policing and the deployment of what Skolnick calls 'aggressive intelligence', while the management of the supergrasses themselves is likely to be high-status police work.[50] It is also clear that, as in the case of Skolnick's informers, what motivates supergrasses most is self-inter-est, particularly the prospect of leniency in, or even the avoidance of, punishment. The rewards available to those from backgrounds of both terrorism and of organized crime are, characteristically, the most generous any criminal justice system is prepared to offer informants. They can include: immunity from prosecution; an extremely lenient prison sentence, and comparative luxury while serving it; money; and new lives with fresh identities, away from the original sphere of operations.

Although each supergrass process, or quasi-supergrass process,

[50] See Ch. 1.

will have its own unique features, the Northern Ireland variant differs sharply from all the others surveyed here since only it failed to be successfully institutionalized. The key to successful institutionalization lies in minimal levels of respect for values of due process and the early establishment of effective channels of political accountability. Only properly accountable supergrass systems can be justified in a democracy. Ironically, because of their high public profile, supergrass systems will be much more accountable than informer systems. But the manner in which this public accountability is exercised, and its effectiveness, varies. In England the controversy over the first supergrass trials in the early 1970s was largely dispelled by the abandonment of immunities from prosecution in favour of lenient sentencing and early release by exercise of the prerogative of mercy. The prosecuting authorities also quickly learned that both juries and the Court of Appeal were reluctant to convict without corroboration. In the United States the Witness Protection Programme was created by the legislature and has been monitored closely by it ever since. It has also operated in a criminal justice system where the accomplice evidence warning is still taken seriously and where jury trial continues, notwithstanding the difficulties posed by organized crime. In Italy the *pentiti* process was also a creature of statute, while the legislatures in France and Germany have ensured that no supergrass systems have developed in these countries at all. In Northern Ireland, on the other hand, the supergrass system emerged from the murky world of intelligence-gathering, which parliament has had little interest in seeking to regulate. It was grafted on to a special non-jury court system, where a compliant judiciary initially gave it the green light. But by the time the public campaign against it had made an impact upon the courts, it was too late for compromise. Either the system had to be destroyed or the judiciary in Northern Ireland had to relinquish any credible claim to impartiality, independence, and rationality.

Anti-terrorist supergrass systems present certain problems for democratic law enforcement, the most serious of all being the reliability of the evidence presented in court and how it can adequately be tested. The gravest danger is that, in his quest for the rewards on offer, the supergrass will exaggerate his role in the movement, while being careful to tone down the precise part he played in murders and other serious offences. This creates an opportunity for names of suspects to be added to the indictment by the police. This danger is greatly increased by inclusion of vague charges of conspiracies which allegedly took place at some unknown point within a long time-period. The risk that the inherent flaws in the supergrass's evidence will go unrecognized are increased when due-process constraints are eroded. The absence, from the Diplock system in Northern Ireland, of both the jury and, initially, the corresponding pressure upon the prosecuting authorities to find adequate corroboration for supergrass evidence, provides a sharp contrast with the English and American parallels, where both the jury and the need for corroboration have always been central.

Supergrass systems create some risk of police profiteering, but only in relation to organized acquisitive crime. But the possibility of corruption of the rule of law is an inherent danger in any supergrass process, because without proper and effective supervision by legislature and courts, the police will be able to bypass more mundane and painstaking police investigations and to determine who deserves punishment for which offence. Without adequate supervision, there is a further risk that the police may attempt to extend policing based on informers and supergrasses into other areas of police work because of the amount of time and effort it can save.

It could be argued that the supergrass process in Northern Ireland has been so different from those found elsewhere because the broader political system lacks effective democratic institutions. Clearly, the extent of democratization varies between liberal democracies, and it would be difficult in a study of this kind to attempt to determine which is the most 'democratic'. However, there appears to be a relationship between the availability of political institutions for the maximization of consensus and the peaceful management of political conflict on the one hand, and, on the other, the possibility of effective institutional constraints upon law-and-order strategies which might otherwise be dominated by crime-control priorites. In Northern Ireland both legislative control and effective standards of due process in terrorist trials have been weak at best. The region is governed by a department of the British government, the Northern Ireland Office, which is only indirectly accountable via the Westminster parliament in London. Parliamentary supervision has also, in general, tended to be indifferent and ineffective. Moreover, the advice of 'professionals', such as the police and the army has generally been given greater weight in the determination of law-and-order policy than any other opinion. Stripped of the jury, the Diplock courts have lost a vital safeguard in the trial of the most serious offences. The result was the establishment of a largely ineffective supergrass system destroyed by the judiciary in an attempt to save the legal system from further damage to its credibility.

APPENDIX A

Chronology of Key Events: 1970–1993

1970		3 trials of 10 alleged UVF activists based on evidence of self-proclaimed Chief of Staff, Sammy Stephenson, end in acquittals.
1974		8 loyalists acquitted in trial on evidence of UDA supergrass Albert 'Ginger' Baker.
1979	August	Sir Maurice Oldfield appointed Security Co-ordinator for Northern Ireland in wake of succession of security disasters.
1980		3 of 7 defendants convicted on evidence of IRA informer Stephen McWilliams.
1981	June	8 of 10 defendants convicted on evidence of IRA informer James Kennedy.
	5 October	Republican prison hunger-strike for political status ends after deaths of 10 prisoners.
	21 November	Christopher Black arrested. Conventional starting-point for 'supergrass system'.
1982	12 January	Kevin McGrady gives himself up to the police.
	February	Formation of Relatives for Justice, representing friends and relatives of those implicated by republican supergrasses.
	March	Robert McAllister retracts evidence against 13 alleged members of INLA.
	3 April	RUC Special Branch Detective Sergeant Charles McCormick convicted of armed robbery on evidence of alleged IRA accomplice Anthony O'Doherty.

	20 May	Joseph Bennett arrested by police.
	July	Clifford McKeown retracts evidence against 29 alleged members of UVF.
	August	IRA supergrass Robert Brown withdraws evidence against 18 suspects.
	September	Jackie Goodman (alleged INLA operations officer for Belfast), Sean Mallon, and Patricia Hughes, retract evidence against some 30 suspects.
	September–November	RUC abandons policy of offering immunity from prosecution to those who have 'pulled the trigger' in murder.
	6 December	Black trial (*R. v. Donnelly*) begins.
1983	16 February	Bennett trial (*R. v. Graham*) begins.
	March	The Chief Constable of the RUC, Sir John Hermon, strongly defends the use of supergrasses in his annual report for 1982.
	11 April	14 of 16 defendants in Bennett trial convicted.
	5 May	McGrady (*R. v. Gibney*) begins.
	August	IRA informers Charles Dillon and Walter McCrory retract evidence against some 13 suspects.
	5 August	35 of 38 defendants in Black trial convicted.
	September	Formation of Concerned Community Organizations, republican anti-supergrass pressure-group and Families for Legal Rights, representing friends and relatives of those implicated by loyalist supergrasses.
	13 September	Grimley trial (*R. v. Connolly*) begins.
	19 October	Robert Lean retracts evidence against 28 IRA suspects.

24 October	The Attorney-General, Sir Michael Havers, issues the first of two major parliamentary statements on the supergrass phenomenon in Northern Ireland. IRA supergrass Patrick McGurk retracts evidence against 9 defendants.
26 October	7 of 10 defendants in McGrady trial convicted.
November	IRA informer William Skelly retracts evidence against 10 suspects.
24 November	Morgan trial (*R. v. Davison*) begins.
25 November	Grimley trial ends with acquittal of all 7 defendants charged on Grimley's uncorroborated testimony. 14 others convicted on confessions and guilty pleas.
19 December	Morgan trial ends in acquittal of all 5 defendants.

1984	12 January	Quigely trial (*R. v. Crumley*) begins. Highly critical Gifford report on supergrass system published. Conviction of RUC Sergeant Charles McCormick on evidence of IRA informer, Anthony O'Doherty, quashed on appeal.
	February	Annual report of US State Department to Congress on human rights violations throughout the world warns that the supergrass system in Northern Ireland is overburdening the legal system by its 'sheer numbers'.
	March	Sir John Hermon repeats his defence of trials on supergrass evidence in his annual report for 1983.
	15 March	Sir George Baker defends supergrass system in review of operation of Northern Ireland (Emergency Provisions) Act 1978.
	2 May	Quigley trial ends in conviction of all but one of 11 defendants.

	8 May	Gilmour trial (*R. v. Robson*) begins.
	22 August	Announcement of early release of Anthony O'Doherty, who turned Queen's evidence in the case of RUC sergeant Charles McCormick.
	29 November	Crockard trial (*R. v. Sayers*) begins.
	18 December	Gilmour trial ends in acquittal of all 35 defendants.
	24 December	All 14 convictions obtained in Bennett case quashed on appeal.
1985	29 January	Kirkpatrick trial (*R. v. Steenson*) begins.
	22 February	Crockard trial ends with conviction of 8 accused who had made statements and acquittal of remaining 21.
	March	Eamon Collins retracts evidence against 12 IRA suspects John Gibson retracts evidence against 35 UVF suspects.
	20 March	Allen trial (*R. v. Austin*) begins.
	5 July	Allen trial ends in conviction of 5 defendants who had made statements and acquittal of remaining 20.
	October	19 IRA suspects charged on evidence of Angela Whorisky.
	18 December	Kirkpatrick trial ends with conviction of all 27 defendants.
1986	19 March	Attorney-General, Sir Michael Havers, issues the second of his two major parliamentary statements on the supergrass system in Northern Ireland.
	April	Joseph Bennett arrested by English police in connection with an armed robbery in Midlands
	4 July	Appeal in McGrady case results in 2 of original 7 convictions being quashed.

	8 July	UVF supergrass, William 'Budgie' Allen released from prison by Secretary of State for Northern Ireland.
	17 July	Appeal in Black case results in 18 of original 35 convictions being quashed.
	15 October	DPP for Northern Ireland decides not to pursue prosecution of 19 defendants on evidence of IRA supergrass Angela Whorisky.
	18 November	Appeal in Quigley case results in 8 of 10 original convictions being quashed.
	23 December	Appeal in Kirkpatrick case results in quashing of 24 of 27 original convictions.
1988	15 May	Kevin McGrady released from prison after serving 6 years of 3 life sentences.
	June	Amnesty International publishes report on killings by security forces and supergrass trials in Northern Ireland.
	November	Right to silence abolished in all criminal trials in Northern Ireland by Criminal Evidence (NI) Order 1988.
1989	19 December	*Independent* reports rumours that another loyalist supergrass has appeared.
1991	8 May	Ten defendants, including Sinn Fein director of publicity Danny Morrison, convicted in Sandy Lynch 'rescued informer' trial.
	14 June	James Crockard released from prison after serving 8 years of two life sentences.
1992	February	Army agent in UDA, Brian Nelson, sentenced to 10 years for involvement in five conspiracies to murder.
	10 March	Harry Kirkpatrick released from prison after serving nearly 9 years of 5 life sentences.

14 November   RUC reported to be reviewing informer guide-lines in wake of Nelson case.

1993   27 May   Chief Constable of RUC, Sir Hugh Annesley, calls for increased reliance upon accomplice evidence in Diplock courts.

June   *Daily Mirror* reports allegations by Special Branch agent in IRA, Declan 'Beano' Casey, that he had participated in over a dozen killings and that his final pay-off was £40,000 plus a house worth £72,000

17 December   Two INLA activists convicted at trial in London on evidence of MI5 agent Patrick Daly who claimed that his resettlement expenses amounted to £400,000 and that he had been promised a £40,000 bonus 'if good custodial sentences were handed out'.

Terrorist Suspects and Informers Turning Queen's Evidence in Northern Ireland: 1970–1993

Supergrass	Position re own offences	Number charged	Dates of trial	Outome
William 'Budgie' Allen (UVF Belfast)	Sentenced to 14 years Apr. 84, released July 86	46	20 Mar.–5 July 85	25 tried, 5 convicted on confessions
Albert 'Ginger' Baker (UDA Belfast)	Life 1973 for murder of 4 Catholics, judge recommended 25 years minimum	8	Oct. 74	All 8 acquitted on technicality
Joseph Charles Bennett (UVF Belfast)	Immunity from prosecution for offences committed prior to *Graham* trial, imprisoned for armed robbery committed in England after *Graham* trial	18	16 Feb.–11 Apr. 83	14 convictions all quashed on appeal
Christopher Black (IRA Belfast)	Immunity from prosecution, other details unknown	38	6 Dec. 82–5 Aug. 83	35 convictions 18 quashed on appeal
Robert Brown (IRA Belfast)	Not known	Not known	—	Withdrew evidence 18 Aug. 82, those implicated already in custody on other charges
Eamon Collins (IRA, S. Down)	Acquitted of 5 murders and 50 other offences in Mar. 87 when confession ruled inadmissible	17	—	7 released when Collins retracted 2 weeks after having turned Queen's evidence
Owen Connolly	Sentenced to life for murder of deputy prison governor William McConnell	2	Nov. 86	Evidence rejected, both accused acquitted
James Crockard (UVF Belfast)	2 life terms for 40 offences including 2 murders, 3 attempted murders, 5 conspiracies to murder. Released after 8 years	29	29 Nov. 84–22 Feb. 85	8 convicted on confessions, 21 acquitted
Charles Paul Dillon (IRA S. Derry)	Not known	7	—	2 released when Dillon retracted in Aug. 83; others had made confessions
John Gibson (UVF Belfast)	Life for 4 murders and catalogue of other serious offences	50	—	Charges against 35 dropped when Gibson retracted in Mar. 85
Raymond Gilmour (INLA/IRA Derry)	Immunity from prosecution	41	8 May–18 Dec. 84	All 35 defendants acquitted
Jackie Goodman (INLA province-wide)	Immunity from prosecution	36	—	23 released when Goodman retracted; fate of others unknown

Supergrass	Position re own offences	Number charged	Dates of trial	Outome
Jackie Grimley (INLA Derry, Craigavon, Lurgan)	Immunity from prosecution	22	13 Sep.–24 Nov. 83	11 convicted on confessions, 7 acquitted, 3 pleaded guilty, 1 failed to answer bail
James Kennedy (IRA Belfast)	Immunity from prosecution	10	June 81	8 convicted, some escaped from custody but eventually recaptured
Harry Kirkpatrick (INLA Belfast)	5 life terms, released after serving 9 years	33	29 Jan.–18 Dec. 85	28 convictions, all but 4 quashed on appeal
Robert Lean (IRA Belfast)	Immunity from prosecution	28	—	Retracted within a month, charges against 12 dropped
Sandy Lynch (INLA/IRA Belfast)	Informal immunity	10	Feb.–May 91	10 convicted, but none exclusively on Lynch's evidence
Robert McAllister (INLA Belfast)	Immunity mentioned but not finalized	13		Retracted, charges against 12 sustained
John McConkey (IRA/INLA Belfast)	Confessed to murder, sentenced to life in McGrady trial	—	—	Retracted before anyone charged
Walter McCrory (IRA/INLA Derry)	Not known	6	—	Retracted Aug. 83, charges against 6 dropped
Kevin McGrady (IRA Belfast)	3 life terms, released 1988 after serving only 6 years	10	5 May–26 Oct. 83	7 convicted, 2 had convictions quashed on appeal
Patrick McGurk (IRA Dungannon)	Immunity from prosecution	9	—	7 released with not-guilty verdicts entered on record when McGurk retracted, 1 defendant did not answer bail, 1 convicted on confession
Clifford McKeown (UVF Craigavon)	Immunity from prosecution except for armed robbery	29	—	Charges against 6 dropped after McKeown retracted, 18 others eventually tried and convicted
Stephen McWilliams (IRA Belfast)	Immunity from prosecution	7	Mar. 80	6 convicted, McWilliams later claimed he had lied about 1 of these
Sean Mallon and Patricia Hughes (INLA Armagh)	Not known	3	—	Charges against 3 sustained although Mallon and Hughes retracted
John Morgan (IRA/INLA Belfast)	Immunity from prosecution	5	24 Nov.–19 Dec. 83	All 5 acquitted at first instance
James O'Rawe (IRA Belfast)	Immunity from prosecution	6	—	Retracted, all 6 released
Robert Quigley (IRA Derry)	Immunity from prosecution	16	12 Jan.–2 May 84	11 tried, 10 convicted, 8 convictions quashed on appeal

Supergrass	Position re own offences	Number charged	Dates of trial	Outome
William Skelly (IRA Belfast)	Convicted of murder and membership of IRA	10	—	All released when Skelly retracted in Nov. 83
Stanley Smith (UDA Belfast)	Life for murder, attempted suicide in prison	9	—	Charges withdrawn when Smith retracted on 13 Feb. 84
Sammy Stephenson (UVF province-wide)	12 years in 1969, served in Wakefield, England	10	Feb. and Mar. 70	All 10 acquitted
Angela Whorisky (IRA Derry)	Life Mar. 86 for 39 terrorist charges including murder	19	—	Charges against 19 dropped in Oct. 86 for reasons not made clear
James Williamson (UDA Belfast)	Immunity from prosecution	8	—	6 had charges withdrawn when Williamson retracted, but 2, who had made statements, proceeded against

Supergrass and Informer Trials in Terrorist Cases in Northern Ireland: 1980–1993

Supergrass/ informer	Number tried	Convicted[1]	Convicted on uncorroborated supergrass/ informer evidence	Independent evidence[2]	Appeals against conviction	Convictions quashed	Guilty verdicts extant after appeal
McWilliams IRA (1980)	7	6	3	3 confessions	0	0	6
Kennedy IRA (1981)	10	8	3	1 confession 4 arrested at scene	0	0	8
Bennett UVF (1983)	16	14	11	1 forensic 2 confessions	14	14	0
Black IRA (1983)	38	35	18	2 forensic 15 confessions	22	18	17
McGrady IRA (1983)	10	7	2	5 confessions	4	2	5
Grimley INLA (1983)	21	14	0	11 confessions 3 guilty pleas	0	0	14
Morgan IRA (1983)	5	0	0	0	0	0	0
Quigley IRA (1984)	11	10	8	2 confessions	8	8	2
Gilmour IRA/INLA (1984)	35	0	0	0	0	0	0
Crockard UVF (1985)	29	8	0	8 confessions	0	0	8
Allen UVF (1985)	25	5	0	5 confessions	0	0	5
Kirkpatrick INLA (1985)	28	28	24	3 confessions 1 guilty plea	27	24	4
Lynch IRA (1991)	10	10	0	8 arrested at scene 4 confessions 3 forensic 6 silence	3	0	10
TOTAL	245	145	69	55 confessions 6 forensic 12 arrested at scene 6 silence 4 guilty pleas	78	66	79

[1] First instance.

[2] 'Confession' includes alleged admission. 'Forensic' means number of convictions supported by forensic evidence. 'Silence' means number of convictions supported by inferences drawn from refusals to answer police questions and/or to testify in one's own defence at trial.

Select Bibliography

Alexander, S., *The Pizza Connection: Lawyers, Drugs and the Mafia* (London: W. H. Allen, 1989).

Amnesty International, *7 April Trial—Italy* (London: Amnesty International, 1986).

——*United Kingdom—Northern Ireland: Killings by Security Forces and 'Supergrass' Trials* (London: Amnesty International, 1988).

——*United Kingdom—Fair Trial Concerns in Northern Ireland: The Right of Silence* (London: Amnesty International, Nov. 1992).

Andrew, C., *Secret Service: The Making of the British Intelligence Community* (London: Heinemann, 1985).

Anon., 'Testing the Factual Basis for a Search Warrant' (1967) *Columbia Law Review* 1529, 1532–4.

Arlacchi, P., *Mafia Business: The Mafia Ethic and the Spirit of Capitalism* (Oxford: Oxford University Press, 1988).

Association of Chief Police Officers, *National Guidelines on the Use and Management of Informers* (ACPO Crime Committee Working Party on Informants, unpub. 1992).

Baker Report: *Review of the Operation of the Northern Ireland (Emergency Provisions) Act 1978*, Cmnd. 9222 (London: HMSO, 1984).

Baldwin, R., and Kinsey, R., *Police Powers and Politics* (London: Quartet Books, 1982).

Beccaria, C., *Of Crimes and Punishments*, trans. Juan Antonio de las Casas (Oxford: Oxford University Press, 1964).

Becker, J., *Hitler's Children* (London: Michael Joseph, 1977).

——*Terrorism in West Germany: The Struggle for What?* (London: Institute for the Study of Terrorism, 1988).

Beckett, J. C., *The Making of Modern Ireland 1603–1923*, 2nd edn. (London: Faber & Faber, 1981).

Bennett Report: *Report of the Committee of Inquiry into Police Interrogation Procedures in Northern Ireland*, Cmnd. 7497 (London: HMSO, 1979).

Beresford, D., *Ten Men Dead: The Story of the 1981 Irish Hunger Strike* (London: Grafton Books, 1987).

Bishop, P., and Mallie, E., *The Provisional IRA* (London: Corgi Books, 1988).

Block, J., and Fitzgerald, P., *British Intelligence and Covert Action: Africa, Middle East and Europe Since 1945* (Dingle: Brandon Books, 1983).

Blok, A. A., 'History and the Study of Organised Crime', *Urban Life*, 6(4): 455–74, 1978.

Blumenthal, R., *Last Days of the Sicilians: At War with the Mafia—The FBI Assault on the Pizza Connection* (London: Bloomsbury, 1989).

Bonner, D., 'Combatting Terrorism: Supergrass Trials in Northern Ireland' (1988) 51 *Modern Law Review* 23.

Bougereau, J. M., *The German Guerilla: Terror, Reaction, and Resistance* (London: Cienfuegos Press & Soil of Liberty, 1981).

Bouloc, B., 'Le Problème des repentis: la tradition française relativement au statut des repentis' (1986) *Revue de science criminelle* 771.

Boyd, A., *The Informers: A Chilling Account of the Supergrasses in Northern Ireland* (Dublin: Mercier Press, 1984).

Boyle, K., Hadden, T., and Hillyard, P., *Law and State: The Case of Northern Ireland* (London: Martin Robertson, 1975).

——*Ten Years on in Northern Ireland: The Legal Control of Political Violence* (London: The Cobden Trust, 1980).

Bunyan, T., *The History and Practice of the Political Police in Britain* (London: Quartet Books, 1983).

Cacciani, M., and Bonetti, M., 'Normativa antiterrorismo e nuovi modelli di organizzazione processuale nell'esperienza francese', in *Convenzione per una ricerca su 'Normative ed esperienze di maxiprocessi e sulla utilizzabilita e gestibilita probatoria dei c.d. testimoni della corona e della relative tutela. Confronto con l'esperienza italiana': Rapporto finale I & II* (Milan: Centro Nazionale di Prevenzione e Difesa Sociale, 1987).

Campbell, D., 'Society under Surveillance', in P. Hain (ed.), *Policing the Police,* ii (London: John Calder, 1980).

——'Whisper Who Dares' (1991) *Police Review* 532–3.

——*The Underworld* (London: BBC Books, 1994).

Carter, P. B., 'Corroboration Requirements Reconsidered: (1) Two Comments' [1985] *Criminal Law Review* 143.

Chadbourn, J. (ed.), *Wigmore on Evidence in Trials at Common Law*, vii (Boston: Little Brown & Co., 1978).

Chief Constable's Report 1982 (Belfast: Police Authority for Northern Ireland, 1983).

Chief Constable's Report 1983 (Belfast: HMSO, 1984).

Clifford, B., *The Psychology of Person Identification* (London: Routledge & Kegan Paul, 1978).

Cole, G. F., Frankowski, S. J., and Gertz, M. G., *Major Criminal Justice Systems* (London: Sage, 1981).

Collins, H., *Marxism and Law* (Oxford: Oxford University Press, 1984).

CNPDS: See Convenzione per una ricerca . . .

Compton Report: *Report of the Enquiry into Allegations against the Security Forces of Physical Brutality in Northern Ireland Arising out of Events on the 9th of August 1971*, Cmnd. 4832 (London: HMSO, 1971).

Convenzione per una ricerca su 'Normative ed esperienze di maxiprocessi e sulla utilizzabilita e gestibilita probatoria dei c.d. testimoni della corona e della relative tutela. Confronto con l'esperienza italiana': Rapporto finale I & II (Milan: Centro Nazionale di Prevenzione e Difesa Sociale, 1987). Cited in the text as *CNPDS*.

Cook, S., 'Germany: From Protest to Terrorism', in Y. Alexander and K. Meyers (eds.), *Terrorism in Europe* (London: Croom Helm, 1982).

Darby, J. (ed), *Northern Ireland: The Background to the Conflict* (Belfast: Appletree Press, 1983).

Deacon, R., *'C': A Biography of Sir Maurice Oldfield* (London: Macdonald, 1984).

Dennis, I., 'Corroboration Requirements Reconsidered' [1984] *Criminal Law Review* 316 and [1985] *Criminal Law Review* 143.

Devlin P., *Trial by Jury* (London: Stevens, 1956).

—— *The Criminal Prosecution in England* (Oxford: Oxford University Press, 1960).

Dewar, Lt.-Col. M., *The British Army in Northern Ireland* (London: Arms and Armour Press, 1985).

Dickson, B., *The Legal System of Northern Ireland* (Belfast: Servicing the Legal System, 1984).

—— 'Northern Ireland's Emergency Legislation: The Wrong Medicine?' (1992) *Public Law* 592.

Dillon, M., *The Dirty War* (London: Arrow Books, 1991).

Dixon, D., 'Politics, Research and Symbolism in Criminal Justice: The Right of Silence and the Police and Criminal Evidence Act' [1991] 20 *Anglo-American Law Review* 27.

Doherty, F., *The Stalker Affair* (Dublin: Mercier Press, 1986).

Dorn, N., Murji, K., and South, N., *Traffickers: Drug Markets and Law Enforcement* (London: Routledge, 1992).

Dworkin, R., *Taking Rights Seriously* (London: Duckworth, 1978).

—— *Law's Empire* (London: Fontana, 1986).

Easton, S., *The Right to Silence* (London: Avebury, 1991).

Edwards, J. Ll. J., *The Law Officers of the Crown* (London: Sweet & Maxwell, 1964).

—— *The Attorney General, Politics and the Public Interest* (London: Sweet & Maxwell, 1984).

Eggleston, R., *Evidence, Proof and Probability*, 2nd edn. (London: Weidenfeld & Nicolson, 1983).

Falcone, G., with Padovani, M., *Men of Honour: The Truth about the Mafia* (London: Warner Books, 1992).

Farrington, D. P., Hawkins, K., and Lloyd-Bostock, S., *Psychology, Law and Legal Processes* (London: Macmillan, 1979).

Findlay, M., ' "Acting on Information Received": Mythmaking and Police Corruption' (1987) 1 *Journal of Studies in Justice* 19–32.

Fitzpatrick, W. J., *Secret Service under Pitt* (London: Longman, 1892).

Flackes, W. D., and Elliott, S., *Northern Ireland: A Political Directory 1968–88* (Belfast: Blackstaff Press, 1989).

Gardiner Report: *Report of a Committee to Consider, in the Context of Civil Liberties and Human Rights, Measures to Deal with Terrorism in Northern Ireland*, Cmnd. 5847 (London: HMSO, 1975).

Gifford, T., *Supergrasses: The Use of Accomplice Evidence in Northern Ireland* (London: The Cobden Trust, 1984).

Goldstein, A. S., and Marcus, M., 'The Myth of Judicial Supervision in Three "Inquisitorial" Systems: France, Italy and Germany' (1977–8) 87 *Yale Law Journal* 240.

——'Comment on Continental Criminal Procedure' (1977–8) 87 *Yale Law Journal* 1570.

Goodman, J., and Will, I., *Underworld* (London: Harrap, 1985).

Graham, E., 'A Vital Weapon in the Anti-terrorist Arsenal', *Fortnight*, no. 198, Oct. 1983, 10.

Greer, D. S., 'The Admissibility of Confessions under the Northern Ireland (Emergency Provisions) Act 1978' (1980) 31 *Northern Ireland Legal Quarterly* 205.

Greer, S. C., 'The Seeds of Another Bitter Harvest', *Fortnight*, no. 198, Oct. 1983, 11.

——'Civil Liberties in Northern Ireland: From Special Powers to Supergrasses', *Fortnight*, no. 214, 18 Feb.–3 Mar. 1985, 4–6.

——'Supergrasses and the Legal System in Britain and Northern Ireland' (1986) 102 *Law Quarterly Review* 198.

——'The Rise and Fall of the Northern Ireland Supergrass System' [1987] *Criminal Law Review* 663.

——'The Supergrass System in Northern Ireland', in P. Wilkinson and A. M. Stewart (eds.), *Contemporary Research on Terrorism* (Aberdeen: Aberdeen University Press, 1987), 510–35.

——'The Supergrass: A Coda', *Fortnight*, no. 249, Mar. 1987, 7.

——'Corroboration and Suspect Evidence' (1988) 51 *Modern Law Review* 121.

——'The Right to Silence: A Review of the Current Debate' (1990) 53 *Modern Law Review* 709.

——'The Supergrass System', in A. Jennings (ed.), *Justice under Fire: The Abuse of Civil Liberties in Northern Ireland*, 2nd edn. (London: Pluto Press, 1990).

——'The Legal Powers of the Army', in B. Dickson (ed.), *Civil Liberties in Northern Ireland: The CAJ Handbook*, 2nd edn. (Belfast: Committee on the Administration of Justice, 1993).

——'Preventive Detention and Public Security: Towards a General Model', in A. Harding and J. Hatchard (eds.), *Preventive Detention and Security Law: A Comparative Survey* (The Hague: Martinus Nijhoff, 1993).

——and Morgan, R. (eds.), *The Right to Silence Debate* (Bristol: Bristol Centre for Criminal Justice, 1990).

——and White, A., *Abolishing the Diplock Courts: The Case for Restoring Jury Trial to Scheduled Offences in Northern Ireland* (London: The Cobden Trust, 1986).

——and Hadden, T. B., 'Supergrasses on Trial', *New Society*, 66 (8 Dec. 1983), 330–1.

——and Jennings, A., 'Goodbye to the Supergrasses?', *Fortnight*, 212 (21 Jan.–3 Feb. 1985), 4–6.

Guerri, G. B., *P. Peci, io, l'infame* (Milan: Mondadori, 1983).

Gutteridge, W. (ed.), *The New Terrorism* (London: Mansell Publishing, 1986).

Hadden, T., Boyle, K., and Campbell, C., 'Emergency Law in Northern Ireland: The Context', in A. Jennings (ed.), *Justice under Fire: the Abuse of Civil Liberties in Northern Ireland*, 2nd edn. (London: Pluto Press, 1990).

Haglund, E., 'Impeaching the Underworld Informant' (1990) 63 *Southern California Law Review* 1407–47.

Hain, P. (ed.), *Policing the Police* (London: John Calder, 1980).

Hamill, D., *Pig in the Middle: The Army in Northern Ireland 1969–1985* (London: Methuen, 1986).

Harney, M. L., and Cross, J. C., *The Informer in Law Enforcement* (Springfield, Ill.: Charles Thomas, 1960).

Harris, R. J., 'Note: Whither the Witness? The Federal Government's Special Duty of Protection in Criminal Proceedings after *Piechowicz* v. *US*' (1991) 76 *Cornell Law Review* 1285.

Hart, H. L. A., *Concept of Law* (Oxford: Clarendon Press, 1961).

Hearings before the Permanent Subcommittee on Investigations of the Committee on Governmental Affairs, US Senate, 96th Congress, 2nd Session, December 15, 16, & 17, 1980: Witness Protection Program (Washington, DC: US Government Printing, 1980).

Hearings on HR 7309 before the Subcomm. on Courts, Civil Liberties, and the Administration of Justice of the House Comm. on the Judiciary, 97th Cong., 2nd Sess. 309 (Washington, DC: US Government Printing, 1982).

Heydon, J. D., 'The Corroboration of Accomplices' [1973] *Criminal Law Review* 264.

——*Evidence: Cases and Materials*, 3rd edn. (London: Butterworths, 1991).

Hibbert, C., *The Roots of Evil* (London: Weidenfeld & Nicolson, 1963).

Hillyard, P., 'Law and Order', in J. Darby (ed.), *Northern Ireland: The Background to the Conflict* (Belfast: Appletree Press, 1983).

——and Percy-Smith, J., 'Converting Terrorists: The Use of Supergrasses in Northern Ireland' (1984) *Journal of Law and Society* 335.

Ianni, F. A. J., and Reuss-Ianni, E., *A Family Business: Kinship and Social Control in Organised Crime* (London: Russell Sage Foundation, 1972).

Jackson, J. D., *Northern Ireland Supplement to Cross on Evidence* 5th edn. (Belfast: Servicing the Legal System, 1983).

——'Credibility, Morality and the Corroboration Warning' (1988) 47 *Cambridge Law Journal* 428.

——'Developments in Northern Ireland', in S. Greer and R. Morgan (eds.), *The Right to Silence Debate* (Bristol: Bristol Centre for Criminal Justice, 1990).

——'Curtailing the Right of Silence: Lessons from Northern Ireland' [1991] *Criminal Law Review* 404.

——'Inferences from Silence: From Common Law to Common Sense' (1993) 44 *Northern Ireland Legal Quarterly* 103.

——'The Northern Ireland (Emergency Provisions) Act 1987' (1988) 39 *Northern Ireland Legal Quarterly* 235

Jennings, A., 'Shoot to Kill: The Final Courts of Justice', in id. (ed.), *Justice under Fire: The Abuse of Civil Liberties in Northern Ireland*, 2nd edn. (London: Pluto Press, 1990).

Joy, Chief Baron, *Evidence of Accomplices* (London, 1844).

Katz, D., 'The Paradoxical Role of Informers within the Criminal Justice System: A Unique Perspective' (1981) 7 *University of Dayton Law Review* 51–71.

Kitson, F., *Low Intensity Operations: Subversion, Insurgency, Peace-Keeping* (London: Faber & Faber, 1971).

Klockars, C. B., *Thinking about Police: Contemporary Readings*, 2nd edn. (New York: McGraw-Hill, 1991).

Kolinsky, E., 'Terrorism in West Germany', in J. Lodge (ed.), *The Threat of Terrorism* (Brighton: Wheatsheaf Books, 1988).

Langbein, J. H., and Weinreb, Ll. L., 'Continental Criminal Procedure: "Myth" and Reality' (1977–8) 87 *Yale Law Journal* 1549.

Lawler, L. E., 'Police Informer Privilege: A Study for the Law Reform Commission of Canada' (1986) 28 *Criminal Law Quarterly* 91–128.

Lecky, W. E. H., *History of England in the Eighteenth Century* (London, 1921), iii.

Levin, J. M., 'Organised Crime and Insulated Violence: Federal Liability for Illegal Conduct in the Witness Protection Program' [1985] 76 *Journal of Criminal Law amd Criminology* 208.

Loftus, E., *Eye Witness Testimony* (Boston: Harvard University Press, 1979).

——and Wells, G. (eds.), *Eyewitness Testimony: Psychological Perspectives* (Cambridge: Cambridge University Press, 1984).

Madden, R. R., *Ireland in '98* (London, 1988).

Maguire, M., and Norris, C., *The Conduct and Supervision of Criminal*

Investigations, Royal Commission on Criminal Justice Research Study no. 5 (London: HMSO, 1993).

Malony, E., 'Supergrass Scheme Owes Much to US', *Irish Times*, 8 Oct. 1983.

Mark, R., 'The Disease of Crime: Punishment or Treatment?' (London: Royal Society of Medicine, 1972), 6 and 13.

—— 'Minority Verdict', *Listener*, 8 Nov. 1973.

Marx, G. T., 'Thoughts on a Neglected Category of Social Movement Participant: The Agent Provocateur and the Informant' (1974) 80 *American Journal of Sociology* 402–42.

—— *Undercover: Police Surveillance in America* (Berkeley, Calif.: University of California Press, 1988).

Maxwell, W. H., *History of the Irish Rebellion of 1798* (London, 1845–1903).

McElree, F. and Starmer, K., 'The Right to Silence', in C. Walker and K. Starmer (eds.), *Justice in Error* (London: Blackstone, 1993).

McGuffin, J., *The Guineapigs* (London: Penguin, 1974).

Miers, D., 'Informers and Agents Provocateurs' (1970) 120 *New Law Journal*, 577.

—— 'Agent Provocateurs: The Judicial Response' (1970) 120 *New Law Journal*, 597.

Moloney, E., and Pollack, A., *Paisley* (Dublin: Poolbeg, 1986).

Moore, W. H., *The Kefauver Committee and the Politics of Crime 1950–1952* (Columbia: University of Missouri Press, 1974).

Mosconi, G., and Pisapia, G., 'The Stereotype of the Repentant Terrorist: His Nature and Functions', in European Group for the Study of Deviance and Social Control, *Working Papers in Criminology*, 3 (1981).

Moxon-Browne, E., 'Terrorism in France', in W. Gutteridge (ed.), *The New Terrorism* (London: Mansell, 1986).

—— 'Terrorism in France', in J. Lodge (ed.), *The Threat of Terrorism* (Brighton: Wheatsheaf Books, 1988).

Munday, E., 'Juries and Corroboration' (1980) 130 *New Law Journal* 352.

Navasky, V., *Naming Names* (London: Calder, 1982).

Nunn Committee: See *Hearings before the Permanent Subcommittee . . .*

O'Flaherty, L., *The Informer* (London: Jonathan Cape, 1925).

O'Higgins, M., 'Harry's Game', *Hot Press*, 27 Mar. 1986, 30.

O'Leary, B., and McGarry, J., *The Politics of Antagonism: Understanding Northern Ireland* (London: Athlone, 1993).

O'Mahoney, M., with Wooding, D., *King Squealer: The True Story of Maurice O'Mahoney* (London: Sphere Books, 1978).

Oppenheimer, M., 'The Criminalisation of Political Dissent in the Federal Republic of Germany', *Contemporary Crisis* 2(1) (1978), 97.

Orfield, L. B., 'Corroboration of Accomplice Testimony in Federal Criminal Cases' [1963] *Villanova Law Review* 15.

Oscapella, E., 'A Study of Informers in England' [1980] *Criminal Law Review* 136.

Parker, R., 'Confidential Informants and the Truth Finding Function' (1986) 4 *Cooley Law Review* 566–73.

Parker Report: *Report of the Committee of Privy Councillors Appointed to Consider Authorized Procedures for the Interrogation of Persons Suspected of Terrorism*, Cmnd. 4901 (London: HMSO, 1972).

Pennsylvania Crime Commission, *A Decade of Organised Crime* (St David's, Pa., 1980).

Phillips Report: *Report of the Royal Commission on Criminal Procedure*, Cmnd. 8091–2 (London: HMSO, 1981).

Pollak, A., 'The Strange Tale of the Collapsing Supergrass and his RUC Accomplices', *Fortnight*, no. 200, Dec. 1983, 11.

Pradel, J., 'Les Infractions de terrorisme, un nouvel exemple de l'éclatement du droit pénal (Loi no. 86–1020 du septembre 1986)' (1987) *Recueil Dalloz Sirey, 7e Cahier-Chronique* 39.

Radzinowicz, L., *A History of English Criminal Law and its Administration from 1750*, ii (London: Stevens, 1956).

Raezer, T. A., 'Needed Weapons in the Army's War on Drugs' (1987) 116 *Military Law Review* 1–65.

Rapoport, A. A., 'The Informer in Jewish Literature' (Ph.D. thesis, Yeshiva Univ., 1952).

Rose and Laurel: The Journal of the Intelligence Corps, 1969–74.

Runciman Report: *Report of the Royal Commission on Criminal Justice*, Cm. 2263 (London: HMSO, 1993).

Ryder, C., *The RUC: A Force under Fire* (London: Methuen, 1989).

Saverda, C., 'Accomplices in Federal Court: A Case for Increased Evidentiary Standards' [1990] 100 *Yale Law Journal* 785.

Schliefman, N., *Undercover Agents in the Russian Revolutionary Movement: The SR Party, 1902–14* (London: Macmillan, 1988).

Schlichter, J., 'The Outwardly Sufficient Search Warrant Affidavit: What If It's False' (1971) 96 *University of California Los Angeles Law Review* 96.

Schmid, A. P., *Political Terrorism: A Research Guide to Concepts, Theories, Data Bases and Literature* (London: Transaction Books, 1983).

Seymour, D., 'What Good Have Supergrasses Done for Anyone but Themselves?', *Legal Action Group Bulletin*, Dec. 1982.

Seymour, G., *Field of Blood* (London: Collins, 1985).

Shawcross, T., and Young, M., *Mafia Wars: The Confessions of Tommaso Buscetta* (London: Fontana, 1988).

Skolnick, J. H., *Justice Without Trial: Law Enforcement in Democratic Society*, 2nd edn. (New York: John Wiley & Sons, 1975).

Slipper, J., *Slipper of the Yard* (London: Sidgwick & Jackson, 1981).

Smith, A. T. H., 'Immunity from Prosecution' (1983) 42 *Cambridge Law Journal* 299.

Smith, D. C., *The Mafia Mystique* (London: Basic Books, 1975).

Street, C. J. C., *Ireland in 1921* (London, 1922).

Sullivan, T. D., A. M., and D. B., *Speeches from the Dock* (Dublin, 1907).

Tapper, C., *Cross on Evidence*, 7th edn. (London: Butterworths, 1990).

Taylor, P., *Stalker: The Search for the Truth* (London: Faber & Faber, 1987).

Tenth Report of the Standing Advisory Commission on Human Rights for 1983–84, HC 175 (London: HMSO, 1985).

Thompson, E. P., *The Making of the English Working Class* (London: Victor Gollancz, 1980).

Thornton, P., Mallalieu, A., and Scrivener, A., *Justice on Trial: Report of an Independent Civil Liberty Panel on Criminal Justice* (London: Liberty, 1992).

Trott, S. S., 'The Successful Use of Informants and Criminals as Witnesses for the Prosecution in a Criminal Trial', in *Convenzione per una ricerca su 'Normative ed esperienze di maxiprocessi e sulla utilizzabilita e gestibilita probatoria dei c.d. testimoni della corona e della relative tutela. Confronto con l'esperienza italiana': Rapporto finale I & II* (Milan: Centro Nazionale di Prevenzione e Difesa Sociale, 1987).

US Senate Governmental Affairs Committee (Permanent Subcommittee on Investigations), Organised Crime and Use of Violence, Hearings, April 28–May 5, 1980 (Washington DC: US Government Printing, 1980).

Urban, M., *Big Boys' Rules: The SAS and the Secret Struggle against the IRA* (London: Faber & Faber, 1992).

Vercher, A., *Terrorism in Europe: An International Comparative Legal Analysis* (Oxford: Clarendon Press, 1992).

Viau, L., 'In Canada is the Control over Undercover Police Work a Sufficient and Effective One?' Paper for Conference, Society for the Reform of the Criminal Law: 'Investigating Crime and Apprehending Suspects: Police Powers and Citizens' Rights', Sydney, Australia, 19–23 Mar. 1989.

Walker, C., 'Army Special Powers on Parade' (1989) 40 *Northern Ireland Legal Quarterly* 1.

——*The Prevention of Terrorism in British Law*, 2nd edn. (Manchester: Manchester University Press, 1992).

Walsh, D. P. J., *The Use and Abuse of Emergency Legislation in Northern Ireland* (London: The Cobden Trust, 1983).

Wardlaw, G., *Political Terrorism: Theory, Tactics and Countermeasures* (Cambridge: Cambridge University Press, 1982).

Weinberg, L., and Eubank, W. L., *The Rise and Fall of Italian Terrorism* (Boulder, Col.: Westview Press, 1987).

Weyranch, W. O., 'Gestapo Informants: Facts and Theory of Undercover Operations' (1986) 24 *Journal of Transnational Law* 553–96.

Whyte, J., *Interpreting Northern Ireland* (Oxford: Oxford University Press, 1990).

Wilkinson, P., and Stewart, A. M. (eds.), *Contemporary Research on Terrorism* (Aberdeen: Aberdeen University Press, 1987).

Williams, J. R. and Guess, L. L., 'The Informant: A Narcotics Enforcement Dilemma' (1981) 13 *Journal of Psychoactive Drugs* 235–45.

Wool, G. J., 'Police Informants in Canada: The Law and the Reality' (1985–6) 50 *Saskatchewan Law Review* 249.

Wilson, J. Q., *The Investigators: Managing FBI and Narcotics Agents* (New York: Basic Books, 1978).

Wood, J. and Crawford, A., *The Right of Silence: The Case for Retention* (London: Civil Liberties Trust, 1989).

Workers' Research Unit, *Belfast Bulletin No. 10: Rough Justice* (Belfast: pub. authors, 1982).

——*Belfast Bulletin No. 11: Supergrasses* (Belfast: pub. authors, 1984).

Zander, M., 'Are Too Many Professional Criminals Avoiding Conviction: A Study in Britain's Two Busiest Courts' (1974) 37 *Modern Law Review* 28.

Index

Names in italic refer to cases cited in the text